TEACHER
TIRED

Why They Left and
Their New Careers

TEACHER
TIRED

Intimate
Conversations with
Former Teachers

Dina L. Beavers, M.Ed.

Decree & Declare Publishing

This book presents the ideas of its author and her interviewees. The publisher and the author disclaim liability for any adverse effects resulting directly or indirectly from information contained in this book.

TEACHER TIRED. Copyright © 2025 by Dina L. Beavers, M.Ed. All rights reserved. Printed in the United States of America. No part of this book may be used or reproduced in any manner whatsoever without written permission except in the case of brief quotations embodied in critical articles and reviews.

ISBN 979-8-9928588-2-2 hardback
ISBN 979-8-9928588-0-8 paperback
ISBN 979-8-9928588-1-5 ebook

Deuteronomy 8:18
He has given us power to get wealth
to establish His Kingdom.

James 2:26
Faith without works is dead.

Deuteronomy 28:12
He will bless the works of my hands.

Job 22:28
We can decree a thing and it shall be established.

Isa. 55:11
Your Word will not return to You void.

Eph. 3:20
He will do exceeding abundantly above
all that I can ask or think.

Contents

11	How To Use This Book
13	Foreword
15	Adult Services Program Manager - Phyllis
23	Ambassador of Change - Kelly
29	Associate Director - Dr. Micaela
37	Attorney - Specializing in Education & Special Education Lauren
45	Business Operations Manager, Project Manager - Marc
53	Case Manager (Out of District) - Tia
57	Channel Program Director - Alissa
65	Chief Academics and Operations Officer - Josh
69	Comedian/TikTok Personality & IT Specialist - Albraden
77	Community Solutions Project Mgr. - Jennifer
85	Contractor, Content Moderator Consultancy - Candace
91	Current Teacher - Carrie
97	Customer Success Manager - Sarah
105	Customer Support Administrator - Carissa
115	Cybersecurity Awareness & Communication Specialist - Nina
121	Data Analyst - Oscar
129	Digital Marketing Manager & Executive LinkedIn Strategist/Ghostwriter - Deiera
133	Data Scientist - Tiffany
141	Director of Coach Success Programs & Partnerships - Derek
149	Director of Internal Business Operations and Recruiting - Lisa
157	Director of User Experience - Claire

167	Entrepreneur - CEO Online Business Owner (Full Time) - Lindsay
171	Entrepreneur Classroom Decor Services - Rachael
175	Entrepreneur - Etsy Shop/YouTube Content Creator - Simply Shawna on YouTube
183	Entrepreneur Life & Student Career Coach Dr. Ai
189	Entrepreneur - Life After Teaching™ Facebook Community Page/Course - Zach
199	Entrepreneurs & Social Media Personalities Eddie and Kara
209	Executive Director for Epilepsy Foundation, OH and IN - Dr. Crystal
215	Founder, Youth Soccer Academy - Bill
219	Freelance Community Educator - Ashlee
227	Freelance Law Lecturer - Gemma
237	Global Learning Partner - Elizabeth
245	Instructional Designer and Training Workshop Facilitator - Nicole
253	Instructional Designer - Kevin
261	Instructional Mentor - Kofi
269	Instructional Specialist - Haylee
277	Leadership Development Facilitator - Kathy
283	Learning and Development Advisor - Alex
289	Learning and Development Specialist - Sandy
295	Learning Content Specialist - Dr. Robin
305	Learning Experience Designer - Maria
309	Learning Experience Designer - Ricky
319	LinkedIn & Personal Branding Coach - Angela
329	Market Researcher - Dr. Julia
339	Marketing Analyst - Rak
345	Product Designer - Vanessa
353	Product Designer/UX Designer & Researcher - Amanda
363	Product Marketing Manager - Lisa C.
371	Project Manager (International) - Melissa
381	Public Health Administrator - James
389	Salesforce Administrator - Nika
397	Senior Automation Engineer - Ryan
405	Senior Economic Research Analyst - Laurie

415	Senior Instructional Designer - Tandiwe
423	SOC Analyst - Lance
427	Software Engineer - Ann
435	Software Engineer - Tyler
445	Software Engineer Developer - Michael
455	Solutions Consultant - Jenni
465	Solutions Consultant - Haley
473	Sr. Client Support Specialist - Neta
481	Training Coordinator, Senior- Rozina
489	Virtual Assistant - Nicole K.
497	Afterword
499	Acknowledgements

How to Use This Book

This Book Offers Stories, Not Scripts

This is not a step-by-step on how to leave.

Instead of telling you exactly what to do, this book gives you real-life stories to spark ideas, build confidence, and help you imagine what's possible.

Read with Intention

Read one chapter a day. Each story is part of your arsenal. You'll be inspired and reminded that all kinds of teachers have made the leap.

Think of it like joining teachers discussing their new careers. You eavesdrop on their conversations, sometimes from the start, sometimes midway. Either way, you gain real insight.

Expect All the Emotions

You will relate to more than a few of these stories.

You'll laugh, you'll cry and you may get angry. That's okay. It means this matters to you.

Stay Curious and Take Action

If something is unfamiliar, look it up. Google terms, explore job titles, and read news articles tied to specific industries. Let one story or phrase lead you down a rabbit hole.

Some descriptions are technical on purpose. Research them so you can ask informed questions when networking.

Use LinkedIn to connect. Talk to non-teacher friends and family. Ask what they do, who they know, and if they can introduce you to someone new.

Use This Book as a Tool

Fight the doubt. Fight the fear. Fight the conversations with fellow teachers who say they want out, but aren't ready to do the work.

Foreword

From an early age, we're conditioned to view a career as a destination. When we are young, we're often asked questions like, "What do you want to be when you grow up?" As we enter adulthood, there is an increasing societal expectation and pressure around having an answer to these questions in order to be viewed as a responsible and contributing member of society.

For many of us this leads to choosing familiar, public-facing roles that we learn about as children. At 16, I decided to become a teacher because I knew I wanted to help others learn and grow. Deciding felt so important, so final. It was an investment, and praised by my community. What I didn't know then was that traditional education wasn't the only way to do that, and that choosing a career (while an important decision) was not a life sentence.

I left teaching in 2020. I felt lost, ashamed, like I had failed, and above all else, I was scared. For 15 years teaching was my identity. I didn't know then that teaching was not my destination like I had always believed, but instead just one of the stepping stones in my career. Over the next four years, I transitioned into roles as a senior instructional designer in fintech, a learning technology manager in e-commerce, a learning strategist in healthcare consulting, and a director of product design and delivery.

Four progressive roles, two layoffs, and countless learning experiences later, I realized something critical: can't always control what happens to us or the conditions in which we make choices, but we can always choose how we respond and move forward. Sometimes how we choose can cause our next "stepping stone" to change location and that (while terrifying) is okay, as long as we lean into adapting when that happens.

Through this journey, I held onto a few truths that continue to guide me true:

1. My career choices are for me and my family. I don't owe anyone outside of that an explanation.

2. Time is an investment. I need to invest my time into work that meets the needs of myself and family.

3. I can do anything, but I can't do everything. It's okay to prioritize what makes sense for my life now, pivot later if needed, and trust that I'll be okay.

4. I am resilient. Fear is natural, but I've faced it before. With intentional preparation, I'll be ready when the right opportunity comes along.

5. My career and my identity are not the same. My career is what I do because of who I am and what I need. What I do may need to shift as I continue to grow. Sometimes, it's important to let go of what our lives could be so we can embrace what should be. And that is not always easy.

What ends up guiding you may be different, but here's what I know for certain: teaching has equipped you with resilience and adaptability. Even if these truths don't fit your journey, you already have the tools to figure out what does.

Let go of the idea that a career is a destination. Embrace the journey and lean into the life that happens in between.

Sara Stevick, Former Teacher,
Director of Product Delivery and Design,
Learning Leader, Strategist, and Technologist,
Founder of Teaching: A Path to L&D

Adult Services Program Manager - Phyllis
Taught for 1 year - Grade: 5

I remember that Aunt Nellie (your mom, my great-aunt) was a teacher and I knew that you were a teacher, but after all of these years, I don't think I've ever asked you, why did you go into education?

I got into teaching because I wasn't really sure what I wanted to do. When I started college, I kept asking myself, What should I major in? Since I had a scholarship, I thought, "Okay, education seems like a good path." So, I got a degree in education, in mathematics.

I taught math for one year, but I realized teaching wasn't for me. I was still living at home then, not here in Virginia. When I left teaching, I still wanted to work with kids, so I applied at the YMCA for a role as a program manager in their child development program. My education degree helped make the transition into program management pretty smooth.

What skills did you take from your education into that role?

Well, there I learned more management skills while I was teaching, working directly with the children, trying to help them understand the process and navigate the system because there were so many kids in the classroom.

I think I really learned how to deal with people, how to deal with crazy parents. But I wasn't as confined. Principals have more restrictions than I did as a program manager at the YMCA.

I remember when you worked at the Y in California! What was next?

I liked that we had over 200 children at the site, along with eight other sites, each with its own unique element. Then I received a notice that Parks and Recreation and Healthy Families for the city were going to take over the program before it actually started.

I learned about their work and thought, "I think I'd rather get into that." I saw an opening in Social Services, applied without fully knowing the role, and discovered it was a case manager position in benefits. In this role, I learned how to establish clients for Medicaid, TANF, and food stamps. I did that for about three or four years before realizing there was so much more you could do within social services. I moved up to a supervisor role, still in benefits for a few years, before eventually transferring to the services side.

I became really interested in it and became a family service specialist. I would go out and talk to individuals about the different services we offer, including long-term care services, home health, and companion services.

About a year after that, I became an APS, or Adult Protective Services, worker, and I did that for about a year. Then I got promoted to adult services program manager, which is pretty much where I am now. I oversee the whole department: benefits, adult protective services, and foster grandparents.

What kind of training have you had to prepare for your role as a program manager? Are there specific skills or aspects of the job that your training has helped you with?

I went back to school to earn a master's degree in human services because without a degree in this field, it's difficult to enter. I also completed eight certification courses with the state for the required training.

How did you learn program management skills?

I think I took a little bit from everything I have done. When I was the manager at the Y, it was different. What I did learn at the Y was how to relate to parents and people. When I came to Virginia, I learned how to handle difficult staff. I took a course on having open, difficult, courageous conversations. I also took training in conflict resolution. These were intense, and I took it upon myself to learn how to deal with adults, even though they're adults. Many adults don't know how to manage their own behavior. They might say, "Oh, I'm doing this and that," but when you look at the big picture, they're only doing half of their job. You have to explain to them, "Look at all the requirements you need to meet." They have to manage their time to get everything done. I realized people have a perception of themselves that may or may not be accurate, so I took a course on communicating with staff to help them understand.

Can you walk me through an example of your workflow?

We get calls through the hotline when somebody's being abused, whether it's physical, sexual, or financial exploitation. Then an investigator goes out to conduct the investigation. They talk to the person, people in the community, and, in cases of financial exploitation, the bank. We gather evidence and decide how to help, even if it's as simple as involving the police. Sometimes we need to remove the individual from the situation, or they might have to close their bank account and reissue everything. If the perpetrator lives with them, we might need to have them arrested to get them out of the environment. There's a lot we handle in protective services. My role is to review the investigator's notes after the investigation. I check that everything is included to follow the story from start to finish, and then I let the supervisor know if it's complete.

Who assigns the paperwork for someone to go out there? Once the call comes in, how does it move from the call to becoming a case?

Okay. We have different units under our services, whether it's APS or other programs. APS has what we call an intake unit. Intake takes calls, and each case is assigned in rotation to a family service specialist. They go out and do the APS investigations, while other departments handle different tasks. We have a specific person to arrange services when someone isn't fully safe. In these cases, they'll close the investigation and transfer it to an ongoing worker who monitors the situation to ensure the abuser doesn't return. The ongoing worker checks that law enforcement and others do their part to keep the person safe before closing the case. My role is to oversee all these programs, whether it's reviewing records or managing grants. For example, Foster Grandparents is a grant program, and I wrote the grant a couple of months ago.

How did you know how to write a grant? Where did you learn that?

To be honest with you, I had no idea. This was my first time writing the grant. I reviewed the requirements for the grant, read over what AmeriCorps and CSCF require, and then wrote the narrative. I had to figure out what was needed for each section to create the budget. I drafted it and gave it to our financial officer to ensure I had done it correctly. I completed all the narratives and gave them to my director, as I report directly to her. She read it, gave me a few pointers, and I made updates. Once the budget was finalized, we submitted the grant, and I'm happy to say it was approved last Thursday.

Congratulations! How many services or programs do you oversee?

Five. The largest part of my job is community presentations. I do them two or three times a week to get the word out because people often think they know what we do, but they don't. For some reason, everyone knows what's available for children, but few know what's available for older adults.

Do you set up these community presentations yourself, or do they come through other channels?

They come in different ways. Some of them I search out myself, and some come through my administrative assistant. During our one-on-one, she'll say, "These three requests came in, and they want to know if you would come to their community to talk about adult services." So I'll set those up. Other requests come through the director. People will email her directly, saying, "Hey, we have a triad meeting next month. Could you or someone else come out and talk to us about the services available for seniors?" She'll forward those emails to me, and I'll handle those presentations.

Is there anything else you'd like to share about your responsibilities and the types of duties you handle?

There are so many little things I do. We recently completed a monitoring process for one of our grants. I have to ensure we're in compliance for both state and federal monitoring. The state monitoring covers benefits, while the federal monitoring focuses on the grant. After the monitoring, if there's a CAP or Corrective Action Plan, I am responsible for creating and implementing it.

What is the most challenging part of your position?

Honestly, personnel issues are the hardest part because they involve people. The rest of my job is more energizing. Presentations make me nervous, but once I'm in the middle of one, the nerves go away. I actually enjoy writing grants. It was kind of cool to learn, and it's neat to see what you can accomplish for your agency. The one thing I dislike even more than personnel issues, though, is meetings. I can't stand them. Some meetings are mandatory. I have to meet with my staff as a group at least once a month, and I also have one-on-one meetings with my supervisor. These leadership meetings are required since we have about seven program managers and a director. There are other meetings, like the Mayor's Senior Administration Committee and the City Manager's Senior Citizens Committee, which meet monthly. I want to say there are about twelve meetings like these. What I've done is delegate some of them. I let my three supervisors attend certain meetings, and they report back to me during our one-on-ones. Some of these meetings can last one or two hours, but when my supervisors attend, they can summarize it for me in ten or fifteen minutes.

Are there times when you need to prepare something for them, and if so, what are you preparing?

I usually prepare for these meetings if a presentation is needed. People always want to know what social services or human services do and why they are important. When I go to meetings, they often want a presentation, so I handle that. If it's not a presentation, I let the workers attend.

It sounds to me like the way I want to frame your story is that you got started early and have worked your way up in a specific field. I am often in conversations and circles where I see young career teachers saying, "I might have made a mistake. I don't want to do this." I want to show them through your story that, first, you can work your way up through a system, and second, there are other ways to help people besides teaching. Is there anything else you want to share about your career path?

I've been very blessed. After a conversation with my supervisor, she encouraged me to finish a doctorate program, even though I plan to retire within the next ten years. I'm proud to be going back because it's something personal, not career-driven like my master's degree was. It's a doctorate in human services, so I can draw from my work experiences in my papers and projects. Right now, I'm in a grant writing class, which is funny, considering I just wrote a grant. My teacher even said, "Why are you here? You don't need this class." It feels like I'm coming full circle, as I plan to use this doctorate to teach remotely at the master's level. One instructor told me, "You can teach anywhere, and do it online."

It's funny to think I'll start and end my career as an instructor, just at the college level instead of fifth grade. Teaching fifth grade was intense. I was 22 years old, and the kids were like the ages of my nieces and nephews. My first class had 45 students, which was typical in California back then. They've since reduced class sizes, but when I was student teaching, I had a third-grade class of only 20 students, and I loved it. I thought, "Oh my gosh, I love this." But when I got my own class, I wondered, "Where is everyone to help me?" I had one aide who rarely showed up. The lesson plans were overwhelming, and some parents expected me to handle everything. Then I saw my paycheck and thought, "This doesn't match what I'm doing." When I got older, I realized my mom had managed because her classrooms had only 15 or 20 kids. In that environment, you can focus and think, "This is my noble profession. I enjoy this." I'm glad my experience was different, though, because otherwise, I might have stayed in teaching like my mom did for 45 years and retired from it. I'm grateful my path unfolded as it did. I have never felt "job-locked." Now I know I don't want to stay in one role forever, but I love my job. I get to do so many different things, whether I'm at work, at home, doing presentations, or handling one-on-ones and staff issues. I love the work itself, and I have a lot of flexibility.

Ambassador of Change - Kelly
Taught for 29 years - Grades: K - 5

What is your current title?

I am a Reading Specialist at a K-5 school, but I call myself the Ambassador of Change because I am on a mission to change how we as a nation prepare to continue education delivery, even in an emergency situation.

Why did you become a teacher?

I actually fell into teaching. I wanted to get into fashion from a little girl. I was raising my daughter by myself as a single mom and was on public assistance, and my case manager suggested that I apply to become a substitute teacher. I really got into substitute teaching and excelled, and that's how I literally got into education. But I wanted to be a fashion buyer. I wanted to travel all over the world and attend fashion shows and live in a Chateau in France. But God had another plan, so I got into education almost 29 years ago.

If you could change one area in education, what would it be?

I would change state standardized assessments. I'm just going to be honest. It puts too much pressure on the schools and on our kids. I would remove it and let teachers go back to teaching. When I was growing up and even when my daughter was in school up until 2000, they took one formative assessment. The scores were sent to the state and never affected graduation. As teachers, we used the data as a measuring tool and benchmark. However, we were not teaching to a test. They would give you the fundamental skills that you needed to ensure that you had mastered the skills. I don't think there's anything wrong with performance summative assessments, but we use them for the wrong reasons. We do too much testing. And I think so much emphasis was placed on just a summative assessment that it took away from teaching. That's my biggest issue. We should not have implemented No Child Left Behind. We absolutely needed improvements, but did it get us in the top five for education globally?

Why did you leave education?

I knew that No Child Left Behind had left behind so many kids, and I was tired of the organization. I was tired of the red tape, politics, and I was extremely tired of teaching to the test. Then the pandemic happened, and I watched as our nation failed. I watched as we didn't really have an e-learning plan. There were pockets of the nation that were successful, but nationwide we failed our kids because we did not update our systems. Not long after we were all sent home, I saw the lack, and I was put in a position to train teachers in my building on how to transition to e-learning. I developed a protocol, and as it was unfolding in my local building, I felt a pulling, and I know that the Lord called me to make a change at the federal level. He gave me the vision to create a system so that, as a nation, we would be prepared for an emergency where we have access to the internet, but not the ability to gather in our school building. I continue to pray, and the Holy Spirit impressed upon me to write the e-learning plan for my current school as a model. I created a forecast for e-learning and what should be covered each month. I surveyed 100 teachers across the nation and even had participants from Mexico City and asked them if they had an e-learning protocol in the event of an emergency. The majority of them indicated no, that they were not prepared, and they wanted to participate and felt the need for a drill on a monthly basis.

I know you have talked to lawmakers about your vision, talk to me about that.

I began to talk to people about the plan, and even though I had the drive and desire, I soon realized there is a specific process to get noticed for it to even be considered for legislation. I was able to complete the draft plan and sent it to the US Department of Education Secretary, Dr. Miguel Cardona, who was very kind. I received an email that said, "We like what you're doing, but we don't coordinate this type of program at the federal level." I took issue with that answer because didn't they implement and mandate No Child Left Behind at the federal level? They then sent me to the actual Department of Education in Washington, D.C., where they told me they too loved what I was doing but that I should take it to my state official. A little bit of time passed, and then I heard that my U.S. State Representative, Kathy Castor, was going to be in Tampa. I made arrangements to meet with her and had the privilege of giving her my plan in person. She looked to see if there was any current legislation to which she could tie my proposal. I shared with her that I conducted the survey so that when I go to Congress, I will have my own data and actual accounts when asking for this federal mandate. I am fully aware that in its present form, it may need altering, but as long as the core goal of e-learning preparedness is addressed, then I will have completed my assignment.

You mentioned consulting, talk to me about that.

During the pandemic, I had a dream, and the Lord led me to use my gifts to start a business. I'm very detail-oriented, have great organizational skills, and I'm a visionary. As a result, I created a business where I use these gifts to help women transition into their "next". It is called Kelly E. Laws Consulting Firm, and I have had the privilege of assisting clients in discovering and achieving their goals. In the future, I plan to route consultations regarding the implementation of the eLearning preparedness program from schools through my firm. Additionally, I will establish a nonprofit arm to provide similar services to school districts that may not be able to afford the consulting services.

What advice do you have for teachers who want to switch careers?

You have to find your purpose. Just because you have been in education, does not mean that is your purpose. Education is a calling, not a job. So, if you pursued it for any reason other than being called to it, my recommendation is to pursue your purpose. Because your purpose will open doors for you that no man can shut. It will bring you personal satisfaction and fulfillment; then the money will come. Everyone should live a Purpose Driven life. Even if you're in education and feel it's time to leave the classroom, seek God and ask, "What is my next step? What would you have me do next?" We don't have time to waste. Time is a commodity that you can never get back. So, find your purpose and walk in it!

How did you get the courage or drive to go after this grand vision?

There was a sense of urgency in me that there is something greater. Everyone has it, whether you know God or not. He still has that part of you in Him. You must pursue something greater. It would have been uncomfortable for me to stay in what I know, which I was not called into, as opposed to leaving the classroom and getting out. There is no other option. Actually, you have an option, but you will live a very unfulfilled life. There was such a drive, and I tell people who come to me for consultation that the urge to do something else will push you out of here. And God will make everything around you so uncomfortable that you have no choice. You can stay and be miserable if you want. That's why I tell people when you feel that deep longing that this is not it, you must go. You must let the kids go; it's time to move on. You can't look back. I had fulfilled my purpose. You will know when you have fulfilled your purpose. I knew it was over. Everything had been a training ground to prepare me for what was next. In your next, you may have to transition with new friends. That will be hard sometimes because the people who were beneficial to you in one season will be detrimental in another. So, pray about it. But you can't stay in that place. If it's time to go, you must go; you can't look back.

Associate Director - Dr. Micaela
Taught for 9 Years - Grade: 6 - Subject: ELA

Did you say you had an interview, or are you in the process?

Yes, I've actually accepted a position. I know, Hallelujah! I'm going to be the Associate Director of Diversity, Equity, and Inclusion for the tech department, the IS and T department, at Boston University.

Okay, let's talk about that. You said Associate Director, and that really got me excited because I love the fact that you are stepping into this role, and it's not entry-level. Talk to me about what made you decide, "This is the position I'm going to apply for."

Honestly, part of it was trolling Instagram for the past two years, following every page with advice for career changers. I took a few pep talks from my mom, who reminded me I didn't need to meet every qualification listed. I was desperate and applying to anything, even if it was the CEO of Disney! I was just throwing everything out there to see what stuck. What I found was that universities gave me more callbacks and interviews during this process.

Tell me about your teaching experience. Were you in admin?

No, I don't have any administrative experience. I've been teaching for the past nine years. I started out at a private boarding school, where I worked for two years, and they paid for my master's degree. After that, I had what I'd call my gap year, working about 50 different jobs, including being a TA in an Applied Behavioral Analysis classroom for nonverbal special needs students. Following that, I spent six years at the charter school I just left on Friday in Long Island City.

Walk me through the process of making that decision because a lot of teachers get stuck in thinking, "Oh, I can't leave until summertime," or, "I can't leave because it's time to report back to school." What made you say, "This is it"?

It took me a long time, Dina, and it was such a hard decision to make. I had been toying with the idea and going back and forth on it since COVID. Were there issues before COVID? Absolutely. Did COVID make those issues worse? Yes, it did. After the first COVID year, around 2021 to 2022, I was completely exhausted and didn't know what to do. Then, I went into the following school year, and it ended up being the hardest year I've ever had in education.

When did you all go back after Covid?

We left in March 2020 and went back February or March 2021, pretty much a full year out of the school building.

Okay, so 2021, second semester, is when you all went back. But that wasn't your hardest year?

No, it was last year (2022).

I keep hearing that. What happened?

Number one, we were unbelievably drained. I had nothing left to give. None of us did. Admin, parents, students, no one. On top of that, my school decided to implement a new grading policy during COVID. Many of my kids hadn't been in school for a year or more, so student behavior was unlike anything I'd ever seen before. Combine that with the fact that the adults in charge of them were exhausted and overworked. Even our administrators, who were pretty good as far as administrators go, were given advice that didn't work because a lot of them had been out of the classroom for 10 years. It was unlike anything I've ever experienced, and Lord, I hope I never go through it again.

Give me a timeline for when you started filling out applications.

Last November(2021), so it took me almost two years (June 2023) from start to landing this position.

Wow! You did not give up. Did you keep track of how many applications you filled out?

Hundreds. I was like, "Apply, apply, apply." I had about 15 different versions of my resume and a thousand versions of cover letters.

So you were catering your resume and cover letters to the roles you were applying for, doing that whole scene. What else were you doing? Did you know about LinkedIn when you were still teaching?

I did. I had a LinkedIn, but it was probably the world's lamest LinkedIn. As teachers, we did not really use it or need it because we had our own systems for finding teaching roles. I did not feel the need to develop it until, honestly, a few months ago when the PBS interview dropped. Then I realized people were actually looking at it, and I thought, oh no, I need to fix this now.

Right, because we're in our own bubble as teachers, and we don't know much about things like LinkedIn. So, when you started optimizing your LinkedIn page, did you already know about the screening interview process and the other rounds before leaving education?

Yes, I did, mostly because the application process was somewhat similar. I didn't have to do a demo lesson, but I figured there'd be two or three rounds. For my current position, I actually went through four rounds, which was a lot, but it wasn't out of the ordinary for me. What made it challenging was that I was working full time, pursuing my doctorate, and trying to manage everything else while researching these jobs. It wasn't like getting on a Zoom call to talk about sixth-grade English Language Arts. I had to prepare to discuss a profession I'd never done before, which added another layer of work to be ready for these interviews.

I think a lot of teachers feel stuck because they don't have the internal knowledge or experience to know what else they can do. I know, in my case, I literally typed into the computer, "What else can a teacher do?"

I did too!

It's like we're in this bubble. Other people switching careers seem to already know what they can do, but as teachers, we're often clueless, thinking, "This is all I can do." But really, we have so many transferable skills. It's just about figuring out how to make them work. So, talk to me about the whole resume revamping process. Did you pay someone, or did you do it yourself?

I'm blessed that my younger sister used to be a recruiter, so she took a look at my resume and zhuzhed it up a bit. I also created multiple versions of my resume because I needed to tailor it to each role I applied for. For example, a data analytics resume looks very different from my DEI resume. It's not about lying but about focusing on what's relevant. My DEI resume doesn't need to highlight all the data analytics I've done. The hard part was breaking down and quantifying what we do as teachers. No one really knows how many jobs we're juggling. For instance, no one on the street would think teachers do a ton of data analysis, but we do. That realization was a big part of the process.

What else do you want to convey about the application process?

Do not stop. I got hundreds of rejection emails, some from people and some from automated systems. I did so many first-round interviews tons of second and third-rounds, but you just cannot stop. Eventually, something clicks, and you get it. Once you stop and give up, you box yourself into this profession. There were times when it was so hard, and the last thing I wanted to do was fill out another application or write another cover letter. But that momentary frustration was better than another year of unhappiness.

Did you take any breaks during this process?

No, I did not. I am not saying that was the right thing to do. I am not promoting hustle culture. Everyone needs to do what works for them, but I was ready. I did not get my position until Memorial Day weekend, but I was fully prepared to leave my job with nothing lined up. To me, that was better than going back. I was even ready to drive for Amazon if I had to.

Let's shift to education in general and what you think is going with the teacher shortage and exodus.

An issue right now, and I am speaking specifically for teachers, is that we are not taking care of the people who take care of the students. We talk about the massive issues facing students, and those issues are real, but we have neglected the professionals supporting them. Teacher salaries have been stagnant since 1990. Our country has de-professionalized teaching. The merit has been stripped away, and this has led to students feeling no hesitation in talking back and parents demanding things from teachers without concern. Teaching, a profession requiring a master's degree, has been reduced to customer service. It is less of a partnership and more of a client relationship.. If they asked for something, they would get it, even when it harmed their child. If they wanted their child's grade changed, it would happen. If they requested another test retake, no matter how many chances had already been given, it was granted.

We have turned a vital profession into something unrecognizable. We have boiled it down to calling us glorified babysitters! They told us what they thought of us when they sent us back into classrooms during COVID. They did not have to say it; they showed it. They put me in a

30-by-18 room with 25 kids and made it clear they did not care about my health, my well-being, or that of the students. They just wanted someone watching the kids. If I am a glorified babysitter, then pay me a babysitter's rate. I will take $30 an hour! In my nine years, every single year brought new responsibilities without any additional compensation. It used to be teaching commas, essays, and similes. Now, it is teaching identity, kindness, and social issues. While these are important, adding to our workload without support or compensation would be unacceptable in any other profession. I want people to understand that I did not want to leave. I still love teaching and always will. Leaving was not an easy choice, but it was a forced one. It came down to choosing between my mental and physical well-being or staying in the classroom. I had to choose myself, even though it broke my heart. We sign up for teaching knowing it is exhausting and underpaid because we love it. We accept the challenges because it is meaningful work. But when a profession built on empathy is pushed to the point where even those who thrive on it cannot stay, something has gone terribly wrong.

Teaching needs real support systems for the children, the system, and especially the teachers. If we could lighten the load on teachers, maybe teaching could become a joy again. People always talk about needing support, but what does that really mean to you?

Support starts with respect and pay that matches our workload. Did you know in Pennsylvania, there were over 16,000 new teacher certification applicants in 2012? By 2022, that number dropped to 4,200.

Yes, the system is broken. We know it is broken, but now it is breaking the people holding it up. It has been broken for a long time, but it feels worse now.

Exactly. We hold it up, and now they are kicking us out. Once we are gone, there will be nothing holding it together unless they make big changes.

That is staggering.

It is not just teachers leaving; people are not even going into the profession. A former lacrosse player I coached asked me if she should become a teacher. I told her not to do it. I said, "Maybe try being a TA for a year before spending the money because the pay is not worth it."

I wish I had another skill set sometimes.

So many teachers feel the same. Every teacher I know is exhausted and overworked. My question is, when does it stop? What will it take to make a change? Losing the entire teaching workforce? Kids failing standardized exams? Kids with no social skills who cannot read or write? All of this is happening right now, and still, nothing changes.

And teachers face so much more than anyone outside the profession realizes.

Exactly. Every day, we are managing layers of stress, and on top of that, we could be shot at any moment. People forget about that. What other job has code blue drills? What other job requires you to cram 30 eleven-year-olds into a dark corner and hope for the best? Our jobs are not just harder; they are scarier, and no one is doing anything to fix it.

When I started teaching, we did fire drills, tornado drills, and active shooter drills. At one school, we practiced barricading doors with desks. In another, kids were told to hide under tables in the cafeteria. At my trailer classroom, we lined up against the walls between two doors. We just adapted.

Actually, it's not adapting, it's surviving. My only thought during those drills was, "How do I protect my kids?" We rehearsed trauma multiple times a year but never stopped to process it. If we had, it would have broken us.

In corporate America, they handle change with these big change management plans. Teams spend months planning every little detail when they roll out something new. But for us, they just said, "We are starting these drills. Good luck."

Exactly.

I remember doing A.L.I.C.E. training. We had to run out of the building...some went to the football stadium, others ran up the road to a designated store. They even announced where the "shooter" was during the drill.

When you stop and think about that, it is horrifying! At my ABA school, where most of my students were nonverbal and had special needs, we still had to do shooter drills. We put the kids in a corner and gave them iPads with headphones, but they were still terrified.

I know you're about to start your new position soon, and I'd love to include an update, but what is your final advice for teachers who want to find a new career?

I want every teacher to know that if they want to leave, they can. It is not a matter of "I can't." You can. It will take time, and it will be hard emotionally and as a process. It might take a month, or it might take two years, but it is possible. Teachers are so smart and capable, and we can do incredible things outside the classroom. I am excited that the world is going to start seeing what we can do. We get to step into new opportunities, discover our potential, and achieve amazing things. I am proud of us for refusing to accept the bare minimum.

Resources: Access Micaela's interview with PBS, "A Brief But Spectacular Take on teacher burnout" https://www.pbs.org/newshour/brief/448026/micaela-desimone

Attorney - Specializing in Education and Special Education - Lauren
Taught for 3 years - Grade: HS
Subject: Special Education ages 13-21

How and why did you become a teacher?

I graduated from Denison University with a major in Sociology and Anthropology, but I knew I enjoyed working with young people and had a passion for helping vulnerable populations and students with disabilities. I worked with Special Olympics over the years and eventually decided to start my teaching career with Teach for America since I couldn't get my teaching certificate in my undergraduate program. I was hired as a multi-intensive special education teacher at a school in Denver, Colorado, where I ran a center-based program for students with multiple disabilities, ranging from ages 13 to 21. This position suited me well because I didn't want to just push in and pull out students to serve their minutes; I wanted to be able to provide my students with a holistic approach.

I also served as the work-study coordinator, helping students learn to ride public transportation and participate in job shadow opportunities, as well as getting hired in paid positions. I taught every subject: reading, writing, math, science, social studies, life skills, cooking, financial literacy, and career readiness. Our school was called an Innovation School, which meant that we could operate differently than the traditional public schools in Colorado. We took students on trips across the country that aligned with the curriculum we were teaching each semester, and I designed a class tailored towards each trip so my students could also fully participate along with their general education peers. For example, we went whitewater rafting, where we learned about the pine beetle and water conservation. We also traveled to the Pine Ridge Indian Reservation, and students from both high schools wrote personal narratives and shared them in advance before the trip so they could learn about each other when we visited. The goal was to give them experiences they'd never had and show them what they could achieve.

It sounds like you were right in your zone. Why did you leave?

I was teaching and coaching varsity and junior varsity sports as well as Special Olympics and Project Unify. I was working sometimes nearly 100 hours a week, which meant most nights and weekends, and my school was year-round. I never really got a break to recharge, and, at the time, we didn't know a lot about self-care. My colleagues were great teachers and wonderful parents, but I could see that they didn't have much time for their families. They were on the football field until 10 p.m. and struggling to balance everything. I saw burnout, stress, and a lack of support. I did not want my true self to be lost, and I didn't not want to reach a point where I was frustrated with students because of adult issues.

My husband, Dan, and I knew that one day we wanted children of our own, but we wanted to be able to have careers where we were able to spend a lot of time with our own kids and still serve other kids in the community. In 2014, we decided not to renew our teaching contracts and embarked on a cross-country bike trip with 31 amazing young people from across the country and globe. Through Bike and Build, we biked from Portland, Maine, to Santa Barbara, California, traveling over 4,000 miles and building houses with Habitat for Humanity while raising funds for affordable housing It was not only a challenging trip since there are a lot of hills across the U.S., but it was inspiring to see the country that way and provided us with a lot of time for soul searching while on our bikes.

You mentioned "lack of support." What does that look like?

I will use leadership support as an example, especially regarding student behaviors. When I first started, there were clear expectations and consistency in enforcing them. If a student had a hat on, they were asked to take it off. But when you let one student slide and then another, it becomes impossible to maintain consistency. If a student disrupted the class, they would be sent to in-school suspension, but they would just be sitting there, painting their nails, or on their phones. It felt like we were not supported in maintaining a positive learning environment for students and one that set high expectations for students and staff and then supported that.

So, how did you land on becoming a lawyer?

During our summer bike trip, I reflected a lot, and I remembered that my grandmother had always said growing up that I would make a good lawyer someday. I didn't have any family members who were lawyers, but it was always in the back of my mind since I had a passion for justice. Had I pursued law school right after undergrad, I probably would have done environmental law. But because I was a teacher, I was drawn to education and special education law. After law school, I participated in a fellowship called the Greif Fellowship in Juvenile Human Trafficking. I represented young people, mostly young girls but also boys, who were victims of human trafficking in Ohio. It was hard but incredibly rewarding work. In every single one of those cases, my clients had education issues and were often students with disabilities who were unidentified and not supported in school. As a teacher-turned-lawyer, I could see the gap between education and legal advocacy for young people.

What can you share about attending law school?

I frequently have this conversation with teachers and sometimes even administrators. They always say they wish they could do what I do and go to law school. I assure them that they can, and it may not be easy or a straight path, but that if it is something they really want to do, then they should seriously consider it. I always encourage people to talk with other people in the field, go shadow lawyers, and ask what their day-to-day looks like. It is important in whatever field you choose to understand the different options out there and get different perspectives so you can be as knowledgeable as possible for making the jump. Law school isn't easy, but it is one of the rare professional degrees you can get without specific prerequisite requirements. You just have to have an undergraduate degree in any field and then take the LSAT. Unlike medical school or some other graduate programs where you must meet certain prerequisites, law school allows for a diverse background. You could have been a math, Spanish, technology or even a special education teacher or really have had any other career prior to going to law school, and I believe those experiences make people better attorneys in the long run.

Most full-time law school programs span three years, or part-time programs typically take four years, with evening classes offered for working individuals. The three years go by quickly, but it is still a lot of time and a lot of reading and writing. I think there is a lot of apprehension about going to law school, and I want people to know that if you attend classes, put in the work, and build rapport with your professors, they want you to succeed and will do everything in their power to help you to do that. Statistically, most people who start law school graduate with their Juris Doctorate. They may not all practice law, as some people will end up in JD-preferred careers, but you may be more marketable because of your legal training.

I represent students and families when they have issues concerning education or special education and need additional advocacy and support. I attend meetings and hearings with students and will also represent them if they end up in court with criminal charges I'm not in court all day, every day, though, which I like. I go to schools and work with teachers and administrators to help get students back on track or help families and schools rebuild trust that has been lost. Each day looks different for me, and I love that about the job. When I was a teacher, I went to bed every night knowing that I was making a difference in the lives of young people, and I still feel that way as a lawyer. I represent students and families during some of their most challenging times, and to have the background as a teacher has been a blessing that has made me an even better attorney.

The great part about the law is that it is so broad, and there is probably a job out that that would be in an area of interest or passion. As I said before, here are careers that are often referred to as "JD preferred," meaning you are not practicing law in the traditional sense. Someone may have not taken the bar exam, or even if they did, they are not currently giving legal advice in their role. However, being JD preferred makes a strong candidate for roles in the nonprofit sector and even in the corporate world.. Companies and organizations often someone with a law degree, with that specific training and background, even though they may not be handling criminal or civil cases or offering legal advice. There are also transactional roles, which primarily involve reviewing contracts working in tax law, and similar areas. In these roles, you might still interact with clients, but the majority of your work focuses on the documents, such as reviewing, drafting, and handling various legal contracts.

Tell me a little about studying for the LSAT.

The LSAT is a standardized test with three main components. One of the sections is essentially problem-solving games. They are called logic games and require a different way of thinking. It is not just reading and comprehension. You have to practice these games and puzzles. There are prep courses that people pay for, and looking back, it would have been helpful. It can be a stressful test for people who may not like standardized tests, but you can always take it more than once if you want to improve your score. It is important to familiarize yourself with the test beforehand and then practice a lot and know what score you need to be a sought-after candidate for whatever law school or schools you want to apply to, as well as any potential scholarship opportunities since some scholarships use your LSAT score and your undergraduate GPA as the criteria for their financial award.

What about the grind of law school?

Law school is a grind that includes a lot of reading and writing in a way that may be new to most people. Grading is on a bell curve, which means most students in the class will earn B's, a few will earn A's, and the professor usually has to give out a couple of C's. Your grade might be based on a single exam in some classes, so there isn't a lot of opportunity to know how you are doing throughout the class like a more traditional undergraduate class. As a teacher, it is hard because law professors do not always have a background in teaching philosophy or best practices and strategies to help all learners. Cold calling can still be common practice in some lectures, where the professor opens the book and will randomly choose a student in the class to answer questions. This can be nerve-racking for some students, but worst case, you get the question wrong and you learn and move on. It is challenging because it is not how we teach in most schools leading up to law school, so it can be intimidating, and professors are not necessarily trained in pedagogy, which can make it hard for students who may have a different learning style, but a student can request accommodations and work with their professors to ensure they are being able to engage in the classroom discussions and understand the material.

How do you obtain clients?

I wish I had a better answer—they find me. I don't do any marketing, which is really nice. I run my own law firm now, so a lot of referrals are just word of mouth. Former clients who refer schools, including superintendents and directors of special education, will give my name to families, the school's attorney, or other attorneys in the community. People also find me online since they have a very specific education or special education issue, so they want an attorney who has a background and experience handling those types of cases If someone is hiring an education attorney, it means things are not going well, but I try to help students stay in school and figure things out. My background also helps when I am in meetings with other school staff since once they hear that I am a former teacher, they realize that I am not there to sue the school but rather to work as a part of the team to help everyone get back on track.

Do you have any resources for teachers considering a career change?

Ask for fee waivers for your application. Law school applications can be expensive, and depending on your situation, you may want to apply to multiple schools. I didn't pay for a single application because I asked for fee waivers, that way, I could apply to more schools without having to spend extra money. If you tour the law school prior to applying, you may also get a fee waiver in order to apply, but it's also amazing how a quick email can get a positive response. Also, negotiate scholarships. If you are accepted to two schools that are rated similarly and one offers more money, ask the other to match or beat it. The worst they can say is no. Another piece of advice is to look for scholarships that you might not think you qualify for. As a teacher, you bring a unique perspective and diversity to the law school classroom.

How has transitioning to being an attorney impacted your view on teaching?

I want to encourage people that they can take a different path. I still work with students and families every single day, just in a different capacity. Teachers work so hard, and they do not get the pay or validation they deserve. I respect teachers deeply, and I am so glad I made the change. I am a much better attorney because I was a teacher, and I know my clients feel that as do the other community members I work with

Everyone I have talked to says the same thing, that they are better at what they do because they were teachers. Do you have any final advice?

You can leave, transition, or take a break and always come back to teaching! Teachers do not get the validation or pay that they deserve, but I know when I was a teacher, every day, I felt like I was making a difference.

I still feel that way in my current role; it just looks a little different now. Plus, I guest lecture in a lot of classrooms, and I am an adjunct professor, so I still get to teach, and now I get to share my passion for education and the law with other students!

Business Operations Manager, Project Manager - Marc
Taught for 6 years - Grades: 5 & 6 Subjects: Math & Science

What made you decide to leave teaching for a new career?

What inspired me to leave the teaching profession and pursue a new career was a combination of factors. After six years, I started considering opportunities outside the classroom. I wanted to stay in education, ideally in an ed-tech role, since our school worked with many companies in that space. I applied to numerous positions and tried connecting with people at those organizations, but nothing worked out, and I transitioned into the entertainment industry. During my sixth year, I began taking on additional responsibilities at school, like managing programmatic tasks, coaching a committee, and handling logistics, to try something new. In my final year, I told my principal I did not want to stay in the classroom and was interested in a programmatic role supporting teachers, like curriculum development or instructional design. Unfortunately, there was no budget for that position. That was when I realized I needed to focus on opportunities outside of teaching. Teaching has always had challenges, but every year felt like a fresh start with new students. By my sixth year, though, things started to shift. The students were more challenging, but that was not what made me leave. The real issue was a lack of support from administration and inconsistent expectations among teachers. I maintained strong classroom management, but others let things slide, which caused behavior issues. I encouraged consistency within the team, but it did not work. This imbalance, along with unfulfilled promises from administration, left me drained. The stress affected me physically. My eye twitched daily, my skin became dry, and I dreaded Sundays because of the looming workweek. Eventually, I told myself, "Enough is enough." It was time to move on.

Yes, I think we lived the same life! I was the "no-phone teacher". The policy was clear, students were not supposed to use their phones in the classroom unless it was for an assignment. I told them, "When you come into my classroom, put it in your book bag." Too many other teachers, though, did not enforce it consistently. That made me look like the bad one, like I was over the top. It was not just the kids; even some of the teachers thought, "Oh, that's so extra." If students have their phones, they are not learning or paying attention. Sunday nights became the worst. I dreaded going back. I can laugh about it now, but at the time it was horrible.

For me, it got to a point where I stopped going to the lunchroom to hang out with other teachers. Instead, I would stay in my room during lunch breaks and look for jobs because I just could not handle it anymore.

What skills did you bring from the entertainment company into where you are now?

I think a lot of the skills I learned in that first position were about handling operational tasks in a business setting. One of the struggles I had when applying for jobs after teaching was that being a teacher was the most recent experience on my resume. Employers would see that and often form an image of what a teacher does, which might not align with the skills they were looking for. That made it difficult to get interviews in the first place and then express my transferable skills effectively. By the time I moved into my next role, I already had some experience working with business partners and stakeholders and understanding cross-team processes. I was able to combine that with my teaching experience and present those skills effectively for other roles. My current role also started as a contractor position, but eventually, I was promoted to full-time. To prepare for this field, I took a project management certificate course. I had already completed graduate school for teaching, and I wasn't sure I had it in me to go back to school for several years for something I might not even find work in. The online course was a way to meet myself halfway, allowing me to learn at my own pace. While taking the course, I landed a contract position, so I was able to build experience while completing the program. Even now, in a world where layoffs are common, I remind myself there are no guarantees I'll have this position tomorrow. I continually work to build my skills, taking LinkedIn Learning courses and exploring other areas. Although I'm not currently doing project management tasks, the course I took could still prove useful in the future. I'm grateful I pursued that extra education to make myself a stronger candidate.

Let's talk about your first role after leaving teaching.

It started as a contract role. The focus was less on strategizing and decision-making and more on executing a high volume of work. On this streaming platform my job was to ensure that the art shown to consumers was ordered, delivered, and displayed on the platform. I worked with external agencies to coordinate thousands of assets each week, making sure everything was submitted on time and looked good for the consumer. The contract was initially six months but was extended to a year because my managers recognized the quality of my work. Contractors often experience high turnover, but I was asked to take on additional responsibilities. This included piloting a new tool for the team, which I later helped scale for broader use. While I didn't make major decisions, I provided feedback, identifying what worked and what didn't for the tool, and suggested improvements to benefit the larger team.

I am looking at your resume...what is AVOD?

Ads are a key part of streaming platforms. Some plans come with commercials, which make them cheaper for consumers. Essentially, you're paying for ads in exchange for a lower cost. VOD stands for video on demand, and most streaming services fall into this category. They often offer both ad-supported plans and subscription-based options without ads.

CMS tools?

The content management system I use now is very similar to the learning management system (LMS) I used when I was teaching. I always see that as a transferable skill.

So, let's move on to your current position. Tell me about what you do and again, explain it as if you're talking to a kindergartner.

I work for an entertainment company with a streaming platform, and my job is to ensure our content is available to consumers without any issues. My work is downstream, at the end of the workflow, tying everything together to present it to the consumer. We aim to create a polished, user-friendly experience with well-organized content pages that encourage users to engage by exploring what we offer. Part of my role involves operational tasks like A/B testing, where we evaluate different approaches to drive the best consumer engagement. I focus on setting up these processes, analyzing results, and strategizing improvements to manage the final operational flow. For example, I spend two and a half to three days building and maintaining pages for the platform, such as the homepage or category-specific pages like movies, series, or action genres. These are the pages consumers interact with when browsing content on the app. My work also includes troubleshooting issues like artwork not displaying correctly, features malfunctioning, or other technical glitches. I identify the source of problems, try different solutions, rule out potential causes, and resolve issues to ensure a seamless platform experience. My role is a mix of building, testing, and problem-solving to deliver high-quality, functional pages that enhance the user experience.

What did cross-functional collaboration look like in your role?

For me, I primarily work in operational roles. My team is operations, but we do have other teams like product design, engineering, and many more. I work in a tech company with a lot of different teams and moving parts. In terms of cross-functional collaboration, it's about being able to work with different team members, understanding their workflows, and ensuring that our workflows align to benefit the business overall. Sometimes, what works well for our team might hinder theirs, so it's crucial to understand how all teams operate and collaborate to make the processes functional for everyone.

When I left education in 2021, I mostly worked in a silo despite having team meetings and other collaborative activities. Cross-functional collaboration, as you describe it, feels new to me. In education, we worked with others, but it was different. Can you explain how this works for you? Are you a project manager, or do you have project managers coordinating this?

Yeah, we have project managers handling all the coordination. My role is more like an operations manager, where I focus on a specific area. I coordinate with the project managers or, depending on the task, directly with team members across departments.

Okay, talk to me a little bit about workflows like I'm a kindergartner.

We follow a step-by-step process where each of us has a sequence to complete, starting with step one, then step two, and then step three. I also need to understand the steps of other teams and identify where our steps overlap. That is where we find the best opportunities to ensure things operate as smoothly as possible. If those steps are out of sync, it increases the likelihood of encountering issues.

What is the difference between what you do and user experience research (UXR)? It sounds like you're involved in activities like A/B testing and UI interfacing, but not fully on that side. Could you clarify?

Most tech companies incorporate this kind of work, and while I assist with it, I'm not directly involved in the research or data analytics portion. Honestly, that's not an area I'm passionate about. I'm more focused on the operational side, ensuring that processes are efficient. For example, if I notice two steps in a workflow are wasting time, I work to streamline them and improve the process. That's where my focus lies.

What did your training look like because I want to know how you know what you know?

I was hired for my current position in 2020 during the lockdown, so all my training was done virtually. I learned the basics of the content management system and other tools we use, starting with an overview of what they do and their key functions. After that, I practiced in a test environment where I could build things out and experiment with the tools. Once I demonstrated I could use the tools correctly in the test environment, I moved on to the live environment, where the work directly impacts what the consumer sees. In this role, I am not involved in UI design or coding. My job is to take all the pieces and put them together in a polished and functional way for the consumer. For example, I ensure that everything is working properly by clicking through and testing all the features. If a tool sends you to the wrong page or displays an error message, I troubleshoot to figure out why and fix the issue. Ultimately, my focus is making sure everything works as it should and provides a seamless experience for the consumer.

Is that a sandbox or testing environment or do you call it something different?

Yeah, some people might call it a sandbox or testing environment.

So, let's go back...when you went to that interview, what do you think helped you get the position? Was it knowing someone, or was there a specific skill or part of the process that made them say, "Yeah, you're the one"?

I think it came down to my passion for entertainment. As a teacher, I often connected with my students by discussing movies, TV shows, video games, and other things they were interested in. I tried to incorporate those topics into my lessons or use them to make concepts more accessible. I think that passion for entertainment came through during the interview. They also asked technical questions about how I would handle challenges, like prioritizing tasks or dealing with things not being turned in on time. I was able to draw on my teaching experience, such as managing late assignments or resolving conflicts between students, and translate those into skills relevant to the role. It took weeks of reflecting on my experiences to figure out how to present them as transferable skills, but by the time of the interview, I was able to express that really well.

What was it like transitioning from teaching to your current role? How did you figure out your next steps and handle any challenges along the way?

After I decided to leave teaching, I informed my school that I wouldn't be returning the next year. At that point, I didn't have anything planned. It was June, the school year was over, and I began applying to a lot of edtech jobs. I really wanted to stay in education and help teachers and schools in a different way, but I was burned out from being in the classroom. Unfortunately, every job I applied for resulted in rejection emails, and I was trying to figure out my next steps. One thing I enjoyed at my school was the operational work. I co-chaired committees in high school, organized large events, and handled programming logistics. I realized I really liked that type of work. After finishing teaching and continuing my job search, I enrolled in a project management certificate course at UCLA Extension to gain experience and knowledge outside of teaching. While taking the course, I reached out to my network for referrals. Fortunately,

I knew someone at a major company who referred me for a contractor role. Thanks to that referral, I landed an interview, secured the position, and got my foot in the door.

What advice would you give someone considering leaving teaching for a new career?

I would say it's a leap of faith. Leaving teaching isn't easy, and not everyone has the opportunity to do so. Sometimes, you want to leave a job, but you can't because of dependents, raising a family, or the risk of losing benefits and stability. If you can, take that leap of faith and trust yourself. It's okay to face failures because they help you learn what you are capable of and where you need to grow. Trust your network. There can be hesitation in posting publicly that you're looking for a job, but someone might say, "I know someone hiring," or "We need someone on our team, and you'd be a great fit." It's worth taking that risk. I don't have regrets about leaving teaching, but I did feel some guilt. You're not just leaving a job; you're leaving the kids. Even now, there's a little of that guilt. I remind myself that if I had stayed, I would have burned out completely. Despite the guilt, I'm grateful I took the risk. I'm much happier now, and it has made all the difference.

Case Manager (Out of District) - Tia
Taught for 7 years - Grades: K - 8 - Subject: Special Education

Did you think about other careers?

I saw a lot about instructional design, but I never got into it. At that time, education was something I was debating on whether or not I would want to get back into it. I do miss working with the kids, but there are just so many logistics and people have their hands on so many things; it kind of makes it hard for you to be successful. They were looking for a lot of reading specialists, and since I am also a specialist teacher, I could have gone back to school, but I already have two master's, so I didn't want to do that.

Describe your responsibilities in this new role.

I'm still working in education but now at a parent-choice school, focusing on the same type of students. However, my role has shifted to managing their Individualized Education Programs (IEPs), conducting all their meetings, and overseeing the Transition Partnership Programs (TPPs) to ensure their needs and support are met. I've encountered students who've been expelled, necessitating adjustments to their IEPs to align with their new schedules. Navigating situations with educational surrogates who may or may not be cooperative is part of my job. Legal issues have also arisen, particularly with students absent from school, leading to disputes between parents and the district. Every day brings something new. For example, I might receive urgent calls from parents concerned that their child hasn't received all their services, prompting me to liaise with other districts and schools to verify and document these services.

There are quieter days without phone calls, which I cherish, as they allow me to concentrate on updating IEPs. Of course, when entering that data, it has to be correct and up to date, but the difference is that I can't run down the hall to ask a teacher a question, it requires a lot more contacts. In specific cases, like when a student needs bilingual services, I have to source external contractors. This role has empowered me to advocate for students in ways I previously couldn't, ensuring they receive all necessary services. Some parents, overwhelmed or uninformed about the full spectrum of their child's needs, are simply relieved to work through the day uninterrupted by calls from the school.

What is one of the things that you really enjoy about this position?

Well, the first thing I enjoy is not getting bit, hit, or slapped. I have more control over what's going on and I feel even more knowledgeable.

Why did you become a teacher?

It was actually a fourth-grade teacher who was awful. She was mean to all the students, and I always said that I never wanted anybody to feel the way that she made other kids feel.

What made you leave the classroom?

Typically, when a new curriculum is rolled out, we see it during the summer. We have an opportunity to review it, discuss it with the company and our peers, determine how to use it, etc. This particular year, our district didn't introduce it to us during the summer and just threw it at everybody. There were a lot of teachers who didn't know what to do in terms of following it with fidelity. Because I have been in the field for many years and I am duly certified, a lot of teachers started asking me a lot of support questions. This may not seem like a big deal, but I had just recently revamped the way I was providing instruction and support for my students. I was also the union representative, and there were situations that I had to address as the union representative that consumed time. We were also very short-staffed, and I was being pulled into other classrooms or had additional students added to my room because of the shortage. With my population of high-needs Special Education students who also required 1:1 staff of students, we had to maintain low levels of teacher-to-student ratios. Also, due to our specialized training, we were in the midst of a fight to negotiate our pay. It was a lot at one time and it eventually took a toll on my mental health. I brought my concerns to the attention of my administration, and they just said, "Oh, no, you're fine, you're good," and I'm like, "No, I'm not!". It got to the point where it was affecting my home life. So, after the pandemic, I made the decision to never bring work home, but I ended up just staying late at work. It all got to be too much, and I had to make the decision to not be in the classroom anymore.

If you could change one thing about being a teacher, what would it be?

I think that teachers need more backing from supervisors instead of fear. The country went from "Oh, we love teachers" to "Get my kid back in school. Why is this happening? Why is your teacher out for five days? Oh, they're sick. Oh, let's praise the teacher that taught from a hospital bed," and that's not right. People expect you to be on call at all hours. You're not going to call me at 6:00 PM and expect an answer. I have my own life, I have my own family and when my day is over, my day is over. There's a lot of disrespect from people just assuming that you're going to be there, you're going to answer the question. Families and staff don't seem to believe in boundaries so this is what I would change.

When you left that position, did you leave at the end of or in the middle of the school year?

I left midyear, which was something that I had never thought about doing.

How much notice did you provide before leaving? Did you face any backlash? Many teachers worry about losing their credentials. Was that a concern or discussed in any way?

I gave 2 weeks. In Connecticut Public schools you don't lose your credentials. I know it happens in some other schools and states. Here, I was supposed to gave 30 day leave, but couldn't do it. I also really don't think we are in a place in this country where we should be having teachers lose their credentials when we are a severely understaffed role.

If a teacher is ready to leave, what advice do you have for them?

I want them to make sure they're putting their own mental health and families first. If you have been feeling overwhelmed for a while, it is not a temporary thing. Go ahead and look into how you can determine what you want to do next.

Channel Program Director - Alissa
Taught for 12 years - Grades: 9 - 12
Subjects: English, History, AP Courses & more

It's been four years since you left the classroom. Can you walk me through your career progression and how you transitioned into roles like customer success or sales?

My title is Channel Sales Enablement Manager, and that's been my title for the last two and a half years. However, I've been operating as the Channel Program Director for almost a year now. I started in this role after returning from maternity leave. Before that, I joined as a systems trainer after leaving the classroom. In that position, I taught other educators how to use software in their classrooms, which led to a leadership role on the team.

What qualities do you think helped you move up so quickly?

I think I can organize. This is where I advocate for good teachers because of their unique skills. Teachers are not just grading papers. They are managing personalities, working with colleagues, administrators, and parents. Good teachers know how to navigate and leverage multiple stakeholders. A truly invested educator becomes a master coordinator of relationships, managing dynamics effectively. Teachers are also master diagnosticians. We collect data, fail fast, pivot, and adjust. Efficiency matters because grading faster frees time for self-care or student care, making us better teachers. As a department chair and coach, I learned to lead personalities and manage organizations. Moving into corporate leadership feels very similar to managing high performers.

What do you think about the notion that teaching skills don't transfer to other careers?

I think this is such an interesting topic. If I had all the time and money in the world, I would research it. Teachers are often told, either directly or culturally, that their skills only work in the classroom. There is emotional manipulation to it as well. People say, "You are such a gifted teacher. The kids need you. They need teachers like you." And they are right. But I also need to feed my family, sleep at night, and be healthier overall. I believe this idea that our skills do not transfer is the biggest lie in the world. When I transitioned to training, I thought, "I can do this because I am a good teacher." I am great at working with stakeholders and building relationships. Teachers know how to control a room, connect with people, and adapt quickly. But still, there is that impostor syndrome whispering, "How dare you think your skills will work in business?" That voice is absolute garbage. Teachers' skills transfer beautifully. They are finely tuned and adaptable. The problem is the language. Teachers use teacher talk that HR departments do not understand. Once you translate those skills into corporate language, teachers become the most overprepared and overqualified candidates out there.

How did your teaching skills help you in your corporate role?

When I got my job as a Channel Sales Enablement Manager, I'll admit I didn't know what "enablement" or "channel" meant at first. But when I read the job description, I thought, "I can do all of this." Enablement is corporate teaching, providing employees with the training and resources they need to succeed. As a teacher, I already knew how to build programs, create scope and sequence, and use backward design, like understanding by design (UBD). In my role, I designed a program from the ground up, applying my teaching skills: objective-driven design, stakeholder management, and adapting to different learners. I even taught companies in Thailand how to sell our products, using the same techniques I used in the classroom. That program received recognition as one of the best enablement programs my boss had ever seen with 20 years of experience in Channel, and he couldn't believe this was my first corporate job. Everything I did came straight from my teaching background.

Walk me through a project. It could be a day, a week, or however long. What does it look like when something comes in, you handle it, and then it exits? What do you do in that space?

One of my responsibilities as Channel Sales Enablement was designing a whole program. Now, as the Channel Program Director, I oversee it, but I have transitioned much of the day-to-day work to another team member, another former educator, who is doing an incredible job running with it and expanding it further. I have shifted into a more strategic role, focusing on how the program ties into other areas. About a year ago, before I went on maternity leave, I noticed a learning gap. The resources I was providing did not fully meet the support needs of our channel partners. To bridge that gap, I needed cross-departmental collaboration, permissions, and funding because some of the teams I needed worked on billable hours while I am salaried. Navigating that dynamic was challenging, not because people did not want to help, but because you have to figure out how to make it work within corporate constraints. I spent time exposing and highlighting the gap while doing what I could with the resources available.

Ultimately, I had to propose a bigger solution. That involved getting executive buy-in for collaboration, funding, and the overall project. I went from designing the enablement program to leading a full-scale project. We created a new enablement program, priced it, coordinated delivery with other teams, and ensured everything aligned. I oversaw all the moving parts, balancing project management with individual contributions. From the initial idea to executive approval and eventual launch, the process took about six months. Now, we have two global partners who have adopted the project, and we are preparing to roll it out on a larger scale. It has been rewarding to take a project from start to finish. Program management can feel like firefighting some days, but it is evolving into a more task-oriented, project-driven role. A good example of this process is identifying a problem, applying a Band-Aid, and then making the case for a long-term solution. It requires coordinating with experts and stakeholders, which I genuinely enjoy.

What's the part of your job that's business, not teaching, that you had to learn?

I think it depends on the experience each person had in their classroom or school. I had a good relationship with every administrator I worked with. If I saw a problem and wanted to solve it, as long as it did not cost money, I was told, "Go do it." That approach worked in education, but the biggest culture shock in the corporate world is dealing with egos. We have all dealt with admin egos, department chair egos, or teachers running the same project since the 1980s. Teachers navigate those dynamics because we are getter-doners. In the corporate world, though, you cannot always charge ahead. Paychecks, job descriptions, and egos complicate things. Taking responsibility for a problem might make someone feel their job is threatened. I had to learn the corporate bureaucratic dance. I did not start at an entry-level or have internships to observe how things worked. For experienced teachers transitioning, you might not start at the bottom, but you can miss the culture learning curve.

Is there any preparation you would have done prior?

Preparation-wise, my situation was unique. I transitioned into a role built for educators, giving me an edge in EdTech. Teachers looking to transition should focus on executive presence, project management, and leadership. Certifications like PMP translate teaching skills into corporate terms. Teachers are natural project managers, as seen in classroom assignments where organization and follow-through were essential. If I were still in the classroom, I would research job postings to understand the needed skills and certifications for roles that interest me. Certifications like PMP or LXD can help smooth the transition. Good managers were crucial to my journey. They pushed me along a path I might not have pursued on my own. Teachers often struggle with imposter syndrome, questioning their worth or abilities. Addressing perfectionism and self-perception made a significant difference for me. Personal growth was essential to navigating my transition.

What about work-life balance?

I wouldn't go back. I'm making more money than I've ever made, working from home and raising my child with help from neighbors and babysitters. I've avoided daycare, saving money, and the work-life balance is invaluable. I do miss the students and the reasons I went into teaching, but the last few years were hard. I burned out, and what made me a great teacher became impossible to maintain. Starting a family changed my priorities. I miss the interactions, the emails from kids saying, "My professor says I write the best essays because of what you taught me." I miss helping kids through tough times. At the same time, I don't blame teachers who leave. I'm using the same skills I used in the classroom, but now I'm paid more than twice as much.

Why did you leave teaching?

I left for financial reasons. My husband's dream was to go to law school, and as an educator, I thought, "More education? Let's do it." I figured I could teach anywhere, but even though we did everything right, we could not make ends meet. Part of the issue was coming from out of state. Public schools were hesitant, as it is often a "who you know" situation. I was hired at a private school, but three months later, they changed the insurance. We could not make it work. I started exploring options. I thought, "I have used Canvas as a teacher; I could teach others how to use it." I applied to Instructure, but they turned me down because they needed higher education experience. While worshiping in the Atlanta temple (Church of Jesus Christ of Latter-day Saints), I felt a clear thought: "Money will be okay, and you will have a baby." Two weeks later, Instructure called with an offer that was exactly what we needed.

Since then, I have been climbing the corporate ladder and just had a baby after several years of infertility!

What about summer breaks?

I don't miss summer breaks anymore because I don't need nine weeks to heal.

Heal? Elaborate.

In teaching, the cumulative stress and trauma were overwhelming. For twelve years, I was dealing with daily stress: lesson planning, coming to work sick because it was easier than sub plans, coaching one or two sports after school, worrying about students who couldn't eat, handling difficult parents, or managing emails from administrators that made me feel like I wasn't good enough. It all added up. I spent countless days at school from 6 a.m. to 10 p.m., supporting programs, loving the kids, or doing extra work to make a little more money. By the end of the year, I was emotionally drained, carrying the weight of my personal life, my students' needs, and constant deadlines. Teaching felt like a cycle of burnout followed by summer breaks where I would strategize and rebuild. I spent those breaks lesson planning and preparing for the next year, hoping to make things easier, but the stress always came back.

Now, my work-life balance is completely different. If I have a busy two weeks with a project or major travel, my boss tells me to take time off afterward. I can take breaks to play with my son, go grocery shopping, or even take myself to lunch. When things slow down, I am encouraged to step away and recharge. The difference hit me when I started this job. One Saturday, I instinctively thought, "What do I need to grade or prepare?" Then I realized, I didn't have to do anything. I could read what I wanted or just sit on the couch and watch TV without guilt. That freedom and balance are things I never had in teaching.

Is there anything else you'd like to share?

I believe that one of the greatest benefits of leaving the classroom is my son. I know a lot of women get pregnant and have children while teaching, but he is the result of lots of fertility treatments and IVF. Fertility is hard. I have multiple teacher friends who have struggled to balance fertility treatments while teaching. Teaching is incredibly stressful, but it's also rigid. For example, if a doctor says, "Can you come in Friday morning?" My answer now is an immediate yes. I just block out my calendar and go. That kind of flexibility was impossible in the classroom. I credit my current situation not only with being able to afford the treatments but also with having the flexibility to make it work and giving me the emotional balance to help my body actually respond to treatment. I think that's something people often overlook about teaching. It's not just about the salary but also the lack of flexibility. There are things I couldn't have done if I had stayed in the classroom, and I'm absolutely grateful for where I am now.

Chief Academics and Operations Officer - Josh
Taught for 2 years - Grades: Kdg. & HS

I am often asked how I got to a senior leadership role, and I think it's good to share that it's not always a straight shot and that there are many different paths. Part of it is just getting that first person to take a chance on you. In 2009, Crystal Rountree gave me that chance when I was selected for a role on staff at Teach For America. At 24 years old, sitting in an interview hall at a conference center in Baltimore, MD where all 50 regions of Teach For America had one booth, I interviewed with six regions in four hours.

When I met with Crystal, as a Florida native, I told her that I " wanted to join staff to develop teachers as leaders so kids at Raines and Ribault (public schools) would have the same opportunities as the kids at the Bolles School and Episcopal High School (private schools)." Three days later, I received a phone call offer that I accepted on the spot. As you can see, a lot of my roles deal with organizing systems, people, and resources to help school leaders and teachers focus on what they actually want to do - teaching and learning.

2006: Ahead of my senior year at the University of Florida, worked in the United States Senate as a Press Intern for then US Senator Bill Nelson (D-FL).

2007: Joined Teach For America and moved to Helena-West Helena,

Arkansas to teach music at an all-kindergarten school and band at KIPP Delta High School.

2009: Transitioned to work for Teach For America staff in Jacksonville, FL as a program director, coaching a cohort of 35 teachers teaching K-12 over two years.

2011: Moved to Nashville and worked as Knowledge Manager for KIPP Nashville (one of my favorite jobs of all time) for Rick Theobald, Meghan Mitchell, and Randy Dowell, helping set the infrastructure for KIPP to expand from one school to the largest and one of the highest performing charter school networks in Tennessee.

2012: Joined the founding team of the Achievement School District as the Data and Student Information Manager for a brand new turnaround district through the Race To The Top (RTTT) grant from US DOE. Returned to a full-time teacher coaching role (equivalent of an assistant principal) for two elementary schools in my final two years.

2015: Recruited to lead the academic efforts for Scholar Academies as they founded the Memphis region to contextualize the school model from Philadelphia and build the infrastructure for a rapid expansion to serve three schools and 1,200+ students in two years. Led the academics team and coached principals for four years.

2019: Recruited to Freedom Prep Charter Schools, first as Director of Special Projects, then Chief of Staff on the leadership team, preparing the network infrastructure to expand from Memphis to new sites in Birmingham and Montgomery, Alabama.

2022: Transitioned to the University of Memphis University Schools to serve first as Director of Academic Operations and now as Chief Academic and Operations Officer for the highest-performing school system in Tennessee.

In addition to my career journey, In 2022, I started Josh's K12 Job Blast. I founded, expanded, and currently manage Josh's K12 Jobs Blast, a confidential and free service designed to consolidate, organize, and share K12 job opportunities in school leadership, senior leadership, academics, operations, finance, external affairs, and talent & HR. I tell organizations their teams cannot be diverse if a diverse audience doesn't know about their roles.

With a mission to ensure diverse hiring pools by making opportunities accessible across lines of difference, the service has grown to over 10,000 subscribers nationwide. Through a multi-year marketing campaign, I increased the subscriber base to include K12 leaders across all 50 states. I've built relationships with over 527 organizations, 92 of which have become paying clients to elevate and promote their searches. By streamlining and consolidating content, I expanded the newsletter's reach from an average of 10,000 views per month to over 45,000 views for five consecutive months.

Additionally, I established consulting services to provide organizations with wraparound support, including talent search, process development, data and student information system integration, and academic thought partnership consulting.

So, keep networking, keep looking, and know that your chance is out there or maybe you can create your own chance!

Resources: https://www.k12jobsblast.org/

https://www.linkedin.com/in/josh-czupryk/

Comedian/TikTok Personality & IT Specialist - Albraden
Taught for 8 years - Grade: PK

How did you decide to get on TikTok and what has it been like for you?

TikTok started during the pandemic. At first, I was doing skits about growing up, like funny stories about my dad. My wife suggested I share some of my pre-K stories, but I did not think anyone would care. She said they were hilarious and insisted I share them. I told one story and figured that would be it, but then I told another, and it snowballed into something bigger. Years before, when I started working in after-school programs, my sister told me to write those stories down because they were so funny. Over time, I jotted down 18 years of little things kids said and my reactions to them, thinking someday I might write a book. Eventually, I decided I would never actually write it, but when TikTok came along, I realized I could share those moments in videos instead. Sometimes I go through my old notes and come across things I forgot even happened. It has been a great way to connect and share those experiences. About Bradley, he is one of the students I talk about a lot. I actually ran into his mom last weekend at Chipotle. It was such a strange moment.

I was going to ask if he was real!

Yeah, Bradley is almost 20 years old now. He really was an actual student in the after-school program. He just came in one day and was like, "Mister, guess what?" I said, "What's up?" He said, "My mom married a Black man." He said, "Yeah, so you know what that means?" I said, "No, what's that mean?" He said, "That means now I'm Black." He was dead serious. You would have thought I told him Santa Claus wasn't real when I told him he couldn't be Black.

Is comedy your aim...Is that the main goal?

Yes, absolutely. I tell people all the time that my first comedy gig was in fifth grade. My fifth-grade teacher saw something in me. At least, that is what I tell people. What I think really happened is she was tired of me being the class clown, so she gave me 10 minutes to do stand-up skits. But the way I like to tell it is that she saw potential in me and gave me 10 minutes to make people laugh. Either way, that was my first comedy gig.

Would you say that there is something in all of us, like a gift or a passion, that we either recognize early on or maybe it gets buried over time? I want to tap into that for teachers. They might read this and think about something they have always had in them but never acted on, like for me, people have always told me I have a great voice for voiceovers. I have heard that since I was in my twenties. I never did anything with it, but it makes me wonder, is there something that we all could revisit or pursue even after all these years?

I think we get so focused on making ends meet that we put our dreams and ambitions on hold. We worry about the next paycheck or trying to avoid money issues, and we push aside the things we are passionate about. The truth is, money will always be there in some form, but you might as well do something that makes you happy and fulfills you. I tell my wife all the time that I wish TikTok had been around 10 years ago. I feel like I started too late, but it is never really too late. Even when I was still in the classroom, I could have started pursuing this, but now I focus on what I have and bringing happiness to people. That is my goal. I love what I am doing now, telling stories, making people laugh, and creating content.

What I love about TikTok is that I do not need to audition for anything. I am the writer, creator, director, entertainer, and talent, and I get to share my work the way I think it should be shared. There will always be reasons not to start or voices telling you it is not the right time. The right time is whenever you decide to start, and that time is now.

Talk to me about that first gig and how it all started for you.

I remember my first gig. It was the most terrifying and amazing feeling all at once. I hated it and loved it at the same time. It was terrifying, but getting that first laugh was incredible. I have never done drugs, but I imagine it feels like that. You get the reaction, and then you want more, and it drives you to do better the next time. TikTok has done that for me too. When I read the comments and see how people relate, how they are laughing, and how they say things like, "I needed this today" or "I was having a bad day until I saw this," it reminds me what it is all about. That connection with people keeps me going. I have had production companies and stations reach out, and one company even offered to buy my whole catalog. They said I could never talk about it again if I sold it to them, and I turned it down. That is not what I am about. I know something else will open up for me, something where I can get what I want at the right price and still stay true to myself. Seeing people happy and knowing I have brought some joy into their day is enough for me. I think about people like KevOnStage, who I have watched for years. He grew from where he started, and his journey inspires me. I love KevOnStage; he is hilarious and so talented.

Why did you decide to become a teacher?

The reason I became a teacher had a lot to do with my experience in high school. I was labeled a "dysfunctional teen," which made me feel like everyone had given up on me. I got kicked out of high school and ended up at a charter school. At that charter school, things changed. The teachers there actually cared about me. I was not just a number anymore. They gave me confidence and made me believe I had potential. It was the first time, outside of my dad always having my back, that people truly saw value in me. That meant so much to me. I did not want to let them down, and that feeling stayed with me.

So then you just went on and got your undergraduate in education?

I had no plans to go to college, but I ended up getting a scholarship. Teaching wasn't part of my plan either; it happened by coincidence. Through a program called AmeriCorps, I was placed in a low-income neighborhood to teach kids how to use computers. Before that, I didn't want to be around kids, but working with them made me realize I was actually good at it.

Why did you leave education?

I initially left because I had a student on the spectrum with extreme behaviors. He would flip tables, throw things, and disrupt the class. He had a therapist who came for about 20 minutes a week, and during those visits, he was calm. I asked her if she could teach me some of her skills, but she said she didn't have time and that she did ABA therapy. By the end of the school year, I didn't feel like the student had made any progress. It felt like I just passed him along for someone else to deal with, and that didn't sit right with me.

After that year, I decided to become a behavioral therapist to gain the skills I needed so I would never feel like I left a child behind again. I planned to return to the classroom once I had those skills. In 2021, I was preparing to go back, but the school company I worked for offered me another position in IT, and I decided to stay.

Another reason I left is the lack of support. I was making barely enough money and often had to spend my own to provide for my classroom. I worked at a government-funded preschool, so resources were even scarcer. I was constantly doing my own research to figure out what my students needed, but we didn't have the tools to support them properly.

Tell me your title and what you do.

I'm an IT specialist. I help employees within the company by fixing their laptops, iPads, and troubleshooting issues like passwords. It's a full-circle moment for me because, during my time at a charter school with AmeriCorps, I learned to build computers for low-income communities and children. Now, I'm back helping people with their technology. There are four of us supporting around 15,000 employees.

How did you move into your current IT position?

I was taking courses in IT because I had learned as much as I could as an RBT (Registered Behavioral Technician) and had reached the ceiling in that role. I told my office manager that I was probably going to return to being a pre-K teacher. She asked if I was still interested in IT, and I said I had a little interest but was planning to leave by the end of the year.

Over Thanksgiving break, she called me and said, "Put your resume in now." I was confused but did as she suggested. I ended up getting the IT job, even though I didn't think I would at first. I love it now, which surprises me. It is funny because I didn't think I would enjoy teaching or sitting at a computer, but it turns out I just like helping people.

What was the training like? If someone said, "This is what I want to do," what training did you do, and how long did it take?

For this job, all my training was on the job because I had no prior experience. Honestly, I was shocked they even hired me! When they did, I was the second IT guy on the team, and funny enough, the first IT guy had actually gone through the same RBT training I did and he was a therapist too. When I interviewed, I had all these notes full of terminology and concepts I thought I'd need, but the actual job turned out to be completely different from what I expected. They trained me on the spot, and I learned everything as I went. Even though I didn't have the technical background, I came into the interview prepared. I was ready to show them why they needed me, and that mindset made all the difference. My dad always taught me not to put myself down because, as he said, there are enough people in the world who'll do that for you. That's something I've carried with me, and it's how I raise my daughters too. I remind them, "You're a queen at all times, no matter what."

Do you know of any training someone should take if they want to pursue your position?

Oh, yes. Google offers IT courses, which is what I was working on. They have all kinds of IT specialist courses. That is what I was taking at the time. I think the course was called "IT Specialist," but it was about two years ago, so I do not remember exactly.

I was also doing Python coding courses because I was not sure what they would need me to do. I wanted to be prepared, so I took anything and everything related to IT. There are many options out there, and IT is a field where there will always be a job.

What is the most difficult or challenging aspect of your current position? If you were talking to teachers considering this career, what would you say is the hardest part?

The most challenging thing for me is communicating technical issues to people who have no technical knowledge. We do not talk on the phone. Everything is done through typing, so I have to paint a picture with words to make sure they understand. That can be really tough, especially when I need to be patient and remind myself that they do not know what I am talking about. Another challenge is when we need to use remote access to fix an issue. They have to accept the remote session, but some people hesitate because they think someone is trying to hack their computer. Then I am stuck waiting for them to open the email or approve the request, which can take 20 to 30 minutes even when they have said it is an emergency.

That said, I know some people at other companies find micromanaging to be the hardest part. Luckily, my company is not like that. My RVP does not micromanage. He trusts us to do our jobs and treats us like adults. I have heard from others how refreshing that is compared to places where managers are constantly looking over your shoulder.

Wow, is there anything else you want to tell me about your position? Imagine I'm a teacher looking at this and thinking, "I want to be an IT specialist." What would you want to share with me?

For me, I never thought I would end up in IT because it is so different from the classroom. When I was teaching, I thought I was not stressed, but after leaving, I realized how much stress I had been under. Living in that world for so long made it feel normal. In IT, at least in my job, there is a lot less stress and fewer physical demands, like picking up kids or sitting down for long periods.

That said, dealing with adults can sometimes be harder than working with kids. I tell people all the time, "I would much rather work with a kid who does not understand than an adult with an attitude because they do not understand."

What final words do you have for teachers looking for a new path?

For any teacher transitioning, I would say that leaving is bittersweet. Most teachers feel guilty about it. But until there is more support and accountability, we usually get the blame and not much praise. Until they are willing to pay and support us properly, you have to do what you have to do. When I left, I did feel guilty at times, especially knowing there is a teacher shortage. But I also know I cannot save the whole world. That is why we have politicians who are supposed to fight for us. Unfortunately, year after year, we find out that many do not have our best interests at heart. I often tell people that you do not see real change until there is a tragedy. Maybe the teacher shortage is the tragedy needed to bring about the changes we have been waiting for.

Community Solutions Project Mgr. - Jennifer
Taught for 13 Years - Grades: 2 & 3

What year did you leave?

I left education at the tail end of 1999.

What feedback have you received from business professionals upon learning about your teaching background?

I know for me, getting out of teaching for the first time, I was scared to death. There's this world of business people. I was afraid of what I didn't know, and how was I going to learn it as fast as I could. But that willingness and eagerness to learn, that is what teachers really can bring. I've always been told that we're a good hire. Many years ago, I had a director say, "Well, Jennifer's a teacher. We know she's not just some pig-in-a-poke," so I thought, okay. That is a really interesting way to say that. In other words, he knew I was coming in educated, committed to what I was going to do, probably could hold a pretty good conversation with people and could negotiate what it is they're trying to get done.

Your career seems to have a common thread spanning various roles in the communications industry over many years. Could you elaborate on the similarities between these positions and how you transitioned from one to the next?

When I started at the 1-800 Sink call center, I was thrown onto the floor as a team lead. Quickly, I learned I had people skills and that there were twelve individuals in front of me needing support and resources to succeed at what I asked of them. Similar to teaching, standing before great minds and ensuring you prepare them for the future with the needed resources and tools. The key difference with adult learners is their freedom of opinion. It was fortunate that after only six months of managing people, they moved me to lead the training efforts which were six to eight classes per month with several trainers under me. In this role, I managed the training efforts which transitioned me into what I loved which was writing curriculum to fill gaps I noticed when agents finished training but still lacked vital call-handling skills. I suggested implementing "transition training" which would give new hires two weeks on the floor taking calls, then returning for supplemental gap training. A really cool experience that is still used today in that transition department. I provided the same transition training for new managers as well.

I quickly became an expert on identifying "what I don't know" from my own early experience, ensuring new leaders didn't struggle with that same feeling. There were lots of commonalities across those roles. Then at Cox Communications, I built their sales department from the ground up, developing curriculum, hiring salespeople, and analyzing desired skills. I found myself analyzing call volumes for the Sunday shift, from 7 a.m. to midnight or 9 p.m. Simply voicing that analysis led them to say, "Hey, you need to see the VP/GM!" An exciting opportunity to build something aligning with my passion for teaching and education. After Cox divested to Suddenlink Communications, the trainer began reporting directly to me. In this expanded role, I ran three call center departments covering the full customer lifecycle, Sales, Billing, and Retention. I built out training for issues like rate increases, "How do we handle this? A triangulation approach, you, the customer, the problem," to prepare agents for those incoming calls. Education was inserted into every aspect of my career there. Still aiming to learn all I could, my next move took me to Austin for a regional retention center leadership role with 10 to 12 supervisors reporting to me.

Again, there was that overlap of nurturing through coaching and development, something core to who I am as a person. I was able to watch former reports go on to become VPs at other companies. Knowing they were willing participants, I felt I had done it right. That educational background continued flowing through my work. When I joined the company in Flower Mound, I stepped into a role as Community Onboard Manager, training multi-dwelling properties on our managed Wi-Fi product. Covering "What is it? How do you discuss it with residents? How to market it? This is how it works." Once more, a training-oriented position matched to my experience. Today, I'm in a newer project manager role which has been challenging yet rewarding as I continue learning different aspects of the work. Yes, that educational mindset has always lent itself to what I do both inside and outside of my jobs. For years, I've also served as the Texas chapter president for Women in Cable Telecommunications, mentoring young leaders, again focused on training and nurturing.

As an educator transitioning to the corporate world, you mentioned facing skill gaps since the environment is quite different from a classroom setting. Could you expand on how to identify and overcome those skill gaps, particularly when you may not have an experienced mentor to guide you like in the teaching profession?

That's a great question. I'll reduce it to the ridiculous at first. When I first went into a call center, I didn't even know how to use the desk phone. Back then, we didn't have today's technologies, and most people are very tech-savvy now. I remember sitting at my desk, "Oh my God, I don't know what the buttons are." So I got over that quick because it's a tool I had to use. One thing I could tell teachers about skill gaps is to learn the company's technology. Many teachers grasp technology, but asking for help may not be easy. We are used to giving answers but do not always know how to ask, which is challenging. We often suffer in silence, embarrassed to admit we do not know everything. As I mentor young leaders, I always say, raise your hand if you do not know. If you are made to feel it is a dumb question, you are in the wrong business. There are companies that will not treat you that way. Do not suffer in silence. Quickly identify your resources and start with your immediate manager. I had to watch the dynamics of how things work.

When I hired, I hired people to fill my gaps. I built teams with bench strength to cover different gaps, then developed them and worked as a team. Ask for help. Surround yourself with knowledgeable people. Do not be afraid to ask. Seek out mentors and sponsors, people who will help when you are not in the room, and mentors who meet with you directly. I meet bi-weekly with a young leader, helping them overcome these challenges. Find mentors and sponsors. Ask questions. They will respect you more if you are openly learning and taking responsibility for professional growth. That is most important because you will think everybody knows more, but they do not. They may know policies or processes, but those answers are easy to find. As a teacher, you already have many of the ingredients for that "secret sauce" for success.

Tell me about your current role as a Project Manager.

Years ago, I was tasked with a project that introduced me to the importance of asking the right questions from the start. Knowing the end goal but not the resources available taught me to map out a plan and familiarize myself with project management tools like Microsoft Projects and Gantt charts. Fast forward to the present, I'm managing a far larger project where we are replacing obsolete video equipment nationwide. This involves logistical planning, technician coordination, and customer communication. It's a complex task with numerous moving parts, making it both challenging and rewarding. What makes it less challenging is that I have some "partners in crime" across the country, and we are using our collective expertise to navigate through the project. The essence of project management, as I've learned, is understanding the project's goal and then filling in everything in between. This requires leveraging expertise to ask the right questions and employ technology tools for tracking progress. In an ideal world, the processes and tools are clearly laid out, but reality is often messier. Projects are dynamic, with continuous changes and unexpected hurdles. In this role, I've had to adapt, teaching myself new systems and proactively learning.

For instance, using Smartsheet to manage updates across various departments. Project management is never perfect; it's about navigating ongoing changes and improvements, particularly in technology. This job has pushed me into new territories, like learning the billing system, illustrating that beyond planning and coordination, a project manager's role also heavily relies on adaptability and continuous learning. You're tasked with making something happen, and typically, you'd expect a clear process flow. Large companies often outline key milestones, emphasizing the importance of identifying stakeholders, understanding available resources, and setting timelines. You need to establish triggers for follow-ups and revisiting unfinished tasks, akin to addressing a "dangling participle" that requires attention later on. Generally, there's a guide outlining what project managers should do, the desired outcomes, and recommending technology tools to facilitate tracking and progress reporting.

For example, I'm responsible for overseeing calls within my region, updating stakeholders on the status of 462 properties. In an ideal world, these guidelines would seamlessly integrate all project components, from departmental updates to field technicians and regional project management, ensuring efficient oversight and smooth communication. However, the reality of project management is that perfection is unattainable. Projects are dynamic, with goals, processes, and team members changing, and people forget aspects that affect the project. This fluidity means that even with the best planning, unexpected challenges will arise, from process updates to technology improvements.

Why is it that you left education?

I left because my then husband was offered a new position in another city in West Texas. So that was kind of the trigger to try something new. He always said, "You have no idea what you could accomplish in the business world because he had faith in my skills and ability." At that time, I didn't know what I didn't know. To me, the 'secret sauce' that educators have is our innate ability to negotiate, to set realistic expectations, and to explain the 'why,' 'how,' and 'when.' These skills are critical in the business world. As educators, when we present something to our students, we ensure they understand we love it and we want them to love it too. This involves getting excited about the subject matter, which is what I always did as a school teacher. I found ways to make math engaging and to think outside the box, which I believe educators excel at. It's not sufficient to stick with the expository teaching style anymore. We need to mix it up, making learning an engaging and desirable experience. This approach is crucial in the business world as well; being passionate about what you do and how you present it to others is key.

Educators have a built-in structure and time management skills. Being in business has taught me to further refine these skills due to the constant flow of tasks. This is somewhat akin to the pressure felt in teaching, where you're responsible for the development of numerous students. Now, in the business realm, there's a similar pressure but it's related to projects and teams that depend on your accuracy and output. Transitioning into the business world has required me to fine-tune my delivery, considering we're dealing with adults, this can be a real "sticky wicket" at times. I think that waking up excited about what the day holds and maintaining a positive attitude significantly influences what you bring into a room. People who possess these 'secret sauces' start with a leg up.

Could you recommend any specific resources, such as books, podcasts, or other materials, that have been particularly helpful to you?

Yes, over the years I have read the John Maxwell books and other leadership development types of books and loved them. They were very inspiring. Today, as I'm in the grind, if I come across something that I don't know, I will Google it and teach myself how to do it. Our company is really good about providing resources, and I have taken courses on leadership development that are available to us as part of what the company provides, which is beautiful. Additionally, I learn by observing others, identifying mentors for specific inquiries.

What else would you like to tell teachers who have been thinking about discovering a new career?

What I would say to teachers thinking about leaving the field is this: I didn't leave because I fell out of love with teaching; I still loved it and do miss it today. However, if you're considering leaving the educational field, know that there are many opportunities out there that you might not yet realize. Don't be afraid to ask questions or to take the leap. Just know that the aspects you enjoyed about teaching can be transitioned to different areas in the world, and I don't regret making that change. I've been able to apply my teaching experience to my current roles.

Addressing the elephant in the room: teachers, unfortunately, do not get paid their worth. We all know this. For me, moving into the business world proved beneficial as I now earn significantly more than I did as a teacher. This was particularly helpful following my divorce, enabling me to support myself independently. While staying in teaching would have brought me closer to retirement, I observe retired teachers struggling to make ends meet. We don't enter teaching for the money, but the financial benefits of pursuing a career outside teaching are undeniable. To those contemplating a departure due to fear of the unknown: yes, it's scary, but do it...go for it. There are people out there that are willing to help and mentor. I'm not sorry at all that I sought a new career, but I do miss teaching every day.

Resources: Books by John Maxwell

Contractor, Content Moderator Consultancy - Candace
Taught for 12 years - Grades: 9 - 12
Subjects: English, History, AP Courses

What is your title?

I am the CEO and Founder of The Candid Consultant, LLC, an Educational Innovation Consultancy; and specialize in content moderation for a global social media company.

I'm so proud of you. You have decided to use your skills and talents and start a business. Let's get into it.

Well, the transition was a little unbelievable. Upon transitioning from the nonprofit space, I started reaching out within my network, asking about opportunities, and getting insight on where I'd land next. I appreciate my colleagues who supported and offered salient advice. I applied for numerous positions for a solid 2 months and nothing panned out. By October 2023, I stumbled upon a posting on Indeed's website, marked as confidential yet, underscored high-level support minors in an online, technological space. Truly, I envisioned the role would be instructional design-related or something in the EdTech space. I completed the application and thought nothing of it. About a month later, I received a call from a recruiter, stating they received my application. When the recruiter named the company, a global social media company, and they were very interested in interviewing me for the role, I couldn't believe it! "Lord, I didn't ask for this! Lord, really, what are you doing?!" is what I was thinking as I continued the phone conversation.

So to your point, I didn't "prepare" for the role - it came to me. I also received an approach from a local couple who needed help building their businesses. In the interim, pertaining to my role as an entrepreneur, I was approached by a husband and wife team that intended to establish a presence in the beauty industry, acquire property, and invest in franchises. I was willing to help them create a foundation for these initiatives while leveraging my network of business leaders to make their dreams a reality. Unfortunately, the funding they were expecting never materialized. While disappointed, I realized this was not a setback but a set-up for personal success...this was an opportunity to focus solely on creatively establishing my consultancy. I realized this could help me with looking at general business consultancy. I've been fulfilled in it and have had a lot of on-the-job training.

I think educators sometimes become misguided in their thinking: "Well if I studied Humanities or a "non-technical" field of study, then the (only) professional choice is teaching." But did someone, per se, teach Bill Gates or Tyler Perry? Not to make comparisons, but within their examples, we see these ultra-successful men utilizing their inherent traits to manifest their passions.

Looking back, what did you learn from that experience? Is there any wisdom you've gained that you'd like to share?

Wisdom! Remain optimistic, set personal and professional boundaries, and surround yourself with individuals honoring your best interests and vice versa. The art of entrepreneurship can present its own set of challenges. How one responds to these challenges determines a positive or not-so-resilient outcome. Also, there are 7.951 billion people on the

planet! Find your tribe. I think there's an interest in world language instruction in a unique way that this company was able to secure contracts in three states already. It's a business that leverages the skill set I have in world languages. Companies need that. I've been told many times that I can consult with companies on developing their training materials in another language. It's not necessarily physically being a teacher in a classroom in front of students, but using that skill can definitely bring in other opportunities.

Okay. So then let's talk about your consulting. Where it's at now and what is your vision?

It is "official-official" as of three weeks ago! My LLC is still a work in progress…I am still working on the landing page and other aspects. I have joined up with a former teacher and colleague and we are in the process of collaborating on a few things with training and development.

Our primary focus is targeting diverse audiences with my language skill set, background in communication, and business experience.

How did you get into education?

Wow! I'm blessed to come from a long line of educators, including traditional teachers, community leaders, and pastors. On my maternal side, I can count at least 50 educators across generations. One of them is my mother's brother who was the principal at Little Rock Central High School in Arkansas during the 1990s, when they filmed the Ernest Green story. He later became a district superintendent in a small Arkansas district. One of his brothers also had a successful career in education as a science teacher. Additionally, my grandmother's first cousins were pioneers in education. My great cousin Carrie began her career as an elementary school teacher and later became the first, Black superintendent of Davidson County Schools. Her sister, Lillian, also had a successful career as a home economics educator. They were local and national leaders in Alpha Kappa Alpha Sorority, Incorporated.

I think it's important to highlight these examples, as they become part of your DNA and influence your life. On my father's side, I have family members who are pastors and a cousin with a high-ranking role in Full

Gospel. My mother was a leader in her field. Although neither of my parents were formal educators, they were leaders in their professional roles. Leaders are teachers and vice versa. I gleaned attributes such as fairness, firmness, and organizational skills from my parents - my mother with a long-standing career in the insurance industry and my father an entrepreneur, postal worker, and little league baseball coach.

What grades did you teach and for how long?

My career spanned roughly 15 years, from 2004 to 2018. During that time, I taught primarily middle and high school students, as well as the post-secondary level at my alma mater, Fisk University. Non-traditional adults have been my students, studying Spanish and Written and Oral Communications. I also taught non-traditional adults in Spanish and Communications. Although I'm certified to teach K-12 in public schools, I've had a highly qualified quotient in terms of teaching.

Why did you leave teaching?

I was ready for change. I was disinterested in following the traditional educational leadership route: first, springing from a classroom teacher role to the suspected, "natural" path to school administration, resulting in a district-level role, and then, retirement. While these steps led to success for many of my family members and former colleagues, with all due respect, I refused to conform. In 2018, I transitioned into a Regional Project Manager role with a non-profit, educational organization and ultimately, Manager of Secondary Schools. This opportunity allowed me to work with schools as a coach and trainer - my first assignment was with schools in New York, Massachusetts, and Illinois. Additionally, in this role, I leveraged strategic, analytical development skills to initiate partnerships within the K-12 educational landscape, leveraging the organization's social-emotional learning model. In May 2022, after nearly 4 years in this role, I transitioned and became committed to building my consultancy. The reasons for my departure were multifaceted on my end...I won't go into all the details, but let's just say that with the recent emphasis on diversity, equity, and inclusion, this organization needed to demonstrate "diversity" by hiring me - a highly skilled, educated, and talented Black woman.

As a former teacher, what advice would you give to teachers who are still in the classroom? You mentioned something about leveraging your skill set, and I really liked how you put that. Can you talk more about how teachers can figure out what they're naturally good at and use those strengths to grow in their careers?

As educators, we are inherently passionate because we would not be in the profession or step away from it if we weren't passionate about something. If viewed through a self-interest lens, I hesitate to use the word "selfish" because I don't think we are selfish people. We look out for our own best interests.

If that means leveraging a passion, what is that passion? How can it firstly help others, but also, how can you monetize it? We have to be realistic. I would say, look at what drives you. If money was truly not a factor and you could do anything you wanted, what would that be? Why? Ask yourself that, remaining true and authentic to who you are. Because as educators, we can often be pigeonholed into doing one thing when our profession lends itself to many things. In this society, we are criticized for trying an exorbitant amount of things: "You should only stick to one thing and do it well." But we don't tell Steve Harvey that, the proponent of having seven to eight streams of income, and everybody glorifies that. But when an individual without that status does it, "Oh, they're doing too much. What is their motivation?"

We have to tune all that out. Sometimes you are your own best cheerleader. Through God's grace, it takes us to get our vision rolling. I didn't know what I would do after leaving that nonprofit. All I knew was I was being inauthentic to myself. It was a great paying position with things I enjoyed, as mentioned earlier. But if I'm going to trust what God gave me, it won't be in this position because they're not aligned with my true self to help others. Get in touch with your true passion and really go through the who, what, when, where, why - ask those concrete questions. Then think about how you'll execute it when you have a plan to truly make your passion a SMARTIE goal: Strategic, Measurable, Ambitious, Realistic, Time-bound, Inclusive, Equitable.

Current Teacher - Carrie

Taught for 19 years - Grade: 4 - Subjects: General, Gift/Talented Program Specialist and Art

Currently you are looking to leave the classroom, but you haven't left yet have you?

I made the decision to resign from my classroom teaching position this summer. I am currently working on a few contracts with educational publishing companies as a content editor, and I want to use this time to dedicate myself to seeking a job in instructional design.

Let's go back to why did you become a teacher?

I have always loved learning. And I started playing teacher from a young age, and I would make my brother be my students. And he did not like having homework assigned to him. It's kind of funny because I have children of my own now, and my oldest is already showing some of those signs she'll tell me "I'm a teacher now," and she wants to play-act like her daycare teachers. I love learning, and I think honestly, probably even when I was in College, what I was kind of thinking was becoming a teacher was I kind of wish I could be a student forever. That process of learning school and getting to read books and write. And I do love working with children. I realized I had the opportunity of going K twelve or even getting a Master and going on to become a college professor, but I really did love the younger children.

Why do you want to leave the classroom?

The reason I give in job interviews is that I need to be intellectually stimulated and have more opportunities than I had in teaching to diversify my skill set and work on different projects. I'm very interested in the design aspect of instruction and learning new technologies. But if I'm truly honest, like I tell my teacher friends... over the years, I felt a continued loss of control over my ability to affect change, not just within the career field but even in my own day-to-day responsibilities. I lost control over how I could teach students in a way that felt developmentally appropriate and purposeful.

The final straw was when they made changes that would put extreme time limits on my art lessons. You can't rush students through the creative process it's not appropriate, and it's not doing them any service. It's almost like learned helplessness you know how we talk about that with students? That's how teachers are feeling now. We're the ones directly working with the students, but nobody asks us. And the ones who get frustrated and speak up end up being the ones who leave. You just reach a point where you realize things aren't going to change.

Walk me through how you made the decision to transition into your new field.

Looking back, this journey started a couple of years before the pandemic. I was married and we were thinking about having our first child. For years, I had known that by the time I had children of my own, I didn't want to be teaching anymore but I didn't know what I wanted to do. I knew I could combine my love of writing with my love of learning and developing curriculum. But I decided I didn't really want to stay in the school district arena to do that. A friend of mine got me a job writing an assessment for a local charter school. I really enjoyed it and thought maybe I can get more of this gig work.

When I had a baby, I wanted to find a way to work half-time. Through a Facebook group, I met a lady who had been a teacher and had gotten into project work when her kids were little. She coached me through updating my resume and shared resources for freelancing. One of my goals was I didn't want to have to get another master's degree. I already had one. Very expensive. So I thought, what can I do where my master's in education would be valued? Looking through job descriptions, I stumbled upon instructional design. Through informational interviews, I was introduced to this whole career field where organizations employ people to create learning and training. You don't necessarily have to be the person who does the training, you just create it.

I found groups like Teaching: A Path to L&D and connected with people leading that teacher transition movement. I realized that instructional design was something I could do remotely without travel and without lots of meetings with customers. I'm more of an introvert. I like to be able to think and focus. I decided I could benefit from some formalized training, so I joined an Academy. Some content services companies started emailing me about projects. The first one, I didn't get, but the next one that came through, I thought, I cannot say no to this. I need the experience. That job is what got me this contract with the same company. I think my increased interactions on LinkedIn and cleaning up my profile helped. But I'm hoping now that I can blend these two career directions curriculum writing and instructional design.

Your resume. Did you create your own resume, or did you get assistance with it?

I created my own. I did look at a lot of examples. One resource that I use was The Resume Repository. I was following her on LinkedIn when she was starting to build that when she first published The First Bank of Portfolios or Resumes.

That was really helpful and then last fall with Teaching: A Path to L&D, I volunteered on this big project to create resources for teachers who were wanting to become instructional designers. Through my team there, I met someone who had just gotten her first job without even having a portfolio. I asked her how she did it. She shared her resume with me. I used that mostly to help me with formatting and deciding what order to put the information in. I don't have a fancy looking resume. I feel like right now my resume is not really going to get any better until I gain more experience. At this point I need more experience.

Your teacher resume and your current resume. What would you say are the biggest differences? How did you translate your experience? What was the biggest hurdle in creating that resume before you got the experience?

They're very different. My teaching resume had gotten to be like three pages long because I would list everything. I had a section about my actual teaching experience, and I listed every single job I'd had. I had a section about my professional development experiences. What I was trained in doing. That's not important for instructional design. If you want to put something like that, you're going to need to put things like authoring tools you can use, or potentially soft skills that you have.

I moved my education to the very bottom because I was told that if you've been in any industry for more than ten years since you've gotten your degree, put that on bottom because that's old news at this point. The major change on my resume now is that I list authoring tools that I can use at the top. I tried to include actual numbers and statistics where I could. I wanted to put my experience with instructional design at the top, even though it was volunteer experience. Now I have my freelance work at the top. I tried to use more industry terms that talk about project management and the instructional design process. Things like QA testing and working with an LMS.

As a teacher, if you can say that you've built lessons or courses in an LMS, that's always good. Being able to quantify the results that you have achieved in different jobs. If you've been teaching for as long as I have, try to call upon anything that you have done working with adults, working in leadership positions. That's going to be more important than listing every single job. They don't care about all the different schools you worked at. Some people have even advised me to use "instructor" instead of "educator" because that sounds better to a recruiter.

What advice would you give to other teachers who are wanting to transition?

First of all, do research. Get on LinkedIn if you're not on there, and don't worry about the fact that you only have like 20 connections so far. Just start searching for the types of jobs that you think you might want. Read those people's profiles. Read if they have a resume posted. Read the job descriptions and think about whether that sounds like a job that you want to do. There are some career coaches who have free resources, short little questionnaires that will walk you through what are the types of skills that you have as a teacher that you really enjoy. You think you're really good at. Those questionnaires will help point you to the types of careers you might be most interested in. For instance, I knew Sales wasn't for me, but I know plenty of teachers who are super bubbly and extroverted, who are always helping each other and always learning new tech apps. They might be perfect for that kind of role.

Carrie's update:

In Fall 2023, I got two job offers in one week. I started a position as an instructional designer with an online education company. I was part of a small design entity which creates eLearning courses for K-12 educators. It was a great chance for me to increase my design skills while working with content I knew well. After a layoff in February 2025, I am happy to report that I will be starting a new instructional design job only a month later. I attribute my ability to quickly transition into a new role to the extensive network I have developed over the past 4 years. If you are seeking a job, reach out to your connections. Engage with influencers who post inviting people to connect and share their interests. Be specific about your strengths and the type of position you're looking for. Repost about job openings and other job seekers, and try to post your own content at least weekly. These actions really do make your profile more visible and make you seem more current in your profession. Continue to both refine and broaden your skill set, and add to your portfolio regularly.

Once you get the job, keep track of your accomplishments and update your resume every 6 months. It took me 2 years to fully transition out of the classroom. Keep focused, and know that there are lots of former teachers out there who are happy to support you.

Customer Success Manager - Sarah
Taught for 15.5 years - Grades: 6-12 - Subject: Math

Walk me through a typical process from start to finish.

When I first started, the company was much smaller. We had fewer than 200 people overall and fewer than 30 in customer success. There weren't onboarding or professional learning teams, so I managed everything.

After a contract was signed, I'd meet with the salesperson to gather information about the customer. We'd schedule the initial launch and onboarding, train the buyers, and ensure every site received training. I also handled marketing materials, social media, and paperwork to ensure the customer had everything they needed.

I conducted training sessions, worked with the rostering team, and managed the onboarding process to ensure everything stayed on schedule. Delays could push back the time to value, which is critical for customers. Once onboarding was complete, I shifted to maintaining the relationship long-term.

What does time to value mean?

Time to value is the first moment the customer sees the value of the product. You have upfront costs and the onboarding process, but then there's a point where the customer says, "Oh, this is what we purchased it for. We see the value now." It's important to reach that point quickly.

If it's a twelve-month contract and it takes four months to roster and get everything running, you've already lost a lot of valuable time. That delay can really affect how they perceive the product.

So what happens after that?

That's when you start identifying champions, the people in the customer's organization who support and advocate for the product. Some will push the initiative forward, while others might not fully buy-in. Champions are critical to the product's success because they keep things moving and help build momentum.

Got you. So it's you, a salesperson, and other people helping in this process. What are their roles?

Initially, we had what we called an implementation team, now our rostering team. They handle the technical setup, making sure that everyone who needs access to the platform has it. They're the ones I contact when, for example, someone can't log in. They handle the behind-the-scenes technical work. We now also have an onboarding team that focuses on transitioning customers from the sales cycle to customer success. They bridge the gap between me and the sales team and ensure a successful launch at the customer's location.

Champions on the user end?

Yes. On the customer side, you often start with a purchaser, someone who discovered the product and approved its purchase. Depending on the customer's size, this might not be the same person who signs the contract. The purchaser is usually the initial champion because they brought the product into the company.

But they're not always the long-term champion. For example, a superintendent might approve it, but they're managing many other responsibilities. Over time, you identify new champions within the organization, people who push for usage and engagement, and keep moving the needle forward.

Once the product has been purchased, and implemented, and everyone has access, what happens next?

We move into regular check-ins. In non-EdTech industries, these are called quarterly business reviews, but we meet more frequently, monthly or bimonthly, because of education's shorter timelines. Contracts and school years are shorter, and when you account for summer and transition months, there are about six months of active engagement. During check-ins, I review data, discuss usage, and evaluate if we're meeting their goals. If progress isn't where it should be, we plan adjustments. I also interact with teachers, share updates or new features, and ensure they're prepared for the next year. For example, if we've developed a Chrome extension for Google users, I'll coordinate with their IT team to implement it.

When you share new products, is there pressure to upsell them?

Not in my current position. I know some roles in other sectors involve managing onboarding, renewals, and expansion. My company doesn't have much opportunity for expansion beyond adding extra grades, and we don't handle renewals. That's managed by our account managers. Before, the sales team handled renewals, but now account management has taken over.

So sales and renewals are handled separately now?

Yes. Sales used to manage both new accounts and renewals, but they were being pulled in two directions—building new relationships and maintaining existing ones. Now, we have an account management team. They attend our meetings to stay informed and handle renewal contracts when the time comes. That's their responsibility now.

How do you support customers during these check-ins and meetings?

During check-ins, we review data and usage patterns. For customers with multiple sites or subgroups, we identify which groups are performing well and consider whether internal champions from those locations can share their successes. We also revisit the customer's initial goals and assess whether we're progressing toward them at the right pace. If adjustments are needed, we plan accordingly. It's all about making sure we're moving in the right direction to help them achieve their goals.

Is there anything else you want to share about your position or how it compares to roles like customer service representatives? Is there anything about your role you haven't mentioned?

The main difference between my role as a CSM and the senior CSM role at my company is the size of the accounts we manage. It's based on the annual recurring revenue, or ARR, of the contract, which determines how many touch points there are. ARR reflects the value the company is paying for the year, while GRR includes potential growth. For example, a customer with 100 licenses has a much smaller ARR than one with 19,000 licenses. Senior CSMs manage larger accounts, what we call a book of business. They have fewer accounts overall, but those accounts are more valuable.

What did you do to prepare for this field or career? Courses, training, books? Did you need to go back to school or do additional training?

I transitioned when it was easier to get into the field. Now, many companies look for candidates with experience because customer success isn't as entry-level as people think.

Why?

One reason is the renewal aspect, which includes a sales component that educators typically don't have experience with. There's also a lot of BDR and SDR work, which involves cold outreach to people who may not know the product. I reach out to individual users, champions, and upper-level staff, but I'm also contacting busy teachers to check-in. Often, they're focused on their students and don't have time for me. There's a lot more cold emailing than I initially expected.

What are BDR and SDR?

BDR stands for business development representative, which focuses on pre-sales, and SDR stands for sales development representative. Both roles are about outreach to connect people with the sales team. Their goal isn't to sell directly but to set up meetings. For me, even though the sale has already been made, I still have to engage people who aren't using the product and start conversations they might not have otherwise. On top of that, I work on renewals, expansion opportunities, tech issues, and collaboration with the support team to identify what's working and what isn't. I also work with the product team to implement feedback.

To answer your question about preparation, I didn't do much formal training. I worked with a coach, Lynn Juve at Bespoke, to identify how my teaching experience already aligned with customer success skills.

You mentioned reaching out to teachers. What makes it difficult to connect with them?

Teachers are the best at ghosting. They're busy and assume you're offering something that costs money. As a teacher, I knew schools didn't have money. I had no authority to make purchases and couldn't afford anything personally. Teachers might sign up for a free trial but won't respond once it's over unless you're offering another free trial. There's also a disconnect between corporate teams and the education calendar. Timing is critical. For example, I wouldn't schedule training in May because teachers are busy responding to emails, helping students who need extra support, and planning for testing. They won't be paying attention at that point. The short school year also makes it harder to get buy-in and onboard users. Teachers are used to trying new edtech that disappears the following year. Some won't engage because they don't want to invest time in something that might not last.

In the past, I remember you mentioned a boot camp.

Yes, I completed SuccessHacker's five levels of customer success training. It was one of our professional development opportunities. My company provides a stipend for training, so I used it to purchase and complete all five levels, earning those certifications. I wanted to grow and ensure I understood the business side, along with my subject matter expertise.

If someone is interested in customer success management, what resources would you recommend to prepare?

I didn't use LinkedIn Learning much, but I'd recommend starting with an entry-level customer success course. SuccessHacker's level one course is affordable, and I got mine for $20 with a coupon. It's a great introduction to the customer success cycle, the sales cycle, and key terms like ARR, GRR, and NRR. These acronyms are like education's IEPs, if you're in the field, you know them. Understanding these terms helps during interviews and on your resume so you don't seem unprepared when they come up.

Why did you leave teaching?

I started looking for other options before my last year, partly because of COVID. My students were two years behind on standards, and I knew it would take at least six years to catch up, which is nearly impossible for seventh grade. The focus shifted to cramming information, which isn't my teaching style. Some teachers gave in to teaching the test, and I couldn't blame them, but I kept fighting it, and it became too much for me.

Then they switched my grade level, and I had to start over. The final straw was when my daughter was quarantined for COVID. I had to choose between staying home with her or going to work. My admin needed me at school, but my daughter couldn't stay home alone. My husband and I split the days, but the guilt of leaving my class and colleagues to manage without me was overwhelming. That was when I realized teaching wasn't where I wanted to be anymore.

In the corporate world, people seem more adamant about not working while sick. How has that been for you?

At my current job, we have unlimited sick days, and they don't want you working when you're sick. I had COVID once and still took a meeting because I didn't want to reschedule. The response was, "Why are you working? Take the time to recover." It's a very different culture.

You live in a small town where everyone pretty much knows everyone, was there any pressure when you left?

I still feel some pressure, mostly guilt, which is just part of who I am. They had a replacement before I left, and the school was fine without me. I liked my admin, and I think he liked me. He even coached my daughter's basketball team, so there's no animosity. When I see teachers now, they often ask if it's really better outside education. They tell me I look happier, though some say they could never give up their summers. Internally, I feel guilty for leaving midyear, but it was the best decision for me and ultimately for my students. Teachers often ask how I did it, and some reach out to say they need to leave too because it's too much. No one has been upset with me for leaving, except jokingly wishing I'd taken them with me.

What advice would you give someone who wants to switch careers?

For new teachers, especially first- and second-year teachers, I'm sorry that education isn't what you thought it would be. If you're thinking about leaving after one year, I'd advise against it unless you're absolutely sure. My first year was rough too, and that was 20 years ago. Starting something new always feels like, "What am I doing?" That's just work. Unless you're financially independent and can walk away anytime, you'll have bad days. You have to decide if there's enough to keep you in. If you're ready to leave, go for it, but be prepared to put in the effort. The current climate and economy make it harder. When I transitioned, it took me a year and a half to find a new position. I've been out for a year and a half now, but with all the layoffs, customer success has become more competitive. The field has grown, and companies are looking for people with experience, even just one or two years. When companies lay off people with ten years of experience, it makes it harder for someone to come straight from the classroom. It's not impossible, and there are resources and people who can help, but it's different from when I transitioned. My company took a chance on subject matter experts, but now they want more experience. If you face rejection, it's not a reflection of you. It's just that someone else brought something different. You could have the same qualifications as someone who gets the job, or vice versa. It's about personality fit, company fit, or something else entirely. It's hard not to take it personally, but those rejection letters don't mean you weren't good enough.

Resource: https://www.bespokeprofessional.com/ Lynn Juve

Customer Support Administrator - Carissa
Taught for 14 years - Grade: HS
Subjects: Chemistry & Forensic Science

Let's start with your first position out of the classroom, you were a technical support engineer and team lead.

Essentially, that position was a tech support role. I handled cases all day long, email cases, phone cases, and chat cases where teachers, students, and administrators would report issues and ask for help fixing them. Within four months, they promoted me to lead my team.

Why do you think they made you team lead so soon?

I believe it was a combination of two factors. First, my in-depth product knowledge. Second, my sense of accountability. I not only understood how the product worked but also mastered the necessary workflows. I consistently achieved high statistics and maintained good customer satisfaction. It was a steep learning curve, like baptism by fire hose, because I had to learn all the systems.

How did you end up at Instructure?

When my school transitioned to digital learning during COVID, we adopted Canvas as our learning management system. One of the reasons I specifically targeted this company when leaving the classroom was twofold. First, I wanted to remain in the education space, I felt passionate about it. It was my comfort zone, and it provided a clear direction. Second, I aimed to work with a product I had used as a teacher because I believed that familiarity would allow me to contribute effectively. While I might not have had some of the corporate experience that other candidates might have, my background as a former user of the product, I felt was helpful.

I originally went for an entry-level position at this company because many people were leaving the classroom and applying for roles. My goal was twofold. First, I didn't really know what I wanted to do. I knew I didn't want to go into sales even though that is where the money is. I'm a little too honest for that and didn't know if I was built for it. However, as a chemistry teacher with strong technical skills, I felt drawn to the support side. In my teaching role, I often troubleshoot when things broke or helped other teachers figure out how to make things work. I applied to several startups, mostly for mid-level positions, and gained some traction but grew nervous. Many of these companies were rapidly changing in size due to acquisitions. The fear of being laid off scared me. Transitioning from a stable teaching position was a concern, so I shifted my focus to larger, well-established companies instead of smaller startups being acquired.

How many applications did you fill out?

Hundreds of applications.

Hundreds. Yes. That's very common.

Reason why is because I didn't necessarily know exactly what I wanted to do. I did the courses on how to transition out of teaching and all of that stuff. The first thing they say is figure out what your direction is. I didn't know what it looks like to be in that position to know if it's going to work for me or not. You just don't know.

Why do you think you don't know?

My current feelings differ from what I felt then. At that point, I just needed a job. I was even willing to work at Starbucks to avoid going back to that atmosphere. Managers don't want to see desperation either. I would read job descriptions and think, with the right training, I could do that. Teachers stay in teaching for the feeling you get when students understand something. I was ready to trade that for a job where, when the day was over, I could turn off my computer and not think about work until tomorrow. I wasn't looking for the next great love of my life in a job.

I want you to walk me through being a technical support engineer.

Everything was incoming tickets. You get assigned and scheduled based on the volume and how many people were working. Either you were taking phone calls, live chats, or email cases. Sometimes you have a split shift where you work phones for 4 hours and then chats for 4 hours. It was really interesting because when it was busy, the days flew by. It felt like teaching on a busy day where all of a sudden it's the end of your day, and you forgot to go to the bathroom. I don't want to say it's the same kind of tired because nothing compares to teacher tired. During our peak season, like the beginning and end of the semester, we'd have back-to-back calls. But you could pause a call and go to the bathroom, which you couldn't do when teaching. It was harder when taking live chats because you had up to three chats at a time. That workflow took time to get used to and stressed me out because I had to troubleshoot three potentially complex situations all at once. All these people were already upset because whatever they were trying to do wasn't working.

What did the training look like?

We had a full three-week training process. We worked daily with a trainer for 8 hours. The first week was easy for me because it was about how to use the product, which I already knew. I think that's where I started being considered for a team lead position. I was friendly with the trainer, who later moved up to different positions. She said I could have just listened to her, but instead, I took a leadership role and helped enhance the training materials with my input from teaching experience. That was the first week. The second two weeks were about workflows, shadowing, watching others take live contacts, and troubleshooting emails as a team. By the end of the third week, we were taking our own phone calls and chats.

What was the most difficult part of this process?

The hardest part is understanding where the customer is coming from. People don't call you when things are going well. You can't take it personally. You also need to be flexible in your solutions. People often say, "I'm trying to do this thing and it's not working." You have to step back and ask a professor who's already mad about the assignment they're trying to plan. Sometimes the tool they're using isn't the best one, and you have to come up with a solution on the spot. That part is tricky for certain people. My teaching experience made it more natural for me compared to those with a purely tech background who might just say, "That's how the tool works, sorry." Not getting down when people are upset is a struggle, but there are also rewarding conversations. When someone thinks they deleted their whole course, and you recover it in a few clicks, they're crying on the phone because you saved their life.

Have you faced any difficulties transitioning to your new career? If so, can you describe them?

This is funny. I think it's a personal problem that I am hyper-aware of and talk to my bosses about all the time. As a teacher, I developed such bad work-related PTSD, always thinking I was in trouble. I'd see my boss typing to me in Slack, and I'd be sweating, freaking out, watching those little dots on the screen, thinking, "Oh my God, what is he going to say? Am I in trouble? Am I on this phone call for too long?" I'd panic, and then they'd say, "Hey, you just got a good customer report. Way to go." The amount of panic I had about that was significant. Also, the autonomy I was given was new to me. They'd say, "I don't need to worry about you. You're doing your job," and I wouldn't hear from my boss for two weeks. Then, in a one-on-one, they'd say, "Yeah, you're doing great," and I'd be like, "Well, what else do I need to do?"

There's always a what else? There's always more.

Right. And a lot of times, there wasn't an additional ask. There wasn't a "But this is great; we want you to do it this way." Instead, they might say, "You're so good at it, we're going to give you an additional project on top of what you're already doing." When I got promoted and moved to a different team, that didn't change. I felt even more anxious because now I was in a real job, not an entry-level one. They were giving me all these responsibilities, and I thought I could totally screw this up. This is a "me" problem, people trust you to do your job well. You might not get any validation like, "Hey, you're doing a great job," because it's understood. Of course, you're doing a great job; we picked you to do this.

Let's start talking about your customer support administrator.

We have a major tech product that we worked on. We have about 200 support agents at different levels working on different teams. We have CSMS who are managing customers on that side, and then we have sales and renewals that I work with. Essentially, my job is to ensure that people who are paying us are getting onboarded properly and are getting the support they're paying for, and people who stop paying us.

You're in that CSMS space. After the sale, but before implementation?

I'm right after implementation. So they make the sale, the sale goes to implementation, and then implementations will assign them a CSMS. The CSMS will then reach out to me and say, "Hey, we need to onboard this customer."

So, what happens after implementation?

The CSMS will inherit the customer from implementation, because then they cut them off from the customer lifecycle. The CSMS will stay with them, and then they'll work with me. Every time a contract comes up, I have to reevaluate their contract. Did they stay the same? Did they drop a support level? Did they churn entirely? All of those things are things that I'm weeding through their contract on a daily basis.

I thought you would have customer contact on a daily basis.

No. CSMS will sometimes bring me onto their calls if they have a question about some sort of indexing with case routing or with what their phone trees or something. That's beyond the technical scope of the CSMS. Where they need to be on a Zoom and need somebody to really explain the nuts and bolts of something.

Define case routing for me and book a business.

Sure. So, case routing is when somebody tries to call in or make a support ticket, how do we make sure that it gets assigned to the right person? Does it come to us? Does it come to them first? And then they have to send it to us? There are all sorts of different ways that we can have that set up in order to work with their workflow. Also, does a teacher directly reach out to us? And then if it has something to do with something at the school, then we have to send it back to the school. Who do we send it to? Is it sent to the right person? All of those sorts of things are all backend associations that I have to make manually.

You're saying that you're not directly interacting with customers?

That's correct. I'm more of a behind-the-scenes person, making sure that everything runs smoothly. Also, for each account with Tier 1 Support, when teachers and students are able to reach out to our support team directly, we manage a knowledge base for them. So when we have the ability for students and teachers to reach out to us directly, we also manage a knowledge base for them, or they can add information about institution-specific things like if they have a question about enrollments, who do they talk to? If they have a financial aid question, they're calling us instead. Or where do we direct them to? I also manage all of our knowledge bases. And we did a massive project last summer where we consolidated them and made them go to a standard set of ten entries. I did a lot of audits to clean up the messy ones.

What do you mean by a standard set of ten entries?

We developed a set of ten questions that are common cases we encounter. For example, if someone has a question about enrollments, who do they contact? If someone has a question about financial aid, who do they reach out to? Teachers also need training. Who do they contact? Who is their LMS administrator? We also provide additional questions for unusual situations. However, we were struggling with these knowledge-based documents that our agents need to read every time they have a new customer from a different school. This document is lengthy and explains the historical reasons behind different college acronyms. It was overwhelming, and people got frustrated. Based on my experience, this was one of the first projects I took ownership of in my role. I focused on our biggest case driver accounts to improve workflows for our agents. In terms of our book of business, we have a diverse range of accounts. These accounts are involved with me, as they're creating cases. Teachers, admins, and students can all reach out to us. These accounts also have knowledge bases that I maintain, but we also have other support levels with many customers. I recently inherited two interns who work with me. I'm currently training them because they're new to the role.

Is there anything else regarding this position?

I enjoy the mix of routine tasks and solving unexpected problems. It's comforting to handle both and plan my day with simple tasks during low-energy moments. I also have ownership to propose and act on solutions, which is very rewarding. I've suggested protocols and received support to collaborate with others, which feels refreshing compared to teaching, where ideas often weren't valued. My work depends on others completing their tasks, and when they don't, it impacts mine. My boss jokes about this and often reminds me when it's time to log out.

What advice would you give someone considering leaving teaching for a new career?

I think that you need to know and be realistic about what your expectations are. Figure out what your why is. My "why" for so long was to be present for my students. I felt like every year my school was pulling more of me in order to do that. Then I couldn't split myself anymore. I was not able to be present for my family and things like that, which was hard. When I became a mom, I was told my daughter had such and such at her school. They said I couldn't go because there was testing that day and we didn't have enough subs. I couldn't go. That's when the light bulb started to go off for me. I love this, and my students are my babies, but what about my actual baby?

What part of education is so jacked up that teachers taking off for their own children's activities or a daytime doctor's appointment totally thwarts the system?

Much of it is the hours of preparation required outside of work. I had a family, and every weekend, I had to spend at least 8 hours planning lessons. If I had a Saturday wedding and my daughter had a Sunday birthday party, I would panic. How could I get everything done? I became unpleasant to be around. It's important to step back and figure out priorities, understanding there are trade-offs. I work all summer now, but my husband is off on Mondays. Last summer, I took every Monday off. Nobody made me feel bad about it; I got to choose when to use my time, and no one was upset.

Is there anything else that you would like to share?

My biggest advice for teachers leaving the classroom is to target companies with a history of hiring former teachers because they understand. At least 25% of my company has classroom experience. Even on our Executive Board, like our head of Customer Experience, a former New York City public high school teacher, they get it. When I visited our Utah office in March, we talked about New York State testing, and it was so validating to connect with people at that level who share similar experiences. While education companies often value teachers, many non-education companies also recognize their worth, but it can be hard for them to fully understand until they see teachers' skills in action.

Cybersecurity Awareness and Communication Specialist - Nina
Taught for 6 Years - High School - Social Science Courses

You can't just go from teaching one of the social science courses to working in cybersecurity! Walk me through the upskilling and reskilling process.

It was early 2021 when I started seriously thinking about cybersecurity as a career. I knew you had to put anti-malware on your computer and stuff, but I didn't know it could be a full career. I learned about it during an in-service. I attended a local info session on different career opportunities coming to the area. The idea was for us to be able to advise our high school students, but I came away with a new interest. I started doing my own research and found a boot camp I thought would help, but honestly, I regret it. Boot camps are expensive, and you can build a solid foundation without the debt. While it gave me a good start, it wasn't necessary. I joined a professional cybersecurity organization that helped me network and connect with others in the field. They host events where you can learn more about different roles in cybersecurity. I also attended a Security+ study group, which was a great resource for building my knowledge. Security+ is a CompTIA certification, and it's a big test with a lot of material. I'd definitely suggest learning about networking before starting that journey. It took about two or three months to finish. After that, I took the test, kept networking, and applied for jobs. My boss posted on LinkedIn that he was looking for a communications person for security. I thought, "Well, I know how to communicate." That's definitely a skill you develop as a teacher. So, I applied, and within a month or so, I got the job and moved to another state.

Wow! Can you walk me through the specific part of cybersecurity you work in? I assumed I'd need a new degree and have to learn something like Python or Ruby on Rails. What skills did you actually need to learn?

To really keep up and have solid conversations, you probably want to know a lot of what's in the Security+ exam. But I don't use everything from the exam. It was good exposure, though. I wouldn't say Security+ is necessary to get into an awareness role, but it helps a lot in understanding basic security principles.

What does your job actually look like?

I run the entire security awareness program for my company. Depending on the company, you could focus on a newsletter or phishing simulations. I do both. I also conduct training. I'm an admin on our security education platform. Large companies often invest in email security systems or awareness platforms, especially when they're global or national. I also do in-person training because I work for a manufacturing company with a lot of plants. Employees can't always leave their day-to-day work because they've got to keep the lines running, but I can go to the plants and pull them away for training. I also help with open events like town halls.

Did someone in this position before you develop the system, or did you?

I had to develop the system.

How did you know how to do that?

It's been a learning process. My director has been in security for a long time and gave me a lot of guidance. The biggest learning curve was adjusting to the corporate environment, which is very different from a school. I create processes, draft materials, review them with others, and test equipment to make sure it works. We make changes as we go along, finding what works and what doesn't. In a way, it's still like teaching . When I started teaching, they gave me a textbook and said, "Here, teach what's here." It's the same here. They said, "Here, run security awareness."

Do you deal with change management at all?

Not a lot. That's mostly IT and security when they're implementing new processes.

How often do you communicate with IT?

I communicate with IT and security all the time. We have to ensure clear communication, especially when we do phishing simulations. I let IT know what's coming so they aren't caught off guard if employees call with questions.

What keywords should someone use if they're interested in a career like yours?

"Awareness" is probably the biggest keyword. You can also search for "security communications" or "human risk," which is a newer term for cybersecurity awareness.

How do you stay current in your role?

I come across books and articles on LinkedIn, and LinkedIn Learning has good training for different tools I use. A great book for this type of role is The Security Culture Playbook. Being part of professional groups helps me stay updated on current threats because cybersecurity changes every week or month.

Where do you get updates on threats?

Some government groups track threats across industries, but a lot of what I learn is from cybersecurity intelligence people I follow on LinkedIn and

Twitter. They're on the forefront of what's happening. Some of them used to be hackers, so they have a good idea of what's coming.

What's the career path for upward mobility in this field?

Running my own program is a big accomplishment. Most people don't start by running their own program. They either work with a managed service provider or are part of a bigger security awareness program, only doing a component of what I do. Moving to a larger company would probably be a move up for me, but there are other areas within cybersecurity that I'm interested in, and my current role has given me some experience with those areas . I've been really interested in governance, risk, and compliance (GRC). Writing policies and doing some human risk management has given me experience that could transfer over to one of those positions. I'm also interested in the role of a Business Information Security Officer (BISO). There's some overlap with awareness because you're working with business units to integrate good security culture and practices. This is a relatively new role, and not a lot of companies have it yet, but it's something I'd like to explore.

That sounds like a lot of opportunities for growth.

Yes, and some of those roles require an MBA, so that's eventually going to be a goal of mine.

That makes sense, especially with how specialized some of these positions are. Like you said, it's not like in teaching where you can just move up to assistant principal and then principal. There are only so many of those positions.

Exactly.

Why did you become a teacher?

My mom recently retired from teaching, so I grew up with a teacher in the family. She did special education for the most part. I was always in her classroom growing up. What drew me to teaching was that it seemed interesting. Your day-to-day really just kind of depended on the students. I just remember my mom always coming home with tons of interesting stories, and it just seemed like something that could lead to an interesting life. Even now, coming out of teaching, I still think all of that holds true. You meet a lot of new people and have a lot of novel experiences. I also enjoyed the fact that you're part of a community. My mom was always getting stopped by people and having little reunions, even when we went to Walmart. I really enjoyed that. And I still run into former students of mine and enjoy that feeling of being part of a community.

Why did you leave teaching?

There wasn't any particular event at my school that soured me. It's more about the general experience of not really seeing an avenue for promotions or career opportunities. I've never been interested in administration work. That kind of seemed like a part of the job I had no interest in. After a while, even though the kids always kept it interesting, the lack of a clear career path made me feel kind of stuck. There weren't any ways to move forward. You just come in, teach, and that's that. On top of that, all the politicization going on around teaching and education, especially in my former state, was a real mood killer.

Do you have any final words?

My biggest piece of advice is to not be afraid to reach out to people on LinkedIn who are where you want to be. People love talking about themselves, and a lot of them are willing to share how they got to where they are. That kind of connection can spark opportunities or at least give you some good guidance. There are also a lot of other teachers who have made the transition to private companies, and there's a bit of a community around that.

Resources:

Women's Society of Cyberjutsu: https://womenscyberjutsu.org/

The Security Culture Playbook: https://www.amazon.com/Security-Culture-Playbook-Executive-Developing/dp/1119875234/

Transformational Security Awareness: https://www.amazon.com/Transformational-Security-Awareness-Neuroscientists-Storytellers/dp/B08CJQXHRR/
Develop Your Cybersecurity Career Path (Highly Recommended): https://www.amazon.com/Develop-Your-Cybersecurity-Career-Path/dp/1955976007/
Breaking into Cybersecurity (podcast): https://www.youtube.com/c/BreakingIntoCybersecurity

SANS course: https://www.sans.org/cyber-security-courses/managing-human-risk/
Follow on LinkedIn: Lance Spitzner, Ashley Chackman, Gabriel Friedlander, Lauren Zink, Meghan Jacquot

Data Analyst - Oscar

Taught for 2.5 years - Grades: 11 & 12 - Subject: Financial Literacy

How did you get into education?

Education was my first real job. Out of college, I did small jobs to make ends meet, like security and stuff like that. Once I graduated, I began teaching. Much of it started because there was a need in my community. I grew up in North New Jersey, and there was a shortage of teachers in Newark. I do a lot of motivational speaking, so I was already speaking to students. There's a need for teachers. Let me step in.

Why did you leave education?

The reason I left teaching was that I was always passionate about the financial markets and being connected to them. My ultimate goal was to get my foot in the door to work for a big financial institution, whether that be an investment bank, a hedge fund, a financial data firm, or something similar. That's what I was passionate about and aiming towards, even when I was teaching. As I began teaching, I really saw how hard it was to educate and uplift youth in the inner city. Growing up, I experienced it as a student. I saw how I was and how my friends were, but being on the other side, I didn't understand how difficult it was to teach until I got into it. A lot of students in the inner city come from broken homes. Many students are the heads of their households at the junior or senior level. Their parents work all the time to make ends meet, so these students look after their siblings and tend to the house. There's a lot of pressure that comes with that. There's also the lack of financial resources in the household. Many students came to school every day in the same clothes. Many students didn't have food to eat. School was their way of getting food; they didn't have it at home. A lot of students were leaving school and going to unsafe neighborhoods surrounded by gang violence. I come from that background as well, which is why I was able to connect with the students more and reach them better. It is a difficult job.

How does the current situation in schools differ from when you were a student?

That's a great question. When I was in school, I felt that teachers cared more. I can remember all my teachers from pre-K through high school. They were invested in me and had my best interests at heart. Nowadays, teachers seem increasingly stressed and underpaid. The rising cost of living and inflation have worsened the situation. Back then, the economy was more stable, but now, teachers face more pressure as their wages don't stretch as far due to inflation. They teach students from families affected by economic shifts, leading to deeper poverty. In public schools in the inner city, students might be experiencing these pressures more acutely. Their parents may work harder or lack financial resources. Many students come from gang-related backgrounds and are already troubled, engaging in behaviors like smoking and selling drugs. Teachers are trying to teach students who are in survival mode, which adds significant stress to the job. Many teachers mentally check out and are just there for the paycheck, struggling to push students forward when they aren't following rules. A noticeable issue is that many teachers can't relate to their students. A lot of teachers are not people of color and commute from outside the city to teach in these challenging environments. Students often sense this disconnect. When I began teaching, students connected with me because I shared similar experiences and spoke their language. Teachers who had been there for years, often white and from outside the community, faced disrespect from students. They asked me how I managed to get students to listen. It's all about relatability, and students can see that.

I understand you can't provide specifics about your company, but let's imagine you worked for McDonald's. What would your role look like there?

In that role at McDonald's, my job would be to turn numbers and information into useful ideas that help improve the business. I would start by collecting data from different places, like sales numbers, customer comments, and market trends. I would use tools like Excel to clean and organize this data, making sure it's accurate and easy to understand.

A big part of my job would be looking at sales to see which menu items are popular and which ones might need changes. I would create reports and charts to show this information clearly to managers and executives. I would also check how well promotional campaigns are doing and suggest ways to make future marketing efforts better. To check the effectiveness of promotional campaigns, I would gather sales data and customer feedback, analyze trends, and compare results before and after the promotion. I would identify what worked and what didn't, then recommend improvements based on the data. For example, if a buy-one-get-one-free deal boosts sales, I would suggest using it again or refining less effective strategies. This would help McDonald's optimize future marketing efforts.

Another important task would be keeping an eye on customer feedback to find out how satisfied people are and where we can improve their dining experience. As a data analyst, my role would be to identify issues and provide actionable insights, not necessarily to implement the solutions myself. For example, if many customers mention long wait times, I would highlight this trend in my reports. I might suggest areas to investigate, like staffing levels during peak hours or efficiency in the kitchen. However, I would rely on the expertise of the operational teams to develop and implement specific strategies to speed up service. My main contribution would be providing clear, data-driven evidence to guide their decision-making. By sharing these insights, I would help the company make better decisions, from changing the menu to planning new marketing strategies.

How did you get started? Did you attend a boot camp or take any specific courses? Let's start at the beginning.

No, I didn't go to any boot camps or formal training.

Walk me through how you figured out how to become a data analyst. I know you initially wanted to go into finance, but how did you focus on data analysis and the skills needed for that?

My path to becoming a data analyst was quite unconventional. I started out as a financial product analyst within my company. While it was an analyst role, it wasn't specifically a data analyst position. In that role, I dealt with clients and taught them how to use our financial product. About 90% of the job involved interacting with clients daily, which I found draining since I'm more introverted and prefer working behind the scenes. I decided to use my company's resources to learn coding languages on my own. I started with DataCamp, teaching myself SQL and Python through various introductory and intermediate courses. Over time, I built up my skills and made it clear to my manager that I was passionate about data and wanted to transition to a different role within the company. Fortunately, I was able to apply my self-taught skills to a new position in a different department, which is how I moved into data analytics.

How long did it take you to go from deciding to pursue data analysis to completing your self-study?

It took about a year and a half. I was studying even before I knew I'd be transitioning to a different department. I used my early mornings, late evenings, and free time at home for studying. I'm still learning and improving my skills, but it was roughly a year and a half before I made the transition.

Are you in front of a computer all day, or do you have meetings?

I do have meetings, but my work is project-based. I spend most of my time in front of a computer, focusing on my tasks. It's more independent work, so I can listen to music and work at my own pace without client interactions.

How much data do you handle, and how long does it usually take to complete a project? It's hard to imagine spending all day, every day, on data tasks. What are the typical timelines?

Every day is different, especially at my company. The duration of a project depends on the size of the data set and the scope of the project. Some transformations are straightforward and can be completed in a day. Others, involving more complex access or security issues, can take several weeks or even months. It varies widely depending on the project.

How do assignments come to you?

We have a stakeholder who communicates our tasks. They outline what needs to be done, and then my manager assigns the work among the team. We start working on it from there.

Do you use Jira or another project management tool?

Yes, we use Jira.

Let's go back to when you first started. With your new skills, did you know exactly what to do on your first project, or did you have a mentor? Describe that transition.

We had onboarding training and team members who showed us various aspects of the job, like loading data, setting up Python scripts, and using Superset. My first project wasn't too difficult, and I had a supportive manager who assigned me tasks appropriate for my skill level. As I progressed, my responsibilities increased gradually. It was a smooth transition, building up from there.

Did you create a portfolio, and did you use it during your interviews?

I started a portfolio on Kaggle and GitHub with some projects I worked on, but I didn't use it extensively in my interview.

Did you need to do any coding for your role?

For this role, there wasn't any coding required during the hiring process. It was an entry-level position without coding interviews. However, for some internal roles, there were coding assessments. For my current role, coding wasn't necessary.

What is DataCamp?

DataCamp is a valuable resource for anyone interested in data analysis. It offers courses in various coding languages like Python, SQL, Power BI, and Tableau. You can learn about machine learning, automation, and Apache Spark. It's one of my favorite sites for learning new coding skills.

How difficult was it to learn?

SQL was relatively easy due to its straightforward syntax. You can grasp the basics in about four hours. Python was more challenging because of its broad range of applications, from building apps and websites to data analysis. I'm still learning and improving my skills in automation and building specific UIs. Python's versatility means you can be proficient in one area but less so in another.

What are the best and worst parts of your position?

The best part is my passion for the work and the enjoyment I get from it. It doesn't feel like work to me. I also appreciate the flexibility, as I'm no longer client-facing. I can set my own schedule, take breaks as needed, and wear comfortable clothes. The worst part is dealing with imposter syndrome, especially as a person of color in a field where there aren't many like me. It can affect confidence and project work.

What's your next move? I see you recently earned a certification. Congratulations!

Thank you! I'm considering moving into an engineering role, though I'm unsure whether it will be software engineering, data engineering, or data science. It will likely be one of these areas.

What advice would you give to teachers who want to leave the classroom and pursue a different career?

To teachers considering a career change, I'd say just go for it. There's never a perfect time. Network, put yourself out there, and trust your intuition if you feel drawn to something else. Surround yourself with people who have made similar transitions or who are interested in making a change. It's crucial to be around those who are on the same path, as that has been very helpful for me.

Resources: Datacamp.com, hackerrank.com, Stack Overflow, LinkedIn Learning, Coursera, Udemy Google Analytics, Microsoft - Training for Data Analysts, Harvard University CS50 (YouTube, edX OpenCourseWare), O'Reilly Learning, Alex the Analyst, CS Dojo, Tech with Tim

Digital Marketing Manager and Executive LinkedIn Strategist/Ghostwriter - Deiera

Taught for 4 years - Grades: 6 - 12 - Subjects: Business & Marketing

How did you connect the dots of your teaching experience and leverage it into your new career starting your own business?

I taught business, marketing, career development, personal finance, and technology courses, so it wasn't difficult for me to connect the dots. I knew that my unique experience in business and education would be an asset to clients and teachers. I started out just writing resumes, but I transitioned to coaching when I realized that a resume could only get them so far. Transitioning teachers need help with the job search, interview process, etc. as well. Teaching six different grades at a time helped me explain how I can change my tone and voice to match different audiences. As a LinkedIn ghostwriter, I ghostwrite for people who are completely different from me about topics I never knew existed. Teaching definitely helped me strengthen that muscle because I sometimes taught subjects that I didn't even know.

How does the current job market's competitive nature, with thousands of experienced and qualified candidates, impact the likelihood of teachers getting interviews for new positions, despite meeting most job qualifications?"

As I see many posts on Facebook and LinkedIn from teachers who don't understand why they aren't getting interviews despite meeting most of the job qualifications. Unfortunately, not everyone who meets the qualifications will get an interview. Many jobs that teachers transition to attract thousands of applicants, making it likely that at least a few hundred are qualified. Realistically, they can't interview every single qualified applicant. When that's the case, they look beyond the minimum qualifications and look at who has the most relevant experience. Yes, there are jobs for which teachers are qualified without upskilling; however, if other candidates have upskilled, you might not be chosen over them. It's not about meeting the basic requirements. It's about showing why you're the best candidate.

How important is an education degree in the corporate world?

Raises and promotions aren't based on your degree in the corporate world, so don't get stuck on finding jobs that ask for an education degree. They care about a degree, but the major just doesn't matter as much. Every teacher has different strengths, responsibilities, and accomplishments, so take time to figure out what you like and what you're good at. Don't limit yourself to education just because that's what your degree is in.

What is your advice for applying to various types of roles in their job search, the "pray and spray" method?

It's important to choose one role to focus on so you can upskill for it and tailor your resume for it. You don't have to stick to the same job forever. In fact, most people don't stay at companies for longer than five years (and that's a long time).

What are some of the hurdles that you experienced in making the transition and/or that you see some of your clients overcome?

I used to have a career consulting company where I helped transitioning teachers. The biggest hurdle my clients faced was that they didn't understand how things worked outside of education. Passion was great, but companies didn't hire you for passion. They didn't hire you to give you a chance or because they liked your personality. They hired you because they believed you would make them money, save them money, or save them time. Salary was based on your ability to do that, not what you hoped to make. That was important to know because I saw some teachers who had unrealistic expectations of what to expect from the transition. They should absolutely have gotten paid a fair amount, but it was unreasonable to expect a company to pay you for your years of experience in education if your new job had nothing to do with education. That was like a medical doctor transitioning to education and expecting to get paid the same amount because they had years of experience in medicine.

Why did you leave teaching?

I left teaching for a few reasons. I never planned to stay long. I couldn't see myself staying in one career for my whole adult life, so I planned to leave after 4-5 years. I saved money the entire time I was teaching so that I could afford to not work for a year after having kids. It worked out that I had a baby at the end of my 4th year, so I was able to take that year off which is when I started the business, started freelancing, and began working for a branding agency as the in-house LinkedIn strategist for their clients.

Do you miss not having a summer break? Explain why or why not.

No. I'm self-employed, so I'm an independent contractor for the branding agency and Edtech company. I'm able to block off my schedule when necessary. I'm paid based on projects, so if I block off my calendar and don't take projects, it impacts my income. That's the downside, but I'm pretty good at planning ahead to cover for it.

What is one critical piece of advice you have for teachers looking to transition out of education and improve their resumes for non-teaching roles?

Make sure that everything on your resume aligns with something in the job posting. Test scores aren't relevant unless something in the job posting mentions test scores or the effectiveness of training. Your resume should be based on the job posting, so don't just throw everything you've ever done on a resume and apply. Recruiters don't have time to read through irrelevant information, as it implies a lack of understanding of the job requirements. Also, research and be prepared to put in the work. It's not quick nor easy.

Resources: Transitioning Teachers Facebook Group

Hubspot Academy courses for professional development.

Data Scientist - Tiffany
Taught for 20 Years - Grade: HS - Subject: Math

You're a data scientist. If I'm a teacher at home thinking, "This is what I want to do," what specific skills do I need?

The first thing, and I cannot stress this enough, is strong communication skills. As a teacher, you're already used to explaining things in simple terms, and that skill has been invaluable to me as a data scientist. When you're dealing with data, models, predictions, or decision-making, you need to explain it in a way that the people signing the checks can understand. A lot of people focus on the technical skills which are important, and I'll get to those in a bit, but soft skills matter just as much. You'd be surprised how many people in this field struggle to take something technical, like a graph or a concept, and break it down for others. Communication is huge, and as a teacher, you already have that foundation.

What steps did you take to enter the field of data science?

My journey started in July 2017 when I enrolled in a one-year program in applied statistics and data management at a reputable local university. I learned SAS programming and a lot of statistics, but after finishing the program, I realized I needed to learn a programming language like Python to truly break into data science. That's when I started teaching myself

Python, which has been essential for my career.

Do you need a technical degree or expensive programs to become a data scientist?

Absolutely not. You don't need another degree or to spend a fortune on boot camps. One of my co-workers is a lead data scientist, and her degree is in costume design! Let's say you don't have a technical background... maybe you majored in history or something else...you can still gain the skills you need. Learn programming languages like Python, get familiar with data tools, and practice through projects. The key is to build the skills, not to go into debt chasing another degree.

How did you learn all of this...it sounds so technical...how did you put it all together?

I learned from my team when I started and adapted their system. In an agile, iterative process, we begin with a minimum viable product to address immediate needs then refine it over time. For example, you might first build a basic shelter for a family, later adding windows, shingles, or a garden. This approach ensures progress while improving in steps, which I explain clearly to stakeholders during meetings.

What is the first deliverable you provide to customers? Can you break it down for me so I can better understand?

The first deliverable is usually about organizing the data. Let us say we have data from multiple sources, and it all looks different. The first step is to get it into a consistent, readable format, like a table or spreadsheet. For example, if I am working with fast food data from McDonald's and Burger King, they might structure their tables differently. One might label dates in one way, while the other does it differently. I make sure everything aligns so we can actually use the data. This process includes transforming the data, adding labels, and ensuring all formats are standardized. Once that is done, we can pull insights. For example, we might discover that more people choose burgers over chicken sandwiches. From there, we start storytelling with the data. This means identifying trends and creating visuals like charts to make the information easy to understand. Finally, as a data scientist, I take it further by building a model. Using all the cleaned and organized data, I can predict trends or solve specific problems for the customer. The entire process starts with cleaning and organizing the data, which is the foundation for everything else.

You just used a term; model give me more context.

The type of data you are working with usually guides your choice of model. For example, if you are working with text, you might use natural language processing models. I work primarily with text, so I use those models frequently. There are different levels of complexity depending on how deep you need to go, but the data itself helps you make those decisions. It really depends on the data, but I would say that by learning Python is to your advantage. You also want to focus on solving a specific business problem. That is what it is all about. Finding a problem relevant to the career path or industry you want to pursue. For example, if you are interested in healthcare, you might analyze patient data, or if you are in education, you might examine test scores and teacher evaluations, like I did. In my current role, I work with legal documents and text because I am in a legal and professional services company. Data science is a broad field, so it is important to narrow your focus to a specific domain. This helps you build expertise and solve problems that matter in that area.

I remember you mentioned BERT before. Can you explain it again?

Sure. BERT is a large language model used for natural language processing. It is a transformer model, which means it can understand context in text, much like how the human brain processes language. You feed it data, and it identifies patterns, extracts insights, and even draws conclusions from the text. For example, BERT can recognize that the word "bank" refers to a financial institution in one sentence but a riverbank in another, based on context.

You mentioned meeting with your team multiple times a week. Are you remote? Also, have you had the opportunity to attend professional development?

Yes, I work remotely, and one thing I love about my team is their focus on continuous learning. They provide free resources and even allow time to learn during work hours, as long as we are not swamped with bugs or other urgent issues. Last year, I took a course that opened up a big opportunity. The instructor liked my work so much that I became a course facilitator. I ended up teaching an AI course, which gave me the chance to bring back what I learned and share it with my team and global data science community at work.

How does AI fit into your work? Are you doing prompt engineering? Can you share more about the AI course you mentioned?

The course I took is called "Building LLM Applications," and it focuses on creating systems using large language models. It is very practical, teaching how to design and implement AI-powered applications.

In layman's terms, what should I understand about large language models and AI if I am interested in becoming a data scientist?

A great starting point is learning natural language processing techniques. This includes classification, text summarization, and named entity recognition, or NER. For instance, if you have a page of text, NER can identify specific entities like judges, dates, or locations within that page. These techniques are the foundation for working with AI and large language models, so I would definitely focus on mastering them first.

Would it be advantageous to transition from a data analyst to a data scientist? Or if someone is interested in data science, should they start in a different role?

If I could do it over again, I would have started as a data analyst. As a teacher, you already have many transferable skills, so the data analyst route feels like a natural fit. I do not want to say you must become a data analyst and then work your way up to data scientist, because the work is different, but for someone with a teaching background, starting as a data analyst might be the best option. If I had focused on technical skills like SQL, and Excel, and data visualization tools like Tableau or Power BI, I could have started as a data analyst without needing to learn Python. Python is essential for data scientists because coding is a big part of the job, but for data analysts, those other skills are enough. Looking back, that route might have been a better starting point for me.

What advice would you give to others transitioning to data science?

I was a high school math teacher for 20 years, and that was my only career for a long time. Networking and job searching had changed so much over those years. It is never too late to pursue a career in data science. I left a 20-year career in teaching and transitioned into data science in my 40s. Do not let age or a non-technical background stop you from following your passion. Once I settled into my new job, I made it a priority to come back and help others like me who are trying to figure out how everything works. My advice is to leverage the skills you already have, get your foot in the door, and then take advantage of opportunities to grow once you are in a new role.

What is the first step to accelerating your data science journey?

To accelerate your journey, use the skills you already have. Get a job, even if it is not your dream role yet, and build from there. Once you are in the door, you can explore other opportunities and continue developing your expertise. This approach will help you grow faster.

How can a teacher find the resources and build experience?

My biggest advice is to focus on project-based learning. Instead of taking long, generic courses, jump right into building something practical that uses skills you will need daily, like Python libraries such as pandas and NumPy. Python is essential for data science, and job descriptions show it is in high demand. Working on meaningful projects helps you learn more effectively than starting from scratch with introductory courses that may not be relevant to your goals. You also do not need to spend a lot of money to get started. There are so many free resources available. Coursera is my top recommendation because you can audit courses for free, and they offer guided projects. YouTube is another great resource, with free boot camps and tutorials from excellent content creators. I wish I had known about these options earlier; it would have saved me over twenty thousand dollars. When it comes to showcasing your skills, projects are key. One challenge I faced was getting people to see me as Tiffany, the data scientist, instead of Mrs. Teasley, the math teacher. My projects became my experience. On my resume, I included detailed descriptions of what I accomplished. By the time people noticed my teaching background, they already understood the scope of my data science skills. Building a portfolio with your projects will speak volumes about your abilities and help you stand out.

How can continuous learning help overcome challenges in your data science journey?

Embracing learning is essential. When I interviewed for my jobs, my manager asked if I knew about BERT, a large language model. I had to admit I did not, and I knew I had failed the interview. Instead of giving up, I learned about BERT through a short Udemy course, applied my knowledge to a project, and emailed the manager to show what I had accomplished. He was so impressed that I advanced to the next round and got the job. Learning never stops. Use it to navigate challenges and seize opportunities. Do not let a no stop you. Keep going and keep growing.

Is there anything about being on the job as a data scientist that surprised you? How does it compare to teaching and being in the corporate space?

There is a lot that is different, and it feels great. First of all, I feel respected as a professional. I cannot speak for every school system, but for me and my teacher friends, that was not always the case in education. In this role, I feel valued for my work, and it is such a refreshing change. Another thing I love is that I am only responsible for myself. It feels good to focus solely on my own work, and as teachers, we know what good work looks like, so we deliver. The stress level is another huge difference. In the tech world, the stress is nothing compared to what I experienced as a teacher. It feels like years have been added back to my life. I feel refreshed like I am just getting started.

Resources: https://linktr.ee/datasistah

Director of Coach Success Programs and Partnerships - Derek
Taught for 4 years - Grades: 11 & 12
Subjects: Business, Geography, History, Phys. Ed. - Location: Canada

Walk me through a project or a process.

I just wrapped up developing a suite of asynchronous training videos specifically for the Youthfully Admissions program. Youthfully helps youth coaches, who primarily work with high school students, identify their post-high school plans. If students aim to go to university, the coaches assist them in choosing suitable programs and guide them through the essay-writing process to maximize their chances of success once their goals are clear. Since universities constantly change their application processes, we want to ensure coaches are clear on what they're coaching students to do. A coach can't do an interview for a student because that's unethical since we want them to understand the criteria schools use to evaluate applicants so they can help students prepare. Coaches also help students decide which story to tell in their essays based on what the universities are looking for. We're creating a suite of resources that coaches can use to improve and maximize the quality of service they provide to students. Before my involvement, the team created blogs used by parents, students, and coaches to understand the latest on university programs, competitiveness, cut-off averages, etc. This was a multipurpose resource. I was then asked to develop resources specifically for coaches, refining our focus and making it more time-efficient. Long blog posts take a lot of time, so we want coaches to spend more time coaching and less time preparing. We now provide 10-12 minute training videos specific to these programs, offering practical coaching tips and walkthroughs. These videos are application-focused, tailored for coaches rather than a broad audience. Creating these resources required user research to understand coaches' pain points and current sources of information. We developed templates, conducted research, built the resources, and released them quickly, considering that admission season is now. We don't want to deliver them three months after the primary admissions work is done. Once uploaded to the Youthfully Academy, coaches can engage with these resources. We'll track engagement and completion levels to understand their helpfulness, popularity, and value. We'll support this data with follow-up conversations with coaches.

Can you walk me through a recent project you worked on and the processes involved?

The first role that I took after leaving teaching was nontraditional education. I conscripted my teaching role a bit. I took a job as Head of Career Services for a digital skills training boot camp. As Head of Career Services, I was asked to create a standardized process for what we call the Career Success Program. If someone's leaving their career in accounting to become a software developer, they go through this training, primarily technical training on how to code. They also need to understand how to get a job. There's a storytelling piece, CV, LinkedIn, and other soft skill professional development elements beyond just the hard skills of learning to code. I also took product management and UX design courses. I took the initiative to get these free certifications, which were part of what we helped people learn. I had the privilege to enroll in these for free. I applied my understanding of education and UX design, realizing it isn't just applicable to designing digital products but to the design of anything. Often, we think, "Here's what we need to do for standardized assessment," and we backwards map from that. Instead, we should understand where our students are and then design something effective for them. The starting point needs to change a little bit. Not having a standardized test to accommodate really frees you up to learn more about who you're working with and design something better suited to them. By iterating through the design of this career success program, I learned and developed those skills. It became a significant part of my process.

What tools do you use? What types of authoring tools are you using?

We have an LMS called Northpass. We have the academy's internal tool built by our technology team. I'll start with a Google slide deck. This can change, but it's typical. I do my research, take that information, and put it in a Google Doc. I then distill that information and start to organize it mentally, still in a doc, but then transition it to a deck. I go through that deck using either Screencastify or Loom to create a walkthrough, including specific teachable moments. Not just a description, but examples of how I've done this with a student. Here are some specific examples of activities you can do with students to achieve this goal versus just saying, "achieve the goals." I then upload all that to our LMS Northpass, and our technology team pushes it to the Academy, the coach-facing platform. I still use other tools, but that would be specific to development and training resources. I also worked in a sales capacity at Brain Station. The short version is I did the career service work for a year. I resigned because my wife had an opportunity over here. At the time, we were in Toronto, moved to London, left that job, and they reached out a couple of months later and asked if I'd like to lead the expansion into Europe. It was a very North American-based business. I was employee number one on the new continent and led the expansion for about two and a half years.

Understanding the pain points of the student is crucial because they're coming to me, saying, "I need this because of these pain points or goals." Having those conversations, understanding their perspective from an earlier stage in the experience, versus just being focused on delivery, is important. Understanding the business of education is a key thing that's often lacking in teachers. They're like, "I don't want to talk about money and numbers; I just want to focus on teaching." Not everyone is a numbers person. I didn't consider myself a numbers person, but understanding the business of education is a key skill that can open many doors. Being willing to talk about things like, "That student has a budget of X dollars per student," is crucial. It's not about maximizing profit and not caring about the quality of education; it's understanding that it's a business like any other. Understanding the pain points and creating suitable solutions rather than jumping into solutions assuming you know the problem is vital. Both the design certification and my time working in a sales capacity in education helped me uncover the importance of this approach.

I want to talk a little bit about sales and education. A lot of teachers see positions on the sales side in EdTech. Do you have any pointers or anything else you think teachers should know if they're considering a sales role in an EdTech company?

Teachers are uniquely positioned to sell education products because ultimately, people don't want to hear the type of language that someone in software sales might use. When I first got exposed to an education sales role, I was working for a private school. Part of my role was being a teacher, designing curriculum, leading trips abroad, and teaching courses. When I wasn't doing that, I was recruiting students. Having that dual role helped me understand the business of education and the language. Talking to a guidance counselor about the value of these programs, talking to a student or a parent about the value of these programs, being a teacher put me in a unique position to talk about the value students would get from this experience. Someone just coming from a sales position wouldn't have that perspective. To translate that to teachers in EdTech, being able to talk about learning outcomes is key. What people are purchasing from an education experience is a future state. You're not talking about features like with a digital product; you're talking about what future state they want to achieve, what blockers they have, and how this education experience can help.

Do you work remotely? If so, tell me how you like or dislike it. What are the advantages and disadvantages?

Yeah, my wife and I both work full-time from home. When I left teaching, I went to a full-time, in-office job at Brain Station. I met the Head of IT and Head of recruitment in HR, and we played ping pong together. That was working at a tech company with the benefit of socializing. The flexibility to work from home would've been nice, but it wasn't possible then. I transitioned over to the UK, and I was the only person on the continent here for a while. It wasn't only remote since someone else was 20 minutes down the road while I was five hours away from anyone else. At times, that was isolating because if I had a problem, I had no one to talk to except my wife, who would just say, "Sounds annoying," but didn't have the context. That was tough. Post-COVID, we started going into an office about three days a week, which was a nice balance.

When I started at Youthfully, we were a fully remote team. Time zones can be challenging because I'm the only one here. Everyone else is in Canada. I was quite firm on my hours because I learned the hard way that if everyone else is in Canada or on the West Coast, that's a five to eight-hour difference. What I learned is the importance of setting boundaries, which I don't think teachers would initially be great at because you're constantly marking on your weekends.

The flexibility of working remotely is great. Teachers have to be at school almost every day, so the ability to go for a walk if you're not feeling it or do a quick workout if your energy is dragging is lovely. If I want to mix up my environment, my wife and I will go to a cafe for a scenery change. It also allows for better gym routines. We can connect more during the day. If she wants advice on something because she's going through internal recruitment, we can talk about it. I see that as a benefit, but every relationship is different.

What advice would you give to someone considering leaving teaching for a new career?

Number one, I think teachers often limit themselves. It can be a very intimidating thing to change a career. It can be very hard to know where to start. You start looking on Indeed or some job recruitment site, and you start scrolling through all the different things and highlighting, "I don't have that. I don't have that." You start to feel very insecure and anxious, and you're like, "I can't leave." You go back to what you're doing, and that can be a really emotional and negative experience. I'd definitely encourage people to start by doing a bit more internal reflection. What do I like about what I do? What do I not love about what I do? What are the push and pull factors to my situation? Why am I even considering doing something else? What's brought me to this Google bar, saying, "What can teachers transition to?" What prompted that? I'd certainly encourage people to do that to avoid the Indeed experience. I've been there myself, and I've worked with many people in that career services role. Instead, do that personal reflection, have a few conversations, and be willing to ask for help.

Number two, no matter what type of transition you're looking to navigate or something you're feeling uncertain about, we have two types of thinking. We have our creative brain and our filtering, logical brain. Writer's block is a common example of this. What do you want to do? You're staring at that page, and that cursor is blinking at you. You don't know because you might think of something, but then you think, "Oh, no, that's stupid." Your filter brain applies immediately. You need to turn your filter brain off and put things down on the page. Don't criticize it, don't judge it. You're just in ideation mode. Let it go. No idea's too stupid. Get into idea generation mode and let the stream of consciousness flow. At least you then have something to evaluate. Then you can invite your critical, filter brain, and logical brain to look at those options. You've got to have options on the paper to take any step forward. It's like, "Great. Now that we've learned something from that, let's turn that off again and get into ideation mode again." It's sort of flip-flopping between them because if they're trying to compete, that's why that cursor just sits there blinking at you. Another thing is to give yourself space to come up with ideas and not judge them so you can move forward. Otherwise, you're just sitting in place, in that same spiral of, "Oh, if I don't even know, maybe I shouldn't leave." Then you start getting into this headspace, and you'll start spinning about it being a bad idea. Off you go back to the classroom.

Number three, teachers will see job postings. Teachers often box tickets. They're typically fairly type A. I'm generalizing, but there's a certain personality that's attracted to teaching, someone who values safety, someone who feels the need to check assignments off a list. If they see a job description and don't have 100% of the things on that list, they'll rule themselves out. They also self-disqualify. "I don't have any of those qualifications. I can't afford the certification. I don't have the time or energy for the certification, so I'm stuck." Certification, if not more education, is probably necessary. There's probably some guilt associated with that because any time you're taking for yourself is less time for your students. Then, are you delivering the best for your students? That's hard, but ultimately, you need to realize that if you have 80% of the qualifications, you're in the same boat as many others.

Teachers put up this huge barrier: if I don't have 100%, I don't even try because I have no chance. Realize that it's worth taking a shot. Ask for feedback, just like you encourage your students to do. If something disqualifies you, great, work on that thing or at least question if it's something you really need to work on. That's helpful feedback. Gather that feedback and then take action. If you don't have 100% of the things such as two years of work experience for a junior position in learning design or user research, many people are in that same position. If they can't find the person with two years of experience because they're asking for the perfect person who doesn't exist, then they'll default to who they find. It's a perfect state and the world. Realize that on the other side of that barrier. It's tough because teachers typically haven't been part of any business or recruiting process. Having hired plenty, I can tell you it's hard to find good people. It's hard to tick all the boxes. Often, you make compromises for the person who's 80% good and has potential.

Any final thoughts?

Almost 100% of teachers are undervaluing themselves and their skills. Teachers are typically not paid relative to other industries or the time they put in. It's something I learned the hard way. I won't get into specific numbers, but I almost tripled my salary in a couple of years post-teaching. There is some context, such as lower cost of living, but ultimately, my earning potential could have been higher if I hadn't chosen to go into education. I have no regrets, but talking to other people in other industries, understanding again, it's kind of bypassing that taboo you will find that people want to help. However, asking directly, "How much do you make?" can be too blunt. Instead, provide context and allow them to share information more comfortably. For example, they might say, "I won't share my exact salary, but someone in digital marketing with three years of experience at this company earns within this range." This approach gives you more valuable insights than what Glassdoor can offer. If you're making $50-60k as a teacher, your skills in a different industry could be worth $90k. Without this knowledge, you might undervalue yourself and accept less than you're worth.

Director of Internal Business Operations and Recruiting - Lisa

Taught for 6 years - Grades: 3
Taught for 11 years (pt) in the Gifted & Talented Program

Let's talk about what it is you do.

My official title is Director of Internal Business Operations and Recruiting. A large part of that is recruiting, but I also work on streamlining company processes. I am a huge process enthusiast and love operations. My goal is to make work easier for the person doing it while delivering a consistent, elevated experience for clients, candidates, or colleagues.

During the day, that is my focus. I also have a side business, Executive Empress Coaching, that I plan to move into full-time. It's focused on executive/leadership coaching. I primarily focus on two groups. One is executive coaching, which is closest to my heart. It is something I wish I had when transitioning from teaching. Having someone guide me through the corporate world and help with politics and red tape would have been invaluable. I enjoy helping people aiming for leadership roles. I do not like to say "climbing the ladder," but I love assisting people in moving into management and leadership. The other side of my coaching focuses on job seekers. I feel obligated to help in this area because of my experience as a hiring manager for ten years and a recruiter. When I was laid off, it was overwhelming. You wonder what to do first, and self-doubt creeps in. I empathize with candidates because I have been through it. I work with clients on selecting jobs to apply for and tips on applying. There is a right way to apply for jobs, and many people do not know that. I also help with interviewing. I had a close friend who was a mentor when I was navigating the corporate world. She was a huge benefit, but unless you truly understand it, it is hard to prepare for all aspects of interviewing. That is why I help with everything from practicing interviews to providing the right follow-up verbiage and knowing when to follow up.

You've kind of answered this a little bit, but why would someone need executive coaching?

I think anyone can benefit from it, just like I believe everyone can benefit from counseling or marriage counseling. Having a coach helps you navigate the challenges you're facing at work. A lot of times, we focus on leadership skills, but when life challenges arise, those leadership skills might take a backseat. A coach helps you navigate both. Anyone who wants to grow and develop can benefit from coaching. Some people struggle with follow-through and need accountability, while others might not even know what areas they need to work on. They want to move up but feel stuck. So, whatever the client needs, that's what we'll focus on. Once I worked with my first coach, my only concern was that I hadn't started doing that sooner.

You're in the corporate world...Think back to when you were a teacher and tell me what teachers might struggle with in terms of understanding the difference between how things operate in a corporate space.

Well, one thing we touched on was working with others. As teachers, we're around little people all day, shaping them. In the corporate world, you need to collaborate differently. Teachers might spend one or two days a year in small groups for professional development or on a committee, which is helpful but typically aligned with a common goal. In the corporate world, you might work on a project with someone from another department who has different goals. While you share the same objective, the approaches might differ. For example, a sales leader might push in one direction while you work with the account management team to balance things out. That's the biggest difference. As teachers, we often chat with colleagues during lunch, between classes, or after school. In the corporate world, it's different when you work closely with people who may not share your interests or goals.

Okay. Now, the type of recruiter you are. You're the director, so you have team members underneath you?

In the past, I have led teams of 12 +, but right now, I just have one independent contractor recruiter on the team. As the business grows, we'll need more support.

So, in terms of your carer and trying to address what teachers need in their resumes and interviews, what's one thing you'd want to tell teachers about resumes?

There are so many things you can do, but The biggest tip is to include relevant metrics on your resume. Tailor your resume for each job application by presenting your experience in a way that matches what the employer is seeking. This does not mean adding things you have not done, of course. Over 10+ years, I have done a lot, but not everything is on my resume. Choose bullet points that highlight the skills and experiences they are looking for. They do not need to know everything you have done, just what applies to the job. And I highly recommend getting help from someone who has been a recruiter.

Does it bother you if you see a three-page resume?

No, it doesn't bother me.

Sometimes, I see guidelines saying resumes should be one or two pages and not to exceed two pages.

There are definitely guidelines, and I say this as a coach. Sometimes, coaches can make things more stressful by saying, "Don't do this, don't do that." As a recruiter, I'm looking for ways to qualify someone, not disqualify them. So, if it's three pages, I'll see if they're qualified within those three pages.

How long have you been in your current role?

I've been in this role for six months. While my LinkedIn identity is a recruiter, I've only been in recruiting for a couple of years. Before this in-house role, I was an agency recruiter. And before that, I was in senior leadership roles for many years. I love developing people and processes most.

What's the difference between an agency and an in-house recruiter?

Great question. So, an agency recruiter works for a recruitment agency. They find companies that need help hiring, often because they're struggling to fill specific roles. The agency will set up a contract with that company and then recruit for those roles. Typically, if a candidate that the agency provided is hired, the agency gets paid 20% of the candidate's annual salary for the first year. In-house recruiting is different. You're responsible for filling all open positions within your own company. When a role becomes available, you work to find candidates and present them to the hiring managers, working together until the right candidate is hired.

Did you go back to get any HR-related qualifications when you transitioned from teaching, or did you just jump right into it?

Honestly, I feel like I kind of lucked into my first role after teaching. I had a connection who helped me get the interview, which gave me an advantage. I still had to do my part in the process, but that connection definitely opened the door. I had not been searching for very long before being introduced to this company. Before that, I found the phone interviews to be rough, and I felt completely out of my comfort zone. But eventually, I got to the point of interviewing with this company and took it from there. They had interviews, personality assessments, and projects to complete as part of the process.

I didn't know if you went back to get your certification in HR or anything.

I didn't, but I do recommend things like that, especially when you're preparing to leave teaching. Once you've decided to leave, I think it's important to start getting certifications, taking LinkedIn Learning courses, and doing things that will make you feel more relevant. It's not just about looking more relevant—it's about feeling more confident. When you're transitioning, you don't always know the language, and you don't even know what you're supposed to say. I highly recommend hiring someone to work with when you do decide to make the transition. Look for someone with recruiting experience because they know what opens doors. If they have experience as a hiring manager, that's a bonus.

Right. LinkedIn has wonderful content.

Even just being on LinkedIn and lurking around, you learn a lot that way, too. I wish I'd done that more myself. I recommend that teachers get active there. Follow other teachers who have transitioned, but don't let that be the bulk of who you follow. Follow people who talk about the corporate world. And follow a lot of active recruiters. Be cautious of those who message you trying to help; do your due diligence.

Sometimes, we didn't have much autonomy. Tell me how that has changed for you.

When I was teaching, I felt like I had a lot of flexibility in my day. My responsibilities were a lot less in the last 10 years of my teaching tenure due to teaching the gifted and talented groups and doing it part-time. The stress was just different. You don't have the same pressures as in regular classroom teaching, like being evaluated from the standardized testing results. I taught third grade for a long time and found it to be a lot of work. But in all my teaching roles, I had a lot of flexibility in how I ran my classroom. I was lucky enough to work with principals who trusted and supported me. I know a lot of people don't have that kind of freedom, though, and things have changed in the teaching world. Once you leave teaching, you realize the difference. You don't have little people around you who depend on you. If you feel sick, you can call out or even just go to your office and close the door, but teachers can't do that.

We talked a little bit about the skills, but knowing what you know now, what would you have changed about your preparation?

If I were preparing for a job in the corporate world again, I'd definitely get a coach. It helps navigate the changes. Though it might feel like an extra expense, you get that return on your investment by getting hired sooner.

The other thing I would've done differently once I started in the corporate world is asking for help. I felt like I had a lot to prove. As a teacher, you know that feeling. I was hired at the same time as someone else with the same title. This created a competitive environment between us, even though we were doing the same job. I would never ask her for help. I just tried to figure it out myself. One time, the CEO asked me to create a label for a champagne bottle to celebrate a company milestone. I spent the whole weekend trying to figure it out, even though I had no experience with the program. The other girl knew how to use it—it was part of her job. I spent the whole weekend printing labels and making mistakes. Now, I realize that even experienced people don't know everything. When you're new to a position, it's okay to ask for help. No one has it all figured out. But I felt like I had to figure it all out to avoid seeming like "just a teacher."

I totally understand. It wasn't until I left the classroom and started seeking a new career that I stumbled upon fields like instructional design, UX research, data analysis, and so many more.

We often think our next career must be directly related to teaching, but teachers now have technology experience that translates well into other jobs. Customer service is a natural progression because we are skilled at handling people and resolving issues. I started in marketing for a home builder as an executive assistant to the VP of Marketing & Sales. I was able to move up to become the marketing manager. After multiple promotions, I was asked to start a customer care department, which involved frequent complaints like incorrect paint colors or misplaced doors. I focused on solving issues proactively and created every process from scratch. It involved collaborating with all of the company departments. This led to becoming the Director of Customer Care and eventually a vice president. Later, I joined a mortgage company to create a customer experience and training department. I enjoyed developing programs and addressing recurring issues.

I wrote down "empathetic recruiter." Tell me why you call yourself that.

When I was laid off from my last job, the process was awful. I came from a customer experience leadership role, where my focus was on elevating experiences. Applying and interviewing for jobs made me realize how terrible the process can be. That mindset shaped my approach as a recruiter. When I was job searching, I made a list of things I wanted to do differently as a recruiter. I prioritized proactive communication and empathy, ensuring candidates feel seen and respected, even if they are not the right fit. I believe a recruiter's job is to provide clarity and support throughout the process. Now, I also use knockout questions strategically to make the process smoother. For example, if a job requires three years of outside business sales experience, I might adjust the requirement slightly to explore other relevant experiences. This approach helps me evaluate candidates holistically while still meeting essential job requirements.

Do you have anything else you want to share with the audience?

Yes, I want to tell them that they are capable of handling any corporate job. Do not let anyone convince you otherwise. If they think you are not qualified, do not let that stop you. Teachers bring fresh perspectives and unique value to any company, often seeing solutions others might overlook. Teachers have to figure things out all the time. How many times do you Google something as a teacher to solve a problem? I still do that today. If you can figure out teaching, you can figure out any job. Second, do not be afraid to ask for help. Anyone new to a job would also ask for help. Do not feel like you need help just because you are "just a teacher." You need help because you are new to the job and company. Third, get coaching or find a mentor. As a woman in business, this is especially important. I enjoy mentoring those who report to me and those I help through my coaching business. Women leaders are happy to help, but you need to take the initiative. Do not just ask; set up regular meetings with your mentor. Often, experienced people do not realize they have valuable knowledge to share. Everyone has something valuable to offer.

Resources: https://executiveempress.com/

Update:

Since this interview, Lisa has resigned from her full-time job and is now working in her coaching business full-time. She works with clients who want to elevate their performance and develop an executive presence. As someone who transitioned from teaching and worked her way up to Chief Experience Operations Officer, she loves helping others uncover things that took her years to learn so they can earn their promotions sooner. She still works with those who are job searching as well.

Director of User Experience - Claire
Taught for 6 Years - Grades: 4 - 7 - Subjects: Multiple

You have done what I call, "master the art of the parlay". It's when you are able to advance in your career in short amounts of time and continue to increase your pay. If you feel comfortable, could you share, not the exact amount, but the percentage increase, if there was one, from the first position you left teaching?

Minus forty-five percent.

Wait! What?! I wasn't expecting that! Why?

That's because my first job out of education was a part-time contract role. However, I was able to get up to almost full-time hours, but initially, I was only working maybe 15 hours a week, if I was lucky, and the pay was hourly. Even when I got up to near full time I was still at about maybe 55 or 60% of my original salary.

I'll have to change my definition, it can be with or without an increase in pay. Let's start at the beginning. Why did you leave teaching?

I had a baby in 2018 and another in 2020. I was given responsibilities that made me really concerned about my safety and the safety of my young children. When I asked for clarity on health and safety guidelines, the answers just weren't reassuring. After several difficult conversations with school leadership, I ultimately decided to leave. The uncertainty and potential health risks were too significant, especially considering the needs of my family. It was heartbreaking.

Did you have the endgame in mind? Because right now, you're a director. You're a director!

Not at the beginning. I did not have the endgame in mind.

So you got the contract position. How long were you in that contract position?

I was in the contract position for nine months from June 2020 to April 2021. In February, I was promoted to lead teacher trainer, a role my boss had previously held as a full-time employee. However, they had already decided to give the customer success manager position to someone else, so I trained the new CSM lead. While I was disappointed, it was clear that decision had been made long before I stepped into the role. Once I realized there wouldn't be a full-time position for me in that department, I began searching for other opportunities. In 2020, transitioning out of education was tough. Teachers leaving were often treated poorly. I received emails from recruiters accusing me of abandoning my students, which was unfair since I finished the school year. The only people I prioritized leaving for were my own children so they could grow up to be the kind of students teachers would appreciate. In one teaching interview, I was asked about my greatest strength, and I said it was that I didn't have to love every kid to teach them effectively. That is a significant issue in education now, the belief that teachers need to coddle every child. I can teach a student well even if I find them difficult, and they will still have many other teachers to connect with. This savior complex many teachers feel pressured to adopt is neither necessary nor practical. I ultimately left Illuminate after being offered a full-time customer success manager role at PowerSchool, which included a salary and benefits.

So you're at PowerSchool and you're a CSM. What skills did you need, and how did you get that position?

PowerSchool receives thousands of applications daily for roles like the one I applied for, so my chances seemed slim without an internal connection. What helped me were two factors: internal politics, as PowerSchool and Illuminate are rivals, and my ability to communicate as someone who understood their customers. At the time, they didn't have any former teachers in CSM roles, which I saw as a major oversight. Teaching gives you a unique ability to understand and address customer pain points. I explained during the interview process that my value wasn't about using tools like Salesforce but about interpreting customer needs and relaying them effectively to teams like support, product, and sales. I had been in their customer demographic and spoke the same language. During my final interview, one person rudely asked, "What makes you think you're qualified since you were just a teacher?" By then, I was tired of that question. I replied, "I could do your job tomorrow. You couldn't do mine for a day." He was removed from the call, and Michael, who would become my boss, asked me to elaborate. That confidence and directness worked in my favor.

I want to tap into that energy and perspective today. I want to hear what helped and what made the difference. You're now at PowerSchool as a CSM. Let's talk about that.

I had another role I almost forgot about that's on my LinkedIn. It was great because I used skills from teaching, like conflict resolution, identifying best practices, and problem-solving. Assertiveness was key, especially in EdTech, which is male-dominated. If my customers needed help, I made sure they got it. Engineers quickly addressed support tickets because they knew I would follow up. If I didn't hear back by the end of the day, I escalated the issue. Being a former teacher helped me see how delays impacted students and teachers, which pushed me to be effective. My reputation became, "If Claire needs you, Claire's going to get you." I built business cases to get what was needed and didn't let obstacles stop me. I loved that role. Both my managers, Jen and Desiree, supported me in different ways. Jen helped me take breaks when needed, often reminding me, "There's no such thing as an emergency in customer success." Desiree gave me the autonomy to do my job while looking out for my well-being. That balance and support allowed me to thrive, and building that reputation early on was the best thing I could have done for myself at that company.

Did you have any autonomy in education?

No, I didn't. My moral injury with teaching came from being blocked from doing what I knew was best for my students, often for petty reasons or parental interference. Parents naturally advocate for their children, even if their requests aren't educationally sound. My role was to advocate for the child as a professional, not as a parent, and that's hard to do if you're emotionally attached. Loving every student can cloud judgment and make it harder to advocate accurately. I didn't have autonomy or freedom in the classroom. Unhealthy work behaviors were encouraged. If I worked late, the janitor would praise me instead of telling me to leave, and principals would guilt teachers who clocked out on time, implying they didn't care about the kids. What I loved about the customer success manager role was how different it was. It wasn't perfect, and I missed working directly with teachers, but I found ways to support them outside of work. I had respectful conversations with administrators and colleagues who valued my input. Even if my suggestions weren't implemented, they were taken seriously. I also had the freedom to approach my work in the way I thought was best, a stark contrast to my experience in teaching.

What were some of the roles and responsibilities that you assumed outside of the classroom?

I was the district technology lead, where I helped develop technology standards for K through 6. I also served as the curriculum lead for fourth grade, creating a full science curriculum, supplemental math materials, and literacy resources for our student population, which included a high percentage of English language learners. I piloted various platforms like Illuminate, DNA, STAR and IXL, testing new features and providing feedback. Additionally, I was a lead teacher, mentor, and curriculum advisor at the district level, focusing on K through 3 schools. Balancing these responsibilities with classroom teaching was challenging, especially since many of these roles were unpaid.

I'm looking at your LinkedIn page, let's talk about Neuromaker?

I was headhunted for a CSM lead position at Neuromaker. At first, I laughed since I had only been a CSM for three months. I loved my job at PowerSchool and valued the incredible leadership there. Good managers were important to me after previous challenges, and leaving for better pay alone wouldn't have been enough.

So when that opportunity came to you, what made you finally decide, "I'm going to do this, and I have the skill set to lead?"

I had the skills for the job, but I knew nothing about the company. Coming from a place where I was familiar with my managers, colleagues, and customers, transitioning to the unknown felt daunting. Initially, I declined the CSM position, telling the recruiter, "I'm super flattered, but no, thank you." Two weeks later, she returned with a curriculum manager role at a STEM startup. She described it as a small, close-knit team and asked if I'd reconsider. I consulted my bosses at PowerSchool, and both encouraged me to explore it. My supervisor assured me I could return if it didn't work out, saying, "This could be your chance to work directly with teachers instead of admins." Her boss asked, "Will you regret not taking this job in a year?" My answer was, "Probably." During my three-hour interview with the company, I started by saying, "I'm 90% certain I'm not taking this job. What are your questions?" I critiqued the curriculum, pointing out gaps and suggesting improvements, then left saying, "Let me know if you need more input." Two weeks later, they asked me to meet with their sales and engineering teams. I agreed, but told them, "I'm 80% sure I'm not taking this job." That two-hour meeting focused on marketing strategies for the curriculum, and I remained transparent about my reservations. Ultimately, they offered me the role with a salary slightly higher than PowerSchool. It was a step forward after the significant pay cut I had taken transitioning from teaching in California, where my credentials didn't transfer to Ohio.

You accepted the new position. Walk me through how you got to the director position.

Transitioning teachers often don't realize they can negotiate salary and title. Initially, I was offered the role of Curriculum Associate, but I declined unless the pay increased and the title reflected my experience. They agreed, and I started as a Curriculum Manager without direct reports. My role involved adapting a dense Brain-Computer Interface curriculum for grades 5 through 12. In the first month, I created lesson plans, documentation, and marketing materials. By the second day, I was already on a sales call as the curriculum expert. My responsibilities expanded to include developing marketing content, creating curriculum progressions to integrate our materials into schools, and supporting customer inquiries. This work naturally evolved into areas like customer success and user experience. In early 2022, we needed a new website. The existing one was outdated, and the marketing and sales teams couldn't continue the project. Despite my workload, I volunteered, eager to learn web design for its relevance in EdTech. It became a massive undertaking. Although they had purchased a template, it was unsuitable. I ended up designing, wireframing, and customizing nearly the entire 250-page website from scratch, completing all but two pages myself.

Whoa!

The website project consumed me. I worked long hours to ensure it launched by the end of July for the back-to-school season. In a startup, everyone pulls their weight, and I thrive on being productive and completing meaningful projects. While working on the website, our marketing manager left, leaving a gap. I took over marketing in April, balancing both responsibilities to keep things moving forward.

What do you mean you took over marketing? Drill that down a little bit more because you don't have a marketing degree.

I don't. First, I created a brand book. It included dos and don'ts for speaking about the company, design guidelines, and language consistency.

How did you know to do that?

I researched brand books from other EdTech companies, found examples, and pieced one together. It was straightforward, choosing colors, language, and branding elements to create consistent content. Teachers notice when marketing materials lack cohesion, which can undermine credibility. My teaching background helped with the attention to detail and problem-solving needed for this work. In addition to the brand book, I created flyers and later managed social media. A recurring issue was the "give it to Claire" mindset, which increased my workload to an unsustainable level. When I was expected to maintain the same output despite added responsibilities, I began advocating for myself, making it clear I could not do everything. Advocacy, something I learned in teaching, became essential to managing my workload effectively.

Now, have we officially crossed over into your current position yet?

Not yet. In April 2020, I was promoted to Associate Director of Curriculum. While the title did not reflect everything I was doing, I gained additional responsibilities, managing areas like the website, marketing, curriculum, and recruitment, much more than the typical workload. By September 2022, I realized my title no longer aligned with my work, so I proposed a restructuring plan for a more accurate title. After layoffs reduced the team size, my supervisor approved a promotion to Director of Experience. I also advocated for a customer success team, crucial for retaining customers in our hardware-focused STEM startup. Now, I oversee customer success, support, eLearning, and a professional development platform with team-created courses.

There are a lot of responsibilities embedded with these positions...was that your end goal?

I didn't have an end goal at the start and couldn't have imagined this role three years ago. Initially, I just aimed for something better than teaching. Over time, I became strategic. After my promotion, I saw the opportunity to define a new role, Director of User Experience, and shaped it to fit my strengths. I identified tasks I didn't enjoy and shifted my focus to those I valued most. In smaller startups, that flexibility is possible, unlike in larger companies. Eventually, I thought about what I wanted the role to include, the team I wanted to build, and the kind of supervisor I preferred. Giving yourself time to figure out where you want to go is key, and that clarity helps you focus on what to prioritize and what to let go of.

Do you have any resources, like books, podcasts, YouTubers, or periodicals, that you find helpful?
Yes. There are two women I am now friends with that I started listening to when I was pivoting from customer success to startup life: Annelise and Erin Luber. These two women have been critical to me. I have bounced ideas off them and found their advice invaluable. I read interesting things on LinkedIn and in EdWeek, but what I find most helpful is talking to someone and discussing specific topics. Early on, I spent time recognizing who were good connections, mentors, and friends to have. Those two women, in particular, have been incredibly helpful.

How can we explain to non-teachers, parents, or society why teaching is so hard? People think teachers are just complaining, but they don't understand. I've interviewed dozens of people, and I still struggle to articulate it. Can you address it in a way that non-teachers would understand?

Imagine running a child's birthday party without any support. Why is it frustrating? Because it's the same as teaching. There's no discipline, you lack resources, and midway through, you realize you're out of something crucial, like forks, but the kids are eating cake. Then, while trying to settle everyone for an activity, one child decides it's piñata time. If hosting a chaotic, unsupported birthday party sounds stressful, welcome to teaching. You have limited resources, no backup, yet you're still expected to deliver an excellent experience. Now add the fact that parents often drop off kids at random times without walking them in. Imagine all of that but with a test at the end where your job depends on their performance. It's chaotic, overwhelming, and stressful, and the students know it too.

Do you have any advice that you would give to teachers who are in the classroom and want to leave?"

Sure. A couple of things come to mind. First, there is no dream job. Any job that's better than the one you have is a dream. Take it. It doesn't have to be perfect, and it probably won't be what you do long-term. I'm a great example of that. I've had seven different positions at four companies, five if you count a contract I did on the side. I'm still figuring out what I want to do. It's a work in progress. Don't wait for the perfect job. Find something better, take it, and know you can pivot. Once you get some experience, you'll be in a much better position. Even a little experience makes you more effective and valuable. Second, don't resign unless you're prepared to pay your rent and handle being unemployed. I've seen too many people resign without a backup plan. I've worked with teachers who were days away from being homeless because they decided not to return, ruined their relationship with the district, and now have no options. If you're single, sure, quit if you want. Good luck. But if you're a parent or the sole provider, it's a selfish decision I can't understand. Quitting without a plan shows a lack of strategic thinking. When teachers tell me, "I quit last year, and I haven't found anything," I think, "You're impulsive, do not follow through, and make poor choices." Many people, including me, see it that way. Teaching, while hard, is better than being homeless.

Resources: https://clairesmizer.com/resources/

Entrepreneur - CEO Online Business Owner (Full Time) - Lindsay

Taught for 8 years - Grade: HS - Subject: Math

Walk me through what took place right after you decided to leave the classroom.

I decided to leave the classroom at the end of my eighth year in May 2019. I was due with my baby in October, so that summer I got to work. I already had a Teachers Pay Teachers store, which I had started in 2017, but I had not taken it seriously. Once I found out I was pregnant in January, I revamped my store and updated my geometry resources to look more professional since we did not have a textbook. At the end of the school year, I decided to create a course called Secondary Math Squad. The course taught math teachers how to create classroom resources using PowerPoint and Excel. These were skills I had taught myself and often shared with coworkers. I realized I could record my lessons and help teachers beyond my school. I talked about the idea with my friend Kayse (kaysemorris.com), who encouraged me to move forward. I launched the course in June 2019, earning about $1,000, which felt amazing. Over the next year, I immersed myself in learning about course creation and marketing. I joined a mastermind with Kayse Morris, which helped me a lot. By the fall, I was not making enough to replace my teaching salary, but I had earned enough to stay home for the semester. Once my baby girl was born in October, I was determined not to leave her with anyone else.

During her newborn phase, I took every opportunity to learn by listening to podcasts, participating in masterminds, and studying entrepreneurship whenever I could. In summer 2020, during COVID, I relaunched my course with a new name, Math Resource Academy, which better reflected its purpose. That launch earned $47,000 in seven days, solidifying my decision to stay home for good. Since then, I have continued to grow my business and started a new one, helping people create their own courses on any topic they are passionate about, including baking, social media, and photography. Four years later, I am still working from home and have never gone back to the classroom.

Do you have any resources that you use to stay current in your field?

I read a lot, listen to podcasts, and use Audible for audiobooks. Some of my favorite books include anything by John Maxwell, who is a Christian leadership guru. His work is amazing for learning about servant leadership and leading a business. Jeff Walker's Book Launch is a great resource for launching courses or memberships, and Donald Miller's Building a StoryBrand helps you understand your customers and how sharing your story can resonate with the right audience. I also enjoy podcasts by female entrepreneurs like Amy Porterfield and Jenna Kutcher. I do not use social media much for learning. My main sources are books, podcasts, and Audible.

Is there anything that you have learned now, specifically in the preparation for your new career, that you would have done differently?

I would have invested in a mentor before leaving the classroom to help me understand how business works. I was scared to invest early on because I wasn't earning much, but I have learned that investing is essential for growth.

Why did you become a teacher?

I became a teacher because I've always loved helping people. Even when

I was in school, I was pretty good at explaining things, especially math. I originally wanted to be a music teacher but switched to math because I enjoyed it, and there was a shortage of math teachers when I was in college. I loved being a teacher. It was fun building connections with the kids, creating relationships, and seeing that light bulb moment when they finally understood a math problem.

Why did you leave teaching?

I decided to leave the classroom when I found out I was pregnant with my first baby. Teachers only got six weeks of maternity leave, and I was due in October. I would have had to come back before Christmas break, and I just couldn't do that. I was very anxious about leaving my baby in childcare. I wanted to find a way to earn money, because we needed two incomes, and still be present with my daughter.

What advice do you have for teachers who want to switch careers?

Do what feels right for you and your family. Teaching is important, and students need great teachers, but your mental health and family come first. For me, becoming a mom and staying home with my daughter was more important than anything else. It was a difficult decision, but it was the right one for us. Think about what truly matters to you. Whether it's starting your own business, finding a job with flexible hours, or better pay, make a choice that brings peace to your life. And remember, teaching will always be there if you decide to return. You deserve a career that works for you and your family.

Resources: www.LindsayBowden.com

Entrepreneur
Classroom Decor Services - Rachael
Taught for 13 years - Grade: EC

How did you come up with the idea for your business?

My business is called Classroom Bloom, and I decorate schools and classrooms. I also host professional development on how to create engaging environments throughout schools and within classrooms. It all started when I was teaching. Every year, I was known as the teacher with the all-decked-out classroom. My principal would bring in other principals and teachers to see how engaging my classroom was. Eventually, my coworkers offered to pay me to decorate their classrooms, and I thought, "Light bulb!"

I started in the summer of 2022, and it did well. I did maybe seven or eight classrooms, but then I had to slow down because I was still teaching. This year has been much different because I'm no longer teaching. I'm still decorating classrooms and even have one scheduled for next week. That's how it all came about.

So, you left the classroom?

Yes, I left at the end of June of 2023.

What aspect of starting your own business is difficult?

I would say finding your niche, because as educators, we have a lot of skills. We multitask in many areas and wear a lot of hats. Finding your niche and what you do best is crucial. Make sure you're working in your dominant field. You need a clear vision because a weak vision creates chaos. Make sure you're focusing on what you do best.

Did you consider any other career choices, or are you considering any other career choices?

Yes. I'm also getting my certification in UX design.

Let's talk a little bit about how you are going about learning UX design?

I'm almost done with my courses. With UX design, we basically enhance websites and apps to make them more appealing to the user. If it's hard to navigate, we go in and fix it so it's easier for users. I could actually use this within my own business as well and freelance with different districts too.

Are you going to a boot camp or did you get a certification?

I'm getting a certification with Google UX Design.

Do you miss teaching?

I do miss it at times. What I miss the most is my relationship with my students and being there for them. The students were the hardest part of leaving because I actually looped with some of them from kindergarten to fourth grade.

Tell me why you became a teacher?

I became a teacher because I started working with kids at a local daycare while I was in college, and I realized I liked it. Even though I was pursuing a degree in music, I kept working in daycares and preschools. Then, I relocated to Charlotte, North Carolina, and I was still at a preschool. I decided to further my education and get my master's in early childhood education.

Why did you leave teaching?

There were a lot of factors that contributed to my final decision, mostly the politics of it all. It wasn't because of the children. They were the reason I stayed as long as I did. It was really the politics that pushed me to leave, and it's just complicated. So, I'll leave it at that.

Can you explain a little about why you think so many teachers are leaving the classroom?

There's a lack of support. Teachers are often overworked for little pay. Teaching is one of the few fields where there's no reasonable yearly pay raise. Without teachers, you wouldn't have any other profession. So, I'd say that's the biggest reason.

Can you elaborate on the lack of support?

As I mentioned before, having more resources within the classroom and more people coming in to help. Also, providing better professional development instead of irrelevant training sessions.

Do you miss summer breaks?

I technically have summer's off now that I work for myself, so I choose when to work and when to take a break.

What advice would you give someone considering leaving teaching?

Don't be afraid. Step out on faith. It wasn't an overnight process for me, but when the time is right, you'll know.

Resources: Google - UX Design Professional Certification, www.Class roomBloom.org

Entrepreneur - Etsy Shop/YouTube Content Creator - Simply Shawna on YouTube
Taught for 18 years - Grade: 4

Did you consider any other careers or did you immediately decide on Etsy?

I could not live on my teacher income. I don't know how anyone does. I am in a good situation because I bought my grandmother's house from my dad and uncles at a good price, which is really cool, but I don't know how people just out of school now can afford to buy a house. I couldn't afford to live comfortably on my teaching salary. I struggled to cover groceries and gas, let alone going out, traveling, or doing anything enjoyable. So, I took on tutoring and did it regularly for years. Every day after school, I would be constantly hustling. I'd finish my lesson plans, think, "Okay, who am I tutoring today?" and pack my bag, grab my computer, and head out. By 3:30, I'd say goodbye to the kids and parents, then rush out the door. Fifteen minutes later, I had to be at the next house, and my afternoons were packed with back-to-back tutoring sessions. I'd get home around 7:00, too wound up to relax, and I'd go run three miles just to unwind. I was so tired of living like this. Over the summer, I took on extra projects to make money, but I felt exhausted from constantly hustling to pay bills.

During COVID, everything slowed down. With only one online tutoring student, I saved some money but lacked the energy to return to that constant hustle. My dog, Tucker, gets anxious when I leave, and the thought of going back to school and tutoring all afternoon, leaving him alone for twelve hours a day, led me to consider alternatives. I'd been in my career for so long that giving up teaching or tutoring seemed impossible. But during this time, I started redoing my house and learned how to use tools, cut wood, and even make a mirror for my bathroom. Similar mirrors sold for $600 on Etsy, but I made mine for about $50. I thought, "If I could sell just one of these a month on Etsy, I wouldn't need to tutor." I could work from home, keep Tucker with me, and live a better life. That's when I began researching Etsy. A video on Etsy and print-on-demand changed everything. I thought, "People are actually making a good income doing this." It opened up possibilities I hadn't considered. I realized people often follow a set path, but watching more videos shifted my mindset. I wasn't making money yet, but I saw the potential. I knew I'd need to make a lot of products before making substantial income, but I thought, "It's not just possible to replace tutoring. I think it's possible to be a millionaire!" That thought was a revelation for me. I believed it was possible to be a millionaire, even before I had broken a hundred dollars in profit.

Have you always had an entrepreneurial spirit, or did it come to you in this season?

It came to me in this season. You might say, "Oh, you were tutoring, so you were hustling." But that was just out of necessity, and it's still trading time for money, right? I wasn't thinking, "I'll start a tutoring business and hire tutors to work for me." That's how you build a business. I didn't have any thought about getting out of that time-for-money exchange. I didn't understand that concept until Etsy. Even my closest friends didn't get it at first. I was pretty quickly convinced as I listened to the Life Hackers couple talk about that concept, and my mind was like, "Holy cow," and it made me think of it in a whole new light. Even with my closest friends, I kept saying, "You gotta do this, you gotta do this." Now, they're jumping on board, but it took a little while.

It's hard to understand because, with Etsy and with a lot of businesses, when you first start you're getting nothing for your time, which seems a lot worse than trading time for money. You're getting absolutely nothing for months and months of hard work, and there's this unknown factor because it's something foreign to you. You think, "Maybe this isn't going to work, and maybe I'm wasting my time." That's the thought that's going to run through your mind the entire time. The YouTube channel I was watching was able to break my mind free from that and show me the possibilities. It's like breaking someone else's mindset and saying, "Yeah, you're going to be working for free, making nothing for a while, but don't you see what's possible after you break through this and get good at it?" You are opening the door to these huge, mind-blowing possibilities for later.

And it's kind of like college. We expect to go to college and come out in debt. So it's surprising that this should be hard to shift over to because, with college, you come out owing money, and you're not making any money for those four years, five years, or however long you're there. With Etsy, you're putting in all this free time, but after a year of that, you could be making really good money.

What do you do when you quit your job and now you have no health benefits?

Yeah, that was super scary, and it was one of the things I had to figure out that summer. I was like, "Oh no, how do I do this?" I was really fortunate because I didn't know where to find that information. But, as many teachers don't just teach, they are side hustling in some way to make enough money to survive. One of my good friends at school, a fellow fourth-grade teacher, had a side hustle in insurance. So I called her and she was able to help me enroll in a plan and I would end up paying about $512 a month.

Once I had that number, I was able to look at what I was making on Etsy at the time and what I projected for the next six months. It made sense. I thought, "Okay, I'm going to make enough to cover that cost and still come out ahead. Plus, I would be putting full-time hours into this business and growing it even faster, so next year, I'll be in an even better place, right?

Do you have any other people that you listen to for inspiration?

Yes. Cassiy Johnson and Life Hacker Couple are Etsy-related YouTubers that I like and another person that someone put me onto is Alex Hormozi. He's all about business in general. He's super successful and has a lot of great information on entrepreneurial topics. I also read a book that was one of the things that helped me make my decision. Last summer, when I was deciding whether or not to go back to school, I was hoping that this summer I could make the choice not to go back. I read a book in July, and I quit my job in August.

The Four-Hour Work Week was another one that really inspired me. One of the phrases in the book says that successful people don't run away from risk. They assess it. They look at the worst-case scenario and the best-case scenario. They focus on that worst-case scenario. They assess it by asking, "Okay, if the worst-case scenario happens, how long would it take me to get back to where I am right now?" When I thought about going full-time on Etsy and considered how long it would take me to get back to where I was if it didn't work out, the answer was clear. It wouldn't take me long. Maybe a month of searching for a job and getting one again. It was really inspiring in helping me take that leap into entrepreneurial endeavors.

Why did you become a teacher?

I became a teacher because, from the time I was a little kid, I played school and loved imagining being a teacher. I had my brother, friends, or animals in my little class. I took mental notes in class, watching my teachers and thinking about what I liked and didn't like, and how I would teach when I grew up. In high school, I started thinking about becoming an animal trainer or a teacher. The idea of training animals came after seeing The

Jungle Book, which inspired me. But ultimately, being involved with the youth group at church influenced my choice. Working at a daycare and enjoying time with kids reinforced my decision. I wanted to be someone who could inspire them to be the best versions of themselves.

Why did you leave teaching?

First let me say, I loved teaching and my school. I was at the same school the entire time, building deep friendships and connections with people. I felt accomplished and supported by my colleagues and administration, and I loved the parents and students. But the pay scale was stagnant while expectations kept increasing. They even reduced the pay scale, removing steps that others had. I saw colleagues retiring with much higher pay, knowing I'd likely never see more than $53,000 to $55,000. My retirement would be a fraction of theirs. I earned my National Board Certification to improve myself, expecting a pay increase, but even that was taken away. I saw very little benefit for the three years of work it took to earn.

The school environment was also declining due to extra demands. It became difficult not knowing who would show up in our classrooms, looking for something to criticize. The focus shifted to test scores, and students were treated more like numbers. I used to measure success by the relationships I built with students, inspiring them, making a difference in their lives, connecting with parents, and helping to shape human beings. That no longer seemed important. It was all about test results. The emphasis on scores ignored each student's situation. Some students were dealing with major life events, like a lost parent or a divorce at home, but these circumstances were never considered. That became very discouraging for me.

Are there any other things someone should consider as an entrepreneur?

Retirement. That was the other big piece. I thought, "How can I generate income to replace my retirement?" For me, I figured that if I live to nearly

100 and retire at 55, I'd get around a million dollars in total, about $25,000 a year. And I thought, "Is $25,000 a year worth it?" It felt like I was stuck in quicksand for such a small return. If I hadn't learned how possible it is to make money online, scale up, and potentially double my income each year after starting a business, I wouldn't have seen the options. Once you have a successful business, it opens your mind to new ideas. You start to understand things you didn't before, like how a business can eventually require less of your time, letting you open other ventures. Last summer, I thought, "All I need to do is replace a million dollars," which sounds crazy now. If you'd asked me before, I'd have said I had to stay because most teachers feel that way. They think they're stuck with their retirement plan and won't get much if they leave early. So, my thought was, if I could buy three houses, rent them out, and have them paid off in 15 years, I'd have replaced that million. That was my retirement plan back then. Now, I have other ideas, but planning for retirement, insurance, and saving for the future is essential.

You just tapped into something. When you have one idea that works. It begets other ideas that would not have come to you had you not done the first idea. That's something that I've learned. Just seeing other entrepreneurs and how it all works. What final advice do you have for teachers who want to leave and become entrepreneurs?

My advice to every teacher? Entrepreneurship is possible. The more I hear others, the more I see it's not about trading time for money. It's about creating something that keeps earning, like a t-shirt design. I wish I'd started this three years ago. If I hadn't heard the right words at the right time, my life would be different. I even talk on YouTube about inviting close friends over every Thursday for Etsy, and my teacher friends join me once a month. I say, "Open your stats; this is what you need to do next." Teachers put so much energy into their students, learning new skills, technology, and curriculum. Their dedication is inspiring, but sometimes, we feel unfulfilled, whether it's from pay, life quality, or a tough school setting. I think if they put that energy into learning something like this, they'd see how doable it is. The scariest part is thinking, "I don't know how to do this." Well, you don't know it...yet. But once you do, it's amazing how learnable it all is. I didn't go to school for this, yet I'm on track to make $200,000 a year on Etsy. That's mind-blowing and growing. Many teachers feel stuck because of retirement and benefits, but something like this can be built on the side until you're ready. Just start learning. It's possible, repeatable, and amazing.

Resources:

Alex Hormozi on YouTube

Cassiy Johnson on YouTube

Life Hackers Couple on YouTube

4 Hour Work Week by Tim Ferriss

Entrepreneur Life & Student Career Coach Dr. Ai

Taught for 15 years - Grades: Higher Education

Tell me a little about yourself.

My name is Dr. Ai, and I am a first-generation immigrant from China. I came to the United States 20 years ago for my studies. Currently, I'm based in DC. I earned my master's degree from Syracuse University, but the intense snow was too much for me. That's when I decided, "I need to move somewhere else." So, I ended up at the University of Maryland to pursue my PhD, focusing on communications and later expanding into public relations, social media, and digital marketing.

Walk me through a little bit of some of the reasons why you left teaching.

Definitely. Part of it was about the students. I just got tired. The most common question I received was, "Dr. Ai, will this be on the exam?" Rarely did I see a spark in many students' eyes. It seemed they were learning solely to earn an A, with very few genuinely interested in intellectual discussion. Initially, I thought it was the student's fault, but after talking with teachers from various schools, including Ivy League and state research universities, I realized it wasn't just my experience. I was advised to get used to it, but that approach wasn't enjoyable for me. I disliked it when students, upon missing a class, asked if they missed anything important, or when they celebrated class cancellations due to me attending a conference. To me that is a reflection of the system, where students are conditioned to value grades over learning. During this time, I also became a mother, and when he was about eight years old, I asked him what he enjoyed most about school and he said recess! I laughed and told him we don't have to pay that much money for you to just enjoy recess. I also realized, while working on my publication, that nobody else outside of my field was really interested in the very small, unique angle that I was doing my research on.

Another concern was that academia also felt increasingly toxic, and I didn't enjoy that either. In order to be in line for a promotion, I felt that I had to be visible and serve on committees as I had seen others do. One committee, deciding on where to put trash cans, another for decision on parking. All of these trivial activities further distancing me from meaningful work. I continued to ask myself, What's the purpose of my existence? Growing up Chinese, the expectation is that you must get your terminal degree. Doctor, lawyer or failure. What I wanted to do with my life? Did I really want to get a PhD? If my community, my culture, and my parents didn't really influence me, what would I be doing? During my sabbatical I stumbled upon a podcast called Entrepreneurs on Fire with John Lee Dumas. I heard the passion, the excitement, the joy in those people. They said things like, I love Monday. I was like "liar!" I couldn't even conceptualize that. If it's Sunday, then I am dreading Monday. I was so serious and curious because I was on the other end of the spectrum.

For all of those reasons combined, I closed that chapter and really explored my life and what I wanted to do in life. I was reflective and knew that education was my calling even though, as a student, under so much pressure to perform, that I developed an eating disorder. I struggled with learning, but I enjoyed learning. "Your mess is your purpose" and my miss was trying to get good grades. My purpose is now to help students enjoy education as well. In the model that I have developed, I have taken out the parts such as politics, evaluating students through grading and standardized exams. As a life and career coach, I assist students and graduates in gaining confidence, clarity, and direction, teaching essential life skills (resilience and self-regulation, emotional intelligence, critical thinking, creative problem-solving) to navigate their paths to success.

What areas did you teach?

I have taught in higher education for almost 15 years. After my sabbatical, I experienced a brutal awakening. I really started asking myself, "What's the purpose of my life? Do I want to spend the rest of my life doing publications that nobody outside my field seems to be interested in?" It felt like a really stuck and broken model, overworked and underpaid.

What sparked your decision to make a change? What were the key factors that gave you the confidence to take the leap?

When I look at my life and my friends, they don't really enjoy their lives. They are miserable, yet they are comfortable. I really think you can be comfortable and miserable at the same time. Looking at life change, it's always hard, right? Change will always bring some level of pain. But in my case, several years ago, the pain of staying in that uncomfortable position was much greater than the pain of quitting my job. Dealing with uncertainty, where I was, is ten times greater than the uncertainty and risk of quitting my job. It was so painful, I couldn't stand it anymore. And I knew, in my gut feeling, that I was meant to do something bigger. I didn't know what it was, but I knew there was something bigger I needed to figure out. I also knew I didn't want the second part of my life to be a repeat of the first part. And those were the reasons that inspired me to make that decision. So, I quit my job in the summer of 2019. My very first business launch was a disaster, a failure. I lost a lot of money. I thought, "Oh wow, you know what? I taught marketing, public relations theories for so many years. I knew how to start a business. Piece of cake." Wrong. Theory and practice are totally different. It wasn't working. I organized an event, and from the outside, it looked great. But from the inside, I made so many mistakes.

But that mistake gave me the clarity that I needed to invest in coaching.

So that was the summer of 2019 and in 2020, I decided to invest in coaching. I thought, "If other people have figured this out, then I must learn from them and not repeat the same mistake." In 2020, I started getting more clients, making more money. And every year, it's been getting better and better. I continue to invest in myself, and the more I do, the more my bank account reflects that investment. I've truly learned that our life is a reflection of us. The more we grow, the more everything else in our lives grows.

Going back to education, I think what's missing is that students are not spending enough time learning about who they are, their identity, their core values, and truly investing in their own personal growth. They spend hours learning physics, chemistry, history, which is fine, but they spend no time learning about who they are. A big part of what I do with students in my program is start from within, and that serves as the foundation to build their roadmap for success. I continue to invest, and every year it gets better. I recently did a talk where I shared my story, highlighting everything that happened in the last three years. I was amazed at how much I accomplished compared to the three decades before that. It was life designed true to my authenticity. Before quitting my job, I had to pretend to be someone I wasn't, which was so inauthentic and part of the pain. I thought, "Enough of that." Why did I have to serve on this committee? I had to do things that made me look good but felt awful. I'm so happy to have stopped that. Nowadays, it takes no energy for me to be me, but I couldn't say that about my old life. It took a lot of energy to be someone I wasn't, a social construction of an amazing scholar.

Who is your target audience?

I attract two groups of students. One is the super smart, straight A students but outside the classroom, they have no life skills, and they are feeling they have no confidence, because their confidence is tied to their grade. Another demographic I track is students who don't fit in with the rules and they are not enjoying school. Some of them are from private schools, homeschoolers and even international students. But it's so fascinating; it doesn't matter where they are, the challenges are exactly the same.

Did you obtain your accreditation as a coach from any institution?

One thing about coaching is that it is not regulated; it is not licensed, like being a psychologist. I participated in different coaching programs and launched a course, which turned out to be my very first failure. I found myself questioning again, "What do I really want to do?" I actually did lots of small products to test my market. I tested lots of different ideas before I finally realized, "Oh, my God. It is actually coaching." I really want to encourage people that you can spend hours sitting in a room, making a perfect business plan. What I've learned is that in order to gain that clarity, you must take action. Planning won't give you clarity; action gives you clarity, including wrong actions. All the wrong actions including the fact that 0% purchased my course. I pivoted and said, "Okay, eliminate that". Eventually, the path is given to me. I didn't wait until I had that perfect condition and all of the correct advice. It was through different versions of design that I landed on a powerful, impactful, relevant curriculum. Yesterday, a mom gave me an amazing testimonial. Her son has only been working with me for a few months. "Thank you so much. You gave me my son back. My only regret is I wish I invested in your program sooner." I'm so glad that I stuck with it and kept experimenting and making the changes. It is now my own intellectual property, and I have my own business that is meaningful to me and helpful to my students.

What is one thing that you would change regarding our current education model?

We must pay teachers more money. This is, like, no joke. Now I'm in the coaching space. I have so many friends who are millionaires, self-made billionaires, and they teach online classes and programs. Looking at how much those people get paid versus a teacher, I'm like, that is a joke. So, if we are talking about keeping more qualified teachers in the classroom, we must double at least how much they're being paid. From the student perspective, I really think we must allow diverse alternative ways to evaluate our students. Standardized exams are for the masses. Learning has to be personal. Every kid learns differently. I think that is really critical and we must figure out ways to evaluate our students. Albert Einstein said a very famous quote that "...everyone is a genius. But if you force a fish to climb the tree. The fish will spend the rest of his life believing that he or she is stupid". I think that is our classroom situation. We have fish. We have elephants, we have monkeys, we have many students who feel so stupid, but they are actually very smart.

Your energy is so great, you've said so much! You are very inspiring...

When I think about my own journey, I am like, "Wow!". If I took all the business required classes. I wouldn't even launch a business because you just get so overwhelmed. In school, the courses may not be in a sequential order that I needed. First, I needed to figure out what I wanted to do. So, for me right now, I'm really learning one thing at a time. For instance, who's my audience? How do I present my offer? As the business has grown, I began to learn the next things that were needed. In the beginning, I'm growing myself to start this business, but now my business is growing me. As I learn one thing at a time, it is a healthier approach as opposed to saying, "I need to learn all those things" about how to start a business.

Resources:

Books by Dr. Benjamin Hardy and all books by Dr. Joe Dispenza.

Podcast: Entrepreneur On Fire - https://www.eofire.com/podcast/

Entrepreneur - Life After Teaching™ Facebook Community Page/Course - Zach
Taught for 7 years - Grades: 5 - 8 - Subject: Social Studies

Can you share the reasons behind your decision to step away from teaching?

Most teachers have plenty of reasons for leaving teaching, and I'm no different. For a long time, I thought teaching was the perfect career for me. I was young and idealistic back then, but two defining moments made me realize it was time to move on. The first moment was purely logical. I had a conversation with a teacher who had been in the profession for almost 30 years, about 25 years longer than me. He told me he was only earning $8,000 to $10,000 more than I was. That hit me hard. I looked at the salary schedule and thought, if I stay in this profession for another 25 years, this is what I have to look forward to. At the time, I was already struggling to make ends meet. I could not afford to take my family on trips or do much beyond the basics. To make it work, I was working nights and weekends at a fast-food restaurant. It felt like I was working extra just so I could afford to keep working as a teacher. When I thought about my future, I realized this was not sustainable.

The second moment was much more personal. My wife had a health scare. Her doctor initially told us she had cancer. Those words hit me like a ton of bricks. Thankfully, it was a misdiagnosis, and it turned out to be pre-cancerous cells that could be removed with surgery. But during those two months of uncertainty, I started to question everything. If she had actually been sick, would I have been able to spend the time with her that I needed to? The answer was no. Teaching consumed so much of my life, over 60 hours a week, including nights and weekends grading, planning, and preparing. I had no time to focus on my wife or my own well-being. That realization stuck with me. If I was not prioritizing what mattered most, what was the point? When our daughter was born, it became even clearer. I wanted to be present for her and for my wife, but teaching made that impossible. It was time to find a career that gave me the freedom to prioritize my family and build the life I truly wanted.

Why do you think there is a growing awareness among teachers about the challenges of the profession, and do you think something like COVID or another shift has changed how teachers see the job, even though issues like low pay and long hours have been around for decades?

My family has a deep history in teaching. My mom was a teacher, my dad is a principal and a college professor, and my aunts and uncles are teachers and principals. My wife's dad was a teacher for over 30 years before he retired. It kind of runs in our family. For a long time, teaching was romanticized. People would say things like, "If you become a teacher, you're a hero. We appreciate you because we know we don't want to do that job." Then there are those sayings like, "A teacher is a candle, burning themselves out to light the way for others." I think those sayings are awful, but they reflect how people viewed teaching. It was seen as noble, even if it came with low pay because you were making a difference in kids' lives.

What they don't tell you about teaching until you are in it is just how many problems there are. Teachers are expected to work hours well beyond what they are paid for. No one warns you that you might end up crying after lessons because students threatened you or completely disregarded you. They don't prepare you for the possibility of encountering toxic administrators. There are good administrators out there, but there are also people who should never be in positions of authority over teachers. The stress and toll on mental and physical health are also left out of the conversation. My father-in-law had a stroke that ended his teaching career. His poor health and constant stress as a teacher were major contributing factors. Teachers care deeply about their students and want them to succeed, but the pressure from administration, standards, and everything else makes it impossible to focus on that without sacrificing your own well-being. The problems with teaching have become more visible, which is why fewer people are choosing this career. Education programs are shutting down because they aren't attracting as many students as before. Teaching is no longer something you can do for low pay and still enjoy. According to a recent NEA study, over 50 percent of teachers are considering leaving the profession. That is a staggering number and speaks volumes about where teaching is today.

What do you think teaching is going to look like in the future, especially with so many people leaving the profession and not being replaced?

That's a great question, and I wish I had great answers for you. I know there is a teacher shortage in most states. In my state of Florida, the shortage is significant, and there are a lot of creative solutions being proposed to address it. However, the education system in the United States is very outdated. While some states are trying to increase teacher pay or offer incentives to stay, the money is not the main reason teachers are leaving. The system needs a fundamental shift in how teachers are supported and what is required of them. I think AI and emerging technologies might help alleviate some of the burdens teachers face, such as spending an extra 14 to 30 hours a week at home on grading and lesson planning. These tools could create possibilities for streamlining tasks, but that alone will not be enough.

We need to reduce the hours required of teachers and offer practical strategies for working within contract hours. Most teachers are expected to teach in the classroom and then continue working at home. That needs to change. The system also has to rethink practices like assigning excessive homework that teachers must grade. Teachers need to work normal hours, and until that happens, it will remain an unattractive job. Beyond that, the structure of education itself is outdated. The current model of keeping kids in a classroom for eight hours a day does not work for today's students, especially in the TikTok generation where attention spans are so short. This is contributing to student misbehavior, which has become harder to manage, even for experienced teachers. If seasoned professionals with 25 or 30 years of experience are saying they cannot do it anymore, how can we expect newer teachers with only a year or two of experience to handle it? The education system has to be updated. It is not just about making teaching an attractive job again but also about creating a system that works for both teachers and students.

Let's talk about how you transitioned out of the classroom.

My wife and I are entrepreneurs, though she is a much better entrepreneur than I am. Our journeys are interconnected because we were both teachers, and she left the classroom before I did. I never imagined myself as an entrepreneur when I started teaching, but I was always starting side projects. In 2015 or 2016, I started my first blog focused on helping non-teaching majors transition into teaching. It was short-lived, as were the other blogs I started, but I gained valuable skills from those experiences. My wife always encouraged me to keep trying. Eventually, I started a teacher store, and my wife and I even launched a custom sign-making business while still teaching. We tried many ventures without much direction, but we knew we didn't want to stay in teaching or transition into a traditional nine-to-five. We wanted careers that allowed us to travel and control our schedules, something teaching and corporate jobs couldn't offer.

Networking with entrepreneurs was a turning point for us. Surrounding ourselves with people who were doing what we wanted to do helped us gain direction and clarity. My wife left teaching first to pursue graphic design, and I followed shortly after. In 2019, we started Life After Teaching, the first project that really stuck. We wanted to help other teachers navigate the transition we had struggled with which was figuring out resumes, job searches, and the next steps. Life After Teaching provides the support and skills teachers need during this process. Now, my wife runs a marketing company specializing in email marketing for small business owners. I support her by managing the books, but my focus remains on Life After Teaching. I am passionate about helping teachers transition into new careers and navigate the process with confidence.

What's something unexpected you've learned or experienced as an entrepreneur that you think teachers considering this path should know?

We run an active Facebook group, which was one of 33 groups selected for the Facebook Community Accelerator Program from tens of thousands of applicants. The nine-month program, led by Facebook employees and coaches, focused on improving the group and monetizing it. A highlight was learning that the Facebook employees who accepted us were former teachers, showing what is possible after leaving the classroom. Entrepreneurship has been a challenging but rewarding journey. Failure has been a key part of growth, teaching us to adapt and improve. While entrepreneurship comes with risks, such as losing money in some months, it offers freedom, higher income, and fulfillment. Teachers have great potential as entrepreneurs if they embrace failure as part of the process. For those uncomfortable with the uncertainty, a nine-to-five might be a better fit, but for me, the rewards far outweigh the challenges.

A lot of teachers feel overwhelmed by the sheer number of options and advice available when they start exploring career transitions. What do you think is the best first step

for a teacher who is just beginning to consider leaving the profession?

That's a great question, and I think it ties into something important. Right now, a lot of people see the teaching market as a lucrative opportunity because so many teachers are looking to leave. There are roughly 3 million teachers in the U.S., and about half of them want to leave as soon as possible. That's a million and a half people. Naturally, you have all kinds of new programs and services popping up to cater to this audience. We've been in this space since 2019, and it's interesting to see how much has changed. Back when we started, there were very few people doing what we do. Daphne Gomez, who runs Teacher Career Coach, is one of the other well-known names in this space, but beyond that, it was a small field.

What sets us apart is our experience. Life After Teaching, the website, has been around since 2013. We acquired it in 2017 or 2018 from Sarah, the original founder, and we've been helping teachers transition ever since. Our Facebook group is another key differentiator. It's the largest U.S.-based Facebook group for teachers looking to leave the profession. If you're a teacher seeking support, our group is the place to be. It's highly active, with a community that understands exactly what you're going through. I've personally seen nearly every post in that group, so I know the challenges teachers face, from mindset hurdles to practical issues like building a resume or navigating LinkedIn. Another thing that sets us apart is our affordability. Career transition courses can cost hundreds or even thousands of dollars. Most teachers cannot afford that. We've structured our offerings to be accessible. For example, our all-in-one course costs just $37. It's designed to provide the same level of value as more expensive options but at a price point that every teacher can afford. Whether you're a single parent or someone in a low-paying district, we want you to have access to resources that will help you succeed.

I have a friend who used to teach in Florida. When she told me her salary after nearly 10 years in the classroom, I was shocked. She left teaching to become an instructional designer and nearly doubled her income. I was so happy for her, but it is unbelievable how low teacher salaries are in states like Florida, Mississippi, and West Virginia. Is there anything else?

One thing I want to emphasize is that teachers should not feel limited by the subject area they teach. A lot of teachers think if they taught math, they have to go into a math-related field, or if they taught science, their next job has to involve science. That is just not true. Companies do not care about your subject area. They care about the skills that make you a great teacher, such as adaptability, communication, and the ability to analyze and adjust. These transferable skills are incredibly valuable in many industries.

For example, I taught social studies, and now I run a business helping teachers transition to new careers. My wife taught science, and she now works in email marketing. Neither of us stayed tied to our teaching subjects, and we have found success in entirely different fields.

If I could convey one message to teachers, it is this: Do not feel trapped by your subject area. The skills you developed in teaching are versatile and can open doors to so many opportunities. You are more than your subject, and your potential is far greater than you might realize.

That is true. Thank you for clarifying. Is there anything else you want to add?

I think for teachers who are considering becoming entrepreneurs, it is important to address this. If someone reading your book is thinking, maybe I want to be an entrepreneur, they should be aware of what that journey entails. There are a lot of people selling courses that promise quick success in entrepreneurship. You will see claims like, "Pay me this much, and I will show you how to make even more." I want teachers to understand that being an entrepreneur is not that simple. That said, teachers have so many skills that make them great entrepreneurs. You are used to working hard, you adapt quickly, and you know how to create solutions on the fly. Those are invaluable traits in entrepreneurship. However, it is also a path that requires a lot of upskilling, learning, and facing challenges. It is a different kind of struggle, but teachers are no strangers to struggling through hard work. I would absolutely encourage any teacher to pursue entrepreneurship, but they need to go in with their eyes open. It is a decision that requires commitment, and it will be uncomfortable at times. The rewards are there, but they come from persistence and growth, not from shortcuts.

I say this all the time: everyone has a money maker, a skill, idea, or talent that could make them money. My son's preschool aide from over 15 years ago started painting as a hobby, displaying her work in local restaurants. Now she's an artist whose designs are featured on Birkenstock shoes! Watching her journey has been amazing. I want teachers thinking about their own journey and what they have to offer.

Absolutely, I love what you said about teachers having a money maker inside them. Teachers are so resourceful, and there are endless opportunities for them to turn their skills or passions into a business. Take painting, for example, or teaching classes, creating content, or even building a presence on platforms like YouTube or TikTok. There are people who make millions of dollars creating content, and teachers are already experts at creating engaging material. The key is learning how to translate those skills into something outside the classroom.

I once read about someone making six figures a year designing outfits for chickens. It goes to show that if you are good at something, whether it is art, bookkeeping, or anything else, you can find a way to make money from it. That said, it is important to upskill. You need to learn marketing, branding, and other entrepreneurial skills. You also have to be prepared for failure, because it will happen, but that is part of the journey. Do not be afraid to go for it, because, like you said, there is a money maker inside all of us. Teachers are uniquely equipped to succeed as entrepreneurs if they are willing to take the leap and learn along the way.

Resources: Life After Teaching: Educator Options Beyond the Classroom (Facebook)

lifeafterteaching.com

Entrepreneurs & Social Media Personalities
Eddie and Kara

Eddie: Taught for 17 years - Grades: HS - Subject: Art
Kara: Taught for 11 years HS - Subject: English/Broadcast Journalism

You've left the classroom, so what are you doing?

Kara: We do junk removal and property cleanup. It's a business where literally what it says it is - we pick up people's junk that they don't want, and we take it to the dump or recycle it. We clean up properties - that's the basics of our job. But we also do some content creation, which wasn't something we had planned on. When we saw how unique some of the situations that we were getting into were, we thought, "This could be lucrative online." And so, we've started showcasing what we do online

Why did you leave teaching?

Kara: Isn't it crazy how traumatic it is for so many teachers? It's just like you think that you're going to be doing this for your whole life until you retire, and then that's not what happened. We want to be respectful of the privacy of others involved. The bottom line for us was we no longer felt safe in our classroom. When student needs are not met, things can get out of hand, and everybody is in danger. This includes the student, the teacher, and other students.

Eddie: It was just a fragile situation, so it was extremely difficult for us to convey what was going on and respect everybody. It's a very long story, so when you ask, it might start getting it going.

Kara: We didn't have the support that we needed to deal with these situations at hand. It wasn't just a lack of support; it was complete ignoring of situations from the people that should be helping. And in our opinion, there is a level of corruption in small-town politics that enables negligence.

Eddie: It just went from people that we trusted to people that we no longer trusted very quickly.

Everybody has their own lack of support story. That's really sad. What does lack of support mean?

Kara: If you need to wash your car, but you don't have any water, towels, or vacuum. That's a metaphorical way. I don't know if something shifted at some point, but I will say my first five years were amazing. Then in my last six years, it's like a shift happened. Not only is there a deficit in students needing support, but teachers don't get compensated for a lot of the things that they do. With our school, we would have to cover classes, and we were just told that was what we were supposed to do. It was multiple times a month. That may seem reasonable to those outside of teaching, but if I am covering a class, then I am covering it during my planning period when I am supposed to be planning for my students.

Eddie: For a while, we were told there's no substitutes available. For a good chunk of time, we were all covering each other's classes during our planning periods. That's part of our job. But then, over time, it's already overwhelming with all of the demands.

Kara: When we approached administrators about problematic issues, they were fairly quick to discipline students, but when students needed help for diverse needs, it was like they didn't know what to do. Or if they did, they didn't want to do it because it was a hassle. The situation we were in caused major health problems for us. I was experiencing severe heart palpitations every day, sometimes panic attacks, and high blood pressure. I started wearing a wig because my hair was thinning. There were just so many things. I thought it was normal. I thought, this is what we're supposed to do. It's just not an easy life out there, and I've got a good job. I've got insurance. I should just deal with it for a long time. Until there was the straw that broke the camel's back, and I chose to protect my health and my life, because our superiors certainly weren't going to. When we resigned, the hardest part was facing people in our community, because nobody knew the full story. We're decent people, people respect us in the community, but you could tell people were still curious and not sure why we resigned mid-year and left those kids hanging. That was really hard because we couldn't talk about it. It was such a sensitive situation. I do want to make clear that no student or students were to blame for our resignation.

Eddie: We couldn't explain ourselves in any way, so we had to just generalize. Those generalizations can make people spread more rumors.

Kara: There were a lot of rumors. Honestly, I'd rather there be rumors about us than cause any rumors regarding any student. We feared for our lives. I know that sounds dramatic, but I would go to school scared that something was going to happen. Not necessarily for me to die, but for our lives to be ruined and possibly for us to be physically harmed. I would go to school feeling that way every single day, and it was terrifying.

How did you come up with this idea?

Eddie: How did it come about? While we were teaching, we were hoping to do something on the side. We saw a couple on YouTube, based in California, and we thought we could do what they're doing. We just thought we'd be doing it in the summer, not like we are now.

Kara: We've always enjoyed cleaning out houses and doing similar tasks. My family has moved several times, so we've done that a lot. Initially, we planned to do it on the side. However, when things happened at school, we realized we needed to take action immediately.

Eddie: Our side plan became our main plan.

Did you think of doing anything else?

Kara: No. We did not. I think part of that was because we didn't plan on leaving. Our resignation was very abrupt; we hadn't thought about getting into anything else full-time at all. When we resigned, we had to do something where we could start making the money we needed to make in a short amount of time. This just seemed like the easiest thing, and we love to be together all the time.

Eddie: It didn't require us to spend a lot of money to get the business started.

How has your teaching background hindered or helped you get clients?

Eddie: I think working at the school, you have to multitask a lot. There's a lot to do there.

Kara: But then how do we get clients?

Eddie: Because you're good at advertising. She's good on computers, so she was a journalism teacher. She makes videos and cuts them up superfast. I have no idea how to do it. That really helps because I don't have to handle any of that.

Kara: Since we were teachers, people trusted us a little more. That was really helpful. Even though a lot of people were curious and maybe a little judgmental, I think they also had a soft spot for us, so they wanted to help us with our small business. A hindrance would just be there were some things that we were hesitant to do out in the community just because of the nature of how we resigned.

Now that you're out and you're doing this, is there anything else that you envision either for this business or just in general? Do you dream and say, oh, this is what I'd like to do?

Kara: A nonprofit for sure, for people that need their properties cleaned up. Around here, we see a lot of properties that are just so bad. People don't have money to have them cleaned up. They're depressed, and they can't get things done, so it just sets them back even more. If we, in five to ten years, can start a nonprofit or do something to help those people, that's one of our big goals. We would like to have a more established presence on social media, bringing in a good stream of income, too, so that maybe as we get older, we don't have to work as hard. Also, we want to travel and do this cleanup service in every state. We've done three states so far. Recently, we traveled from Kentucky to clean out a huge warehouse in Lockport, New York!

Eddie: It's very rural here, and all the other companies that do what we do say you've got to be in a city with lots of people. We don't have that here, but we've been really blessed. There's still plenty here.

I saw your videos and Kara, you were in a dumpster without a hazmat, and I said to myself, how is she tolerating that!

Kara: Honestly, I'm the masked queen, so it's really funny that I didn't have one on. The smell wasn't as bad as you would have thought. It wasn't as bad as most of the stuff you get. I should have had it on to protect my eyes, at least my goggles. It wasn't that bad because it was really cold. There was a stench, but it wasn't too odorous like a "hot stink." It was just stenchy.

Starting a new business, then talk to me about some of the upsides and downsides of starting a new business.

Eddie: The upsides are having our own schedule. That is amazing, and it's very stress-free. The worst thing that can happen is we go somewhere, and we can't take a piano or something crazy for somebody. It's so different from teaching. I don't think we realized how much stress we were under when we were teaching until we stopped, and we're like, wow, this is amazing.

Kara: Yeah, it was beautiful.

Eddie: We thought it almost felt kind of selfish to stop teaching. But then once we got into this, we realized how much we could help people because a lot of the situations are sad. Like somebody passes away and the family takes over an estate. Taking stuff that's just a lot of memories so the family doesn't have to. It's been very fulfilling. We still get to see our students in the drive-throughs.

Kara: Struggle-wise, we've been pretty fortunate. The business we've started is really basic. There are a lot of variables, but we remove trash. It's not a super complicated concept. I would say our struggles were mostly before, as we were planning to start the business. Our struggles were knowing who we were going to be trying to reach. It's a completely different world than teaching. We know our audience as students. But starting this business, our audience was not going to be kids, it was going to be adults. That was a struggle, learning how to transfer what we knew about educating because we do educate people a little bit on stuff. But transferring that to adults was a little bit of a struggle. Seeing our insights on social media has helped with that because we're like, oh, these people like us. A lot of middle-aged women, 45 and up. It's like, okay, that's our group now. Everything has been very positive about starting our business. We needed it. The Lord knew we needed it. It was a fresh new thing for us to do. We got to work with each other in a different way. There were a lot of positives.

Eddie: We've gotten in a lot better shape.

Kara: I don't want to be super Pollyanna about it, because people need to consider things before, they do this. We didn't have the luxury, and it was really a blessing that we didn't have time to think about it more. We might have ruined it.

You brought up insurance. How do you all approach that, as much as you're able to share? Is health insurance expensive? Some might want to start a business... We looked into many insurance options. One advantage of starting a business is the expenses in that first year, so in year one, doing it our way, the Marketplace...

Kara: Starting a business is new territory. We're still navigating it. Some months will likely be more profitable than others. Spring and summer should be better than winter. Insurance will be a new adventure this year, as well.

Eddie: It was all so scary starting out. We had a steady paycheck, and then nothing. We went from knowing our income to worrying if no one called within three days, "What if no one hires us?"

All things work together for the good. What advice would you give to new teachers who want to enter education?

Kara: Well, we've talked to some of my former students about becoming teachers. I would still say that if you love it, then do it to your best ability if it's something that you're passionate about.

Eddie: I think even if you don't have good experiences as a young new teacher, it's still worth trying to do it for a year or two. If you can do it because you have good or bad experiences while you're teaching, you're going to learn a lot from it, and it's going to be good. I had no idea what it was like. Both my sisters were teachers, she's a teacher. I used to coach college baseball in Cleveland, Georgia before moving here.

(This is when we discovered that Eddie's former neighbor from his time in Cleveland, GA was someone I'd gone to church with years earlier in Dayton, OH. Small world!)

Kara: It's funny, because usually when I'm asked that question, it comes from a teacher's perspective. Classroom management is crucial, and building relationships with your students is so important. That would still be my advice because they're going to be teachers, so they need to know those things. However, as someone who resigned due to a toxic environment, my story is different. I don't want to discourage people from pursuing something they feel called to do. I was that person led to teach, and I loved it for years. My discouragement would be to take care of yourself. If it gets to the point where your health is being affected, step back and know that you can do something else. You're not stuck.

You mentioned there was a shift?

Kara: It wasn't Covid necessarily. Covid was unpleasant, but that wasn't the main issue. It was something else.

Eddie: If they're at peace with leaving and have made up their mind, I'd say just do it. I don't think you'll burn bridges. There will always be a way back into teaching, even if it's in a different district. As long as you've done what you were supposed to, an administration can't claim you're unqualified or inadequate. Just go for it - don't waste time. I always like to have a plan though. When this was all going down, I thought, "This is horrible. But will it get worse if we resign without insurance or income?" I have just gotten my master's degree. I felt like I had wasted it because we wouldn't be using it, but resigning was the best decision we ever made. It's awful to think we could still be there, dealing with those daily issues. I love the kids, but this has given us more opportunities to help others than even when we were teaching. We can determine our own paths now and reach people who need it.

Kara: That's a good point. If they're truly considering leaving, I'm not saying resign mid-year - that was a necessity for us that I wouldn't recommend unless your health demands it. If you're considering it, consider it seriously. Know there are other options; find your passion and pursue that. Make it a positive career move, not an escape from fear. We were lucky to have that chance. It would be harder if we had time to really think it over. For those who do have time, focus on it being a positive step rather than a negative one. Build it up in your mind as a good thing. The sadness and guilt can be overwhelming.

Resources:

Facebook: Junk Lovers Junk Removal & Hauling LLC

Website: https://junkloversky.com

Instagram and TikTok: junkloversky

Executive Director for Epilepsy Foundation, OH and IN - Dr. Crystal
Taught for 22 years - Grade: Preschool

Why did you become a teacher?

Honestly, at this point, I don't know. I think I just always liked kids and always wanted to be involved with them. And remember, teaching years ago, was the way to go. But then I also thought that I wanted to go into social work. So, I went back and forth. And I remember, my pastor (Pastor Samuel Winston, Jr.) said, "What's wrong with being a teacher with a social worker's heart?". So, I pursued and stuck with it and to be honest, I was good at it.

Why did you leave teaching?

It was a mixture of reasons. I was spoiled at working at a private school. Therefore, it was an eye-opener to go to a charter school. In my experience, the parents who paid for their children's education and a vested interest. They had a different set of questions vs the parents at the charter school (this is not a blanket statement). Quite frankly, at a private school, if you are not doing your part academically, you run the risk of either losing your scholarship or being asked to leave. That is just not the case with charter schools.

In my experience with charter schools, if a student's behavior was off the chart, there was little that was or could be done about it. Also, academically, these students were low and it was extremely difficult to bring them up to grade level when for many years, they were just passed along. Many of the students' struggles mirrored those of the students who had been diagnosed with learning disabilities. I was in more than one situation, where I called for assistance because of student behavior and that assistance did not come. I don't like to be in a potentially dangerous/physical situation with a child, nor did I want the other students to deal with that either. Because I had taught in such a supportive environment in the past, it was very difficult to remain in a school system that had so many constraints, lack of support, and really just chaos. So I decided that I didn't want to teach anymore.

What was your first position when you left the classroom?

One of my first positions was as a Program Manager, working with adults with disabilities. I was responsible for hiring and training aides to work with this population. But I had to be trained to work with them as well, in the event that someone did not show up. This was an office position, but I was occasionally in the field with the clients. I was responsible for the strategic planning and development of programs. For instance, ensuring that our vocational and social skill programs were available and equitable. I was also in charge of hiring, overseeing the budget and always looking for ways to improve the programs that we offered to our clients. Financially, I was responsible for overseeing the budget and seeking out funding opportunities, such as talking with local businesses to build partnerships for our support. Even though I didn't always work directly with our clients, I enjoyed being an advocate for their needs and had the opportunity to represent our organization in the community.

What was your next position?

I started at Marriage Works in Ohio as a Program Assistant, handling logistics and daily support. After three and a half years, I became the Program Manager and took charge of the entire relationship education program. I developed and managed the curriculum and class schedule, working closely with our instructors to ensure that each course met its learning objectives. I also recruited and onboarded new instructors, reviewing resumes, conducting interviews, and providing orientation to ensure they were a good fit. Managing the class registration process was another key task, which involved optimizing our website and marketing materials to make enrollment straightforward. I also coordinated facilities, supplies, and resources to ensure classes were organized and efficient. To maintain high-quality standards, I implemented a system to collect participant feedback and used it to refine the content and support our instructors. I tracked and reported on participation rates and graduation metrics for leadership and stakeholders to show our program's impact. I managed program partnerships, coordinated guest speakers, and explored ways to expand our offerings. I also handled the program budget, monitored expenses, and ensured all costs, like instructor fees and supplies, aligned with our financial goals. Ultimately, I focused on continually improving the program's quality and reach while maintaining its mission and objectives.

After we lost funding for that program, I obtained a position as a secretary for a non-profit program focused on fatherhood, but after a month, they asked me to be the Program Supervisor. That program ended and I found myself back in the classroom. I will say that this was the worst experience that I had as a teacher. There were times when I felt physically threatened, there were times when I felt that my safety was in jeopardy and there was nothing that could be done about it. Everyone knew the behaviors of certain students and we walked on eggshells. I began to feel a "certain type of way" about the students and I didn't like that…that was not who I was, but no one, not the parents, not the admin, and no one addressed these behaviors in a constructive way. The only benefit was at this time, I was continuing to finish working on finishing my doctorate.

What made you say, "I want to get my doctorate degree"?

Because I love education and I was like, I might as well do it. I might as well go to the end. I love education. I wanted to be more reflective of my community and so I got my master's in public health administration.

Now, let's talk about your current role.

Yes, in 2019 I joined The Epilepsy Foundation, in Ohio and Indiana as an Education Manager. In this role, I was responsible for conducting training regarding epilepsy for adults, students, school personnel, school nurses, and the community. So my job was to go out within the community and within the schools and do those training programs. It was very eye-opening, because looking back on it from a teacher's perspective, we didn't receive this type of training. Out of all the training that we did receive, we should have definitely been trained in this area because there are many students who are diagnosed with epilepsy and it benefits teachers to know what to do until the school nurse arrives. In some instances, the school nurse is not on the campus every day. Many teachers don't know that they may have someone diagnosed with epilepsy, but based on the statistics, there is a probability you have a student with epilepsy.

How did you get that role?

When COVID hit we went through a restructuring and in that restructuring, the role for Indiana was absorbed by my supervisor. Eventually, the decision was made to consolidate the Ohio and Indiana roles. When the position was posted, I interviewed for it and was promoted to Executive Director for both Ohio and Indianapolis.

Tell me some of your duties and responsibilities.

I am still involved with the education part, which I enjoy, but I am responsible for cultivating the relationship between both the Ohio and Indiana advisory boards. Whether it's partnerships through education or partnerships through sponsoring. I am still responsible for it. Make sure that we all attend the national training once a year for the Seizure Safe education training. However I have gone one step further, where they have asked me to be one of the main trainers for in-person events such as the Black Nurses Association conference that I will be attending in Atlanta to conduct training. Also the Society of Public Health Educators. I am also responsible for being on different types of committees such as our DEI committee and our Public Health Institute committee. I also ensure the progress of various advocacy initiatives. So, for instance, Indiana has passed Seizure Safe School legislation but Ohio has not. I have been to the state to give testimony about the importance of the legislation for the school systems in Ohio.

What's next for you?

I go back and forth about that, honestly. I used to want to open my own wellness center. I think I still do. But I also have a heart for diversity and health equity. In the meantime, I've been taking different training courses and attending webinars on health equity topics. So I really think it'll be more towards health equity.

What advice do you have for educators who want to leave the classroom?

Leave. Make a plan. If it's going back to school, just know that you might be tired. I was tired, but I went to school the whole time I was teaching. I just had to. Now I wasn't married. I didn't have children, and there are teachers just like me who have full lives with community service and family that we help and you say you are tired. Yes, you are, but it's possible. Find the program that works for you. If it's not going back to school, find a certification program. Start doing the research and make the plan. "Write the vision. Make a plain" - Habakkuk 2:2 (King James Bible)

Founder, Youth Soccer Academy - Bill
Taught for 18 years - Grade: HS - Subjects: Communication Tech., Media Studies & Yearbook - Location: England

What inspired you to want to do to start your soccer academy?

One specific thing actually happened outside the classroom, but it resonated for me inside the classroom.

I was coaching a rec soccer program and I had not realized the landscape had changed since the last time I was coaching. The issue with parents and mandates and politics, all that stuff that's always been there. But what I found, though, there's kind of a meanness that is prevalent. When my son, who was gifted at soccer and loved the game, came to me one day and said, "Dad, I don't want to play soccer anymore," it felt like a dagger. I just thought I had failed him. I couldn't get it back, so I started my own academy. I tried to do whatever I could to help make restitution.

With this academy, we had a lot of kids come in. The local association, the powers They said, "You won't get coaches." At the end of it, I had 24 coaches. I had about 400 kids signed up, and it was basically a nonprofit. My journey from teacher to academy founder has been about learning and my passion for helping kids reach their potential. It's not about fitting into the system; it's about creating systems that fit the needs of the children we serve.

It sounds like you have a unique perspective on education. What influenced that? Tell me more.

I got clues from my father, Charlie Howe, not from the education system. My father was born and raised in England and grew up during the Second World War. He did a stint in the army and was a professional boxer for two years. His diverse experiences shaped his perspective on learning and problem-solving. I recall, one day when I was sitting at the table, frustrated with my algebra homework. My father noticed and asked, "Are you having trouble?" I explained that I didn't understand the algebraic equations we were working on.

He then asked, "What are they asking you to do?" I said, "Solve the equation." He inquired if they had explained the process, to which I replied that we were simply told to memorize parts of the formula. He was outraged. "They're teaching you to memorize, not to think," he said. He then sat down with me, guiding me through breaking down the problem into simpler terms. We translated the algebraic question into plain language, used diagrams, and worked through the problem step-by-step. He didn't give me the answer; instead, he asked questions that led me to find the solution myself. By doing it this way, he showed me how to solve problems and use critical thinking skills as well. In the program, that is what I try to give to the players. Anyone can come and everyone can try and keep working on their skills. I remember one young girl, her parent's didn't think she would make it. The skill set just wasn't there. But I encourage her and her parents to allow her to stay and keep trying. She came out the following week, and she said, "Coach, I got to show you!" She juggled the ball five times, did it ten times and you could just see the light bulb. What was key for me was she discovered that she could do it if she put her mind to it. I didn't have to tell her. It proved to this girl that she could juggle the ball more times, and she found out that she could improve through her own efforts.

I didn't realize it at the time, but I created a space where the children can succeed on their own terms. I didn't like how the traditional school system treated students in terms of placement and assessments. At a very young age in England, they called it the eleven-plus exam. When you turned eleven, you did an exam. If you did well, you went to a grammar school. If you did not do well, you went to a technical school. There was a clear division. Similarly, in soccer, decisions are being made at very young ages. Who a child is at a young age isn't who they will be when they grow up, without acknowledging their potential for growth. Starting the academy was my own way of letting them know, they can be successful through their own efforts and abilities. Starting the academy felt like the right thing to do. I wanted to create a place where children could grow and learn without pressure. It's been challenging, but has been very worthwhile.

Freelance Community Educator - Ashlee
Taught for 9 years - Grade: PK - 2nd (Autism, Reading Intervention)

Tell me about your transition to your new role?

Actually, I initially went to community college and started their two-year physical therapy assistant program because I didn't want to go to school for four years. I wanted to get a job and get out in two years. I thought making $35,000 a year sounded fantastic! So, I took the first year of classes, but when it was time for clinical, 75 people applied that semester and they only accepted 20. I didn't get in. It was my dad who noticed that I enjoyed working with kids and suggested I become a teacher. We relocated, and after taking all of my extended, paid leave, I resigned. I had no idea what I would do and just wanted a "normal", no heavy responsibility job. I spent six months in room service at a 3-star hotel. I realized how out of place I felt: 32 years old with two degrees and a wealth of knowledge and experience in education, but never learned how to operate a cash register. Navigating the nuances of a non-professional, non-female-dominated workplace had its own transitioning challenges. I wasn't happy but my time at the hotel allowed me to reflect, and figuring it all out involved literally using index cards, notebooks, and self-help journals to write down my ideas and find some sense of what I still deeply loved - education and children.

What is your current position, and how does it align with your career aspirations?

I wanted to get on with the library. I first interviewed for a position with the Adult Collections department, which I was not that selected for, but six months later, there was an opening in the Children's department, they reached out to me, and I said, "Yes, absolutely!" As a homeschool family, we were at the library all the time. Since my brother had special needs, we had a bookmobile stop at our house once a week. Going to the library was a big part of our education. I truly enjoyed being there in an educational setting without the responsibility, helping patrons find the books they want. I've gotten a ton of ideas through their outreach programs and from working there. I really love working with the little ones. That's what my master's degree is in—Early Interventions. I also love STEAM subjects and enjoy writing. My professional opinion is that the best and earliest intervention comes from a well-educated and advocating parent. I've seen it in my own brother's educational journey. I love helping my community, and my new home in Arkansas is riddled with poverty and the effects of drug abuse and lack of literacy. 60% of our county cannot read functionally above a third-grade level. We have a large homeschool population from all walks of life. There were so many directions to go it was overwhelming.

In January 2024, I launched Mobile Teacher's Corner. I'm offering free small-group community education classes for all age groups, parents, colleagues, and young adults. I work with some low-income families to offer affordable intervention and tutoring, as well as offering a wide range of professional and educational services freelancing locally and on Upwork's platform. I'm creating my own developmentally appropriate PK/K curriculum and continue to maintain a page on Teachers Pay Teachers. My webpage evolves and includes free parent resources, a blog for my STEAM garden club, original hands-on teaching packets, even a podcast channel on YouTube. I even plan to branch out with senior (ages 60+) classes and do outreach in surrounding areas. My time at the library allowed me to plan ahead how to operate on the logistical side of things.

Since joining the library, have you encountered any professional development opportunities that have pushed you further towards your career goals?

This library, in particular, goes out of its way to connect with the community and provide a holistic approach to community services and education. They provide so much more than just books. When I saw what they were doing, I realized I could take part. I could do book readings, mobile tutoring, demonstrations, and consulting services for parents with special needs. The longer I worked here, the more I knew I wanted to do something for myself. now have settled on the title of independent community educator. Working in the children's section, interacting with the little ones, and hearing the parents talk about their needs—needs that schools aren't meeting—was been enlightening. My launch of my volunteer services could not have been possible without my experiences in the Garland County Library. I am in year 3 of 5 and my goal is to have a small transit and non-profit to truly go mobile. This year the library added a community garden, and even got to host Mychael Threets, he's that famous PBS librarian. I got the chance to meet hime and it was so motivational. He helped me harness some of that library joy for education. I have recently learned that I do indeed have undiagnosed autism, and this is rekindled an interest in one day pursuing a PhD in autism and education. (If I ever pay off those pesky student loans!)

Where are you now with this process?

I'm a two and a half into my five-year plan. I would still say I'm building a client base right now, focusing on my page and community awareness and who I am. I'm offering free services, which isn't a huge money maker right now, but it's fulfilling my Ikigai and allowing me to see all the free stuff I can do. The website is fully functional. I am offering free consultations to parents to answer their questions on how to best support their children with special needs. This year, I've been focusing on doing YouTube videos for parents and teachers, focusing on my books that I self-published, and I have an official book release for middle-grade fantasy in September.. I am truly learning what it means to work for myself, building good work habits, and being in the mindset of getting things done without being stressed. Lately, I've been going out in the community and networking. I went down to the Garland County Literacy Council and was informed that approximately 50% of adults can't read above a third-grade level. Although I don't want to work with adults right now, I'm going to be working with the families who need to work with the children, and being cognizant of that has helped me build further compassion I also have the exciting opportunity to teach non-credit classes at the community college, when I can dedicate the time. My next writing project will focus on my (predicted best-selling) memoir about my education journey, which I am always taking mental notes on. My biggest professional aspiration is having a Ted Talk.

You mentioned Ikigai. How did you come to discover Ikigai, and how has it influenced your career decisions?

It was then that I discovered Ikigai. It's a Japanese term that means "a reason for being." Ikigai represents what you love, what the world needs, what you're good at, and what you can be paid for. All of those elements combined form your Ikigai. So, I thought, I need to focus on what this is and what I could accomplish in my new, smaller, more relaxed mountain and lake community It's a moving goal post but it's resonating now more than ever, especially with the increasingly political and unsafe school environments that have become normal in education. I also remembered the wisdom I received from the strong black women who were truly my betters in my classrooms, and their passion for education, even through old age or a challenging season. I knew I could channel what I knew into something wonderful.

How long were you a teacher before you decided to leave the profession?

I had my own classroom for eight and a half years, but I'd been in the classroom for about ten years. I knew within my first six months that "this" was not going to be sustainable.

What led you to leave teaching after all those years?

I would say the biggest reason was that I was just worn out. But I knew within my first year of teaching that I was not going to last 25 years. I spent my first four years at a Title I school in one of the poorest areas of Shreveport, LA teaching pre-K. I had a wonderful paraprofessional, Ms. Lewis, who had been there for at least 30 years, teaching the grandchildren of the kids she taught before. She taught me quickly all I needed to know for teaching 4-year-olds, and also the unique challenges of being the only white person in the school and understanding the varied dynamics of the families I served. I really, truly loved being there, in my classroom. Unfortunately, it was an extremely negative, punitive climate towards the staff and students alike. I left there because I felt administration only cared about test scores, and I was completely overwhelmed having to navigate what I knew to be developmentally appropriate practice to Preschool and what I was being asked to teach and base my professional performance on. In retrospect, I also didn't receive the proper professional development or staff support needed to coordinate services for students with speech IEPs, which I even had no idea I was legally obligated to implement in my own classroom. I frequently had to buy my students food to supplement our daily snacks and even lunch, for the few students whose only nutrition was at school, or who forgot their 30 cents for lunch and only got 3 nuggets and a milk for lunch. The pressure was so overwhelming that I had an extreme panic attack and had to take three weeks off. My principal dinged me on my evaluation for being out because my students' end-of-year goals weren't up to the impossibly high and inappropriate standards that I was forced to set

What advice would you offer to other teachers considering a career change based on your own experiences?

I would say, even if you do want to leave teaching or education completely, you have to look and see what within your experience brought you joy and fulfillment. Maybe it was networking with your peers, helping families, connecting with the community, or the constant drive (grind is inherently negative my bad lol) of doing something purposeful. Every teacher I've worked with has their own strengths and personal passions. Sadly, there are only about three teachers left from my graduating class who are still teaching. Most are stay-at-home moms with their own children. One of them turned their passion for detail orientation into owning a craft business, another became a home real estate agent, and a dear inspiration to me has, herself, become a mid-life transition coach.. If you entered education, you likely have a passion for connecting with people and wanting to leave a lasting impact. One colleague I enjoyed went into art therapy. She wasn't an art teacher, but she enjoyed when students would draw pictures and explain their stories. Sometimes those pictures were a little rough, and they would talk about them. She ended up going into art therapy because that was her passion. So, focus on what brings you passion and hone in on that, then just look for it. You're not going to find it sitting on the couch. That's another thing that came about from working at. I wanted to be a writer, but I knew I couldn't make steady money being a writer and illustrator. But that's another thing that's going to be a big part of being an author. I do want to write a memoir about my experience. I already have a title for it, Just Another Dropout - My Experience as an American Educator" It will cover my college experience, my first four years, my second four years, why we didn't learn this stuff in the bachelor's program, and then post-COVID anecdotes I'm still collecting, including my finding of my Ikigai. Some of it will have to cover the negative realities, but the lessons I have had time to learn, helped me learn that I really love teaching.... Just my way., but it's definitely going to be a bestseller!

Resources:

Teach like Finland by Timothy D. Walker

Who Moved My Cheese by Spencer Johnson

Autism & Education, The Way I See It by Temple Grandin

https://www.instagram.com/martitarobbins (personal friend/colleague and my inspiration to do something on my own)

Freelance Law Lecturer - Gemma
Taught for 17 years - Grades: KS5
& Undergraduate - Subject: A-level law - Location: UK

Tell me about the education setup in England.

I did my law degree and then qualified as a solicitor. I spent some years in private practice specializing in property law. When I wanted to move into academia, I started providing continuing professional development for solicitors. From there, I transitioned into lecturing at a university, teaching law. As I saw my career progressing further into education, I began teaching 16- to 18-year-olds studying for their law A-level, which is the qualification they need to enter university. In my last positions, I was in leadership, serving as head of law, politics, and criminology. I also oversaw a qualification called the EPQ, or extended project qualification, which is similar to a mini-thesis students can complete at age 18. I held these roles before ultimately leaving the classroom.

You mentioned that students can go in different directions. In order to get into that program at 16 to 18 years old, do they need to take a test, or can they simply choose to enroll and be accepted?

No. At 16 in England, students take GCSEs (General Certificate of Secondary Education). Every student takes about nine GCSEs, including English, math, and science, along with a variety of other subjects. After that, they specialize by selecting three A-levels. One of the subjects I taught was law. Students take their three A-levels, receive their grades, and those grades serve as their passport to university.

The students you encounter are those who are aiming for more professional careers, correct?

Yes. They were pursuing professional careers, and because of the nature of our law A-level, we had specific requirements for students entering the program. They needed to have performed well in English since the subject required extensive reading, analyzing cases, and writing structured arguments. Strong English skills were essential to handle the subject's demands, which were quite rigorous.

That leads me to a key point, but I have a few questions before we get there. You mentioned that law A-level is heavy on reading and case studies. In the U.S., students complete high school and then pursue an undergraduate degree before attending law school. It seems like in England, students start focusing on legal studies much earlier. Is that correct?

Absolutely. I earned my law degree in England, but I also studied part of my degree in Canada at Osgoode Hall Law School in Toronto. In the U.S., students complete an undergraduate degree before going to law school to specialize in law. In England, however, students do their undergraduate degree entirely in law. By the time they graduate, they can immediately begin training to become solicitors. So yes, law content is introduced much earlier in England.

Very interesting. Now, let's get to the reason why you laugh at this side of education. Let me put it this way, many teachers leaving the profession say it is not just about the pay, and it is not entirely about student behavior, even though behavior is often a symptom of larger issues. It sounds like your students had a different experience. Let me ask this directly, I might be making assumptions here, what are the positives in that sector

of education? Do you have support? Are the students well-behaved? Do you receive support from your administration and parents? Talk to me a little bit about that.

I was well paid in education. The job provided good money, especially when taking on leadership roles, which came with additional pay. In schools, you do get a mix. I worked in an inner city Manchester school, and you get a variety of students. Some parents are engaged, and some are not, to be honest. You would think that by the time students have chosen their courses, they would be interested in doing them, but that is not always the case. I was always quite good at managing behavior, but I understand how that can be a problem for some. I think post-COVID, there have been more issues because students were out of school for so long, missing exams and structure. In some schools I have worked in, there has been massive underfunding. I have worked in schools where we did not have enough chairs for students, where we only had one textbook and I had to personally buy additional resources. Sometimes, you have nonspecialist teachers delivering subjects, which is tough for everyone. I do think most people go into education because they enjoy it, but there is an expectation that it will be stressful due to constant data collection and analysis. Everything is data-driven because of exams. However, your school day is not really your school day because there is so much more to do, parents' evenings, extra paperwork, and various other responsibilities. I reached a turning point when I realized I had been there for so many other people's children, helping them and supporting them at the start of every term, but I was not present enough for my own children.

I understand. That is a common theme I hear in all of my interviews, teachers dedicate so much time because they want to, but the way the system is structured does not provide the necessary support for them to teach effectively and still have a life outside of work. Is there anything else you would like to say in terms of comparing the systems? I would love to

highlight those differences. Also, are there any final thoughts on why you left?

I do not know what your class sizes are like, but we were seeing an increase in class sizes, which makes it difficult to get around to every student and provide individualized attention. While differentiated learning is important, you simply cannot always implement it effectively because there is not enough time to get to every student. I understand leadership positions come with responsibilities, but when you are constantly being observed, asked to fill in reports, complete forms, and analyze data, you start wondering, when do I actually get to teach and spend time with the students? It takes the joy out of it, really. It becomes very stressful, and unfortunately, we are losing some of the best teachers because of that. They are losing the love of teaching because it has become all-consuming.

Of course. When I taught high school, I taught 10th grade. My students were about 14, so they still had a few years left in school. My class sizes were usually around 28 to 32 students, but it was common to have between 30 and 35. When did you decide that you wanted to transition out? What year did you say, I want to go back into another field? Do you call it corporate, publishing, or something else?

Now, I am in a bit of a hybrid role between education and other fields. I do not work in the classroom anymore, but I write exam materials, mark exam materials, and work for exam boards. I write textbooks, and I also work in court. I could not leave education completely because I love it so much. I am still involved in it, just not in the classroom. I also do guest teaching. Recently, I have traveled to cinemas across the country to run full-day revision courses for students. I also provide CPD (Continuing Professional Development) training for schools and work as an inspector. I do many things, but I am not based in the classroom.

I think the realization came during Covid because we had three lockdowns. We were teaching online, and I was prioritizing my students while telling my own children to manage on their own. There was nobody there to help them. One day at work, I got a call that there had been a Covid outbreak at my daughter's school, and I was asked to take her out for testing. Public Health England had intervened, so I went to HR, showed them the notice, and they told me that testing centers were open until 6:00 PM, so I could work my full day and then take her afterward. I had done so much extra when others had been out sick, but there was no flexibility for me. That lack of give and take was frustrating. I worked at a Roman Catholic school that promoted religious values, but I felt those values were not reflected in how they treated staff. That was the moment I decided I was done.

Let's get into what it is that you do now. If you have had a progression, like leaving the classroom and holding a couple of positions before your current role, we can discuss that as well. But first, give me your title and break it down for me. I am not sure if you have kindergarten there. In the U.S., kindergarten is the first level at five years old. Can you explain your work in a similar way?

Well, because I could see the writing on the wall, I knew I wanted to leave. I started considering what I could do, but I did not want to leave education entirely. I began looking into working for exam boards and writing exam papers. I started working with an exam board on some of their most serious malpractice issues, such as when a student or teacher is accused of cheating on an exam. That can have serious consequences for both, as a teacher could lose their job. I applied for a position and got it. I think my legal and education background made me a good fit. I now sit on a panel reviewing these cases. I also work in court, sitting in magistrates' court in both adult and youth cases, sentencing individuals. Additionally, I work with the police and crime commissioner in Cheshire while continuing education work, writing textbooks and exam papers. Because I am well known for my work in exam boards and writing, I often receive requests for guest lectures, exam writing, and other related projects. It is fantastic because I am in control of my work as a freelancer. I choose what I take on rather than having decisions made for me by people who do not understand the field. I enjoy the variety, and while it can be pressured at times, I like working hard. I would not go back to classroom teaching because I now have the best of both worlds. With my legal background and courtroom work, along with my involvement in education, I get to do what I love without the challenges that come with being in the classroom.

When you say developing exam papers, what does that mean?

I write the exam papers. I am the lead examiner for England and Wales for criminal law papers. It is a privilege, and I feel very fortunate. Right now, it is exam season, so I am very busy. I enjoy it, and I think it is important for someone who has been in the classroom to be setting these exams. I know what we can expect an 18-year-old to write in two hours under exam conditions. I also know what a teacher can reasonably teach in that time. At 18, students will not get everything perfect, and we need to allow for that. It is important that someone writing these exams understands the reality of teaching and the stress students face. I really enjoy the work.

I love that you bring that perspective. Let's dig into the process a little more. Walk me through the timeline of writing an exam paper. Not necessarily the writing itself, but the process and meetings involved.

Exam papers are set two years in advance. First, we do an initial draft while reviewing previous years to ensure differentiation. We need to make sure we are assessing different parts of the specification and revisiting areas where students have struggled in the past without making the questions identical. In law, we also have to be mindful of safeguarding concerns. For example, if we include a question on theft or murder, we must consider how it is worded. The paper then goes through several revisions. Revisers go through the content, scrutinizers check for accuracy, and proxies test the paper. The proxy is a teacher who reviews the exam and determines if it is achievable within the time limit. Multiple meetings take place throughout this process. Exam chairs oversee everything, making final revisions. It takes a small village to create an exam paper. Once everything is finalized, the paper must be formatted correctly before being used. Students often do not realize how much effort goes into writing an exam. Every word in a paper is there for a reason because each phrase has been debated and refined to ensure fairness and clarity.

Earlier, you mentioned some of your duties, and I want to clarify something. In the U.S., we have private education companies that develop tests. Is the system similar in the UK? Are exam boards private or state-run?

Exam boards are private companies. They administer exams, but they are regulated by JCQ (Joint Council for Qualifications), which ensures that exams are administered fairly and consistently across England and Wales. JCQ monitors the process to maintain high standards. That is what I meant by going into corporate. I did not leave education, but I am now on the other side of it.

I also wanted to clarify something else. You mentioned dealing with cheating cases. I got the impression that students who cheat could end up in juvenile court. Is that correct?

I do sit in youth court, but that is separate. In education, if a student is caught cheating, their exam paper may be canceled, and they could receive a mark of zero. If a teacher is involved, such as in coursework grading, they can also face consequences. For example, some exams have coursework components where teachers grade student work and submit the marks to the exam board. If a teacher falsifies grades, they can be brought before a panel, and sanctions can be placed on them. These sanctions may prevent them from being involved in exam administration, which could affect their ability to teach certain subjects. Additionally, if someone leaks an exam paper on social media or shares it inappropriately, they may no longer be allowed to work with exams, impacting their career. I sit on a panel that reviews these cases and determines appropriate sanctions.

In the States, we get June and July off, along with holidays. Do you miss those breaks from your time in education?

Well, I think it was a bit of a fallacy saying that we had those breaks because we really did not. Some of that time was spent marking, and some of it was used to go in early to prep. Even though the term would not start until the second week in September, you would have already been in two or three weeks from mid-August. Now, when I take time off, I pick my time off. I have children, so I do want to take a lot of the summer off. That means right now, I am working pretty intensely, but I do not mind because I know I can take that time off and it is actually time off. Toward the end of my teaching career, there was increasing pressure to run extra sessions and revision classes, particularly in August and Easter. I remember one year, an email went around asking if we would volunteer to come in and run a revision session. It was framed as voluntary, and I think they offered some time back, but I said I could not do it. Then I got asked again, and again. By the fourth time, I had to say, if it is voluntary, I can say no, but the expectation was that you would come in. I think those holidays were being watered down, so I do not mind not having them now. When I take time off, it is proper time off. There are no emails asking me to do something else, and I appreciate that.

That is the same answer I hear everywhere. I have yet to meet anyone who says they miss summer breaks. Everyone says the same thing. All right, if you have any advice or final words about your journey or for someone who wants to transition, what would you say?

I think you see a lot of things on social media with people saying they want to leave, but if you are not completely disillusioned with teaching, you do not have to leave the education sector entirely. I have not. You can work in different areas within education. You can work for exam boards, write textbooks, be involved in exam production, or work with local governments in schools. You do not have to completely reinvent yourself. If you enjoy education, there are still ways to be involved. If you do want to leave, I understand how daunting that can be. I started by finding opportunities and getting on board with different types of work. You can take on smaller projects, like working for an exam board, while still teaching. Start building something up on the side and potentially go part-time to ease into a transition. It can be busy while you are doing that, but it gives you a chance to see what interests you. One thing often leads to another. It is easy to say, "Have the courage", but you also need financial stability. You need to see where your income will come from, so you can build yourself up before making a full transition.

Global Learning Partner - Elizabeth
Taught for 10 years - Grades: 6-8 - Subject: Science

Walk me through how you obtained your first position after leaving teaching.

I interviewed for a long time. There were no resources to help me translate my teaching experience into something valuable outside the classroom. I only knew what a teacher's resume looked like--no idea what one for a different role should include. They're very different, and at that time, there just weren't resources available.

I wasn't aware of coaching or resume writers. I knew about recruiters because my husband was in healthcare, and they were always reaching out to him, but I didn't know how to get noticed by them.

It took three to four years of applying to every type of role I could think of. I did LinkedIn Learning courses to try and upskill in different areas. Finally, a company took a chance on me right when I hit my breaking point. I was so desperate that I accepted the first offer without negotiating and said, "When do you need me to start? I'll be there."

And what was that position?

It was an instructional designer role, a contract position at that, but I knew taking a contract role would lead to more because I was not willing to fail. This was my chance, and I wasn't going to mess it up.

Tell me about that first position...how did you upskill so quickly?

The contract was for six months with the possibility of an extension or conversion to full-time. I wanted that extension or conversion because I was not willing to fail. I worked on training content for a gas and electric company, an industry I knew nothing about. I had never even thought about how power goes from a substation to your house, and here I was, creating training content for people who work in it.

Fortunately, there was a project team. It's not just you; there's a whole team working together. I built relationships with my team, which included quite a few other former teachers. That was exciting because I could talk to them about my experience and learn how to do this job. I was creating PowerPoint presentations and using some fundamentals of instructional design without even realizing it, pulling from my classroom days. I remember creating a Venn diagram, which turned out to be a hit at the company.

A lot of my learning came from speaking with subject matter experts to understand what needed to be taught. Outside of instructional design, it was about building relationships--something that comes naturally to teachers because we do it every day with our students, even the challenging ones.

Why did you leave?

I left because of the lack of support and resources, and the pay was unacceptable. In San Francisco, I was making $40,000 with a master's degree, while rent was over three grand--it just wasn't doable.

Student behavior became a big issue, and there was no support. On my final day, a "good student" brought mace to school and sprayed it in my classroom. It wasn't directed at anyone, just at the wall, but the spray spread. At first, I thought the kids were just clowning around, but then I realized something was seriously wrong.

I called the principal, and we had to evacuate the entire school. The administration's response was to have the student apologize to each classroom. That didn't sit right with me. I had already been interviewing for other jobs, and that same day, I received a job offer and immediately accepted it.

I felt unsupported in dealing with real issues. My training didn't prepare me for the trauma and crises my students were going through-- parents involved in crime, abusive situations, even a parent who'd been murdered. Some had parents in jail or dealt with other unimaginable horrors. Support also means tackling practical challenges. I had students who had to ride four buses, leaving at 6:00 a.m. just to get to school. When they acted out, instead of getting real help, they were sent back to my classroom with a candy bar. I had non-English-speaking students (Spanish and Korean), but when I asked for help, they sent someone who spoke Portuguese. I had to explain that Portuguese isn't the same as Spanish!

There was also a lack of basic resources--pencils, paper, and books that many students couldn't afford. I ended up buying supplies out of my own pocket. In the end, I finally stood up for myself and my mental health. I was depressed, I was anxious, and that had been going on for years. That last incident was the final straw. I said, no more. I'm taking care of Elizabeth, and I won't be back.

Considering how much more information is available now, what do you see as the difference between what you had to do and what people are doing now?

The difference is there's a ton of resources out there for teachers now. TPLD (Teaching a Path to Learning and Development), for example, feels like a one-stop shop for everything you need. It has mentorship, upskilling guidance, and resume workshops--or at least it used to. There's a giant network of people in the same boat, trying to figure things out. There's power in numbers, in collective knowledge, and in working together towards a common goal.

Back then, there were no options like that. No "Teacher X, Y, or Z" resources out there.

What has changed for you most in your new career?

What's changed most is my growth in the role and my ability to work fast. I've developed a strong understanding of building relationships, whether with teammates, stakeholders, or subject matter experts. I've also learned to set boundaries and push back with confidence. I like to say, "I can say no and still make a friend." There's a nice way to say no. You're going to have to say no at some point in your career, and it's important to do it while maintaining positive relationships.

My confidence has also grown. When I started interviewing, I was shaky and did a poor job because I wasn't used to those types of interviews.

Walk me through the end-to-end process of a specific project or workflow in your current role. Explain it so the reader will understand your position or career.

In my most recent role, I was responsible for all product training for the sales team. Each quarter, around 20 to 40 folks from the product team come together, pitching their products and debating which ones we should prioritize. Some products might bring in the most revenue, while others are more applicable to certain markets.

The stakeholders, including myself, prioritize the products based on business outcomes--what's it going to mean for our bottom line? What's it going to do for our customers? Is it urgent, or can it wait until next quarter?

Once we have our products prioritized, we figure out which ones need training. Everyone thinks their product needs training, but that's not always the case. If it's just awareness, that's marketing. But if they need people to do something specific, that's training. I can only create about three trainings per quarter, so we have to get creative. For the others, I might suggest a huddle, a one-sheet, a job aid, or work with marketing to put out a video.

Once we've identified the trainings, I go back to the stakeholders to clarify--what exactly do they need people to do after the training? These become our performance objectives. We focus on those instead of overwhelming people with too much information.

Next, I create an outline, breaking down the key topics. Stakeholders review this outline, and once we've made revisions, they sign off. Then, we polish the training, add assessments tied to our performance objectives, and roll it out. We collect assessment results to see if learners grasped the material. If they didn't meet certain objectives, we figure out how to improve--whether that means tweaking the training or providing additional resources.

Finally, we look at business outcomes. Did the training help sellers pitch the product effectively? Did customers adopt the product? How much revenue did it generate? While training isn't the sole factor driving revenue, it's correlated with successful product pitches. We assess whether training contributed to this success and make necessary adjustments. That's the whole process, end-to-end, for me.

Teachers don't typically have to deal with being laid off. Talk to me about reorgs and layoffs. What advice do you have for teachers who want to switch careers?

One of the things that I think is true for the teaching profession--and many professions--is that the only constant is change. Every year in teaching, something new is thrown on your plate while nothing else is taken away--new policies, new curriculum, new rules--always something changing.

That's true for my instructional design career as well. Everything at the company always changes. The products are changing. The templates are changing. The software we're using is changing. You're getting new teammates all the time.

So, career advice for anyone--go into any job knowing that the only constant is change. Be adaptable and flexible, open to change, and keep a growth mindset. Be open to things evolving, to hearing other perspectives, to doing things in new ways. If you can do that, you'll be successful and able to adapt to those changes.

Re-orgs are a big part of that change. A re-org means that your team is changing--the makeup of your team is changing. Maybe your team is moving into another team, or combining forces with another team. That happened frequently in my last role.

Having a stable manager helps. In my last role, I had the same manager for two and a half years. It's helpful to have a manager you have a great relationship with, someone who sees your magic. That advice came from Fidji Simo, who used to be the head of Facebook app, and it's served me well.

Your manager is the one who makes sure you have the resources you need, that your workload isn't too big, that you have time for life outside of work. They help you navigate challenging situations and go to bat for you when it comes time for a promotion. Your manager is your biggest advocate, so having a good one is crucial.

As far as layoffs go, my team was recently laid off, and it's been a wave of emotions. At first, I was almost euphoric in my optimism, which shocked me because I'd been having weekly therapy sessions for my anxiety leading up to the news. We knew the day was coming, kind of like teachers getting a pink slip--you hope you don't see the principal that day.

When I got the email that morning, I had to remind myself it wasn't personal. It wasn't about my performance; I was a high performer. But they no longer wanted to support that project or organization. The L&D and recruiting industries have been hit hard by layoffs across the tech industry, so the job market is challenging. There's so much great talent out there, and we're all competing for the same jobs.

I feel for teachers right now because they're competing with people like me, who have more experience in the corporate world. It's not impossible, but it requires tenacity. I used to say I had enough rejection letters to wallpaper a mansion. Even in this job market, I've got quite a few. I could probably do a powder room or something at this point.

My former manager's father, a VP of a major company, said, "If you're trying to progress your career to become a VP, and you haven't been laid off, you will at some point." It happens to everyone. It's outside your control. Don't attach your whole identity to a job. Your job is just a job.

What advice would you like to share with teachers who want to leave but are apprehensive?

Teaching is different because students might see you out in public and judge you based on what you're doing, who you're with and what you're buying, but you're a person outside of your profession. If you need to be at Walmart buying condoms, go do it. You've got a life too, outside of those kids. And if you need to go have a drink and you're at Applebee's, and there's a whole classroom there, have your drink. You deserve it. It's been a long week.

Since I left teaching, I've never led with the companies I work for. Because then that becomes part of your identity, and people associate you with that company, and that's not what I want.

I help create training programs and strategies that help learners get the information they need to be successful in their job or with a product. It's not my company. I don't claim it. Because they can make decisions I don't agree with. They can make decisions that directly impact me where I'm no longer a part of the company, and it can happen so quickly.

I was lucky to get a severance payout, like a leaving bonus, so that's something different from teaching.

That's right. And I love how you said that as teachers, we have that identity. And that was one of the freedoms that I have now. When I go to my son's school, if I don't agree with

something, I feel more comfortable in voicing it. There's just freedom in not being a teacher sometimes.

Resources: The Jr High Dropout Podcast

Instructional Designer and Training Workshop Facilitator - Nicole

Taught for 8 years - Grade: HS - Subject: English and Honors African American History

What did you do to prepare for this career?

Honestly, it was unexpected. One day, I was frustrated with teaching and discussing my woes with a fellow teacher friend. We prayed together asking God to help us remain grateful and in service to His Call and I kid you not, the next day, I received an email about a free master's program for teachers in instructional design! The scholarship I received was in honor of Dr. Deborah Kantor Nagler, who lost her life in April 2020 to COVID-19. It was for an online program at Full Sail University and it was intense. Each month, there was a new course and a new professor, essentially cramming 16 weeks of work into four. But, all of the professors had real-world experience. Before that, for about a year, I was watching YouTube videos and attending webinars about transitioning from teaching to instructional design. While I was in preparation, about four months into the program, I was offered my present position, even before I finished by way of a friend and networking connection who was already an instructional designer and encouraged me to apply for an open position he got wind of where he worked. I then researched how to put together a portfolio and learned how to translate my current teaching material into pieces with ID principles.

Walk me through the end-to-end process of a specific project or work and tell me as if I know nothing.

So, I'm in HR, it's a unique intersection because we handle training and organizational development within human resources. We provide learning and development for the entire university, which has about 31,000 employees. The process for a project usually starts with my supervisor, who manages all requests departments make for new training.

A recent project I worked on was a complete revamp for one of the older courses in our library. It was a training for leaders on emotional intelligence. This course was an ILT which means instructor-led training. So, rather than creating an e-learning or online course using authoring software like Articulate Storyline, the deliverables in this case was a PowerPoint and a handout. This course in particular is a vILT (virtual instructor-led training).

The process involved me attending a session of the course in its current state where I took notes on participant questions, where they got confused or stuck, and places where the content did not flow or the design was not conducive for grasping the material. I then met with the subject matter expert (SME) and we discussed the leadership model that the course is based on and the institutional updates that needed to be incorporated into the new design. I storyboarded the course by physically printing out the slides of the old course and re-arranged the slides into new topical chunks that would aid learner retention.

Next, I set up regular meetings with the SME who is also the instructor of the course to discuss the progress and get feedback. I also designed activities and scenarios that participants would solve together in breakout rooms to reinforce the content and offer time for self-reflection of their own emotional intelligence awareness as a leader. Once complete, my SME gave me their final edits and I designed an interactive handout with fillable text so participants can have a lasting resource to grow their skills. From there, I hand off the file to the instructor and they teach it!

How are you keeping track of your projects? What are you using? SmartSheets, Monday, or whatever? What is it that you use? Do you block time on your calendar? How does your boss know you're busy with a project?

That's a really good question. I just use the Outlook calendar. We use Microsoft Teams, specifically the Planner tool. It works like other project management tools, and we use it to track our work. At meetings, especially on Mondays during check-ins or stand-ups, we'll pull up Planner to see the status of projects, whether they are to be started, in progress, or completed. It helps keep everything transparent and accountable.

What tools and strategies do you use to collaborate with subject matter experts (SMEs) and manage the project flow when developing e-learning courses?

For managing projects and working with subject matter experts (SMEs), we primarily use Microsoft Teams. Teams has a feature called Planner, which is very similar to other project management tools like SmartSheets or Monday.com. In Planner, we organize projects into buckets: 'to start,' 'ongoing,' and 'completed.' This allows us to track the progress of each project and make sure that everyone is on the same page. During our weekly check-ins and stand-up meetings, we pull up Planner so everyone can see the current workload. It's a transparent way to redistribute tasks if necessary, and my boss adjusts priorities based on deadlines or any delays.

When I start working on a project with an SME, I usually schedule a standing meeting through Teams. What's great about Teams is that when you set up a meeting, it automatically creates a chat and a Files tab, keeping everything organized. Throughout the week, I send screenshots of the course and ask for any clarifications via chat, which helps speed up the process through asynchronous collaboration. By the time we have our weekly meetings, I already have feedback and updates in hand, so we can make changes together in real time. This approach is efficient and helps build credibility with the SMEs because they can see progress happening consistently, even when there are delays.

In terms of tools for e-learning development, we recently transitioned to Storyline. Before that, we used Captivate, but it didn't quite fit our needs anymore. , With Storyline, we now ask the SME what level of interaction and technical functionality they want for the course, which helps manage expectations and timelines upfront. Of course, as instructional designers, we ultimately analyze to know what methods are best for learning, but having earlier conversations about limitations and possibilities is important for level-setting.

As far as time management goes, I block off chunks of focus time in my Outlook calendar for specific projects so I can concentrate on them without interruptions. Overall, the combination of Teams, Planner, an up-to-date calendar, and an intuitive course authoring software, along with regular communication and feedback from the SME ensures that our projects stay on track and are delivered successfully.

As you're creating the content, for instance, in this project, is it just you and the SME, or are there other people involved to make this come together?

Sometimes, after my boss tells me about a new project, she sometimes decides to join the kickoff meeting, but other times, she'll let me handle it and work directly with the SME. Once I start the meeting, I have a little autonomy over how I work with the SME. My boss suggested in a previous project that I hold a standing meeting with the SME, and I kept that practice. It works really well, especially since I do it through Teams. The chat feature allows me to send updates, screenshots, or questions throughout the week, so when we meet for the standing meeting, everything is clear, and we can make decisions quickly. I find this process helps me keep things moving faster because I don't have to wait for the weekly meeting to update the SME on something.

Why did you become a teacher?

That's a great question. I actually always thought I'd be a teacher, but when I went to college, I was planning on being an advertising executive. That was the dream. I studied advertising, and then the recession hit. Advertising is a tough game, and it's pretty lucrative, but suddenly jobs were hard to find. My professors always said advertising was for young people because you age out quickly. I figured I'd do that first, make a great living, and maybe teach later, you know, as a second career. But with the economy the way it was, it became clear people needed teachers more than advertisers, so I started teaching much earlier than I'd expected.

I come from a family of educators. My grandfather was a teacher, my aunt and uncle, even cousins. So, looking back, I don't think I could've avoided teaching even if I tried. It was just meant to be, and the recession of 2008 to 2009 really pushed me into it sooner. It was a gift passed down and ultimately, I wanted to teach The Higher Lesson, be an example of Christ while uplifting and equipping students.

Why did you leave teaching?

I knew my time in teaching had to end when I started encountering things I can't really talk about. But I do think people need to know. I could talk about the workload, and that was definitely part of it. Working 12-hour days, grading on weekends, sometimes 60-70 hour weeks, not having much of a life. That's one piece of it. The lack of balance really wore me down. But ultimately, what pushed me out was the trauma of my students, none of which was their fault. When people hear that, they think, "Oh, you must have taught in a really rough school." But it wasn't. ; Students from various socioeconomic backgrounds walked through enormous trauma that we weren't trained to handle. I learned quickly that secondhand or vicarious trauma is a very real thing. There was no support to handle this reality, no structures in place or investment in teacher mental health.

It was so hard seeing what kids were going through. In my eight years of teaching, I watched the issues kids were facing get worse and worse. I nearly broke. I remember after I left teaching, I found out a girl I had taught in ninth grade was killed in a home invasion. At the time, I had been out of teaching for two years, but the trauma stayed with me. I cared about her life, but I was so angry — not at her, but at the situation. It felt as though the trauma was following me even after I left.

A year to the day after her death, I lost another student in a motorcycle accident. I started realizing that no matter how much I gave, I couldn't stop these tragedies from happening. This is not to say that there weren't triumphs. I have many stories of students who turned out successfully. I am grateful for the tremendous privilege of hearing students tell me that I changed their lives for but better. But, after about 1,000 students, I finally realized I had fulfilled my purpose in teaching. It wasn't that I had failed them, but that my time was done. Teachers are human beings too - not martyrs. They are allowed to exit, expand, and evolve.

What advice do you have for teachers?

There was a Haitian educator, Ashley Toussaint, who once told me, "Somewhere along the way, someone told us we were just teachers, and that's a myth." That really struck me. People often think all we do is sing songs and color with kids, but they don't see the science, the data, and the hard work behind it.

My advice is to stop thinking of yourself as "just a teacher." Start quantifying what you do. Track how many students improve, how much content you create, how many hours you spend on curriculum, the different learning modalities you specialize in, calculate learning gains and detail your strategic approaches. Chronicle your journey. If other teachers use your materials, count their students too. This isn't selfish; it is showing your impact.

For example, I once led a workshop for 140 teachers and realized that made me more than just a teacher—I was leading professional development. Look at what you do beyond the classroom and recognize your value. Focus on the numbers, because they matter. Those are real accomplishments, and they count.

Instructional Designer - Kevin
Taught for 10 years - Grades: MS/HS History, English, AVID

I know that you have talked a lot about teachers and mental health on your podcast and LinkedIn page, but tell me your initial thoughts.

When it comes down to it, I want them to understand two simple words: you matter. Because let's be honest, these days, teachers are an afterthought in education, and their mental health is not very well looked after. They're told to practice self-care rather than being given actual avenues or resources to address their mental health. It leaves us feeling like we're alone a lot of the time. Get the help that you need and understand that you're not alone. A lot of the time, we don't really talk to people. We teach students, we grade papers, we're stuck in our rooms, and we don't take time to address ourselves. Once you pop your head out of the classroom, you realize things can be different. There are people out there to support you, and it's waiting for you if you want to take advantage of it.

Do you feel like this was the case before COVID?

I think the way I looked at it is that COVID just exacerbated the problems that were already there. By all means, we always had mental health issues. We always had declining levels of respect and salary and all these other things that made teaching difficult. But after COVID, I think a lot of teachers woke up to just how bad things were, especially when they got to teach from home during distance learning. They realized there could be work-life balance and times where you don't feel stress coming home, allowing you to cook dinner, pursue hobbies, and take care of your mental health.

After COVID, administrators and policymakers forced teachers back into the classroom in an effort to return to some semblance of 'normal' and tried to do away with what little progress was made to improve our working conditions during the pandemic school closures. The issue was that teachers had awoken to just how abnormal and out-of-touch education is now in comparison to the corporate workforce while remote and started to leave the profession in droves when their basic needs and desires for change were not being met. A basic example would be that companies should understand when someone says, "Hey, I'm sick. I can't come in today," and allow that rather than gaslighting them into thinking it's their problem and they need to show up regardless. And we've all done it as teachers.

What do you see as a solution?

When it comes down to it, the first problem we have is that there are so many things wrong with education, many of which result from society rather than education itself. Over time, teaching has unfortunately come to be seen as professional babysitting, a fallback career rather than a meaningful and important job. I always say that teaching is a great career but a terrible job. Teachers create future citizens, nurture good people, and open students' minds to their interests. Yet teaching has become a profession where educators feel disrespected and unhappy, and no one understands just how bad it is. We have deprofessionalized education, turning it into a career viewed with skepticism rather than admiration, often seen as what people do when they can't do anything else. This perception is inaccurate and harmful. Many teachers have multiple master's degrees, certifications, and expertise in their fields, excelling at reaching children. Educating people about the professionalism and dedication of teachers is key. Once people recognize what teachers truly offer, they will stop deprofessionalizing them, which is necessary to address deeper problems in education.

Teaching has often been seen as a job for women, and historically, it has not been the primary income that supports the family. For those who are married, it can certainly help with the household income, but for individuals maintaining a household on one income, especially with children, it is extremely difficult.

When it comes to salary, I want people to understand one thing I always talk about. Salary is never the first reason why teachers leave, but it is a significant part of it. People don't realize that when you enter the teaching field with your degrees and certifications, you are often loaded with debt, and teaching simply doesn't pay enough to cover it. Even in my area, where we are paid more due to the higher cost of living in California, it still wasn't sufficient.

I left teaching well over two years ago and even though I'm making about the same as I made as a teacher, I actually see that money go further since I'm being paid a yearly salary rather than one that only covers a 10-month period. The pay is still on the lower end, but I make about the same, if not slightly more, with nothing but a certificate in my field and with far less stress. It's amazing to look back and reflect on all the money and time I spent obtaining degrees I'm no longer using and which never really advanced my career or salary in a meaningful way. However, the issue is not just about the pay itself but the underlying deprofessionalization of teachers. The mentality is, "Oh, because it's not a real profession, we can pay them less."

People need to understand how much education and training we go through to become teachers. We've earned higher pay not just because we want more money, but because we deserve it. Without fair compensation, teachers can't live in the communities they serve, which creates significant financial strain. As retention issues continue, schools are hiring people without the necessary degrees or certifications, as we've seen from teacher certification scandals across the country recently. I even made a video talking about that over on my YouTube channel actually. This ultimately reinforces the idea that teaching isn't a professional career, which only deepens the problem.

You have a podcast. What is one of your favorite topics to talk about?

I'll talk about the gaslighting one because that relates back to the mental health issue we started with. One of the many problems in education is that it's always made out to seem like these issues are our problem as teachers. For example, teachers are blamed with comments like, "Do you have any idea the situation you're putting us in by taking a day off? We need to find a sub." It makes it seem like it's our problem rather than acknowledging, "No, I'm sick. I need to stay home." Or even something as basic as, "I need to go to the bathroom." And then there are situations where students are throwing desks across the room or being violent and they just end up right back in our classroom because administrators give them no tangible repercussions. They just say that the student 'was in crisis' as an excuse to not really do their job and that we should help them because 'we're there for the kids.' Yes, we're there to teach the kids, but it shouldn't require the complete sacrifice of our mental health and autonomy in order to do so. All of these things encourage us to break contracts, stay longer hours, and take on jobs that aren't in our job description. When it comes down to it, education would not function without the unpaid labor of teachers.

Wow. Right there. That is so true. Let's talk about your position as an Instructional Designer. How did you learn to use the authoring tools?

There are many ways to become an instructional designer and learn the necessary tools. I completed a college extension course where I earned a certificate in instructional design. I also learned Storyline and Rise, part of the Articulate suite, through self-paced courses on Udemy. During the program, I created projects to practice what I learned. Over the last year, I've become very interested in video editing and have taken a shine to Camtasia where I create training videos for learners, particularly those with disabilities. That experience even helped me secure my most recent job with Hanger Inc.

When it comes to adult learning theories and Gagné's nine events, how did you learn the other pieces? You have the practical side, but how did you approach learning the actual process, like ADDIE?

I learned a lot of that in the certification program, where I picked up the lingo and jargon of the discipline. Afterward, I got into instructional design work, which is generally contract-based. I completed my first contract and began creating content, improving my skills along the way. Eventually, I got a full-time position with Cruise, where I created training using these tools for Customer Success Agents who worked with our riders and customers. Now, I work with Hanger in a full-time position creating training for clinicians and fabrication specialists who help our patients who've lost limbs and need prosthetic or orthotic care. I routinely follow that process to create coursework.

Now walk me through one of your projects. Do you have a kick-off meeting?

I have a learning and development manager who identifies needs, assigns training to the best instructional designer for that job, and then starts working. Usually there is a kickoff meeting with the SMEs involved on the course and then we keep them in the loop during the design and development phases. After beginning the course, I get questions answered from SMEs as needed and have weekly meetings with my manager to keep them updated on the progress or if I've run into any blockers. After the course is done, it gets reviewed, edits are made, and then it is posted to our LMS for learners. As time goes on, we review feedback and make changes as needed if the training isn't working. There's a similar process for when I create training videos, which I'm mainly the one responsible for doing in our group. I have a learning and development manager who identifies needs, assigns training to the best instructional designer for that job, and then starts working. Usually there is a kickoff meeting with the SMEs involved on the course and then we keep them in the loop during the design and development phases. After beginning the course, I get questions answered from SMEs as needed and have weekly meetings with my manager to keep them updated on the progress or if I've run into any blockers. After the course is done, it gets reviewed, edits are made, and then it is posted to our LMS for learners. As time goes on, we review feedback and make changes as needed if the training isn't working. There's a similar process for when I create training videos, which I'm mainly the one responsible for doing in our group.

Walk me through the review process.

I create the course in its entirety and then send it out for SME review as an Alpha. Occasionally, I might involve them during development if there is something I want to get their feedback on but generally that leads to them getting bogged down in the colors or pictures rather than the content I need them to review so it's best to wait until the end. After their Alpha reviews, I action any needed changes and comments the SMEs left, have them approve those alterations, and then we publish it to our LMS for learners. After it goes live for a few weeks, we evaluate user responses. If users report issues, such as unclear sections or struggles with specific questions, we revise the content and republish it.

Do you feel that you got everything that you needed through the program?

There were some things I didn't feel like I learned beforehand, and I had to pick them up on the job. But that is normal. When I was teaching, we walked in without any onboarding or information. I just had to dive into the deep end and figure it out. Here, although I had gaps in knowledge, the job helped me develop those skills and improve. As a result, I felt supported. When I started at Cruise and Hanger, I had no experience with autonomous vehicle operations or prosthetics. Once I learned the acronyms, the information, and the needs of the audience, I thrived and continued to grow. That support encouraged me to keep learning and building my knowledge. No program, even a great one, is perfect. There will always be things you need to learn on the job, but having support makes all the difference. That was something I did not have in teaching.

What else can you tell me about your position?

I really do enjoy my job. I have a good manager and a good company that I work for. I get paid what I am worth. I also have support when I am struggling. If I do not understand something, I can ask for help, whether it is a video call or a group meeting to work through the project. The answer is always yes, and we get things done. Unlike in teaching, where they use phrases like "we are a family," to gaslight you into putting in more time and effort than you should. I actually feel like I am part of something here. In teaching, I felt like a cog in the machine. Now, I feel like an important and valued part of the team. Not every job is like this. My first job outside of teaching was not the best. It was okay, and I did not love it, but I still felt better and more valued than I did as a teacher. I think every worker needs to feel like they have control over their own environment, and I feel like I do now.

What final advice do you want to share?

My advice is, if you are questioning whether you should continue teaching or leave education, the fact that you are asking likely means it is time to leave. I have had dozens of teachers come to me and say, "Should I come back next year and then look for something the following year?" I always respond by asking, "Can you see yourself in the classroom next year?" There is often a pause, and they say, "I don't know." I tell them that uncertainty is their answer: it is time to move on. Transitioning out of teaching is not easy or quick. The average transition takes six to twelve months, not including the time needed for upskilling. However, once you make the change, you will be happier, your mental health will improve, and you will feel more valued not just as a worker, but as a person.

Looking back, you will realize how much you tolerated and put up with that only served to hurt your mental health and work-life balance. If you are unsure whether you can keep teaching, it likely means you can't. Staying will only do a disservice to yourself and your students in the long run. Even though you've been educated into believing that your needs aren't important as a teacher and that you should give up everything for the kids, you need to rid yourself of that 'Savior-like' mentality. It's okay to be selfish sometimes and realizing you need to leave teaching is an inherently selfish, but needed decision. Your personal and professional growth is just as important and shouldn't be neglected for the sake of a system that doesn't care about your well-being.

Resources: https://www.youtube.com/@KevinTheID/, "Breaking the Fourth Wall of Public Education" found on: iHeartRadio, Apple Podcasts, Google Podcasts, and Spotify.

Instructional Mentor - Kofi
Taught for 17 years - Grades: K-8
Subjects: ELA, Social Studies and Science

You're still in education...but in what role?

Well, I taught for 17 years and have been in education for 27 years. I work for a teacher residency program through Georgia State University under the College of Education. This program supports teachers starting in their senior year, which is their student teaching year. We provide wraparound services into their second year of teaching. Essentially, we support these teachers after they graduate from college and enter their first year in the classroom. What's unique about our project is that we partner with districts. We only place our teachers in schools that are part of these partnerships. Within Atlanta Public Schools, the mentors, cooperating teachers, and university supervisors who work with these student teachers are all trained and developed by us. That's why we describe it as wraparound support because it's a comprehensive system. Our goal is to streamline everything. Our vision is to help create and facilitate teachers who are compassionate, critically conscious, and skilled. In my role within the project, I observe, debrief, and support my teachers. What makes our program stand out from a traditional school system is that we get the opportunity to truly walk alongside the teacher. I always tell my teachers: You're in the driver's seat, and I'm in the passenger's seat. You're driving your own development. You determine your goals and the direction you want to go. We have a framework curriculum for them, but they ultimately take the lead. It's not about mandating that they learn a specific pedagogy or teaching strategy. Sometimes, we might just focus on their well-being because you can't show up as an effective math teacher, or any kind of teacher if you're not taking care of yourself. That's what sets our program apart. The residents drive their own development to a large extent, and we facilitate their growth. My role is to guide them as a reflective partner. They tell me what they want to work on, we identify their next steps, and then we reflect together on how things went. We discuss any barriers they faced and brainstorm how to overcome them. It's a collaborative process.

Got it. If I am a teacher reading this, what can you tell me about what you do that give more insight on your position?

I think what's different now, as a coach, compared to when I started in education 26 years ago, is that there's much more opportunity for teachers to feel empowered. My approach focuses on empowerment. I don't come from a place of pointing out what someone doesn't know. Instead, I approach it from a strength-based perspective. I look at what they already know, what they bring to the table, and how they can contribute. I really try to get to know each teacher and their unique strengths. I focus on how they can maximize those strengths while addressing areas for growth. For me, the starting point isn't What do you need to do? But rather, How are you?

How did you find out about this position? Or, if someone else were interested in this type of position, what should they be looking for?

I'd say I didn't actively look for this position. What I've always done, though I didn't realize it at the time, is network in different ways. I found this position through a mentor of mine who was already working with the organization. It just so happened that I was looking for a part-time job, and they needed someone.

So, I'd say it was more about networking. I think teachers are often underestimated when it comes to the skills we bring to the table. We're one of the few professions where people view us as limited by what we do, rather than recognizing the broad range of skills we actually have. When I first left teaching, I didn't immediately realize the value of my skills. My first job outside the classroom was with Teach For America, and that experience really started me on a journey of understanding what I bring to the table. Now, I feel like I'm on that journey again as I think about what's next after this position. I ask myself: What skills do I possess? What can I offer? The first step for me has always been figuring out what I'm good at and how I can use it. I'm good at a lot of things, but I've realized I'm not passionate about all of them. That clarity is so important.

For example, I love strategy. I love helping people align with goals and ensuring everyone is on the same page. I really enjoy strategic planning and seeing how everything connects to a larger vision. But I've also learned what I don't enjoy. I don't like being involved in the middle of the process. I prefer to coach people through it. I want to step in at the back end, audit what's been done, and evaluate how things went. Another example of how networking has helped me is when I picked up a contract while looking into a program for my own kids. They were in an after-school program that was a little disorganized. I ended up talking to the owner about their training and onboarding process for facilitators. That conversation led to me helping them improve their systems, and it eventually turned into a contract. It all came from just being willing to help and share insights.

Has your new career impacted your work-life balance compared to teaching?

Okay. It has provided me with more balance, but I don't have the story of being a disgruntled teacher or experiencing burnout. That wasn't my story. I left teaching for a couple of reasons. First, my daughter was about to start kindergarten in the same charter system where I worked. I didn't think I could be the best teacher and the best mom at the same time.

The other reason was that I had simply been there too long in a sense. By the time I left, the person who was my assistant principal was someone I had hired. I had been her grade-level chair, her team lead, her assistant principal, and then we became peers again when I returned to teaching. It wasn't a bad situation, but I knew she wouldn't be able to grow in her position with me there, and I wasn't going to grow either. Yes, I also faced a major medical challenge the year before, but transitioning out of teaching has given me a lot more margin and stability in my life. It has allowed me to stay connected to the field of education, which I still love. At the same time, I'll admit it has also broken my heart.

Meaning it's broken your heart in regards to just leaving or just the way that it's going.

The way it is going, I think we missed a great opportunity with the pandemic to really make changes in education. We decided to go back like the pandemic never happened, doing the same things we did before, and it felt like we were punishing kids and teachers. As if it was their fault. It was like, "Let's just make these kids do more," or, "Let's just make these teachers do more." But how about we stop and ask, "What are we doing? Is it even working?" What really upset me was this constant focus on "learning loss." Everybody kept saying kids had "learning loss," but that's not what it was. Learning loss is when a student doesn't have the chance to keep up, like homeless kids or military kids who are moving around, but the rest of the class keeps learning. That's not what happened here. During the pandemic, students didn't have the opportunity to learn, period. The system just wasn't there for them in the same way, and it wasn't about kids or teachers doing something wrong. We should've looked at it as a chance to rethink how we teach and learn, but instead, we acted like it was their failure.

And then we tried to fix it by piling on more, instead of stopping to ask if what we were doing even made sense. That's what made me so upset. We haven't addressed where the real loss was, which was in social-emotional learning. I'm not referring to a specific program, but strategically thinking about how to support students and staff through their post-COVID syndrome. Instead, we turned to "programs to facilitate this process. In addition, we bought into the narratives from the media and curriculum companies about "learning loss". We didn't take the time to identify the things in education that needed to be left behind and what is needed for this next generation. We just rinsed and repeated the same perspective we had before. That, for me, is heartbreaking as both a parent and an educator.

You've kind of touched on it, but what would you change in education? Is there anything you want to elaborate on? Is there one thing you'd highlight?

The biggest thing is that we need to build more instructional leaders. We have a lot of managers, but instructional leaders are what really make a difference for kids. The second thing is to listen to what teachers are saying. For example, over the last 20 or 30 years, Lucy Calkins was considered an "expert" with her writing program, but it wasn't based on sound research. Now, people are finally realizing that. When you talk to teachers who taught during "the Lucy Calkins era", they will say they always felt like the program wasn't supporting kids with writing and shouldn't have been implemented. Teachers oftentimes see these issues long before they're acknowledged or displayed in the data.

Another critical change would be focusing on what kids truly need to be successful in the 21st century and cutting out all the unnecessary fluff. What do kids need in terms of wellness and holistic development? I've worked in both predominantly white schools and predominantly Black schools, and I'm so tired of the disparities. In Black schools, the focus is on controlling kids and teachers, whereas in white schools, it's about fostering a love of learning. In Black schools, it's all about teaching the skill of reading. In white schools, it's about nurturing a love for reading while teaching the skill. That's heartbreaking. The last thing I'd say is that everything starts at the top. When leadership builds strong relationships with teachers, and teachers build strong relationships with students, everything changes.

I hear that a lot, and the way I often hear it framed is as a lack of support.

Yeah, but I think it's deeper than just support. When people talk about support, it feels too broad. I think it's more about centering people. At my last school, I was there for ten years with the same principal and most of the same staff. That's rare, especially in Black schools. And that school performed well. A lot of it was because the principal and admin, including me when I was an admin, centered the people. For example, when I went on maternity leave with my daughter, they accommodated me when I returned. When I had my son, they accommodated me in a different way. We always talk about differentiating for kids, but we don't differentiate for adults. We want teachers to differentiate for kids, but we don't differentiate for adults. That's what I love about my current role. It gives me the opportunity to do just that. For example, last week, one of my teachers broke down and cried. She hit that wall, which happens around September. I could've said, "Let's keep pushing; let's focus on getting your math groups together," but instead, I told her to step outside. We did a mindful moment together.

Do you have any advice for someone considering leaving the classroom?

First, know why you're leaving. Have a clear exit strategy. I understand that some people are ready to leave without a plan because they're at their breaking point. But if you can, plan ahead. When I left the classroom in 2015, I spent almost a year preparing. I researched the kinds of jobs teachers could transition into. Things are different now. Another key step is to update your LinkedIn profile. Activate your network and really work it. That was huge for me. When you're in education, you can easily update your résumé because you already know what to highlight. But when you leave, it can be hard to see the value of your skills. I had an HR consultant look at my résumé, and she pointed out things I'd never thought of. For example, I'd been involved in talent acquisition for years but never framed it that way. I'd even helped create the hiring process for my school, but I hadn't included it on my résumé. Also, begin capturing your impact- student data, facilitation data, etc. As teachers, we will utilize many gifts, but not capture them. When I left, I felt guilty...guilty for the kids I left behind and the educators still in the trenches. But I had to do what was best for me and my family.

Dina, let me ask you this: If they doubled your salary, would you go back?

Dina: No. If they did that, I would make well over $125,000. But things would have to change drastically. I don't have the mindset to just go through the motions. Right before I left, I'd gotten to that point, and I hated it.

Kofi: That's the thing. People always say, "They need to pay teachers more." But money isn't the number one reason teachers leave. Many teachers leave because they don't feel empowered (through intentional professional development & coaching), they don't have community (a mentor, grade chair, team) and they don't feel like they have a voice.

Instructional Specialist - Haylee
Taught for 7 years - Grades: 7-12 - Subjects: ELA & Spanish

When I look at your LinkedIn page, I see something about EdCafe. Tell me about that.

EdCafe is a professional learning organization founded by teachers for teachers. It's a passion project that doesn't generate revenue; everything is completely free. The goal is to provide professional learning opportunities for educators and Friends of Education. It started when colleagues in mid-Missouri invited me to present at an event they were organizing. I loved the concept so much that I started a chapter in Southwest Missouri. While the original founders became less involved, they supported my efforts to grow it in my region. EdCafe focuses on fostering collaboration and networking among educators. Every summer, we organize and promote professional learning events. I have other colleagues who help obtain speakers and spread the word to market the events, and the mission is to inspire collaboration and professional growth, making a positive impact on educators.

What did you do to prepare for this career?

One of my biggest steps was hiring a company called TopResume to update and revise my resume. I also subscribed to various email lists and followed social media accounts focused on helping teachers transition to other careers. One of the subscriptions I found particularly helpful was the Teacher Career Coach. Through their resources and social media content, I gained ideas about which of my skills were transferable to other professions. Additionally, the same company that helped with my resume also revamped my LinkedIn profile. Looking back now, there were probably free resources like public higher education institutions, and I could have received the same resume and LinkedIn revision help. When searching for jobs, I specifically looked for remote positions that allowed me to use my education degree and training skills while staying within or adjacent to the field of education. My husband also periodically helped me search for jobs, which is how I found the position I currently hold. The hiring process for this role involved three rounds of interviews—the first two were virtual, and the final round was in person. For the final round, I had to deliver an in-person lesson, so I spent a significant amount of time preparing for that.

Can you describe the onboarding and training process you underwent for your current role?

My onboarding process was a gradual integration into the role. Initially, I completed the required University compliance training and worked on getting familiar with the new position. Transitioning from a rigid bell-to-bell classroom schedule to a more self-directed, work-from-home environment required prioritizing tasks effectively. My supervisor, who also serves as my mentor, guided me through this transition. I was under a six-month probationary period, although the formal onboarding process took a few weeks. As for training, all staff at eMINTS participate in a two-year program called the Affiliate Trainer Program. This program, based on the book Mentoring Matters by Lipton and Wellman, trains us to be effective facilitators, coaches, and mentors. I completed this program in April 2024 and am now a certified eMINTS Affiliate Trainer. Additionally, eMINTS funded the Cognitive CoachingSM certification for staff to enhance our instructional coaching skills, and I completed this training in July 2024.

Could you walk me through the end-to-end process of a typical project or workflow in your role?

In my current role as a professional learning specialist, I work for the eMINTS National Center, which we are now rebranding as eMINTS Professional Learning. We are a grant-funded organization under the University of Missouri's College of Education and Human Development. While we are technically part of the University, we are self-sufficient and sustain our work through government grants, primarily from the Department of Education. This funding supports our outreach initiatives. When it comes to project initiation and planning, the process usually begins with securing grants. These grants determine the type of projects we undertake and the participants we work with. Educators and schools sign up to participate in our no-cost, grant-funded programs. In exchange for providing us with data during the project's data collection phase, participants receive professional development (PD) and technology tools to enhance their teaching practices. My role in the planning phase involves identifying the specific training needs of participants based on the objectives of the grant.

Once needs are identified, I collaborate with my team to design the training content, schedule sessions, and coordinate logistics. This includes creating or updating training materials and ensuring all resources align with the goals of the project. Within eMINTS, I work closely with everyone in the organization. We are a small but mighty team of 15 people. Since we are grant-funded, we occasionally collaborate with faculty members for our grants. However, most of our collaboration is with our internal team members. Our training programs are tied to grant projects. Participants, who are typically active K-12 school teachers and personnel, opt into these grant-funded research projects. The training we provide is based on the objectives outlined in the grant. For example, my current work focuses on a grant called Prosocial and Active Learning. My role is to teach educators how to help their students develop prosocial skills, which involves intentionally teaching students how to collaborate and work effectively with others. In other words, we aim to guide students to become kind, cooperative individuals.

On a typical day, if I'm working from home, I start by walking my dog and then begin work around eight. My tasks include responding to emails, updating materials, and attending virtual meetings with my team. These meetings help us stay aligned and address any challenges. When I'm preparing for a training session, I focus on ensuring the materials are ready and that the content supports adult learning principles. If the session involves travel, I usually arrive the night before to prepare the venue and finalize arrangements, such as seating and materials setup. During training sessions, which often span two days, I lead the participants through the prepared materials and facilitate discussions and activities. My role doesn't end there. For ongoing coaching visits, I schedule times with participants to provide hands-on support in their classrooms or virtual calls to help meet their needs. This might involve helping with lesson plans, administering tests, or creating resources. My goal is to ensure that teachers feel supported and have the tools they need to succeed. This collaborative work extends across our team as we design and execute these training sessions.

Regarding the training materials you develop, what forms do these take? For example, are they primarily PowerPoint presentations, facilitator guides, or participant workbooks?

That's a great question. The format of our training materials depends on the program. For participant guides, we adapt the format to how participants will access the materials. In the past, we have used Google Sites or Google Slides as participant guides. We also create facilitator guides to ensure consistency in how sessions are conducted. The materials vary depending on the grant or project. For example, I have developed asynchronous virtual platforms as well as live in-person participant guides. We also focus on embedding strategies and technology tools into these materials to show teachers how they can implement them in their classrooms. This way, we make sure that the training is applicable to the teachers and immediately implemented in their classrooms.

How do you get feedback on your performance?

I work for the University of Missouri, where we have a structured performance review process. This includes a formative mid-year review in the fall and a summative progress check at the end of the year, typically in June. These reviews are based on a self-evaluation that I submit to my supervisor. My supervisor then provides comments, and I can respond to those comments. Beyond these formal reviews, I have weekly check-ins with my supervisor, who I consider a mentor. If there were areas where I needed improvement, I would likely hear about them during these regular check-ins rather than waiting for the formal evaluation process.

How do you assess the impact of your training and coaching on teachers and their classroom practices?

For the grant I'm currently working on, we test the effects of the training on the teachers' self-efficacy, stress, and burnout levels using pre- and post-surveys and video observations. We don't assess the coaching, although I have a strong interest in coaching and mentoring. I began an educational doctorate program, and my dissertation in practice will likely focus on coaching and mentoring and their effects on teacher stress, burnout, attrition, self-efficacy, and retention. While we don't have that data right now, eMINTS is uniquely positioned to explore these areas. I'm hoping to gather data to better assess the impact of training and coaching on teachers.

Coaching teachers is a significant part of my role. Through the Affiliate Trainer Program and cognitive CoachingSM certification, I've gained the skills necessary to mentor and support teachers effectively. Our coaching cycle typically spans a school year. Teachers participate in professional learning sessions throughout the year and receive ongoing coaching and mentoring. The first coaching visit is always in person. We use this time to get to know the teacher and their school environment. After that, we schedule periodic 30-minute virtual check-ins, usually monthly. These sessions focus on key topics such as how prosocial education is being implemented, identifying struggles, celebrating successes, and encouraging teacher self-reflection through Cognitive CoachingSM methods. The year ends with another in-person visit to reflect on progress and provide any additional support. The goal is to build their capacity as self-reflective practitioners while providing the tools and strategies they need to succeed.

What are some of the biggest challenges you face in your role, and how do you address them? Can you share an example of a particularly challenging project and how you managed it?

One of my biggest challenges is transitioning from working with students to working with adults. Having been out of the classroom for about two years, I'm still adjusting to this new dynamic. When I worked with students, I gave them grace because they were still learning. Now, working with adults, it's harder not to impose my own expectations or perspectives on them. I'm learning to acknowledge that adults, like students, may need to develop certain skills, and I can't control their actions. For example, some teachers I coach don't respond to emails in a timely manner. My initial expectation was that they should respond quickly, as I would in a professional setting. However, I've learned to remind myself that they may have personal or professional challenges that delay their responses. To address this, I've started offering alternative communication methods, such as texting or FaceTiming.

Why did you leave teaching?

I left teaching three years ago, resigning in June 2022. The environment wasn't a good fit for me anymore. Despite improving my boundaries between work and home, I was overwhelmed by emotional baggage, such as the struggles my students faced. Being a helper, I internalized their problems, which made it hard to separate work from home life. I also felt constrained by the district's emphasis on standardized testing and its mold for teachers, which didn't align with my philosophy. When I applied for another position within the district and was denied, I asked for feedback. A district leader suggested ensuring my values aligned with the district's focus on test scores. That confirmed I didn't belong there.

My priority was building relationships with kids and supporting their mental and emotional well-being, while the district prioritized high test scores. So, I left.

Is there anything that you've learned now, specifically in the preparation for your new career, that you would have done differently?

I love that question. If I were to give advice, I'd say that if you come across a job that looks promising or aligns with what you want to do, apply immediately. Don't rush through the application; act quickly and intentionally because these opportunities can be few and far between. The competition has grown significantly, with many more teachers looking to leave the classroom now than there were two years ago. If I had to do it all over again, I would still invest in having my resume professionally revised and my LinkedIn profile optimized. I would also have researched the organization I was applying to more heavily before the interview process. Although I did some research, I realize now that additional preparation would have been helpful. Another thing I would have done differently is focus more on learning how to work with, coach, and mentor adult learners. Transitioning from teaching students to supporting adults required a different mindset and approach, and I think preparing for that shift earlier would have made the transition smoother.

Who do you follow on LinkedIn or other social media? Any books, blogs, or websites?

I followed the Teacher Career Coach during my transition out of the classroom. I have completed training programs within my organization focused on improving coaching skills, studying Mentoring Matters by Lipton and Wellman and Designing a Prosocial Classroom by Dr. Christi Bergin. The last text aligns with the grant program we are running. I follow various education organizations, professional development groups, and edtech companies on LinkedIn, as well as individuals I admire. I subscribe to email lists like CharacterStrong, which focuses on SEL and offers free webinars. Another resource I've used is Experience Learning, which specializes in problem-based learning. I grow professionally through research, reading, and passion projects. My employer supports this growth by funding certifications, like the Cognitive CoachingSM certification, and by allowing me to attend conferences. I also recently applied for an educational doctorate program, and if accepted, I'll use the university's tuition discount. This level of support is something I didn't often experience in the classroom.

What advice do you have for others who are exploring career options that align with your experience?

My biggest piece of advice is to check LinkedIn frequently. For me, it was my go-to resource for job listings. Set alerts for specific organizations, school districts, or job types that you're interested in, so you get notifications when new opportunities are posted. Use relevant keywords and cast a wide net in your search. Be prepared for rejection because, unfortunately, you're likely to hear "no" more often than "yes," but persistence is key. I also recommend joining social media groups like Teachers Transitioning Teachers or the Teacher Mass Exodus. These groups are filled with people who are either in the process of leaving or have already left teaching. They can be a great source of advice and encouragement. If you have questions about anything, post them in these groups and see what responses you get.

Leadership Development Facilitator - Kathy
Taught for 27 years - Grades: MS English and MS & HS Librarian

Why did you leave the classroom?

I'm someone who likes to change it up. Often, there's this belief that once you become a teacher, that's your identity for life. That's not true of almost any other career. People change careers, and for some reason, we have this very fixed mindset in teaching that I am a teacher forever. Over the years, I've made several shifts in education roles. I spent a decade as an English teacher before transitioning to a librarian role, first in a middle school where I had a long tenure and then moving on to a high school. Eight years into that role, I was ready for a change. But I didn't have a "plan," and I hadn't figured out how to make a corporate resume. So, if I got mad, I'd rage apply in hopes that something would land. Then the pandemic hit, and I signed up for one more year of teaching because I just didn't know what was going to happen in the world.

However, that was the year I really focused on upskilling and translating my resume. Looking back, had I not changed to high school, I'm not sure what would have happened. I realized that this level was just not a good fit for me. Middle schoolers were my people. So, I think those two things together, I just got really burnt out. Yes, people say, "Oh, I love kids," but for me, it partly was that I didn't enjoy teaching that grade level, and I just didn't love it anymore. I got to the point where I was not my best self, and that's not good for anybody. It was time. There are still lots of students that I keep in touch with, and it's fun seeing them on LinkedIn as they graduate college and get jobs. But, yeah, I was just ready to not work with teenagers anymore.

How did you upskill prior to obtaining this role and what is needed to perform the duties?

During the pandemic there were so many free online conferences and resources. One free course that I took was a DEI course with the University of Florida. I also did a lot of reading and listening to podcasts. I think for this particular position, facilitation skills are obviously very important, but also being able to quickly recall things and make connections because a lot of the work that we do is very much based in research and psychology. So, a big part of the job was familiarity with psychology concepts, which I have no formal training in, but luckily, I'm very interested in. A lot of the reading I do and the podcasts I listen to are around that topic, so that really helped. Even though the content is already there, there are always questions that people ask or examples that are needed that I just have to put together. Then, find ways to feel confident in asking for help when you don't know something.

Walk me through that learning curve and what were the most difficult parts of that?

One learning curve was just the language. The language that corporate America uses is very different from the education world. The other is having the confidence to figure out what to do when you don't know. When you first start out, and someone says something about KPIs, and you're like, "What's a KPI? Do I fake this? Do I try to subtly Google it? What do I do?" You need to have the confidence to say, "I don't know," or to find creative ways to ask for more information. You might say, "I've seen people using KPIs differently in different companies. What does KPI mean to you?" or "How are you using it?" Finding ways that feel comfortable to you to figure out what you don't know is a really important piece of the process. Because trying to hide it isn't going to work; it's going to bite you in the butt.

Let's talk about what you do as a Leadership Development Facilitator.

I deliver workshops that have been developed by the company I work for. As a facilitator, I have to learn all the content. So, when I first started, it was a very steep learning curve. It took me pretty much the first year to learn all of the content, but we're constantly changing and developing new products, so that learning curve continues, but not at the sharp rate it initially was. Typically, each workshop is 2 hours long, and I do between five and eight workshops a week. Sometimes they're one-offs; sometimes it's a group that I will meet with five or six times over the course of several months. It's always fun to touch base with people and hear how they're using the skills they learned. That's probably my favorite thing about my job. When someone shares one of the things they learned in a workshop that they tried and the impact it had.

Could you explain the process for handling new materials when they arrive? How are they delivered to you, and do you have any input in their creation? Additionally, how do you approach learning and rehearsing these materials, and what is the typical amount of time required for this?

With the more established materials, initially, there was a video of someone else teaching it that I could watch. Also, the slide deck contained really detailed notes, Q&As, and all sorts of useful information. But now, as we introduce newer content, it often starts with, "Here's our first draft. Take a look and share your thoughts." So, there's definitely room for input. In fact, over the past few months, I've been collaborating closely with our learning experience design team, spending quite a bit of time with them. This has allowed for more direct interaction with the content, which has been quite enjoyable. Typically, for a two-hour workshop, we're allocated about 10 hours for preparation. This allocation ensures we have sufficient time to thoroughly review the deck, discuss any questions with colleagues, delve into the research underpinning the content, and practice presenting it a few times. So, for each workshop, about 10 hours of learning and rehearsal time are set aside. Regarding the logistics of our sessions, we don't have a physical facility. Our operations are primarily virtual. However, for in-person sessions, we visit the company's location. Being part of the Boston facilitation team, I travel to various businesses in the greater Boston area to conduct sessions at their sites.

What other aspects of your role can you share?

I think one of the key things I've realized is how demanding facilitation can be, especially when it's your main focus. It's surprisingly exhausting. And I've definitely come to recognize that in my own experiences. What's really helped me manage recently is having a mixed role. I've been part of the learning design team for about 10 hours each month. This shift has slightly reduced the number of workshops I need to teach. Finding this balance is crucial, particularly because it demands so much from you. This is especially true if you're an introvert like me. It's all about taking that essential time and energy to recharge. There are days when I'm running three workshops, which means I'm actively delivering content for about 6 hours. It's akin to the life of a classroom teacher in many ways. But, understanding my limits and learning to pace myself has been key. It can get overwhelming, so finding that right pace is important.

What specific responsibilities do you have, particularly concerning AV setup for in-person events and managing invitations for virtual settings?

Our client administration team schedules everything, and the details, like the Zoom link, automatically appear on our calendar. I must admit, I do have a preference for Zoom over Google Meet or Teams, especially because of the filters that make us look better. Here's a funny side story to give you an idea: In addition to our standard in-person or virtual sessions, we sometimes host what we call avatar sessions. In these, all participants gather in one room, while the facilitator, much like the great and powerful Oz, joins virtually on a screen. About a year ago, I was facilitating one of these sessions and didn't realize until just before we started that there are no filters on Google Meet. The thought of appearing on a giant screen without a filter was daunting! It's a stark contrast to Zoom, which offers those Instagram-like filters we've all gotten used to. When the pandemic hit, most of our workshops were virtual, but now we do quite a few in-person sessions and travel to the client's location. Another aspect of my role, possibly influenced by my past as a school librarian (the go-to person for any AV issues), is handling AV problems. I've become quite adept at troubleshooting on my own. Generally, there's usually someone on-site to help with technical issues, but I've encountered a few situations they couldn't fix. When that happens, I just adapt and find a workaround. Being quick on your feet is crucial, especially when it comes to resolving AV issues so they don't interrupt the flow of the session.

Could you discuss any professional development opportunities you've pursued or resources you follow for personal growth, whether formal or informal?

I am a total podcast junkie, always on the hunt for something new. I really enjoy the ones from Harvard Business Review and anything by Adam Grant. They often discuss studies that I can use as fresh examples in my workshops, so I'm constantly looking for those gems. In the L&D world, I follow Sarah Cannistra, Kevin Yates, and Crystal Kadakia. Most of my learning comes from podcasts and reading books and articles. Often, other facilitators will share something intriguing on Slack, like an article with great insights for a specific workshop. It's incredibly helpful to tap into what my colleagues are discovering as well.

I see you're going to be speaking at a conference.

One of the things with my role is that we do a lot of conferences and events as a way to get our brand out there. Getting to speak at HR conferences, company offsites, and other events is a great opportunity that I really enjoy and value. Plus we run our own event that we call Culture Club, which is a free event for those in HR or People Ops. It's a chance for them to network and come and see an abbreviated version of some of our workshops. It's incredible to be only a couple of years into this new career and be given the opportunity to be a thought leader and facilitate conversations about best practices in people operations and learning and development.

What advice do you have for any teacher that wants a change?

When looking at your experience and seeing what other roles you might be qualified for and interested in, I think the key is to take a close look at everything you're involved in, like the committees you serve on, or perhaps you've played a part in organizing a field trip for a special event. Consider all the activities you engage in, even those that might seem insignificant. Maybe there's a hobby you're passionate about, and you're the one steering the related club. It's important to dive deep and reflect on what activities energize you and where your strengths lie; these areas may or may not align. Your goal should be to identify and concentrate on the activities where your passions and skills intersect. Right now, many people are thinking, "I'm done with teaching, I'll become an instructional designer." But let's be honest, that path isn't cut out for everyone. I had a heart-to-heart with a fellow ex-teacher who made me see that instructional design wasn't my calling. It simply wasn't going to bring me joy. So, it's crucial to take the time to evaluate the day-to-day tasks that not only play to your strengths but also make you feel alive.

Resources: University of Florida - Diversity, Equity and Inclusion in the Workplace Certificate

Learning and Development Advisor - Alex

Taught for 14 years - Grades and/or Subject: Qualified Teacher, Language Instructor Teacher Trainer, Trained Sports Apprentice Location: UK

How do you go about finding a job in the UK?

We have LinkedIn and Indeed, which I think you also have. We also have industry-specific recruitment companies such as Charity Jobs and another for higher education, primary schools, secondary schools, and nurseries. Everybody. All education institutes advertise on TES, called The Times Educational Supplement or TES. You can also go to specific employers, like I did, to get job alerts, and there are also recruitment agencies who hire directly.

Tell me about your role.

There's one part of my job that's quite admin-focused, where I oversee the training completed by our workforce and, crucially, what they haven't completed. I then provide them with opportunities to undertake certain essential training, which we refer to as compliance training. This includes courses like safeguarding and fire safety. I'm in charge of this aspect, which forms a significant part of my responsibilities. However, the more intriguing facet of my job involves collaborating with a group of tutors, about 20 in total. We engage in developmental activities monthly, discussing various educational topics, which could range from assessment techniques to strategies for stretch and challenge. I dedicate a month to prepare for these sessions, aiming to introduce new practices. Additionally, I observe individuals, gathering effective practices, and strive to integrate these insights into our sessions. Following these meetings, participants complete a 'growth task,' applying something new they've chosen to undertake. For instance, a few months back, we examined three assessment strategies, allowing each member to select and implement one. They later share their experiences with me, which vary in success but invariably contribute to our collective growth. This professional circle has been particularly rewarding. I've seen individuals who, a year ago, lacked teaching qualifications and came from diverse industries evolve into educators through their engagement and achievements in continuing professional development (CPD). Their transformation fills me with immense pride, reminding me of the impactful role I play in their journey.

Provide any current resources that you use to stay current in your field. Or do you follow anyone? Or is there any professional development that you take on yourself?

I work in a field with people who have learning disabilities. I've taken quite a few courses in dyslexia, ADHD, and autism. I'm taking an Autism certificate now. I look around, and I find the information that gives me my subject knowledge that I need to know about the learners that we work with in my organization. But as a learning and development professional, I use an organization called CIPD.org, which is a learning and development body for the UK. You can join it to take professional development courses, locate jobs, and more.

Leaving and starting your new career, when did you decide to pursue something different? How did you find this new career, and how did you acquire the necessary skills to begin?

I decided to leave education about 18 months before actually doing so. I looked for alternative opportunities, like in teaching. I was training teachers, training newly qualified teachers, and I was training sports apprentices. My first port of call was to go to those kinds of organizations.

However, there weren't a lot of jobs in teacher training. Funding is being cut in the UK. So, there weren't really the jobs available for me to go to, and where I did find them, they were either one-year contracts, which I can't do because I've got kids and a mortgage, or I would have to relocate, which I didn't want to do. After that kind of initial phase, I started to look outside of education. As a teacher, there's always advertising, saying, "Teachers, we need your skills, they're really transferable." When you go and talk to people, the dream is not as good as the reality. There were a lot of jobs with admin and customer service, which I just found really boring. But I came across learning and development, which is sort of a personnel human resources function of a business. It centers around getting people to be able to do things for a company, so it might be just learning new processes or understanding new information, or taking health and safety training, for example. I was looking around and continuing to look for jobs in further education. This job that came up, that's a mix of both. I train all the staff at a charity. Part of what we do is deliver a program for people with learning disabilities to be able to get into work. The young people, aged 18 to 24, do things like working in a cafe, working in logistics, or in a factory. We have tutors who need to be able to deliver math and English. That's my area of expertise, really. But I also oversee other areas of training, like how to conduct a risk assessment, how to do manual handling training, and just managing the admin side of that. Because my job had that component of teacher training or tutor training in it, I was really strong in the interview and I felt like it's something I really wanted to do. I had the right experience for it. Fortunately, I was successful and got the job.

You mentioned there's an agency that could find another teacher. How does that work?

Oh, gosh, we have recruitment agencies all over England that specialize in finding teachers. They charge an incredible amount of money. So, for example, if a teacher is off sick and they've got the flu and they're going to be off sick for a week, you can phone an agency and say, I need a substitute teacher for a week, and they will say, sure, we have someone available. Then the school has to pay the agency £500 a day for that substitute teacher.

Why did you leave teaching?

By the end of my career, I was working a lot, around ten to twelve hours a day, four or five days a week. I dropped a day, I was working four days a week and still clocking 50 hours in those four days. It was unmanageable, despite having holidays. I thought I could manage for six weeks and then get a holiday. However, I felt too exhausted to enjoy the holidays. I wasn't able to recharge my batteries; I was just recovering and bringing myself back to zero, never going beyond that. I also have two kids. When I left, they were seven and eight years old. I had no energy for them, no time. I thought I was putting other people's kids first. I needed to get my priorities in order.

What is one area in education that you would like to change?

Teaching is not perfect, but one area that would help a lot is the approach to inspections. In the UK, we have something called OFSTED, the Inspector of Schools run by the government on behalf of His Majesty the King. It is punitive, and everybody lives in fear of it. An education minister in the UK has said he uses the threat of OFSTED to get leverage over the education profession, it is a weapon. I really disagree with it in principle because they don't provide any solutions. I would create a school performance service, which would potentially work in particular regions like the Southeast of England or the Southwest of England. The School Performance service would conduct scrutiny of how a school is performing, asking questions such as how the students are performing. What's happening with the staff? Are the governors doing a good job? All the things that OFSTED looks at, but out of the back of it, it would provide support to the school to make improvements. It would be a go-to place for teachers to say, I'm struggling with a particular student or this year is really difficult for me. How can I cope with this? Maybe they want to go and talk about their boss if they're under a lot of pressure. Maybe it would be a way of supporting schools and supporting educators and teachers rather than judging them, which is what OFSTED does. I would also make sure that part of their function would be to share good practices. For example, when they see one school is really excellent at dealing with children who have autism, they would say to another school who's struggling, I'm going to link you guys together so that you can share best practice. Now we have created two schools who are really good at dealing with autistic children. That is what I would change.

How long has that been in place? What was the purpose? Has it been in place ever since you first started? What was the capacity or the purpose of it?

OFSTED has been around for my whole career. There is a place for performance review in education. I understand that. It is really important to get things right for children, but doing it in this way is not useful. It doesn't provide any solutions; it doesn't improve it. You get a little snapshot. I've met inspectors who have been really lovely people and then I've met ones who are terrible.

Would you advise anyone to go into education?

I would give different people different advice. This comes from my experience of working with newly qualified teachers. Generally, those people are young, and they live at home. When they're required to work a lot, that's fine because when they go home, their parents may have cooked dinner for them, and they don't have a mortgage to pay. They don't have any children who require energy when they get back to their homes. They can cope quite well with the workload because they have the time at home. They're not trying to feed children and things like that. Whereas, if I was talking to somebody who is a career changer, let's say, my age in their early forties, and has children, I would say, don't go into education because you're going to sacrifice time with your children, and you're going to sacrifice your energy to the school. In my opinion, it's a young person's game now, and I would also agree with your earlier statement that people need a backup plan because it's not a long career anymore. It's a bit like being a professional athlete. Football (soccer) players will do maybe 14 to 15 years maximum. They then need to think about what they're going to do after. Do they become a talent scout, coach, or a manager? I think that's the way you need to think as a teacher now. You have to say to yourself, "I've got five years, ten years, top, and then what am I going to do after?

What advice do you have for teachers who want to switch careers?

If you're at the point where you want to exit teaching, do it. If you feel like you need to get out, then get out. When you leave teaching, you might not find the right job immediately, and that's okay. It's perfectly fine to explore different roles and sectors before settling into a new career. For example, instead of working with children, apply to work with adults. Here in the UK, teachers are treated with respect. They've studied, and they are considered professionals. There are lots of opportunities, maybe more than you actually think.

*In England, the Office for Standards in Education, Children's Services and Skills (Ofsted) is responsible for inspecting a range of educational institutions, including state schools and some independent schools. Ofsted inspections are designed to assess the quality and standards of education these institutions provide the effectiveness of their leadership and management, and their capacity to provide a safe and encouraging learning environment. - site via ChatGPT

https://www.gov.uk/government/organisations/ofsted/about#our-responsibilities

Learning and Development Specialist - Sandy
Taught for 8 years - Grades: Primary

What did you do to prepare for this field/career (i.e.-courses, training, books, etc.) - Have you had to go back to school or receive additional training for your new career?

When I transitioned into my current role as a Learning and Development Specialist, I didn't have any formal training or courses under my belt. However, I did volunteer for a non-profit organization as an educational coordinator, where I developed my organizational and project management skills, as well as gained some exposure to the corporate environment.

Knowing what you know now, what would you have changed about your preparation, not necessarily the experiences that you have had?

My advice to anyone considering leaving teaching for a new career is short and sweet! It is to take the time to prepare properly. Spend time reflecting on your skills, passions, and goals, and use that information to guide your career decisions. It may take some extra effort and planning, but the end result will be well worth it.

What skills or experiences from your teaching career have been helpful in your new role?

As a teacher, I had to be adaptable to say the least! Some days, the lesson plan went out the window, and I had to come up with something new on the spot. That kind of flexibility has been a huge asset in my new career. In my role as an L&D Specialist, I'm often tasked with developing training programs that meet the specific needs of different departments. It's not always a one-size-fits-all approach, and my ability to be patient, creative, and adaptable has served me well. I also know how to make learning engaging and interactive, and I'm not afraid to switch things up if I see people's attention start to drift.

How has your teaching background helped or hindered you in your new career?

As someone who has made the transition from teaching to a new career, I can say that my teaching background has definitely helped me in many ways. One of the most important skills I've carried over is the ability to be patient and flexible.

When you're a teacher, you never know what's going to happen in the classroom. You have to be able to think on your feet and adapt to the situation. In my new career, there are times when things don't go according to plan. Maybe a project gets delayed or there's a sudden change in direction. Having the ability to stay calm, be patient, and adapt to the new circumstances has been a huge asset too.

How has your new career impacted your work-life balance compared to teaching?

It's been amazing. As a teacher, my life was all about the job. I was constantly thinking about lesson plans, grading papers, and always preparing for the next day's classes. Even when I wasn't physically at school, I was still mentally consumed by it all. It was hard to disconnect and enjoy my personal life without feeling guilty or stressed about work. But now, as an L&D Specialist, everything is different. My job revolves around me, rather than me revolving around my job. It's such a breath of fresh air. I can focus on my work during work hours, and then actually disconnect and enjoy my personal life without feeling like I'm abandoning something. It's been so freeing and has definitely improved my overall well-being.

Have you faced any difficulties transitioning to your new career? If so, can you describe them?

So, transitioning into my role as an L&D Specialist was pretty smooth overall, but there was definitely one major obstacle that I had to overcome - imposter syndrome. I constantly felt like I needed to prove myself and do more to feel like I belonged. But, as I got more settled in my new role and started working with my team, After a night out with my team, they told me what they thought of me at the beginning and it was such a surprised. They said they were really impressed on how hard-working and friendly I was at the start. It was a huge confidence boost for me, especially in those early months. I'm grateful for the support of my team and for the opportunity to prove to myself that I had what it takes to succeed in this new career.

What inspired you to leave the teaching profession and pursue a new career?

What ultimately led me to make the decision to leave the teaching profession was the inspiring example set by my partner, who left his banking career to pursue his passions and start his own successful business. Seeing his journey and ultimate success gave me the courage to explore new opportunities and discover my own path. It was through this journey that I realized that anything is possible if you have the determination and willingness to pursue your dreams. So I thought, anything is possible!

Was there a specific event or situation that made you decide to leave teaching?

Looking back, there wasn't really one specific event that made me decide to leave teaching. It was more of a feeling that my skills and passions could be better used in other roles. I remember thinking this as early as my second year of teaching, but I always felt like I should stick with it and keep pushing through. Unfortunately, that led to several years of just going through the motions and not really enjoying what I was doing. Don't get me wrong, I absolutely loved being in the classroom with the children - they were the highlight of my day. But all the other stuff - the reporting, the marking, dealing with other teachers, administration - just wore me down over time. So, in the end, I knew it was time for a change. While I loved teaching and was passionate about my students, I found myself increasingly frustrated with the outdated systems and practices within the education system. Despite my best efforts to innovate and modernize my teaching approach, I often felt restricted by bureaucratic red tape and the resistance to change from certain colleagues and administrators. As they say, "When one door closes, another one opens"

Do you miss teaching, and if so, what aspects of it do you miss the most?

While I definitely don't miss teaching as a whole, there are certainly aspects of it that I do miss. The thing I miss the most is the kids. There's something special about watching them grow and learn new things every day. Seeing their faces light up when they finally grasp a concept or accomplish something they've been working on is truly priceless. And I have to admit, I do miss the occasional influx of chocolates around Christmas time. It was always a nice little perk of the job!

Do you miss not having a summer break? Explain why or why not.

No. As a teacher, I often found myself feeling depleted, and the school holidays became necessary for recharging. However, since transitioning to my current work environment, I now have the ability to work at a more sustainable pace. With regular breaks throughout the day and the flexibility to pace myself based on my personal needs, I am now able to recharge daily, leaving me feeling energized and focused for the weeks ahead rather than counting down to school holidays.

What advice would you give to someone considering leaving teaching for a new career?

If you're thinking about leaving teaching for a new career, my advice would be to take the leap and don't be afraid to step out of your comfort zone. It can seem daunting to leave a profession you've dedicated so much time and effort to, but the rewards of pursuing a new career can be truly fulfilling. The transition from teaching to a different industry may seem challenging, but with preparation and persistence, you can succeed. It's important to recognize that the corporate world operates differently from the education industry, but with some effort and an open mind, you can adapt and thrive.

Learning Content Specialist - Dr. Robin
Taught for 18 years - Grades: HS - Subjects: English & Honors African American History

What year did you come out?

I came out in February of 2022.

Tell me about your role and what you do.

I'm part of the corporate relations group, and I work on the events and training team. One of the main things we do is put on a lot of events in the cooperative space.

The simplest way to think of us is that we are the bank of the co-op. One of the seven cooperative principles is education, making it an essential part of what we do. Education is taken seriously in the cooperative space because it is a core principle. What makes our training for CFC unique is that all of our events, training, tools, and resources are provided at no cost. We view these as added-value services. I design training for rural utilities within the National Rural Utilities Cooperative Finance Corporation, supporting over 900 electric distribution cooperatives. Let's talk about the cooperative space again. Working in a cooperative environment creates specific training needs. As a finance corporation, we focus heavily on finance-related training. Our audience includes CFOs, accountants, controllers, and financial managers, anyone in the finance space. They require specific training because cooperatives follow guidelines and principles different from traditional accounting. Cooperative accounting is very different, even down to the balance sheet, so we provide training for that. Some sessions are for beginners who are new to cooperatives, and I help design those. We also offer training for people who have been in their roles for years.

We offer financial tools like our budgeting system and forecasting program. I help design training to teach people how to use these tools effectively or integrate them into their daily role in their jobs.

Cooperatives are like school districts. Just as every district has a school board, every cooperative has a board of directors, and we create training for them as well. I also design training specifically for cooperative directors. Like school boards, cooperative boards can include lawyers, doctors, or people from other fields. I'll be teaching them about balance sheets, equity, and other financial concepts so they can make informed decisions. I've worked with CEOs, CFOs, controllers, general managers, and plant accountants. It's a two-week intensive training covering cooperative principles, equity, financial policy, and more.

I meet with stakeholders to review presentations, ensuring they're relevant and exploring improvements like adding activities or changing the format. I create activities and provide feedback based on what has worked in previous sessions. For example, I might recommend using a poll to increase interactivity. I review every presentation, collaborating with our sister company and stakeholders to make edits. There's a lot of back and forth, but it's part of the process. After each session, we debrief to evaluate how things went and identify improvements. The programs that I design covers a wide range of topics, which was a learning curve for me. We manage four entities within one program.

A key part of the program is the capstone project. Participants apply what they've learned by conducting a financial analysis, writing a paper, and presenting their findings to leadership, sometimes including the board. I read all the capstones, so I need to understand the financial concepts they cover. After reviewing several, I've become much more comfortable.

For instance, I recently read one on standard cost accounting. Two years ago, I wouldn't have understood it, but now I can provide meaningful feedback. Since I used to be an English teacher, I also teach participants how to write their papers. I designed a presentation guiding them from outlining to finalizing the paper. It's a great way to use my teaching skills while learning about their co-op operations.

When we talk, I hear you mention other aspects of this role. Tell me more.

Sometimes I have to go into the LMS because our courses are hosted online, so I manage that. I handle the technical side, like opening the LMS, setting up the classes, and controlling access. It is the most tedious part of my job. I also create the job aids that go out to participants. With CFPC, it is not just training; it is also project management. Being a teacher and involved in extracurricular activities helped me prepare for this. So much of this role involves managing projects because everything has to be decided, even down to the books we give out. I coordinate that and design them. I had to learn how to use Adobe Photoshop and InDesign for this job since we create what we call the Facebook, a "who's who" book. My role also allowed me to earn my Adobe Certified Professional-Adobe Captivate, which my job paid for and allowed me time on the job to take the in-person sessions, prepare and test.

When you made the transition from teaching to this new role, how did you handle all the unknowns that came your way? Some parts probably felt familiar, but others were completely new. How did you manage that?

Everything was unknown because I didn't even know what a cooperative was. I didn't know they existed.

How did you deal with that? How did you feel?

The first project they put me on was plant accounting, and oh my goodness, I bombed it. I'm not an accountant. I had the chance to learn on the job and appreciated having time to ramp up in some areas. In teaching, you do not get downtime; you just start. Here, I had a couple of weeks to settle in and get used to my job and space. They didn't throw me into a major project right away and say, "This needs to be developed and handed over." In teaching, you get maybe a week to prepare, and that's it. Here, I had real time to adjust. I wasn't constantly in demand, with people in my face, needing me, or calling my name. I spent a lot of time researching. I still have a bookmark on my computer for a website from when I had no idea what a transmission line was, and suddenly I was talking about three phases and transformers.

I had to design a script for that. I found videos and had the time to watch them. Professional development here is self-paced. I could learn on my own time without having to fit it in around my job. Once I found out I could get a free LinkedIn Learning account through work, I signed up. I needed to improve my Excel skills and learn InDesign. I could sit at my desk, watch videos, and immediately apply what I learned.

It was strange. As a teacher, you would get in trouble for that. When would you even find time for professional development? You would have to do it before school, during planning time, or at home. Here, I could do it during the day. When I did not know something, I researched and found resources we already had. I discovered we printed a solution in a newsletter. I found old newsletters and asked people questions. I was not afraid to ask, "What is this? Why do we do this? How is this done?" Everyone knew I used to be a teacher, and I was fine with them knowing that. I asked questions, made friends, and joined Toastmasters. I met new people, learned about their roles, and figured things out. I just did the work, even though I knew nothing.

You said you bombed, but how did you bounce back?

My manager realized that I needed more support in terms of understanding the content and providing incremental support. He also did not hold it against me, which was very different than the environment I came from.

Why did you get into education?

Oh my goodness. I remembered being in my room that I treated like a classroom. My uncle gave me a teacher's edition literature book...I have no idea how he got it. I had my kids line up, and I'd write on my mirror like it was a chalkboard. I've always had the gift. I've never been afraid to teach or stand in front of people. In high school, during my senior year, I worked in the office and asked the attendance clerk about education. She said it was a good idea, especially if you wanted a family. The hours were good. Honestly, there weren't many other options in Mobile. You could be a teacher, a nurse, or work on the shipyard. I chose teaching. Oh my gosh, when I started, I loved it. I loved the kids. I felt like I was making a difference, and it was so much fun. I didn't even want to go home, and I had a child of my own. Carlos was already reading by the time I started teaching. He grew up with me in that first school, where I taught for seven years. Everybody knew him. A few months ago, Carlos went home and ran into a former student. He posted it on Facebook, and all my old students commented about how big he's gotten. They couldn't believe it. Carlos was such a part of my teaching life. I really loved teaching. I promise I did.

That resonates with so many people I've talked to. For a lot of us, it's something we've always wanted to do. Why did you leave education?

Early in my career, by my second year teaching high school, I was already seen as a leader. I became the cheerleading sponsor, and my principal wanted me to be department chair and join the School Action for Excellence committee, which worked on accreditation. He told me I was going to be a leader, and I believed it. My ultimate goal was to become an assistant principal. I was a part of the first cohort of future administrator who earned their certification or Masters degree through the University of South Alabama who got to experience this unique internship. We rotated through high school, middle school, and elementary school. I loved the elementary rotation and found out I enjoyed working with data.

But the last rotation didn't go well. The principal and I didn't get along. In a meeting with the assistant superintendent, she blamed the teachers for everything and threw them under the bus. I saw how disconnected the administration was from the teachers, and it hit me that this was not the kind of leader I wanted to be. When I finished the program and went back to teaching, I realized I no longer wanted to be an administrator. Even though I had the right connections, I didn't fit in. I spoke my mind too much. If something didn't benefit kids, I would say so. I wasn't willing to play the political game or compromise my integrity. I realized I couldn't thrive in that environment.

Then I met an English teacher who was getting her doctorate, and she encouraged me to do the same. I started with organizational leadership but eventually found instructional design. I fell in love with it. It was everything I believed education should be which was focused on effective teaching methods, with structure and purpose. I knew then that I had found something better, and I decided I would leave education when the time was right. Even though I loved teaching and got to work in a program that used innovative, active learning techniques, the move to DC made things harder. The schools there operated in rigid ways that didn't align with my values. I loved teaching, but I couldn't agree with how students or teachers were treated. I knew I had to find something else.

What surprised you the most about leaving teaching and moving into this new role?

You know what Stockholm syndrome is, right? When people start developing positive feelings toward their captors? I feel like all teachers have a bit of that. You know it is bad, you know it is not right, but you keep making excuses for why you stay. For years, I thought I could not take a sick day unless I was actually sick. I squeezed in doctor's appointments early in the morning or during planning because I thought I had to. It was not until I moved to DC that I realized I had flexibility. I could go to the doctor at 7 AM and still go to work, or leave early without worrying about coverage for my class. I remember my first day at my new job, my manager took me to lunch. We were gone for two hours. In my head, I was panicking, thinking we needed to get back, but she just said, "It's fine, just don't abuse it." It blew my mind. At this job, if someone's dog had a vet appointment, they would email, "I won't be in." No guilt. No permission needed. Meanwhile, I used to feel like I had to justify even a dental appointment.

One of my last conflicts at my old school was over a vacation. My family had planned a trip for 2020, but COVID happened. So, we pushed it to 2021. We had already paid for a cabin in Tennessee, and the trip fell on Martin Luther King Jr. weekend. I told my principal I would take the day after the holiday off. She got upset, but she let it slide. At that school, you needed permission just to take a day off around a holiday. Now, I can take vacation whenever I want. I do not have to ask anyone's permission. With my hybrid schedule, I do not even have to rush in the mornings. I was talking to a friend about how needing the bathroom before work used to throw off my whole day. If I forgot something, ran back in the house, and ended up late, I would get in trouble because nobody opened my classroom on time. These days, I do not have to rush. I am never late, but nobody even tracks my hours. Nobody tells me, "Robin, you need to work 8 to 5." I make my own schedule. For the first time, I feel like a professional. That is what I mean by Stockholm syndrome. Teachers get so used to not being treated like professionals that they think it is normal. It was not until I left that I realized how different things could be. My manager told me, "You are a professional. We trust you to make those decisions." I had no idea I was not being treated like a professional for 18 years because teaching was all I knew.

It sounds like schools need better systems in place to support teachers, like having someone available to cover classrooms so teachers can take basic breaks.

I remember my first day at my new job, February 22, 2022. I realized I had been ignoring the urge to use the restroom out of habit because I forgot I could just get up and go.out of habit because I forgot I could just get up and go. In education, you feel like you have to report every little thing. I still catch myself telling people when I'm about to leave, but now nobody cares or needs to know. At this job, there is trust in how we manage our time. I can step away when needed because the focus is on outcomes rather than hours, and we are given the freedom to structure our day in ways that work best for us. One of the biggest questions I get from my friends still teaching is, "What do you do with your day?" Teachers are used to having everything decided for them: when to teach, when to eat, and what to cover. But now, I get to decide. If I have a deliverable due, I know the date, and I can choose how to manage my time. I could finish it all in one day or spread it out. Nobody hovers over me asking what I'm doing every hour. That freedom is what people don't always understand. I design my own day, and that is something I never had before.

As an educator, you work with children, which is naturally time-bound. I understand the need to supervise those who are entrusted with the care of children, but what else contributes to teachers not being treated like professionals?

Think about the superintendent and the principal. What were they before becoming administrators? They were teachers managing students. That's what they know. Most principals don't get much training on how to manage adults. They're good at classroom management, but working with adults is a whole different thing.

In education, we're trained in pedagogy (how to teach students). But adults don't learn the same way. Adults need more freedom, collaboration, and respect. Workplaces outside education focus on adult learning principles, but schools don't train principals to apply them. A lot of principals end up managing teachers like students, talking to us the same way and trying to control us the same way. Even though we're teachers, we're still learners and need support like anyone else. But the system doesn't seem to get that.

Look at professional development. They tell us where to go, what sessions to attend, and what goals to set without asking what we need. None of it fits adults. It's all top-down and rigid, just like managing students.

I know what I'm talking about. I'm a certified administrator in Virginia with a license valid until 2030. In all my training, I never had a class on managing adults or applying adult learning principles. It was all about working with students.

That's the problem with education. Teachers are treated like students, and the people in charge don't see that managing adults takes a different approach. Schools are stuck in pedagogy, and until they apply adult learning principles, nothing will change.

Do you have any other advice?

If teaching isn't fulfilling or purposeful, my advice is to leave. We get stuck because of the sunk cost fallacy, a concept I learned from Quit: The Power of Knowing When to Walk Away by Annie Duke. It's the idea that, because we've invested so much time, money, and energy, we feel obligated to stay even when it no longer benefits us. I left a job I was great at after 18 years, and after 35 years, I moved away from Alabama to start fresh. The truth is, nobody says, "Good job for quitting your job and doing something else." People only celebrate perseverance through hardship, but staying for the wrong reasons isn't worth it. If teaching no longer serves your purpose, it's okay to leave, no matter how long you've been in it. My reason for not going back to education? Yes, it has gotten worse. I hear that kids are more out of control than ever. But that is not what keeps me away. What keeps me away is knowing I was not treated like an adult or professional. I cannot go back to that abuse. I will not return to an abusive environment under any circumstances. If I told you I was in a relationship with a man who did not support me financially, who let me be beaten down physically, mentally, and emotionally, and who worked me to exhaustion without care or respect, you would tell me to leave. You would say, "Get out. That is abuse."

Education was that relationship. And I am not going back.

Resources: Quit by Annie Duke

Learning Experience Designer - Maria
Taught for 17 years - Grades: 2 & 4

I've interviewed a few former teachers in the Learning and Development space, so I want to focus on your path and your new experience in developing content. I know that you went through two learning academies: Devlin Peck's and Anna Sabramowicz's. Which one did you do first?

I started with Anna because you recommended her. I loved her approach to storytelling in e-learning. Then Devlin's boot camp opened up a few months later. I was unsure about taking on a second project, but noticed other members such as Teresa, involved with both, that inspired me to do that too.

Did you finish Anna's project before you got hired?

Yes, I finished both projects. I completed Anna's first, then Devlin's within two months.

What was the project for Anna? What is her academy about?

Her academy focuses on narrative, scenario-based e-learning. Ryan and others helped make it more engaging. My eLearning project involved a character facing a conflict: What is the problem? What is the conflict? How does it resolve? The goal is to help learners apply this thinking to themselves.

What did you learn from her academy that you're using now in your job?

It was instrumental in so many ways. My company embraces storytelling, so I've brought pieces of that into my work. Without that experience, I might not have developed these thought processes.

What did Devlin's program offer you?

He built a community that allowed us to form relationships up until today. We were all creating our portfolio projects, which he calls the flagship project. He also focused on precision, helping me understand how to apply design to business problems.

How often were you able to get feedback?

We had group meetings where he'd use my project as an example to discuss improvements. There were peer review cohorts and one-on-ones with boot camp pros who had already transitioned to instructional design. Nicole, in particular, helped me develop a designer's eye.

Where did you learn the principles of instructional design?

It was a combination of being part of these communities and building collaborative skills that taught me the principles of Instructional design. In addition, the hands-on practice, reading Instructional design books, and listening to your interviews from your podcast helped. I'm still learning, but these experiences gave me a strong foundation.

You invested a lot of money for this new career. What are your thoughts on that?

There was a moment I had to make a decision whether to pay for such programs and/or resources, and I took the risk. One thing I'm sure, I could not have done it without my family's support. I saw it as an investment in myself. There were tough moments, but it was worth it.

Let's go through a project you worked on. How did it develop?

They wanted to convert a previously instructor-led course into e-learning, so I observed the original training to guide my development.

Did they give you any guidance on where to start?

I was given the initial guidance and confidence to be part of the decision-making process. It was a responsibility I took seriously to provide the best possible outcome for the learner.

As I took the training, I thought about how it would translate to e-learning. Some subjects are dry, so I focused on making the topic engaging for the learner. I used the resources given by the stakeholders to lay out the storyboard structure.

So they have a template for a storyboard?

Yes, there is a standard template, but we modify according to the specific needs of the eLearning.

I created a small prototype. It was a bit intimidating at first, but my manager encouraged me. Working with the stakeholders allowed me to build a strong relationship while making the revisions they requested.

Do you work on projects where you do one part and then hand it off?

Yes, there are projects like the one I just shared where I handled everything. For larger projects, my manager assigns parts to different team members.

Tell me about how you landed your current role.

I had always thought I would teach forever and retire. But then I started to feel this urge to explore more. It took me about a year to eighteen months from the time I decided to leave until I got hired. After going through training and starting the interview process, I had at least three positions that I thought were "it." I would make it past the screener, through several rounds of interviews, but in the end, I didn't get the positions. I was extremely disappointed. Looking back, I realize that the other interviews prepared me for my present position!

So, I interviewed with a global corporation and made it to the final rounds, but I didn't get the position. Something happened that I don't think happens often--they offered to give me feedback. I immediately accepted that opportunity for feedback. In that feedback, I learned information that would help me in future interviews. They primarily said I didn't get the position because they wanted someone with marketing experience, but they also mentioned that if something else became available, they would ask if I was interested. I said, of course, and was thankful for the feedback.

We had a vacation planned with my family, so I set the job search on hold. I knew that when I came back, I would need to restart the whole application process, but decided to enjoy the moment. You know how we typically have our apps? Well, I had turned them off, but I did have my email app open, and toward the end of our vacation, I received an email from the hiring manager asking if I would be interested in another position that became available! I was so happy! I couldn't believe it. When you leave things in the hands of God, He takes care of you. He will. The process to transition from an Educator to a Learning Experience Designer was challenging to say the least. However, with preparation, persistence and faith, it is possible!

Learning Experience Designer - Ricky
Taught for 5 years - Grades: 6 - 8

What is your title?

I was hired as a learning experience designer, and then our titles changed to instructional designer. I don't feel like there's a lot of difference in how I performed my role as a learning experience designer versus instructional. However, that doesn't mean that other companies don't view the role of a learning experience designer differently.

Can you describe how you typically approach projects?

When working on projects, we closely follow the ADDIE process. Our manager handles the reception of the intake form and delegates tasks. There are several deliverables that come from the intake form, and if a project is directed to my team, it often means that an eLearning course needs to be created or updated. I review materials, ensure completeness, and prepare for an intake meeting with the requester and all necessary SMEs or stakeholders where we clarify objectives and all related matters.

What's a project you particularly enjoyed working on?

One of my favorites was a five-level, gamified project I recently finished. It was quite cool, but it came with its caveats. This project was already in flight and was originally scripted for an AR/VR (augmented reality/

virtual reality) course, which are technologies we don't possess. Typically, I would inquire about any motivating factors, mistakes observed in the field, etc., during the intake, but this project started off a bit unusually. I presented alternatives to AR/VR, leading us to develop a gamified learning experience that was more scenario-based and experiential than the typical multiple-choice quiz or knowledge dump. The development involved considerable voiceover work, so we utilized AI, which has gotten pretty good. This was a substantial and complex project with voiceovers, scenarios with narration and branches, numerous triggers, and variables. The AI voiceover needed to bring the scenarios to life, not just narrate them, which meant creating videos for each scenario branch and incorporating them into Articulate Storyline with numerous triggers and variables. I created a health meter to measure how many questions the learner got right or wrong, and if you ran out of health, like most video games, it led you to a game over screen and they had to start again. Typically, there is a two-review cycle process, and this also involves both internal reviews by our team of instructional designers and external reviews by SMEs and stakeholders. I used a rapid prototyping approach instead of creating an extensive storyboard. After finalizing the design and development, I tested it and it is now in the LMS (Learning Management System). There are some other decisions that need to be made before it is implemented.

That has happened to me before, where I have created content but "others" have then made a decision not to deploy...

Sometimes when you don't have power in deciding the modality for learning, or decisions reverse work, it can be frustrating. Having been a teacher, you control most of what happens in your classroom. You can change the lesson plan and your modality for teaching. You might not control the baseline curriculum, but you have most control over how lessons are taught. Some of that control is lost when you move to a corporate setting. What I find frustrating is having more expertise than is utilized and knowing a decision may not be the best one, but it's out of your hands because it's not your lane. My manager is great, takes feedback well, and I can express my frustrations and make my voice heard. The answer might still be that it's not our lane as a team. Sometimes there's politics or finessing that has to happen. Sometimes, it's like teaching, figuring out which battles to pick. If you want your opinion respected and heard, sometimes you just have to wait for the right time.

How did you learn the skills to become an instructional designer?

I went through a paid program although I know those may not be for everyone. Doing so allowed me a quick start and guided transition. I do believe that there are plenty of resources out there for free to help transitioning teachers and do not condone taking out loans or overpaying for a program to help transition into Instructional Design. There is a right fit for everyone's time and budget. For me, the program certainly helped me get a kick start, and then I used several free resources and volunteer opportunities to continue upskilling.

How did you find some of your volunteer opportunities?

By searching on LinkedIn and talking to friends. My first portfolio piece resulted from helping a friend who is a realtor. I asked them what kinds of content their clients have trouble understanding, and I created a video and a click-through e-learning. I also volunteered with an org called Designed by Humanity (I don't think they're currently operating), where I got to work with a real cohort on e-learning, which gave me the opportunity to work with a team. This is why I encourage volunteering and networking, because through that, I found one of my first part-time content writing contract gigs, where I got to write some content for e-learning. The person I worked closely with knew I was an English teacher and knew they were looking for content-writing contractors. I had just started working at an insurance company. They called me the regional creative lead, and I was responsible for reformatting their sales materials, primarily PowerPoint presentations. I got into the corporate world through networking; someone created a position for me to help the sales team clean up their materials. While it was not exactly instructional design, it was instructional design adjacent. At the time, none of my other applications were coming through. There is a lot of advice out there about not settling, and I agree with it if you have options. Do not settle for the lesser one. But if you are trying to get out of teaching and there is an offer in front of you that is better than what you are currently doing, see it as a stepping stone. It is okay to settle for the next step. That helped me get my first full-time e-learning job because they liked that I did not just have teaching experience but also a bit of corporate experience, even though it was not in instructional design. That little bit of corporate experience helped me get my first full-time corporate job. They are all stepping stones. I stayed there a few months before landing my first full-time contract position with an airline. From there, I transitioned into what I am currently doing. All of it was just stepping stones, figuring out what was for me, what was not, and what I wanted to do next. I am pretty happy with where I am now. I am not in a rush to leave, and I am not looking for anything new. It took a few steps to get here, but I got here.

It's not like in teaching, where you find a position and maybe stay at the same school for 20-plus years and stay as a teacher for that same amount of time. You may be at your first position for 1-3 years and then move on for various reasons.

Right. If you can find that 20-year job, awesome. Usually, you're not going to do that in your first corporate job, but if you do, kudos to you.

Don't you have a graphics background...is that natural and self-taught or did you go to school for that?

It's mostly self-taught. Natural, I guess. I've been in several church roles previously where we had to put promotional materials out and we didn't really have the budget to pay for a graphic designer. You kind of figure out how to use tools on your own and how to make things look good. I knew Canva and a little bit of Photoshop, Illustrator, and InDesign from previous church projects prior to teaching. Once I was a teacher, I added Microsoft Word and PowerPoint. Do you want your eLearning to look good? Yes. But that is not the end-all, be-all of eLearning. I've seen some pretty effective eLearning out there that doesn't look the best. But it still is effective in the learning aspect. I know there are a lot of people that really stress the graphic design part. I think as long as you can look at something and know what looks good and doesn't look good, then that's a start. I do think investing a little time into watching some YouTube videos or reading a book on the basics of design would be beneficial. I don't think you have to be an expert in design in order to be an instructional designer, even though it's in the title.

Do you have any resources that you would recommend for someone interested in instruction design?

There are plenty of free resources available. Teaching a Path to Learning and Development (TPLD) on LinkedIn is an excellent resource for teachers transitioning and even for those who aren't teachers. Their website and past webinars are worth exploring. Networking was crucial for me; I had a few people review and help reformat my resume. I also found value in volunteering. For instance, I served as the community manager for TPLD for a while, continuing the work already established and eventually passing it along to another instructional designer. On LinkedIn, Cara North shares helpful insights, and Tim Slade offers free content and a community for feedback on portfolio pieces. Following key professionals on LinkedIn helps you discover others in the field, and their posts provide valuable learning opportunities. Additionally, consider adjacent fields like UX/UI design, project management, and graphic design for inspiration and career possibilities.

If you work remotely, tell me about how you like or dislike it. Any advantages or disadvantages?

I'll start with the disadvantages, though I don't have many. If you're highly social, it can get lonely. I'm social but more introverted, so it doesn't affect me much. There are still ways to connect with your team. My team uses Microsoft Teams, and sometimes we have coworking sessions that end with casual chats. Another disadvantage is the lack of immediate assistance. In teaching, you could quickly ask a colleague next door for help. That's not as immediate. The advantages far outweigh the disadvantages. Tasks often take less time, leaving moments for quick chores, brain breaks, or even a walk during lunch. I eat healthier too, as I'm not limited to cafeteria food. Flexibility is another big plus. If you need to step away for an appointment, you can make up the hours later. Most workplaces are more focused on you getting the work done than sticking to rigid hours. There's no bell dictating when you can leave. Work-life balance is significantly better. You can even travel, work during the day, and explore at night. Some wonder if I miss summer breaks or holidays like spring and winter break. I don't! As a teacher, those breaks were never really free time. I was always planning for the next quarter or year. Now, when I shut off my computer, I'm done. Even if I think about a project, it's not as stressful because there's no class waiting for me the next day. Remote work removes the constant pressure of always performing.

What advice would you give to someone considering leaving teaching for a new career?

What's going to help you upskill, and what will you focus on? Volunteering and networking were key for me in building my portfolio. Start by looking at job descriptions to identify the tools and skills most commonly required, and focus your efforts there. My biggest advice is to shut out some of the noise on LinkedIn and similar spaces. While many people have advice to share, you'll often encounter contradictory information, so stay focused on what aligns with your goals. Seek out people who have transitioned recently. Look at what their portfolios are presenting and how they structured their resumes. Because the career environment, the career-seeking culture, all of that is constantly changing. It's a lot different than it was in 2021 when I transitioned. So I can tell you all day how I transitioned but that might not be applicable to today's culture. When we transitioned in 2021, it was a job seekers' market. There were definitely enough opportunities out there for everyone. It's the buyer's market. There have been several layoffs at big companies with L&D teams and so if you're transitioning, you're not just competing against the 10,000 other teachers. You're now competing against some of the people with years of experience who are also looking for their next job because they just got laid off. I am not saying that you can't compete with them, but some of the advice about salary out there is just not as current. They are telling people to negotiate up. Negotiate? You're putting yourself at a disadvantage because you are in the same talent pool as someone who has five or more years of experience. I'm just saying, you can't believe all the hype. There are people out there who will say, as a transitioning teacher, you can get a six-figure salary at an entry-level L&D position. That's just not the norm or that might be outdated information. There may be stories of people who have done it, but how old are those stories? Don't compare yourself to others just because someone else got the position. If you don't get that, it's okay. You're still successful, you're still doing fine. You're valuable, you're worthy.

I had a teacher reach out to me regarding her resume, and I know why she did it, because this was the advice that we got when you are in that vacuum of "transferable skills" and you think that it is ok, not because you're trying to lie, but because this is all that you hear and that is changing our titles from teacher to "instructional designer". Have you seen this happen?

We can translate the skills but not the job. Initially, I put "Instructional Designer" on my resume because that was the advice we had been getting. If you look at the day-to-day duties of an instructional designer and compare them to what a teacher does, it seems like the closest match. However, I found myself in an interview where the interviewer asked me, "Tell me about your experience as an instructional designer." I immediately got flustered because I knew what he meant by instructional designer did not match what I meant. I stumbled through my explanation, trying to align my experience with the role. At the end of the interview, he was really nice but told me I shouldn't feel like I have to hide my experience as an educator. He also said he could see right through the title. Nobody was fooled. After this experience, I changed all my school titles to "Instructor," thinking at the time that this was the closest I could get to a corporate title without stretching the truth too much. Going back to when we were hiring for a position on our team, we saw someone who did the same thing. The first impression wasn't, "Oh, look at all this instructional design experience," but instead, "This person is not being forthright regarding their experience." It was clear they were a teacher who had listed "Instructional Designer" for their teaching experience.

Something I've observed over the last year is teachers on LinkedIn embracing the notion, 'I'm just going to get out there and do it,' without making many changes on my part as a teacher. Have you noticed this trend?

Everyone's looking for the easy way, wondering, "How do I do this without putting work into it?" For instance, we just added a position to our team. So, we've been sifting through resumes and portfolios and initially, the job posting didn't ask for a portfolio; it was recommended. But you have to understand when you're applying for a job and there are 150 people against you, and we've got 20 with portfolios, then which ones do you think we're going to look at first? If you don't submit your portfolio, you're not giving yourself an edge by not including one. I kind of roll my eyes every time I see someone groaning that teachers aren't being given a chance. It's nothing against you, and it's not that this job doesn't want to give teachers a shot. However, I think a lot of that comes from misguided people trying to pass their teaching experience as corporate experience without being upfront. Do I disagree with job descriptions that say, "Don't apply if you're a teacher," or whatever? Yes, I absolutely disagree with that! But I think you can't go to the other extreme of thinking that you should be considered based on your teacher experience without showing any attempt at upskilling or even translating your experience on your resume. You have to show some initiative in your job transition.

Resources: Teaching: A Path to Learning and Development (TPLD)

LinkedIn https://www.linkedin.com/groups/12490007/

https://www.teachlearndev.org/

LinkedIn & Personal Branding Coach - Angela
Taught for 8 years - Grades: K - 5

What is your title?

I am a LinkedIn and personal branding coach, freelancing with founders, CEOs, and small business owners to build their brands on and off LinkedIn. I am also interviewing for a full-time role in marketing and branding.

If you had to put a title to that, if you were at an organization, what would that title be?

It would be along the lines of a Growth Manager or a Brand Engagement Manager.

What would be an entry-level position for someone working their way up to your current role, and what would their responsibilities be?

Marketing is a pretty large umbrella. There are lots of different things you can do - operations, and SEO analytics. What I like to do is the content creation - it's the writing, the storytelling, building relationships, building the brand, developing the audience. There is also being a Social Media Manager when you have your hands in whatever that company wants. Typically Instagram, LinkedIn, some want to do TikTok, some want to do X (formerly Twitter), or Facebook. Another role is Demand

Generation Specialists or Digital Marketing Specialists or Associates. I would recommend that you niche down and figure out what you like and what your strengths are. You can kind of go up from there. When I first got into marketing, I was a Social Media Influencer, where I worked on employer branding. Then I went into Account-Based Marketing.

I heard a couple of things. Building the brand and demand generation to me, that sounds a lot like Instagram and the whole social media scene. How did you begin with social media?

I wanted to break into the corporate tech world, but I wasn't sure what I wanted to do. I unintentionally started building my brand on LinkedIn, and it became a focus of my work. As a social media manager, I've worked with companies to build their online presence. I pivoted into the B2B industry, working with SaaS companies, and focused on LinkedIn as the primary platform. I built my own brand and helped other companies establish theirs. My approach is inbound, relying on people reaching out to me on LinkedIn rather than paid advertising.

My interview process is also inbound, with people contacting me directly after seeing my profile. I work on a project-by-project basis, taking on part-time work with clients who reach out to me. We discuss the project details, and I provide a proposal and deliverables. I believe in sticking to the contract and delivering high-quality work. Coaching clients also reach out to me for one-on-one calls, where I share tips and tricks to help them improve their online presence. Having a strong brand makes marketing yourself or your products much easier, and it's a key step towards achieving your goals.

How did you go from being a teacher to writing proposals for clients and telling them the types of services you would be able to provide?

I think it's important to acknowledge that I'm aware of my strengths and the value I bring to the table, but I also struggle with imposter syndrome and wondering if I truly belong. I've always been a writer and have grown up with technology and social media. However, I had to learn about marketing terms, strategies, and proposal writing through research and online resources like Google and LinkedIn.

I believe it's crucial to connect with people who are ahead of you in their careers and learn from their experiences. I didn't always understand the algorithm and best practices, but I've learned over time. Now, I'm comfortable sharing my knowledge and experiences with others. I try to be authentic and showcase my personality, work, and motivations to connect with others.

Do you follow anyone on LinkedIn or listen to podcasts or books related to this field?

I follow companies and content creator groups on LinkedIn and subscribe to several marketing newsletters. I enjoy the "Marketing Millennials" podcast because they inspire bold and creative thinking. I also follow marketing professionals, including VPs and people at companies I admire. I suggest identifying roles or companies you aspire to and connecting with those individuals. This builds name recognition for future opportunities. For upskilling, I used LinkedIn Learning and free courses on Trailhead and Salesforce. During my transition, I relied entirely on free resources like YouTube, Coursera, EdX, and Udemy because I could not afford to spend money on courses or career coaching.

I've seen your journey and I see the time that you are putting in. Talk to me about that.

It's a lot of work. It is a full-time job. I think this might sound harsh and I don't mean it the way it's going to sound. I am very lucky and kind of privileged on one side. I'm unlucky because I'm on a single income. If I'm not working, I don't have a partner to help me out. But on the other hand, I don't have children or family. Right now, it's me and my dog, so I can devote a ton of time on LinkedIn and job searching. I don't have to make dinner full-time. If I don't do laundry one day, I'll wear sweatpants.

I don't have as many responsibilities as some other people, so I was really able to give this my full attention. I understand other people may not be able to spend all these hours on LinkedIn every day and job search. What I say to teachers, especially if you only have a teaching background and haven't done other things in your adult professional life, is to network. I recommend LinkedIn. Sure, there are other ways to do it. I recommend building your brand on LinkedIn, which means optimizing your profile and engaging with others. If you're just sending your resume out, unless you want to be an educational consultant or give PD, but if you're trying to get away from education, you should show people what you can do rather than just sending your resume out. For example, if you want to go into marketing like me, or if you have friends who went into project management or sales, employers will see that you were a teacher and wrote lesson plans, and you probably won't get the interview. Showing people who you are outside of the resume is really important. Going back to the point of the question, sometimes people think, "I'm a teacher, I do 100 different things, I wear all these hats, all of these are transferable, I am a project manager." Well, that's great. We know that. But they don't know that, so it is up to you to connect the dots. You can't assume people will get it. You have to tell the story, connect the dots, and show, "I did this, which means I achieved this result, and this is how it translates to this." You have to throw your teaching resume completely out the window. No one cares how many papers you graded or how many lesson plans you wrote or things you juggled. You have to quantify and put metrics out there and results, and be very specific and explicit. They should be able to read it and know how your experience relates to the position. You have to really earn that interview. Connect the dots and be clear on what you're good at and what you bring to the table. Focus on one thing. Don't say you're open to customer success, sales, and other areas. That's called praying and spraying, and it's not a good tactic. Really hone in on something. Maybe after a few months, you realize that's not what you want anymore. Great, move on to something else. But don't overextend yourself and try to do everything, because people will think you have no idea what you want to do or what you're good at. So, focus.

How did you become a teacher?

I wanted to teach from a very young age, probably around five years old. I loved being in front of a room sharing knowledge and would play teacher with my dad and sister in our basement, using a blackboard and whiteboard to teach whatever came to mind. Teaching and helping others always drew me in. Over time, I considered other careers like becoming a vet or marine biologist, but I always returned to teaching. In high school, I told my family about my dream, and while they supported me, they encouraged me to explore other options, knowing teachers don't earn much. I attended an engineering camp, which was fun, but it only reinforced my desire to teach and impact the next generation of leaders. I pursued a dual major in elementary and special education, which involved a lot of coursework and student teaching, but I loved every moment. I was the first in my cohort to land a job before graduation. Over eight years, I taught six subjects, driven by a passion to help as many children as possible. Growing up, I had mostly great teachers. My favorite, a secondary teacher, remains a mentor I'm still connected with on Facebook. In contrast, my third-grade teacher was the worst, solidifying my desire to ensure every child has a teacher like the one I had in second grade. I wanted to shape education and even dreamed of working in the Department of Education to influence the system positively.

Why did you leave teaching?

There are so many factors, so many reasons why, but I would say the idea of leaving never dawned on me until 2020, which was Covid. I was living in the Netherlands when Covid started teaching at an international school. Later that year, we went back into school in person until the end of the year, which I didn't mind. I had six students in my class, so we were able to separate and wear masks. I moved back to the states in August 2020 and returned to my old teaching position, which was virtual for the beginning of that year. Then, in February or March of '21, they brought us back into the classroom to do hybrids, which was interesting. Kids were in front of me, and then I'd have twelve on the laptop, and we were supposed to teach them all at the same time. What I realized was that I really love teaching virtually. I loved working from home, being able to walk my own dog every day, and not pay a dog walker. I liked taking a real lunch, sleeping in a bit more because I didn't have to commute, and the flexibility to work from anywhere. In 2020, I lived in Baltimore and visited my parents in Savannah from Thanksgiving break until January. Being able to spend all that time with them while still working made me want to spend more time with my family. Even simple things like going to the doctors or the dentist without taking a half day off work were easier. Unfortunately, in April 2020, I lost my grandmother to COVID, which made me realize what my priorities are and how you never know what tomorrow is going to bring. That's kind of how it all started. All these things started falling into place. I eventually got COVID, even though I was already vaccinated. It was like Christmas of '21 school year, so I couldn't go back to school for a few days. I was actually happy about that and was dreading going back in. That's when I realized, what happened? I used to love teaching, and now I don't want to do it. So in January 2022, that's when I got on LinkedIn, and that's when this whole thing started.

Like you said, COVID changed a lot of people thinking about leaving before. Did you consider any other career choices?

I didn't know what I was able to do. I think many teachers struggle with "what can I do next?" You don't even know because you went to school to be a teacher, and you thought that's what you would do until you retired. At first, I was thinking about educational roles. I can give PD to teachers, be an educational consultant, work at a tech company, or write curriculum. I looked into curriculum development, and then I realized very quickly, that sounds horrible! I do not want to be writing curriculum! I then made a list of what I loved about teaching and what I didn't enjoy. That shaped my job search. I wanted to leave education altogether. I was open to doing something else at an edtech company, but I also knew all the other transitioning teachers were looking at edtech companies. So I was thinking, you know what? I just want to go to tech and get out of here. I went to LinkedIn, not really knowing what I wanted to do. Networking with people, learning how it worked, connecting with people in all different roles and industries. I looked into customer success, something many teachers think about. And I know I'd be good at it because I'm good with people and I can train well. I've done that, I've done PDs, I've done onboarding. But I realized again after spending more time networking and having coffee chats and talking to people that I didn't want to be in face-to-face meetings all day. I really want to be able to go heads down on something and be creative. I've always loved to write, building relationships, all these things happening. I've built this community. Marketing makes sense. It's fine to start your job search thinking, "Okay, this is kind of what I'm interested in," and then learning and growing and changing. I think equally, it's important to figure out what you want to do, what you enjoy, what your skills are. It's also important to identify, let that lead the way. And here I am.

I know you are seeking your next role, tell me more.

I pivoted over a year ago now. I'm searching for my next role. I'm very focused on which roles I want to do. Marketing is exactly where I want to be. I've loved the ride so far. I'm excited to see what I do.

Looking at your LinkedIn page and seeing previous roles, talk to me a little bit about your roles at Canopy.

At Canopy, I worked as an in-house marketer. When I joined, I was the only one. Later, we brought on a Head of Marketing, and I joined her team as an account marketing strategist, focusing on account-based marketing (ABM). ABM involves targeting key accounts and companies in marketing campaigns and outreach efforts. My role included prospecting and conducting market research using various tools like Zoom Info and Salesforce to gather intent signals. I also monitored who was visiting our website, engaging with our emails, and interacting with our LinkedIn page. I synthesized this information to create our Ideal Customer Profile (ICP) and propose targeted campaigns. This approach helped us refine our marketing strategies effectively.

Do you miss teaching?

No, I don't miss it at all. And even if I was unemployed for a while, if I couldn't find a job for months and months, and I was kind of running low on funds and getting a bit desperate, I still wouldn't go back to teaching. I'd bartend or work at Starbucks instead. Teaching is emotionally and mentally draining. You do so much, yet I didn't feel paid or respected enough. While I don't regret the experience, and it will help me as a mother one day, my time, sanity, and flexibility matter too much now. I've almost doubled my salary and gained flexibility without commuting. I couldn't afford my current lifestyle on a teacher's salary. Unless the system changes to pay teachers more, give them more time, and make it sustainable, I wouldn't return. Teaching as it stands isn't a fun experience.

Do you miss summer break?

No, when you tell people that you're leaving teaching, and they say, "But what about the summers and the holidays?" That response makes my blood boil. First off, I wasn't paid for summer breaks, I was a ten-month employee, and summer vacations cost more since everyone travels then. Summers were necessary to decompress after a draining school year, but most teachers work during that time. I worked as a camp counselor, bartender, and more, while also planning for the next school year. Now, being out of teaching feels like a sigh of relief. I sleep in, spend time with my dog, and enjoy creativity, autonomy, and being treated as an adult. I can work on my own schedule, start early or late, and live without the chaos of 25 kids, ringing bells, and disruptive behavior. My quality of life has drastically improved. I have a great social life, go out during the week, and feel energized. The freedom to take breaks on my terms, not by a school's schedule. That to me is worth so much more.

What advice would you give to someone considering leaving teaching for a new career?

My advice would be to start today, even if you plan to finish out the school year. Start building relationships, engaging with others, and learning from them on LinkedIn. Consider free upskilling or LinkedIn Learning. Begin exploring different careers to see if they align with your interests. People often ask me if I would have done anything differently. The only thing I wish is that I had started sooner. I began in January and spent four or five months building my brand and actively job-seeking. I resigned and spent July, August, and September as a true job seeker, receiving offers in early October. Starting early made a significant difference. If you feel overwhelmed or unfamiliar with LinkedIn, consider my LinkedIn and personal brand coaching sessions. I keep my rates affordable, especially for teachers, who often face high costs for career coaching. I offer both 30-minute and 60-minute sessions, and teachers receive an additional discount. Feel free to contact me for support in your transition.

UPDATE:

As of April 15, 2024, I began my role as the Creative Director at Digital Reach Online Solutions. In this position, I lead a talented creative team dedicated to developing high-quality marketing and branding campaigns. My responsibilities include overseeing all content and design production, ensuring consistency and excellence across various deliverables such as advertisements, blogs, ebooks, and print materials. My team produces a wide range of marketing assets tailored to our clients' needs, including ads, blogs, direct mail, emails, social media posts, and web pages. Our client base spans diverse industries, from nonprofit organizations and historical societies to dental implant providers and B2B SaaS companies. Each project is unique, reflecting the client's specific goals and requirements. Essentially, our role is to act as the marketing team, or to augment a company's small marketing team, with the primary objectives of raising brand awareness, increasing engagement, and generating leads.

Market Researcher - Dr. Julia
Taught for 16 Years - Grades: Middle & High School, University
Subjects: French & Spanish

Talk to me about your job search experience. It has not been too long since you went through the process. Do you remember how many applications you submitted? How many interviews did you land? What were your overall stats?

I submitted, I think, 101 applications. I didn't rely on the quick-apply options often. I tailored my applications, including a customized cover letter and resume for each position.

What types of positions were you applying for?

I was applying for different types of research positions. I focused on roles involving qualitative research. Some were university-based research positions in social sciences, but most were market research roles, as that's what I was primarily targeting. I also applied for research jobs with nonprofits. So, from January 2023 to December 2023, I submitted about 100 applications.

Out of the 100 applications, how many granted you an interview?

I think it was three.

That's a very small number. It really highlights how difficult this market is right now, here in 2024. What would you want to tell teachers about the application process and the overall job search?

First of all, starting a new career is doable, but you need to prepare. Research thoroughly before quitting your job, if possible. Spend six months to a year researching, talking to people, connecting on LinkedIn, and doing informational interviews. I learned a lot by hearing about others' career paths. You also need to learn the industry's terminology, which differs from education. For example, transitioning to learning and development may have some differences. Knowing the language of your field is essential. Collect as much information as you can and be prepared for the process to take longer than expected. I was told to start applying four to six months before wanting to work, but it took me a year. Have a backup plan. If finding your dream job takes longer, consider part-time work to make ends meet. Stay flexible and realistic while working toward your goals.

How important was LinkedIn in your job search? Were you using it before you started looking?

For me, it was vital. I got on LinkedIn when I started seriously looking into careers outside of academia. Near the beginning of that process, I attended a month-long virtual event for linguists who wanted to transition out of academia. During the event, I attended panel discussions and talks, and the one thing I kept hearing was how important LinkedIn is. That's how I started connecting with people who had already made the transition. For me, LinkedIn was critical for connecting with others and learning from their experiences. If you're pursuing anything in industry, you really need a LinkedIn profile.

Can you walk me through what you do? I'd like to understand the deliverables and projects. What happens before you start a project? Once you're working on it, what are your responsibilities, who do you interact with, and what happens after your part is finished?

I've been in this role for three months, so I'll explain it as best as I can. There are still some parts of the process before and after my role that I'm not entirely clear on, but I'll give you an overview. I work for a private equity consulting firm. When a corporation wants to invest in or buy another company, they hire us to conduct research to make an informed decision. My company has two sides: the investing side, where the team has a finance background (not me), and the market research side, where I work. If a company is considering adding another company to its portfolio, they come to us. The finance team begins by conducting initial research, often involving experts and gathering data. Once the project reaches a certain stage, market researchers, like me, step in. We work across various industries, which I enjoy for the variety. Right now, I'm working on an aviation software project. When I joined this project, I was given an overview of the industry and the client's objectives. For this project, I conduct research primarily through phone interviews. We're cold calling, so I receive a list of contacts and reach out to them directly. I ask if they have time for a short conversation, following an interview guide provided at the start. The guide outlines key questions, so I prioritize the most critical ones first, depending on how much time the interviewee has. After each call, I type up a summary of the conversation. This includes formatting and ensuring grammatical accuracy, as the write-up becomes the deliverable. Essentially, I capture the voice of the consumer (or Voice of the Customer) to provide insights into what's happening in the market—in this case, aviation software. Each day, I go through my list, conduct calls, and send my summaries to the investment team. At the end of the day, we have a debrief where market researchers and the investment team discuss findings and client updates. Since the investment side communicates with the client, their updates sometimes lead us to adjust our approach. Projects typically last about three weeks but can vary. Once my part is done, the investment team compiles all the research into a summary or presentation for the client. At that point, my involvement ends, so I'm not fully aware of what happens afterward.

Did you get this position through someone you knew, or was it kind of cold?

No, I didn't know anyone.

What skills did you have to demonstrate to be in the running?

I'll say that the market researchers they hire come from a variety of backgrounds in terms of education and experience. Some people come from sales, others from law, so it really varies. What I believe they were most looking for were people who are detail-oriented, very organized, able to communicate well, and who enjoy talking with others. In this role, I'm often on the phone speaking with people, so communication is key. I think my research experience helped, but it wasn't necessarily a requirement. It was more of a bonus than a prerequisite.

Are there pre-made templates for the reports you create?

Yes, I'm given an interview guide that goes through the questions one by one. It's designed to collect both quantitative and qualitative data. For example, there might be a straightforward question like, "How long have you been in this role?" For that, I don't have to write a full sentence; there's just a space to indicate the answer. For most questions, there are text boxes where I write commentary based on what the person said. It's not word-for-word; I can take some liberties to ensure it's grammatically correct and communicates the essence of their response. Usually, I go through the questions in order and type directly into the guide, which is a Word document. Some people prefer taking notes by hand, but I find it faster to type during the interview. Afterward, I polish everything by putting responses into complete sentences, double-checking spelling, and ensuring it's formatted properly. I like to cross my T's and dot my I's.

That's the interview document. When you report out, are you using learning personas or similar frameworks? Or is it more about entities, not people? And the report you give

at meetings, is it a PowerPoint, or do you combine your information with someone else's?

Yeah, that's actually on the investment team's side. I submit the completed interview guides to them, and they're the ones who create the deliverables that are presented to the client. It's a very narrow focus for what I'm doing. In many market research roles, you'd use different methods and be responsible for creating the presentations and reports yourself.

If you wanted to move up, would you become a senior market researcher? What does that progression look like?

That's actually one of the unusual things about this position—there's not really anywhere to move up. I knew that going in, so I'm fine with it. I just know this won't be a 20-year job for me. That said, there are researchers who've been here for 10 years or more. There are opportunities to get raises during your reviews, which happen twice a year, but in terms of moving to a different position within the research side, there's really nowhere to go.

If I'm a teacher, how can I target a role like this? It seems easier to enter than other market research jobs. Any tips, or did it just happen for you?

To be honest, I really just stumbled upon it. One tricky thing about industry jobs is the job titles are so hard to navigate when you're searching. The search term I used was "qualitative researcher" because qualitative research is what I love. Sometimes you'll find roles labeled as "market researcher," but there are so many different titles out there.

This particular job is called "market researcher," like many others, but the job duties are very different from others with the same title. So I don't really know of a way to narrow it down beyond trying different search terms. But yes, this role does have an easier entry point. I found it challenging to get into a new field because I didn't have the specific training or background that other roles were looking for.

That leads me to my next question. Since you've recently transitioned, even though you're three months in, can you walk me through your job search timeline? Did you leave teaching before starting this job, or were you still teaching while you searched?

The most recent thing I did before this role was being a full-time PhD student, which lasted six years. During that time, I had different part-time jobs at the university. For three of those years, I was an instructor of record for French classes, though they technically called me a teaching assistant. Then, in my final year of the program, I was the teaching assistant supervisor. I wasn't actually teaching that year, and it was during those last few months of the program—around January 2023—that I started looking for a job. I hadn't finished my degree yet, but I began applying for jobs as time allowed. I completed my degree in May 2023, and the rest of that year was spent job searching. While I was looking, I did some French tutoring on the side, but I didn't go directly from teaching to this job.

Why did you leave teaching?

I worked for private schools and I left in 2017. It was kind of a two-fold thing. For about four years, I had been thinking about pursuing a PhD in linguistics. I had known for over 15 years that I wanted to get a PhD—I just didn't know in what field. That desire kept growing stronger, but at the same time, I realized that teaching was becoming very draining for me. It was physically, mentally, and emotionally exhausting.

There were different reasons why it was so draining. I started feeling like I had to be constantly entertaining in my classes just to keep students' attention. It was like I was an actress in front of a group all day, and as an introvert, that was really exhausting. I loved the subject material and was passionate about conveying it, but the constant performance, combined with all the accommodations I had to make, made it difficult. I understood the reasons behind the accommodations, but it was just another layer of exhaustion. Teaching isn't a nine-to-five job either, and the demands didn't align well with my personality.

Why isn't it a nine-to-five job?

At almost every school I worked at, I was the only French teacher, which meant I had to teach all levels of French offered. For example, while a math teacher might teach two preps, like algebra and geometry, I had five classes, each a different level. Planning for multiple levels took much more time than grading extra assignments for a single subject. I only had one planning period each day, and while I used it wisely, it was never enough to plan lessons, grade assignments, and meet my own standards. I cared deeply about my students and wanted to create a great experience. I could have relied on the textbook and pre-made multiple-choice quizzes to save time, but that is not who I am, and I do not believe it is the best way for students to learn.

I'm so glad you mentioned books. Many assume teaching relies on textbooks, but in my six years teaching resource geometry, we used created and approved resources alongside our content knowledge.

I will say that I almost always had a book to use, with only one exception. There were even some that I really liked, and I used them. But I never relied on them as the sole resource for my students to learn.

With so many teachers wanting to leave, do you have any comments on the current educational system?

I moved frequently within a 10-year period and changed schools a lot and one thing that was consistent, was inconsistency. It felt like we were always reinventing the wheel.

For example, I wanted to be able to use the same curriculum for several years and improve it gradually, refining my teaching each year. Instead, there were always big changes, whether it was a new curricula, new initiatives, or other major shifts thrown at me. I'm a very self-reflective person, and I had ideas for improving my teaching, but I never had the time or space to implement those ideas because of all the constant changes. That was one of the most frustrating and exhausting aspects of teaching for me.

Update: I have just completed one year in this role. I sometimes work on projects that involve cold calling, but I most often conduct introduced calls now. The interview questions are the same in nature, but the client's target company has reached out to some of their customers and introduced my research firm to let them know that we will be speaking with them. I enjoy these calls much more than cold calls.

Resources:

Market Researcher

To transition into market research, start by understanding the two main areas: qualitative research (e.g., focus groups, interviews) and quantitative research (e.g., surveys, data analysis). Each requires unique skills and tools.

Tools and Techniques:

Qualitative: Use flipcharts or handwritten notes during focus groups to capture themes. Record sessions for review. AI tools like ChatGPT can help summarize, but rely on your critical thinking to interpret insights.

Quantitative: Familiarize yourself with software like SPSS, Excel, or Tableau for data analysis and visualization. Start with simple analysis plans based on objectives and hypotheses.

Learning Resources:

Join professional organizations like ESOMAR, QRCA, or the Insights Association for webinars, guides, and training.

Take specialized workshops (e.g., RIVA for qualitative methods) or online courses for survey design and storytelling with data.

Workflows:

For qualitative work, identify themes through active listening and contextual understanding, not just what's said but what it means.

For quantitative work, structure your analysis with clear goals, focusing on actionable trends.

Actionable Steps:

Build foundational skills in both qualitative and quantitative methods.

Network through LinkedIn or attend industry events to connect with experienced professionals.

Practice asking specific, well-framed questions to improve your understanding and communication.

Start small with tools like SPSS and Excel, then expand to more advanced techniques as you grow.

Books:

The Market Research Toolbox by Edward F. McQuarrie: https://www.amazon.com/Market-Research-Toolbox-Edward-McQuarrie/dp/1452272006

Marketing Research: An Applied Orientation by Naresh K. Malhotra: https://www.amazon.com/Marketing-Research-Applied-Orientation-Malhotra/dp/0134734843

Questionnaire Design by Ian Brace: https://www.amazon.com/Questionnaire-Design-Structure-Material-Effective/dp/0749481977

Free Online Courses:

Market Research by the University of California, Davis on Coursera: https://www.coursera.org/courses?query=market+research

Market Research Essentials on Alison: https://alison.com/course/market-research-essentials

Market Research for Decision Making on Udemy: https://www.udemy.com/course/market-research-/

YouTube Channels:

Qualtrics: https://www.youtube.com/user/qualtrics

Market Research Institute International (MRII): https://www.youtube.com/user/ResearchOnline

Research Rockstar: https://www.youtube.com/user/researchrockstar

Marketing Analyst - Rak
Taught for 6 years - Grade: 3rd

Rak, how did you even get into this career?

My wife is an analyst. At the time, she was a marketing analyst, and I got into it because, when I was teaching, I had some results, and we were getting married. We were paying for a wedding, and she said, "Hey, you can work for my company during the summer." I thought, okay, why not? It was a job working with the White Pages, going through listings and advertisements. I sat at a desk, going line by line through a spreadsheet. I had my earbuds in, listening to music while I worked. She told me, "You can do whatever you want in the office." For me, that felt like winning the lottery. I started out by reviewing advertisements and doing web analytics. My job was to check if a client's website was up to par. It was an upsell opportunity for the sales team. I'd find things missing on a website, hand them a report, and they'd take it to the client. Today, we'd probably call that role a web analyst, though back then, it was more likely part of a web developer's job. Basically, I critiqued clients' websites. I'd check if they had a thank-you page, make sure all the tabs were in order, and confirm everything was properly coded in HTML. These days, a web developer would run diagnostics to get the same information.

In your current role, tell me what i would see as the consumer, what do I see? For example, you mentioned Facebook. What's

the end result of your work that I would notice? You're behind the scenes, but what's visible to me?

Think of it like a two-way mirror. On your side of the mirror, you're scrolling through social media, watching Netflix, shopping on Amazon, or just doing your normal online activities. Whether it's shopping for clothes, buying tickets, or streaming entertainment, that's what you see. On the other side of the mirror, there are people like me who collect data. We gather information about each user's activity. It sounds like a lot, but it happens with every click, every page you visit, and every purchase you make. These actions leave digital footprints, which are collected as data. I track those footprints using metrics like impressions, clicks, and conversions. For example, let's say you're at the mall, and you see a sign for a Nike store advertising a 50% off sale. That sign is the impression. If you decide to walk into the store, that's the click. If you buy something, that's the conversion. My role is to collect and analyze all that data. I might report to Nike, saying, "Dina, a mom of two, age 50, living in this location, made a purchase." Nike takes that data, adds it to their database, and uses it to target you with more ads and opportunities.

What are your deliverable? What are you presenting, and what happens at the meetings you attend?

My deliverable is the collection and presentation of that data. I use tools like Google AdWords and other platforms to manage and track ads. There's also a platform we use to determine where purchases took place, alongside proprietary systems built by the company, often similar to Salesforce. Once the data is collected, we use tools like Power BI or Data Studio to create visualizations. We present these insights to clients, either in meetings or through offline reports. The tools we use include Power BI, Data Studio, Google Analytics, and Google AdWords. AI is massive right now. It's growing quickly, and everyone is diving into it. Web development isn't as central in my role, but it still plays a part. The value of my position lies in staying updated with the constant changes in platforms, algorithms, and technologies. Keeping up with these changes such as troubleshooting and adapting to new tools is what makes the job valuable. If you can stay ahead of these shifts, there's significant earning potential in this field.

What do you say in these meetings, and who are the decision-makers? What are their roles, and how do they use your input?

In my position, I collect user data. Right now, millennials and Gen Z are huge because they're the new "pig in the python." That term refers to the largest and most powerful generation of our time. Boomers have exited the python, and now it's swallowing millennials and Gen Z. A lot of them don't realize it, but we saw it coming years ago. Ten years ago, we knew these generations would become a major force. Colleges, hospitals, and others saw it too. What we didn't anticipate was how the pandemic would escalate this shift. The pandemic gave Gen Z and millennials unprecedented buying power, $100 billion. These generations spend freely, unlike Gen X, my generation, which carries the most debt. We have mortgages, children, and student loans, while they are spending on experiences, shopping, and entertainment. For example, before the pandemic, McDonald's jobs paid $7 an hour. Now they pay $14 an hour, a 100 percent increase. Retail wages have also doubled. And what do people do when they get a raise? They go shopping. I track this data and report it to companies that want to understand how these generations are spending. Data is gold. It's the new oil. It drives wealth generation, and I help businesses leverage it.

Would this you be similar to that of a marketing research analyst?

Yes. If you're looking for a similar position, try searching for roles like "digital media specialist" or "digital campaign manager" on LinkedIn. These positions overlap a lot, and people wear many hats. It's similar to teaching where we were educators, parents, and social workers all at once. In this field, you might start as a digital sales coordinator. It's an entry-level job that supports sales teams. Essentially, you act as an admin for the sales process, handling the logistics of ad campaigns. From there, you can move up. Coordinators learn the products, processes, and relationships, which opens doors to positions like ad operations, trafficking, or production. These roles come with pay increases of $10,000 to $15,000. Trafficking is especially lucrative. It involves taking the ads created by production and working with ad operations to ensure they run smoothly. Ad operations tracks how well digital products perform, analyzing pacing, success rates, and potential issues. This analysis helps sales teams communicate effectively with clients. Many in ad operations eventually become analysts. Analysts get more face time with clients and leadership, analyzing data and providing insights. From there, you can move into roles like associate analyst, director of analytics, or even director of ad operations. The career ladder moves quickly. It doesn't take 5-10 years to advance. You can climb within two to three years if you're proactive and adaptable.

Is there anything else your position involves?

I can join sales calls. Just this morning, a salesperson came to me with an idea, and I helped refine it. Sometimes I ride along with the sales team to meet clients. If a salesperson needs support, I can step in and explain how the product delivers value. Salespeople can't always provide detailed explanations, especially if clients have concerns about budgets or past experiences. That's where I step in. For example, I can tell a client, "If your budget is $15,000 but the project requires $30,000, this isn't going to work." I can provide clarity and avoid unrealistic expectations, which salespeople may struggle to address directly.

What do you listen to? What do you read? Are there any podcasts or resources you'd recommend for a teacher to start exploring this field?

My number one platform is Twitter, followed by Reddit. They're nerd-central for me, and I get a lot of my news and job-related insights from them. On Twitter and Reddit, you can find a lot of valuable information. For example, I've worked with graphic designers and web designers who were hired as directors with just two years of degrees. They didn't need a four-year degree. Their value came from self-learning and staying up-to-date. The thing is, you can go to school and learn the basics, but your real value comes from keeping a pulse on how information moves and evolves. I've met people with two-year degrees who started at $70,000 or $80,000 more than me when I first started and quickly moved into six-figure roles. It's all about self-pacing and continuous learning.

So on Twitter, what should people look for? Are there keywords or accounts you'd recommend?

It's really organic. On Reddit, it's easier because there are specific subreddits like Google Analytics and Ad Operations. Those are great for diving into the topics I've learned about. The key is to get into the habit of reading a lot and following the right people on Twitter. Over time, you'll know which headlines to stop on and which to skip. My wife, who's also an analyst, would tell you to focus on certifications like Power BI and SQL. SQL is huge, and if you get it, you can make a lot of money. Power BI, data visualization tools, and Excel are also essential skills in this field.

What else would you like my audience to know about transitioning or your journey?

My biggest struggle was getting past the thinking and talking stage and actually taking action. I had to push excuses and fear. Reinventing myself was hard, but I had to do it for my kids—they were my biggest motivation. The opportunities are there, especially now. You just need a goal, a plan, and a commitment to execute. You have to move quickly and find mentors to guide you. I won't sugarcoat it. It's hard. It's like hauling a wheelbarrow full of wood across the yard; you're going to fumble before you get it right. But the reward is worth it. There's risk, but there's also great reward.

Product Designer - Vanessa
Taught for 7 years - Grades: HS
Subject: ESOL, Spanish & World Cultures

Can you explain your role in the design process? Do you manage the entire project or just certain parts?

I think it's a little bit of both. Sometimes design is a visual conversation, and it can be the beginning steps to initiating your user flow, right? I'm at a startup company where I'm the only designer, and a lot of it is visionary work. I listen to what the stakeholders want, come up with a design, and ask, "Does this match what you envisioned?" From that point, we document the process and move forward.

Do you manage both user research (UXR) and design (UXD), or do you specialize in one area?

At a startup, I've had the unique opportunity to wear many hats, which has allowed me to gain exposure to different areas of UXR and UXD. It has its benefits and downfalls. I am a jack of all trades, but a TRUE master of none!

It sounds like there's a lot of planning and structure involved. I know that you attended a boot camp (Memorisely) for UX/UD and eventually became a T.A., did that experience help?

Yeah, I would say Memorisely definitely provided the foundation for design and the design process! You can only learn so much in a 15-week boot camp, and you have to apply everything. Luckily, when I was hired, I had incredible mentors who sat down with me and explained how things work in the tech industry. It wasn't anything I hadn't done with teaching or in the boot camp; it was more about fine-tuning the process.

Can you walk me through a project from start to finish?

I'm a product designer, and my team and I are working on a platform--a kind of software service that helps people understand their data better. My job is to figure out the overall plan for the product, like what features we need to create and when, and to make sure all the designs for the screens look and work great.

When I plan the product roadmap, it's a lot like how a teacher plans lessons and the curriculum for the whole year. We divide the year into four parts, just like school quarters. For each quarter, we focus on the most important features first, making sure those are really solid before moving on to the next set of features. By the time we finish, ideally, we have a complete and well-rounded product. It's like a student who starts the year knowing very little but, by the end, has learned a lot and can show it on a test. Our product starts simple and grows into something fully developed and useful.

Where does your part in the process end, and when does the development team take over?

My part ends when the design is selected for development, meaning the engineers are now going to take the design and build it. But I circle back into the loop after they've built the design and sent it to QA (quality assurance). Often, the requirement states that the design needs to match the Figma, so that's when I'm brought back into the loop to say, "Yes, this matches," or, "No, maybe the interaction or behavior of the design doesn't quite match the intention."

How do you handle the graphic design side of things? Is that something you developed along the way?

Long short, I am artistic to a certain degree, but not in the sense of a graphic designer. It's definitely something I think I have an eye for, but I've developed my skills within that by simply practicing. By no means am I the best graphic designer out there--I'm not. But I do know that I'm actively engaging in the community, reading about trends, and learning more every single day. I take 30 minutes a day to learn something new, so that's just my personal go-to thing.

Do you work in sprints, or is your workflow more flexible?

We do kind of operate within sprints, but we're a little bit more fluid. We have this new product, and we don't necessarily work in strict sprints. We work on what we need to until it's done, because it's constantly changing and growing. Oftentimes, we can get things done before the typical two-week sprint.

Has any of your design work been rejected? How do you handle that feedback?

It's less about rejecting the idea and more about tweaking it. "Can we add to this? Can we remove this?" It's iterative, meaning you start with one design, and it might grow or change multiple times before it meets the requirements.

Who's guiding you on your team, and how does leadership influence your design process?

My boss is amazing. He's been a UX designer, an architect, and an engineer for so long. He really leads the way but is probably one of the best bosses I've ever had. He literally says, "You do you. Go and create this thing. It looks awesome, and I trust you fully." That kind of trust and freedom is rare, and it allows me to be more creative.

It seems like your teaching skills are transferable. Can you talk more about that transition?

Now that you say that, what it really boils down to is just having a mentor to help guide you and grow with you, passing down the knowledge. A lot of the skills I used in teaching--like communication, planning, and organizing directly transfer to product design. You just need someone to show you how to apply them in a different context.

What challenges did you face as a junior designer transitioning from teaching? Were there any barriers that surprised you?

Yes, that's one of the biggest challenges for people transitioning from a different career path, especially if you're a junior designer. Many companies want someone with experience walking in versus growing and establishing a person. I was really lucky that someone believed in education and wanted to teach me, which helped ease the transition. But I did struggle with imposter syndrome, feeling like I wasn't supposed to be there because I was surrounded by people with more experience. Understanding the industry has also been a fun challenge. Much like teaching, we specialize in a particular area. This new 'area' for me happened to be the supply chain, and there are a lot of complexities within it!

What did you do to prepare for this field? You mentioned the boot camp but were there any other resources?

I read several design books and I've been active on multiple e-learning platforms such as Udemy and Domestika. There's a great one for designers called Uxcel and I really love to read the NN Group and I'm on Medium.

Knowing what you know now, what would you have changed about your preparation?

I wish I would have known more about the tech industry and how data really influences design, especially big data, which is where I'm at now. When you're in a boot camp and working with smaller companies, redesigning things, it's often not centered around data. And that's the most important part when you're building software for anyone who wants visibility into their data.

What advice would you give to someone considering leaving teaching for a new career?

I would say be brave and do it. Put in the time and effort that you put into education. It's the same principles: work hard, believe in yourself, and just keep going forward--one foot in front of the other.

Why did you leave teaching?

That's a good one. I have an article I posted on LinkedIn that talks about this. I was in a program called Flexible Personalized Learning, which involved quite a bit of design model thinking. The professional development surrounding that required us to think differently and incorporate students into decisions. We were re-envisioning what education could look like for students and redefining what a typical learning day was. We did a lot of cross-curricular work,

Then, COVID hit, and I was unhappy with going back to the traditional form while juggling online, hybrid, and in-person all at once. My partner at the time actually said, "You talk about design processes all the time. Have you thought about user experience design?" I was like, "What is that? Is there another career called that?" Seriously, we don't even let teachers explore different realms or give them the platform to advance in a different fashion than just education. It was them saying that me Googling it and then diving into the internet. That's when I realized, this is my calling. I can feel it!

What skills from teaching have been helpful in your new role?

There's a ton when you think about it. As a teacher, when you are lesson planning, you are designing and you're designing a curated experience for this tiny individual. You take into account their needs, pains, frustrations, desires, and hobbies. You're listening to those and making something worthwhile to them. It's the exact same thing in the adult world, even in the kid world. Also, the ability to quickly think on your feet and come up with different solutions which is the same as iterative design. We did it constantly as teachers. "This lesson isn't working, this activity is failing and I can see it in their faces. But this other thing is working wonderfully," and you have this inspired moment to celebrate. Also, the ability to manage time. Who would have known that decision-making and time management would matter so much in product design? But it really does. You have to think of timelines, of moving forward with something even if it isn't necessarily the best solution.

Is this different from your experience in education?

I would say I did not have anybody looking over my teaching either. My content was Spanish, so I didn't have the same core focus or standards that everyone else had. The autonomy is similar, but the work here is more collaborative and visionary.

Do you miss not having a summer break? Explain why or why not.

I thought long and hard about this, and my answer is no. I don't miss it. I think it has to do with the mental exhaustion of teaching. You're surrounded by tiny humans who need more than just education but they also need social-emotional growth. They have aches and pains; they get tired too. You're constantly "on," and I don't have to be that way anymore. I have the capacity to come home at the end of the day with room to exercise, grocery shop, hang out with friends or go to my pottery class during the weekdays. I can stay up until 11:30 at night and still function perfectly fine the next day. It's been great getting back to myself and focusing on myself instead of 100 different people before myself. So, long story short, no, I don't miss it.

Resources:

Resources prior to job transition (in sequential order):

Udemy: Graphic Design Masterclass

Domestika: Minimalistic Graphic Design for Big Ideas/Web Design with Figma/App Design: Prototyping for Beginners

DesignLab (Bootcamp): UX Foundations

Memorisely (Bootcamp): UX/UI Design

Resources after job transition (helped strengthen skills):

Uxcel: ALL COURSES

Pendo: Product-Led Course/ Digital Adoption Course/ AI for Product Management

Product Designer/UX Designer & Researcher - Amanda
Taught for 12 years - Grade: HS - Subject: French

Walk me through a project.

One example of the things I did was customer journey mapping at a very deep level with our current company. I started with a schema and a discussion guide to go over with the interview participants. We grabbed participants in various roles at multiple client companies and pulled them into interviews about their entire workflow, not just where they use our app, but how their entire workflow happens. How does one thing move into another? Basically, to get an idea of all the different touchpoints and pain points and places they were in the journey. I talk to customers to understand how they use our app and what problems they face. I lead group discussions to gather detailed information, which I use to create profiles of different types of users. This helps my team design a better app that meets the customers' needs and improves how different parts of the company work together. I led the workshops with this. I built the protocol, but someone else did the interviewing, although I was part of all the interviews and asked follow-up and clarifying questions. We did a workshop with the participants. There were product managers, product executives, designers, and even some lead engineers, front-end and back-end, for our app. Because we're enterprise, which means we're a lot more complicated than a normal app. We're a web app too, which makes it even more complicated. We interviewed them and kept them in the workshop with us while we did an empathy map. We examined what they saw, thought, felt, heard, said, or did, and also their pains and gains. The nice part about keeping them in the workshop was that we were able to dig a lot deeper and ask follow-up, refining questions about their flow. This is about their entire job role, not just the one aspect that has to do with our app. In another workshop, which lasted a couple of months because it's quite huge, we dug into "How might we" questions and developed personas from those. We affinity-mapped them, did data analysis, and then pulled that into really deep personas for each of the roles that emerged based on our interviews. We went in with an idea of what the percentages could be, but we changed that a lot based on the interviews. We didn't have preconceptions of what the personas were in their roles. Then we built out touchpoints of their journey and emotional highs and lows and boiled it down into their journey. We went back, analyzed, and pulled quotes from all the interviews for the pains, gains, actions, and experiences of each of those touchpoints. This allowed us to examine the app in a much more holistic manner to see if we were meeting the challenges they needed to meet, if we were solving the right problems rather than just solving a problem because some executives said to solve it. We made sure that it was all aligned going forward. I'm primarily a designer with a researcher role on the side. I took that into design. We went through a design audit, audited the app, audited all the flows, and started coming up with conceptual designs. This led us to building the new app we're working on now. It was several months of a process doing readouts. The stakeholder readouts were so important. We've done this with three different segments now. I've led two of the three, and in the third one, we got all of our Customer Success Managers to be fully invested. Now there's a much better working relationship. Our company is more of an ecosystem rather than independent organisms not working together. There was a dual purpose: the researcher part leading into good design decisions, and the business side of that, which is really interesting. That's kind of a project wrap.

You used the words protocol and empathy mapping, how do you know those terms?

As you know, I've self-studied a lot. These were things that are way past the Google course certificate on Coursera. I did a lot of independent study before I switched jobs. I was already familiar with many of these terms. They may have different terms than what we call them, but they connect back to teaching concepts from my bachelor's and master's programs. It made a lot of sense. The psychology, the cognitive and behavioral psychology taught as teachers completely applies here and gives me deeper insights, putting me at a higher level than I should be for my years of experience. Those terms are just like education terms. They become buzzwords. Maybe they call them something different over time, but it was really just a bunch of research while I was still teaching and connecting it to concepts of teaching.

Walk me through another project/process.

The first thing I do as a designer is look and see if we have any research already. I look at the quality of the research and request more research from my partners, project managers, or product managers as they're called in the tech world. We look at qualitative and quantitative evidence, numbers, and anecdotal evidence. We look for patterns of behavior from our users, analyze those, and define the problems. That's the first key step, figuring out the real problem we're solving. Sometimes, we're trying to solve the wrong problem. We balance business needs and user needs and then take that into solution design and development. Once we have a product brief, which tells me about the problems, the jobs to be done, the challenges, and the research we've done already, we might go into discovery. Discovery is just research, figuring out more and deciding that a little better. We move into solution discovery and solution design, which is just research and actually starting to design. We start with different concepts, check their feasibility early on with wireframes, which are basic designs. We don't use wireframes too much if we have a good design system that works well and has good parts because it's easier to put together snazzy-looking stuff with a good design system. Then we check that with flow, making a flow map to compare to the designs and the technical team, ensuring things are feasible and within scope, keeping the project on budget. We make better designs, refine them, and continue to test them with real users to ensure they're solving their problems. We keep making tweaks. At the end, we make a lot of documentation before handing this off to the developers, letting them know any little things that might not be obvious from the prototypes. Prototypes are the fake versions of the designs that work kind of like a real app so we can test it. Then it goes to the developers, but the job doesn't stop there. We help with story mapping, figuring out how the project will be broken down for the developers, answering any questions during that process, and checking to ensure it looks and works the way it's supposed to. We work with quality assurance people as well, who test all the different scenarios to make sure it works as it rolls out to the public. That is basically what I do on a big scale.

How can teachers, who still have to work and take care of families, prepare to become a UX designer or product designer? They can't do an internship, so how can they prepare?

I didn't have any money for boot camp or really the time to invest full-time in it. I worked on this for almost two years as a teacher before I transitioned. So the two things you need to know about transitioning to UX is that the initial transition is really hard. But once you get that first job, you're set, you're in. So it's worth sacrificing to get that first job. The second thing is you always hear people say, don't work for free. But as teachers, we're used to working for free all the time. So what really helped me was that the pandemic refocused my priorities. I stopped using all that after-school work time, the hours every day for prepping, for teaching, and transitioned most of that into prepping for UX or doing my learning and going deeper. So I did it for free. I even worked for companies pro bono, which was for free for a while. But those experiences gave me the networking that I needed and the ability to interview well and the design know-how way past any courses or boot camps you can take. That helped me land really nice jobs pretty quickly. And I'm already almost in a senior design role and I've only been a full-time designer with no other job for a little over a year. The other thing I would say is don't be afraid to step away from the classroom and take a job in something tangential, like working as a CSM, a customer success manager, or something in the business world. No, they should. They don't take us seriously if we're teachers even though we're powerhouses. And so transitioning into that tech world or business world depending on where you want to be can often give you the leg up to work your way through a company and get the things that you need.

Do you have any resources that you would recommend?

Go deep into your learning. Whether it is a reputable university program or free online courses like Coursera, take the time to read, watch, and practice beyond what is offered. Tie concepts from teaching, especially psychology and sociology, into UX design since the overlap is significant. Tools can be learned over time; focus instead on understanding user needs and running workshops effectively. Seek mentors who emphasize in-depth work rather than surface-level design. While visual design is not my strongest skill, my psychological foundation allows me to succeed. I recommend the University of Michigan's resources and the Interaction Design Foundation's affordable membership, which provides access to unlimited courses. However, learning is not enough, take action. Working pro bono for a startup connected me with a former UX manager who mentored and reviewed my work weekly. Building that community was indispensable.

If you work remotely, what are some the advantages and disadvantages?

I love working remotely. I discovered during the pandemic that I am autistic and realized how overwhelming the classroom environment was for me. While I miss my students, I do not miss being constantly overstimulated, restricted in basic needs like bathroom breaks, or dealing with hidden agendas from adults. Before remote work, I needed therapy every two weeks, but now I have graduated from therapy and require minimal medication. I am healthier, more positive, less emotional, and less drained. Remote work also gives me more time with my family, something I struggled with as a teacher. My husband is also a teacher, which made balancing home life harder. The only downside is the physical toll of sitting more, but overall, my health has improved. My job's flexibility and unlimited PTO have allowed me to engage more with my kids, such as volunteering for Tech Week at my son's middle school musical. I can flex my hours as long as I attend meetings and complete tasks, breaking my day into manageable chunks. Remote work has truly transformed my life for the better.

What skills or experiences from your teaching career have been helpful in your new role?

Everything, honestly. My social skills are much better than most autistic people because of it. My ability to read situations and handle high-pressure situations, my ability to present, especially on the fly, without being stressed about presentations to multiple levels of stakeholders, and to differentiate what I'm saying on the fly. My ability to interview, usually as a designer or researcher, and I get to do both now. Because of those skills I developed as a teacher, skills such as cultural competency, understanding of sociology and cognitive and behavioral psychology, it just really brought a wealth to me and really helped me accelerate my career much faster. I'm often told by my boss that I'm not really a mid-level designer; I perform almost at the level of a senior designer, even though I haven't been in it as long as others. Because of my experiences with teaching and those deep learning moments, I use what I've learned in teaching every single day.

Have you faced any difficulties transitioning to your new career?

Yes. I am open about my disability because I want to avoid the kind of situation I faced with an abusive principal who acted poorly after learning about it. That has been challenging, but most places I have worked are understanding and willing to grow. However, I did encounter a job where I was essentially an order taker, producing poor UX work with no depth or research. The biggest challenge, similar to teaching, has been advocating for what is right. In a company like Click Thrive, which is open to growth and change, it is possible to make a positive impact. Business needs can sometimes take priority, but overall, we can create meaningful changes. On the other hand, some positions require paying your dues, doing superficial work without addressing deeper issues because the company is not receptive. Advocating for your job and pushing for the right decisions is essential. When leadership understands the business value of good UX, it is rewarding, and the work is often more fulfilling with better pay and fewer hours.

Why did you leave teaching?

Part of that was that I was just tired, exhausted, emotionally and physically, especially when I found out that I was autistic and the classroom was contributing to a lot of these things. For me, the pandemic was an eye-opener because it was the first time in my life I wasn't working multiple jobs outside of my house. My whole personality changed because I wasn't overwhelmed. I didn't realize my emotional responses were actually sensory overwhelm, which is so funny because I see it in my kids. I knew what it looked like, but I couldn't see it in myself. It changed my whole life, and I got so much better so quickly. Part of it was the politics and dealing with crappy administrators who didn't want to do the right thing. I'm somebody who can't not live my values. I read a study the other day that said autistic people are likely 98% of the time to continue to act according to their values, even if they know no one is looking and no one ever will, they'll still follow their values and ethical code. Neurotypicals aren't like that; it's a much smaller instance for them. They said that that was a deficit, but for me, that's not a deficit. The whole reason I got into teaching was to help kids and make a difference. Uncompromising moral values, I think that's really important. My ethical value is I wanted to stand up for my kids, I wanted to do the right thing. I was constantly being knocked down by my administrator for my autistic and ADHD traits. I was constantly being told not to do something, and then someone else a month later would get praised and exuded for all of these great things that they came up with, which I had been doing a month before and had my hands slapped for it. There were just a lot of times, which honestly, since leaving teaching, haven't continued. It's not as much of a problem outside of teaching, except for maybe a few ethically compromised professions. That's really sad, but it was the adults that ran me out.

That is the common denominator that I keep hearing. It's rarely the kids. The kids can be whatever they are, but that's just because of adults.

I enjoyed building those relationships. I had my kids for two to four years. I had some of the rougher kids who go on to take AP French and be failing English. It just happened because you have those kids. You build those relationships, you know how it is.

What advice would you give to someone considering leaving teaching for a new career?

Prepare for the grieving process. It hit me a lot harder than I thought it would, especially since I had left teaching for a year at one point and then came back. The grieving process is really hard, especially if you live in the community where you teach and you have children in the community where you teach. I have a husband who is also a teacher, so that was really hard, especially because I didn't feel like I had a great relationship with my main principal, who is now Assistant Superintendent in my district, and I have to see everywhere. At all of my kids' functions and events, that was really hard. I still feel guilty. I sometimes have nightmares, waking up with guilt from leaving teaching. But know it's the right thing in your heart, too. I have had many surprising high school kids, who I didn't think had the emotional intelligence to realize this, but they're still in high school or graduated just a couple of years into adulthood, say to me that me leaving after they saw everything that I went through because they saw it, he did not try and hide it. They say they're proud of me and that I've made an example of standing up for myself and going after my dreams and what's right. It wasn't the right fit anyway, so the guilt is okay. It's normal. It's natural. You're going to have to work through it. Embrace the journey and embrace the networking. The people you meet will come up and help you later on. For example Dina, our relationship is so great. We just met in a teacher forum trying to figure out what we wanted to do to get out of these situations. The people you meet and the things you do and experience are fantastic. Lean into that and embrace the journey. It may take you a while, but ultimately it's worth it.

Resources:

Univ. of Michigan UXR and UXD Coursera Course: https://www.coursera.org/specializations/michiganux

Interaction Design Foundation: https://www.interaction-design.org/

Product Marketing Manager - Lisa C.
Taught for 17 years - Grades: MS/HS Subject: Biology

What is your current title?

I am a product marketing manager for a software company that's based in France. The software company is called LumApps and we sell intranet software, which is a private network that organizations use to securely share information and resources with their employees.

Why did you want to become a teacher?

So, it's an interesting story. I grew up in upstate New York and attended the University of Tampa where I majored in biology and participated in the Army ROTC program with full intentions of going into the military after graduation and working in some capacity in the medical field. However, I injured my ACL and could not continue with the ROTC program. One of my professors knew that I was struggling to determine a new major and said, "You're so good with people; you're so good at just articulating your love and your passion for science. Have you ever thought about being a teacher?" From there I switched majors and realized that I loved teaching!
I graduated with a double major in biology and secondary education with a final internship at a middle school. In this placement, I was assigned to a very sick teacher, and she pretty much gave me the autonomy to teach the classes from bell to bell. That is where I

figured out, not only did I love this, but I was good at it too. Sadly, she passed away that summer and when I returned to the school to seek a recommendation, unaware of her passing, the principal offered something unexpected. Instead of just a recommendation, she proposed, "I can do better than that for you. How about a job?" It was 2001 and I taught at this school for five years. In 2005, I had my daughter, and I didn't want to leave this baby and just so happened to run into a teacher friend that said she was teaching at Florida's statewide virtual school, and I told her, "Get me in!" I was hired and taught with Florida Virtual School for several years. In 2011, I returned to my former district and helped them build their online program.

Why did you end up leaving the classroom?

It's funny because I would have remained in the classroom had it not been for an unfortunate encounter. My husband retired, and we relocated from Florida up north. I was eager to continue working with the virtual school, thinking, "I'm online anyway. Even if I needed to fly to Florida to deliver the state testing and proctor those exams." I proposed, "Even if I have to fly down to Florida for a week to proctor the test, I love teaching and love my students and will make it happen." However, the administrator refused, stating, "No, you cannot do that; we need you here. You need to be in Florida if you're going to teach online." This was challenging because we had just bought a house up north to be closer to my husband's aging parents and my dad. She made it exceedingly difficult for me. I had to resign. I was so sad, because our online staff had formed a well-knit community through online school and in-person interactions. We organized get-togethers with the parents and students at the local park, beach cleanups, and field trips to our local waste management facilities. It was all about going above and beyond. Ultimately, I decided, "If you're unwilling to work with me, I have no choice." Surprisingly, it was challenging to find another teaching position. Despite interviewing for multiple roles within my local community and beyond, it felt as though decisions had been made beforehand about who would be hired. This experience began to disenchant me with the education sector, wondering, "Is this what education has become? Putting dedicated individuals through exhaustive processes?" I've been teaching for 17 years, not a newcomer requiring the proverbial dog and pony show. By that point, I really had developed a passion for building courses in learning management systems, like Moodle, Canvas, or Blackboard. I recognized I had another skill set and decided to explore other roles.

Looking at your LinkedIn profile, I see that you have had a few roles after you left the classroom. Let's go over them.

Yes, I taught at VIPKid for a while, getting up at three in the morning, and it served its purpose financially for me, but I did outgrow it as more roles became available to me. Through a connection with a former colleague, I acquired a Teaching Assistant position with Strayer University. I also did some private tutoring to continue to make ends meet. At the end of 2020, I was doing training and instructional design at Instructure in addition to my full-time role as a Learning Technology Specialist at Strayer University, where I began working towards my Ph.D. in instructional design. In the summer of 2021, Instructure offered me a position as a contractor, where I redesigned over 20 courses in Canvas for their Global Sales Team, which included onboarding, training on the Instructure products, how to use Salesforce, Outreach, and training for all of their tech stack. It was here that I was able to infuse the best practices I had learned about instructional design from my doctoral courses, my role at Strayer, and, yes, my teaching experience to create consistent and impactful online learning experiences for their global sales teams. I worked hard in this role, and when a full-time position (Revenue Knowledge Strategy Manager) became available, I was thrilled to apply. Even though I did not check all the boxes in the job description, the VP who hired me knew my work ethic from the contract role and trusted that I would do whatever it took to not only get the job done but (his words) "knock it out of the park."

As the Revenue Knowledge Strategy Manager, I was tasked with using a new software, LumApps, to design and develop a personalized and regionalized revenue enablement site within the company intranet. I never thought there would be a software that I loved as much as Canvas, but alas, I fell in love with LumApps. It allowed me to create a personalized experience for the Instructure global sales team, so that the sales reps in the US K-12 market, for example, only saw content and news that was relevant to their work. And I basically owned the whole project from start to finish, getting a blank page with LumApps software in January of 2022 and building out a massive knowledge base with all of their sales collateral, pitch decks, messaging, and content in just four months. I met with different teams such as marketing, product marketing, the product team, and solutions engineering to coordinate and build this knowledge base for their sales teams, and that's where I learned to really love the LumApps product! LumApps eventually did a customer story on the work I did at Instructure, and when I discovered they had a position available for a Product Marketing Manager, I applied. Again, I didn't check all the boxes, but my willingness to work hard and do whatever it took to get the job done was apparent. And of course, it was also helpful that I was fortunate enough to have a hiring manager who believes you should hire for attitude and train skills.

So, you didn't have sales training going into this? How are you bringing it all together without the sales experience?

It is about being willing and open, and not putting yourself in this box, right? Because I am not a salesperson. As a teacher, you know how to ask the right questions to probe your students to determine their prior knowledge. So, I knew to ask questions such as, "What do their day-to-day? What do they need as far as knowledge goes? What assets and sales collateral are going to make their lives easier?" I got on calls with the sales team, had one-on-ones, and conducted small focus groups where we discussed their current situation and what they envisioned. I really started to listen to people and understand their needs. Then, I began to build out and map out; as the designer of this site, I asked them, "Does this make sense to you in your day-to-day workflow?"

I see that you have your Prosci-certified Change Management Practitioner. What made you want to get that certification?

What I learned from that project we just discussed is that when you have a global audience of people who are all distributed everywhere and in different time zones, and being able to say, "Here's how to navigate this new site, and here's why you should use it. Here's the value." People need to know what are the drivers. How is it going to help them? What's in it for them? So, I thought, you know what? I want to know more about the people side of change for future projects. I had actually seen it in action at Strayer as well. We brought in a Change Management consultant to assist with the faculty and student side of change for a project. As a Product Marketing Manager (PMM) at LumApps, I wear many hats. There are four PMMs. Two of us are in the US and two are in France, which is very helpful, as we partner closely with Product Managers, marketing, sales, customer success, and even meet with customers and prospects. It's our job to translate the value of our intranet software to customers and to really listen to customer feedback and be the bridge between our customers and the Product Managers and Engineering teams. We create product pitch decks, define the messaging for our products, identify and research buyer personas, and of course, do competitive analysis. Then, we take these learnings and distill them down for our sales team, so they are enabled and feel supported. Most recently, our company made an acquisition of a mobile-first microlearning software, and I was entrusted, as the resident former teacher, to help define the go-to-market strategy. I created the sales pitch deck, did the competitive analysis, and became the point of contact for the North American sales and customer success teams when they had an existing customer or a prospect who was interested in learning more about how this microlearning solution could increase employee productivity and democratize professional growth at their company. I proudly shared with customers and prospects when I demo this product that I was a former teacher, spent 17 years in the education space, and am now in the dissertation phase of my doctoral program. It's like things have come full circle for me. If someone had told me 23 years ago that I would be a product marketing manager, I wouldn't have even known what that was. But I still get to do a lot of teaching in this role, especially during sales enablement sessions for our customer-facing teams. Sales enablement is really just teaching. You are teaching sales teams about the product or a process. I am also invited to speak at webinars, which a lot of times focus on thought leadership.

Talk to me about any similarities or skills for managing projects.

Absolutely, teaching involves daily project management, from coordinating with other teachers in a multidisciplinary team to aligning lessons across grades. In a middle school setting, for example, teams of science, English, math, and social studies teachers work together, integrating curricula and theming activities to enhance student engagement. Additionally, lesson planning mirrors project management, requiring strategic pacing and alignment with district-wide guides, which is especially important in virtual settings to maintain consistency with traditional classrooms. Teachers adopt multiple roles. Not just educators but also role models, caregivers, and leaders.

Do you have any resources that you can recommend?

Liz Wiseman, author of Multipliers and Impact Players, taught me a lot about leadership and self-confidence, as well as recognizing toxicity in the workplace. These books helped me understand that toxic and healthy work environments exist. Multipliers specifically taught me to identify a manager and leader who amplifies their team's impact.

What's next for you, and do you miss summers?

I do not miss summer. I am very fortunate in that I work for a French company because they take the entire month of August off, so I'm still getting used to the slower summer pace, but it's a good time for my colleagues in North America to work on special projects to close out Q4 strong. I am working on my Ph.D. in instructional design because I want to keep learning and apply what I am learning to my current role.

What advice do you have for teachers who want to switch careers?

Going back to a positive work environment. I'm a teacher on paper, right? I have no certification to be a product marketing manager, but I'm willing to learn and embrace learning and try something new. Until you step out of the box that is self-imposed, you won't know what's out there for you. We put ourselves in these little boxes and say, this is what I am, this is what I must do. No, that is not the case. You can do something else. You just have to allow yourself to be uncomfortable for a while. You will then get to the place where you can say to yourself, "You know what? I can do something different if I want." I work for a company that I enjoy, I am fulfilled, it is a positive work culture and a supportive team. I was mistreated in the K-12 setting, not every year and not by everyone, but by some in leadership, by some students, and by some parents. So, I appreciate and know that it's not easy to make that change. As much as you care about the students, you also have to prioritize yourself and your own health and well-being.

Project Manager (International) - Melissa
Taught for 4 years - Grades: 7 and 8
Subject: Social Studes, Dual Language Spanish Social Studies, Spanish, Spanish Language Arts

Melissa, I have been following you since "forever...and we talked about project management, while I was on my journey to figure out what I wanted to be when I grow up, but let's just start at the beginning.

My journey starts with LinkedIn. I was looking to switch careers and get out of teaching. In January, I got on LinkedIn with about 200 followers because I had created my account twelve years ago. I started from scratch, following people and looking for wisdom and advice from those who knew what they were talking about. I connected with people and began posting on LinkedIn. I've always been a verbal processor and someone who enjoys writing and blogging, so I experimented with writing posts for my 200 to 500 followers, getting around 100 to 200 impressions. Then in March, I wrote a post about my resume and some changes I made to it that got me five interviews in one week. That post went viral, getting about 350,000 views within a couple of days. Scott Hinson, who has helped many transitioning teachers, reached out to me and asked what I was going to do now that I was a content creator. At the time, I wasn't planning on becoming one. He pointed out that I had hundreds of people messaging me, asking to see my resume and other resources. He helped me set up a Gumroad account (I've since transitioned to Topmate) to share my resume. I started posting different things, and that's how I got into content creation. I continued sharing my journey as a transitioning teacher, focusing on project management as I worked toward my PMP certification. I posted about the entire process. Several people encouraged me to write a book about my journey. I realized there wasn't a resource for the application process for project management certifications. There were study guides and resources for exam preparation but nothing to walk people through applying. The application process was incredibly stressful for me, especially proving the required 36 months of experience as a nontraditional project manager. I had to piece together information from Google and other searches. I went through the entire process, including being audited and denied. I shared all of this on LinkedIn. Eventually, I made a five-part series. Scott Hinson suggested turning it into an ebook. I thought about it and decided to create the ebook. While putting it together, I considered what else would be valuable for anyone looking for this resource. I created a template to help with the application process since nothing like that existed. I compiled a list of resources for project managers and included specific projects from my teaching experience, demonstrating how I used a ten-month school year as a project, mapping it to the five stages of project management. I also copied and pasted my application into the book so readers could see exactly what an accepted application looked like. That's how the book came about.

I thought you had to show three years of project management experience.

Yes, you need three years to get the PMP. My three years of teaching counted as project management experience. Even though I wasn't titled a project manager as a teacher, I explained how my teaching role involved project management, and I believe all teachers are project managers. Teachers with three to four years of experience could easily get their PMP because every school year is its own project. If someone got it without three years, they were either audited or not honest. You don't need to be a formal project manager, but you must show the experience. Without it, they can pursue the CAPM. What that did for me was make me realize, oh, I have been a project manager as a teacher this whole time. I just didn't know the words to use. By taking that course, I was able to use the right language in interviews and on my resume to clearly show I had that project management experience as a teacher. The Google certification course has six parts. The foundation class is the first one, which is great for someone thinking, maybe I want to do project management. I always say, start with that one. If you love it, do the other five. You need 35 hours, but I think you actually get around 100 hours in the course. That is definitely a good way to work toward the hours you need if you are seriously considering the PMP.

What resources or tools would you recommend for teachers who are considering transitioning into project management?

Yes. Walt Sperling has a podcast called PM Mastery. There's a link to it in my featured content. He interviews project managers, so for someone wondering if project management is for them, it's a good place to start. There are also many teacher transition podcasts. My journey began with listening to all of them, including Daphne Gomez and Carrie Conover. The Teacher Transition Podcast helped me realize there are so many jobs I could do. The project management LinkedIn community is also incredibly supportive. Logan Langen, for example, helps teachers and co-wrote an ebook with a teacher who became a project manager about transitioning from teaching to project management. There are numerous resources and free tools available to help teachers make this transition. LinkedIn is an excellent platform for project management resources. And of course, I would recommend the Project Management Accelerator Program that I helped create.

What is the day in the life of a PM?

A day in the life of a project manager varies a lot. For example, today I had eight calls back-to-back, but other days I might only have one or two. The best way to describe a project manager's role is that they make sense out of chaos. It involves bringing together different people and subject matter experts to work toward one goal, whatever the project might be. At my company, we help organizations update their HR technology or transition from older systems like QuickBooks to an online HR system. My role as the PM is to act as the go-between for the vendor—the HR tech company—and the client, along with everyone involved. I handle tasks like writing agendas, tracking progress, and coordinating communication. While many PMs track budgets, I don't in my role. A big part of the job is constantly monitoring the project's status to keep it moving forward. Today, a coworker compared it to herding cats, and I thought, yes, that's exactly what I'm doing. Right now, I'm coordinating 25 coworkers on a massive project with four divisions, ensuring smooth communication between everyone. Project management involves continuous communication all day long. There's also the role of a Scrum Master. Scrum is a specific methodology, and you can become a Scrum Master through a certification with the Scrum Alliance. Another methodology is Waterfall, a more traditional approach where you complete one step before moving to the next. Agile, which is becoming more popular in tech, is different. Instead of presenting a final product, you regularly check in with the client and share parts of the project along the way. The Project Management Accelerator Program goes into detail about all the project management methodologies.

I want you to walk me through a project. From right before you get it, how does it come to you? Then walk me through what you do during the project and what happens on the other side.

My title is international project manager because I was hired specifically to work on international clients. In my company, my boss, the VP of international sales, is responsible for securing these sales. For example, we might have a company interested in updating their payroll system. Just this week, I was on a call with HR for a company that has employees in the UK, Australia, China, and Brazil. They are trying to make their system more efficient by consolidating multiple systems into one instead of relying on twelve different people to operate separate systems.

At what point do you start research for clients? For example, when you were onboarded, did you have to learn the product so you could contribute effectively in meetings?

Great question. It depends. Our company is only five years old, and right now, it's just me and my boss handling international projects. I often do research as we go. For instance, a client recently asked for help with onboarding compliance issues in Germany, so I conducted extensive research. We also work with a third-party vendor for certain aspects, and I gather information and create resources based on their input. Additionally, I'm the only person in the company of about 150 employees who has a PMP or PM designation. Others, like the person implementing the technology, have acted as project managers but without formal credentials. There's a major project we're working on, the largest in the company's history, involving 25 internal people across different divisions. I was brought in after the project had already started because they needed someone to manage it from a PM perspective with so many moving parts. Several elements had already been initiated, so I've had to recreate the wheel in some areas. This particular project isn't international, it's domestic, but it involves a company with 14 entities in different states. I manage weekly calls with the CFO and the head of HR to coordinate getting all 14 entities into one system. The challenge is that everyone else in my company is an expert in HR technology or implementation. They have experience with systems like Paylocity, Paycor, and other HR platforms. I came into this role with no industry experience. That's not why they hired me. They hired me for my expertise in managing projects. This project highlights that. A project manager often needs to know a little about everything, enough to keep things moving. A good project manager asks questions, admits when they don't know something, and identifies who does. I don't need to know every detail about payroll—that's the payroll specialist's job. My role is to ensure everything functions and progresses.

As for onboarding and research, it's about understanding the basic steps of processes so I can help each division see how their role fits into the bigger picture. I'm learning as I go. There isn't much prep beyond understanding the general framework of processes to support the project effectively.

For someone who doesn't know, can you explain what pieces the certification brings together? I've seen project management in action, so I understand it now, but as a teacher, I wouldn't have understood. What does the certification teach, and how does it help connect the dots for teachers?

That's a great question. The PMP certification teaches the five stages of a project: initiate, plan, execute, monitor and control, and close. As a teacher, I was already doing all of those things without realizing it. The certification helped me understand and name these stages, which gave me the language I needed to describe my experience. For example, instead of saying, "As a teacher, I did this," I could say, "I initiated projects by doing X, Y, and Z, and I monitored progress by doing A, B, and C." This shift in language made a huge difference in how I communicated my skills during interviews. It also gave me practical tools to track and manage these stages effectively, which has been invaluable. The course made it clear how my teaching skills directly translated to project management. It helped me articulate what I was already doing in a way that resonates with the corporate world.

Got it. That's exactly what I needed to hear. It helps teachers understand that the steps they'll learn in the certification are things they already know how to do.

Exactly. The biggest challenge for teachers is explaining their experience in a way that resonates with the corporate world. The certification helped me clearly showcase my skills on my resume and talk about them in interviews using corporate language. That made it easier for interviewers to see that I could do the job. The courses help you articulate your experience in a way that makes sense outside of education.

Before we switch topics, is there anything else the reader should know about being a project manager?

Great question. I heard this on Walt Sperling's podcast, and it's really true. I'm five months into my role—I started May 1—and I'm just now feeling like I'm fully managing projects. Even though I knew how to manage a project, it takes time to learn the specifics of the industry. On Walt's podcast, he talked about working in construction and how it can take a year for a new project manager to understand everything before they're given their own project. That's been my experience too. My boss told me upfront that it would take time to dive in and learn, and that's okay. I spent the first few months learning, listening, and developing my skills. It's important for people to know that you might not manage a project right away, and that's normal. It takes time to get up to speed.

How did you get into teaching?

I didn't take the most traditional route into teaching. I didn't graduate from college at 22 and go straight into the classroom. My undergraduate degree is in history, and I earned my teaching license and a master's in social studies. However, I ended up moving all over the country and living overseas for a while. I kept maintaining my license because I really enjoyed high school and thought I would eventually become a high school social studies teacher. I was drawn to the idea of making history and social studies exciting for students. So many people say history was their least favorite subject in school because it's boring, but I always thought, no, it's not boring, you just had boring teachers. That's what motivated me to pursue teaching—to make the subject engaging. When I returned from Guatemala, I had Spanish language skills, which allowed me to earn a Spanish certification. That opened new doors, and I combined that with dual-language teaching. I taught social studies in Spanish as well as introductory Spanish classes. I didn't start teaching full-time right away because I stayed home with my kids for a while. I only taught full-time for about four years. That's the nontraditional path that led me to teaching, and at first, I really loved it.

Then why did you leave?

By the time I started teaching, my kids were in elementary school. The education industry often takes advantage of single people without families, expecting them to work long hours. For those of us with families, it's a different challenge. I was spending so much time working at home, lesson planning, creating programs, and teaching. It was exhausting. My first year of teaching was during COVID, which was especially difficult. I was constantly creating and recreating lessons for three different subjects. Since I didn't have a teaching partner, it was overwhelming. A year ago, I switched to a new district. I had been teaching in a higher socioeconomic area, but I wanted to work with native Spanish speakers, connecting back to my experience in Guatemala. I thought the change would help, but the same issues persisted and even got worse. My daughter was in middle school, staying home alone for three hours every day because I didn't get home until 5:30. I didn't feel good about what that meant for my family. At the same time, I was creating three courses from scratch in Spanish, including Spanish language arts. By December, I started Googling alternative careers. I didn't know what a social studies Spanish teacher could do outside of teaching, but I found teacher transition podcasts. Those podcasts were key in showing me other possibilities. I listened to stories of teachers becoming project managers and customer success managers, and it opened my eyes. I realized I didn't enjoy creating lessons. It wasn't fulfilling for me. But when I learned about project management, I saw how it aligned with what I loved. Organizing, making sense of things, and turning chaos into order. Listening to those podcasts was a turning point that started me on this new path.

Did you explore other career paths before choosing project management?

I considered copywriting and applied to a lot of customer success roles. That seemed like a common path for transitioning teachers, and I thought it might be one of my best options since teachers often excel in those roles. In fact, I was offered a job in customer success a week before receiving the offer for my current role. While there are many transferable skills in customer success, I just wasn't as excited about it as I was about project management. For a while, I maintained two different resumes because I was applying to both fields, but eventually, I decided to focus on project management.

Do you have any advice for teachers considering a career change?

The biggest thing is to have clarity. You cannot just rush to leave teaching and apply to everything because that approach doesn't work. No one wants to hire someone who says, "I'm open to anything." You need focus and direction. That's the biggest mistake teachers make when trying to leave the classroom. Take the time to figure out what you want to do and research it thoroughly. It will pay off. If you don't take the time to focus, you could spend months applying aimlessly and hoping something sticks. That's not how it works. People often say the average job search takes four to six months, but that's because many lack focus. My job search took about three or four months because I worked hard and applied to over 100 jobs during that time. I completely revamped my resume. Teachers don't really need resumes in the same way other professionals do, so I had to start fresh. My brother looked at my teacher resume and told me it was terrible, so I began again with a blank document. Another key point is that teachers can't assume people outside of education understand what they do. Many people I talked to had no idea what teaching involves. I had to explain everything, like writing tests and creating Spanish content. Teachers need to clearly spell out their skills because outsiders won't inherently understand the value of their experience.

Everyone remembers either their favorite teacher or their least favorite teacher. So when you bring up teachers...

Right. Teaching is familiar to everyone because everyone was in school at some point, but you still have to explain the details of what teaching involves. In interviews, I would walk through how I tracked data, analyzed it, made decisions, and adjusted my plans. These are things teachers do naturally, but you have to learn to articulate them. Companies won't automatically understand your value. You have to show them. On LinkedIn, I try to share what I did during my transition.

Resources:

Melissa's LinkedIn Page: https://www.linkedin.com/in/melissachappy/

Free and Paid PM Resources: https://topmate.io/melissa_chapman

https://pm-mastery.com/

Project Manager Accelerator Program: https://www.bettercareer.org/pm-accelerator

Public Health Administrator - James
Taught for 12 years - Grades: MS/HS - Subject: Mathematics

How did you get that first position after you left teaching?

The first job I had after teaching was part-time, doing research. It was after I got my master's degree. Shout out to my wife (Mashuanda). She helped me find the right program. I always wanted to get a degree in public health, but I just couldn't find an online school. She found it for me, and it turned out to be one of the top programs in the country. For the degree, I had to partner with a health agency. I ended up doing my practicum with the health department in Mobile. My mentor assigned me a project. She asked me to design something for the fathers of the young women coming to their program. Many of them were first-time mothers. They had a lot of services aimed at the mothers, but nothing for the dads. So together, we developed a fatherhood initiative.

After I wrapped up the practicum, she asked, "James, can I use your project for a grant proposal I'm working on?" Honestly, at that point, the only thing I cared about was whether I got an A. I said, "Sure, do what you want with it," as long as I got my grade. Amazingly, from my information, she secured a grant and asked me to spearhead the program. She couldn't offer me full-time work right away, so I started part-time. Eventually, that grew into a full-time role, and that's how I transitioned from teaching to public health.

Tell me about the health service administrator position.

Okay. The fatherhood program I ran was coordinated by a woman who offered me a full-time training management role because of my background in education. I took the position and stayed for a year, but I kept hitting a ceiling and couldn't find a path to advance in public health the way I wanted. I was about to submit my resignation, and then I had a casual encounter in the elevator with the CEO of the clinical side of the health department, a lady named Dr. A. Lewis. I told her I had been trying to get onto her side of the organization for a long time. At the time, I was actually on my way to take the test to get certified to teach again. Dr. Lewis did not know that I was about to leave, but she just nodded her head and did not say much else. I thought, well, I gave it a shot and tried asking her.

Later that same day, I got a call asking me to come in for an interview. It was a chance I did not think I would get. She gave me that opportunity, and she became an unofficial mentor to me. She helped make sure I was doing okay, and she taught me a lot. I made plenty of mistakes, but she was patient with me. As I grew into the role, she guided me along the way. I feel like I had a pretty successful career there. I achieved a lot of things both in the job and in life.

Is this a position that one can acquire without another degree?

No, you would need a public health background. In this role you have to set goals because there are benchmarks from the state that you need to meet. Just like in teaching, there are performance targets to hit. That mindset really translates to being a health administrator, especially for a public health entity.

The funding comes from state and federal governments, and there are benchmarks you have to meet with that, too. Instead of students, you have patients, and you need to make sure they are getting what they need to succeed. I applied a lot of the same skills I developed as a teacher and transitioned them into healthcare administration.

I also had to understand things like budgets, scheduling, and revenue generation. Even though the funding comes from government grants, you still need to generate revenue. You have to train your staff to understand insurance policies and make sure your doctors know how to close encounters properly so you can get reimbursed. Otherwise, you could get in trouble for fraud by not charging patients with insurance. I found that a lot of the skills I learned in teaching, especially classroom management, carried over. People are going to be people, whether they are first graders or adults on a job site. You need to know how to manage them. You have to know how to handle clients who walk in having a bad day because nobody comes to the health department when they feel good. It is all about connecting people with the services they need. I realized I was using a lot more of my teaching skills than I expected, even more than my public health education.

Walk me through some of the specific responsibilities you were in charge of.

I had to make sure the budget was balanced, and I was responsible for meeting it. I had to ensure that the clinic was always fully staffed, which included hiring staff and covering shifts when someone called out sick. I had to move patients around and arrange coverage. It was clinic management. I was assigned five clinics, including all of the dental clinics. I was also responsible for optometry, so I had about nine clinics in total under my management.

Did you learn a lot of this on the job, or was it somewhat intuitive?

No, it was all on the job. There is not a class on this planet that could fully prepare you for running a clinic. But, like I said, I had a great mentor in Dr. Lewis.

She was one of those rare leaders who was both a practicing doctor and an administrator. She ran her own clinic and knew the realities of clinical operations, and she made sure to teach us along the way. I really tried to learn as much as I could from the best.

For the statistics, you were a research project coordinator, but that was just for a little while. Is there anything you want to tell me about that position before we move on?

I have always been interested in research, but I learned from that job that I am not really interested in categorical data. That type of data just did not interest me. It involves things like assigning categories and asking how people feel. For example, you ask one person how they feel, and they say they feel like a three. Then you ask someone else, and they say they feel like two. When you come back later, their answers might be totally different. That kind of subjective data was not for me. Statistically, you could manipulate the data to get whatever outcome you wanted, but I just was not interested in that. Everything I have done in my career, if you look at my resume from a public health standpoint, was aimed at building my skills to get to the CDC. That was always the ultimate goal.

I see here that you worked for General Dynamics Information Technology. Let's talk about your role as a health communication specialist.

That is where my teaching background came in handy. I had to create briefings for public health emergency responses. I worked on responses to situations like COVID, Ebola, Operation Allies Welcome, and even the wildfires. When responders are sent out, you cannot just tell them to grab their go-bags and go. They need to be briefed on exactly what is happening, and the information needs to be presented in a way that is clear and easy to retain. It can feel overwhelming, like drinking from a fire hydrant.

I would run pre-deployment briefings three times a week. If responders were heading out to a polio response in Madagascar, for example, I had to make sure they knew the lay of the land, who their field support was, and how to manage their expenses. I had to explain what to do if they got sick in the field. I was also their point of contact if they ran into emergencies.

If someone missed their flight or had to get home for an emergency, I took over from there, gave them instructions, and handled the situation.

Where did you get the information for the pre-deployment briefs?

I worked with subject matter experts. Sometimes they would present the information at a very high level that was not practical for people working directly with refugees. My job was to tailor the content into something they could absorb and retain. I would meet with the experts and put the presentations together based on what the responders needed to know.

Was this a job you knew about internally, or did you just happen to find it?

Not at all. I used to apply for CDC jobs every day. I would get on USAJobs and just keep applying. I happened to come across this one through General Dynamics. I met with the project manager, who liked me, and then I interviewed with the leadership team at the CDC. During the interview, my teaching background came up again, and they said it would be a perfect fit for the role.

I really like how career-focused this is. I want teachers to hear this because many teachers do not have a clear path beyond teaching, especially if administration is not their goal. I think it is important for teachers to plan ahead so they are not left wondering what to do next.

I kind of fell into teaching. After I graduated from undergrad, I moved to Houston to find a job in statistics or research. My goal was always to get to the CDC as a statistician, but I could not get hired without experience. Employers kept asking what I had been doing for the past few years, and I had just been in school. Then my undergrad advisor reached out and told me Mobile County Schools was hiring teachers. He said, even though I did not have an education degree, they had a program that would pay for my teaching certification if I agreed to teach for three years. I took the opportunity because it sounded like job security.

I moved to Mobile to teach, but I missed the certification deadline, so when my contract was not renewed, I had to move to Mississippi and teach there while sorting out my paperwork for Alabama. That is why my career path shows Alabama, then Mississippi, and back to Alabama. Losing that job gave me a new respect for teaching. Not knowing what is next changes your perspective, and I promised myself I would never take it for granted again.

I see on your resume that there is a transition, tell me about that.

I was with GDIT, and my contract was about to run out because the nation was ramping down the COVID response. COVID was no longer being treated as a major threat in the US. At that point, the response had reached a level where it was becoming just another routine operation. Other emergency responses were starting to wrap up too. You still have polio going on, but large-scale responses tend to bring in a lot of people to manage things. Once the response winds down, staff either go back to their original roles or, for contractors, they are let go.

Since I was a contractor, I was one of the ones who had to move on. But while I was there, I made sure to get involved in everything I could. I even participated in nuclear radiation exercises. That is where my teaching background came in because I helped make presentations for those exercises. A lot of people started to recognize my name. Honestly, that was a blessing from God because nobody is that smart on their own. The real challenge was getting to Atlanta, which is where everyone wants to be since it is the main CDC hub. Atlanta is the hotspot, and that is where the CDC headquarters are. I kept trying to get there but could not break through. Someone finally floated my name and asked if I would be interested in a position in DC. I had been to DC before for conferences and loved it. I decided to go for it, but I had to convince my wife first. I told her that if it did not work out in a year, I would go back to teaching. I kept my teaching license active just in case I needed to return.

I was ready to go back to teaching if I had to because math teachers are making really good money in Alabama now. On the state's salary schedule, you can make close to $100,000 if you teach math, science, or special education. Alabama has really stepped it up for those areas. I thought to myself, if the CDC job did not work out, at least I could make $90,000 teaching math. That would not have been a problem because I have always enjoyed teaching. My only issues with teaching were with bad administration, not the students or classroom management. I am six foot six, a big black guy, so the kids never gave me trouble. I was a troublemaker myself growing up, so I knew exactly what they were trying to pull. I would tell them, "Let me show you how to do this better so you don't get caught," and the kids loved me for that. Right before school orientation was going to start, the CDC called and said they loved the interview I had with them. They asked if I would take the position in DC. I said yes, and I have been here ever since September.

Wow. Congratulations. I bet you were elated.

Elated does not even begin to describe it. It is everything I thought it would be. I love the diversity here. I am seeing people who look completely different from anyone I grew up around, and they are thriving. It gives me hope. Coming from the deep South, you do not see a lot of that. You get used to the way things are and become institutionalized to it. But it does not have to be that way. That makes me really excited.

Absolutely. Diversity in not only cultures and people but also experiences. You can learn so much from that kind of environment. I love it too. Now, tell me about what you do at the CDC.

I work with the Port Health Protection Agency and global migration. We monitor people coming into the US by land, air, or water. If they are sick, we are the ones responsible for handling it. The first case of the most recent COVID response in the US actually came through the station I work at. I am stationed at Dulles International Airport. People come in from all over the world, and we have to make sure that nothing poses a threat to public health.

Thank you for everything you do to protect us. What advice would you give to teachers?

Be a good steward of what you have because it can be taken away from you. I did not respect teaching, and that is why I lost my position. I had to go to another state, get my license back, and start over. I did not value the profession the way I should have, just like many people in the world do not appreciate teachers the way they deserve. I used to believe the saying, "Those who can, do. Those who can't, teach." But teaching is a skill, and you need to take care of those kids because they will take care of you in return. If you do not like kids, though, do not go into teaching. Leave it now because it will only make you miserable. For anyone wanting to transition into something else, be patient. Perfect your craft and take all the skills you learned from teaching with you. There is nothing wrong with going back to teaching if you need to.

Salesforce Administrator - Nika
Taught for 12 years - Grades: K - 3
Subject: Bilingual Language & Special Ed.

I know you're volunteering as a Salesforce Administrator, but I also see that you were an EdTech Consultant. Let's start with the Salesforce position. I see that you have a Salesforce Certified Administrator and Triple Star Ranger Superbadge...that's a mouthful, what's that all about?

Salesforce is a CRM software, which stands for Customer Relationship Management. It is used across various industries such as real estate, education, and finance. Salesforce optimizes business processes, from storing customer information to automating tasks like sending emails or contracts. I have two Salesforce certifications, one from September and the other from October. (Have another certification now, Salesforce Platform App Builder)

There is also Trailhead, an online academy for Salesforce, where you complete hands-on challenges. It is gamified, so you earn points as you go, and Ranger ranks show your progress. Super Badges are part of Trailhead too, but they are more challenging. Instead of guiding you, they give scenarios, and you have to solve them using your knowledge. It is tough but really tests your skills.

Salesforce is popular with many companies, and I often see job descriptions asking for it. I looked into it a year ago. Is the demand still high, or is the market oversaturated?

Salesforce is in demand, but it's starting to feel oversaturated, especially with all the tech layoffs. There are still plenty of jobs, but companies are pickier now. During the pandemic, it was different, but I was still teaching then.

That makes sense. The layoffs might have changed things, and I hadn't thought of that.

Exactly! Now, people laid off are looking for Salesforce jobs, and there are boot camps and academies bringing new people into the field. For example, there's Salesforce Talent Alliance and Talent Stacker. These programs teach Salesforce, help you work on projects, and prepare you for interviews. Many participants land jobs. It's competitive now because there are so many ways to learn Salesforce.

Do you think these programs would help someone with little to no experience, or is Trailhead enough? I know Trailhead is gamified, but does it provide everything?

Trailhead is a great resource, but it's not enough if all you do is modules and watch videos. These programs offer real projects and teamwork. They help you build a portfolio, which is important when job hunting. Trailhead is good for learning, but it doesn't give you the teamwork or portfolio-building opportunities these programs do.

Where did you find freelance gigs?

I haven't done paid technical writing yet, but I realized that writing instructions for my Salesforce projects qualifies as technical writing, which I could use for freelance work.

Why does Salesforce need technical writing?

It's needed to document processes like standard operating procedures and user manuals, so others can easily follow them. For me, it was also a way to showcase my writing skills.

Did you have any training for creating workflows, or did you learn it on the job? How did you develop that skill?

I definitely didn't just know how to do that! It's something I learned through a program called Clicked, which is sponsored by the Self Worth (remove Self Worth, should be Salesforce Talent Alliance) Talent Alliance. Clicked offers real-life projects--unpaid, but great for learning. They have these things called "team sprints" where, once or twice a month, you're grouped with random people to work on projects together.

I think I've heard of Clicked! Is it project management-related?

Yes, that's it! They taught me how to ask the right questions, understand workflows, and figure out what departments need from Salesforce. You're basically acting like a business analyst. These sprints are for Salesforce business and admin analysts, and I've practiced interviewing people and translating their needs into software solutions. Best of all, it's free. A lot of programs charge, but not this one.

How long is the program?

One sprint was four weeks, the last was three. It varies. Sometimes there are daily challenges that last an hour or two, but they still offer good experience.

Is there anything else about Salesforce you want to add?

One last thing: Having a portfolio really helped me, especially coming from education. Many companies don't see the value of teaching experience unless it's learning and development.

Right, they think of their own school days.

Exactly! Convincing them was tough. Even with certifications, they'd say, "But you were a teacher, how do you know this?" My portfolio helped show I was serious.

What did you include in your portfolio?

I started with a boot camp. Some assignments were portfolio projects, similar to Trailhead, but with extra steps. I also added things like screenshots and slideshows, whether for security or creating profiles. It didn't take long, but it showed I went beyond the basics.

What made you pursue Salesforce?

I did not choose Salesforce by myself. It was part of a boot camp I joined last June. One of the programs they offered was Salesforce. Before that, I took a course on ServiceNow because they offered free exam vouchers. Then Salesforce was introduced in the boot camp, and that is how I got started.

What was the boot camp called?

It was called "My Tech Best Friend" (MTBF). If you search for it online, you will find news articles about it. It was a great experience, and that is how I got into Salesforce. (I'd like for this to be removed, or at least remove the name of the bootcamp. It was not a good experience and the news articles that I referenced were regarding how the bootcamp was more of a scam than a legitimate bootcamp. I was in the bootcamp for a little under 2 months before we discovered this and ended the boot camp. Many complaints have been filed and there are still students who are trying to get their money back and recover from that experience.)

What made you decide to go into tech?

The boot camp was a six-month program that covered several different skills, including Salesforce administration, software testing, technical writing, and even a little bit of JavaScript. I liked that it offered a wide range of practical skills that seemed useful for transitioning into the tech industry, especially since I wasn't entirely sure which area I wanted to focus on.

Why choose that path instead of something like accounting or another career path?

I had always been interested in tech. Before I seriously looked into it, I had been exploring other fields like learning and development, trying to figure out what teachers could do outside the classroom. At one point, I considered grant writing, but as I looked into tech more, I noticed how well-paying these jobs were. That got me interested, and I started researching teacher-to-tech transitions. I found some good resources and narrowed it down from there. The boot camp I joined stood out because it combined so many different components into one package.

Got it. And what about your work as an EdTech consultant with Houghton Mifflin Harcourt?

I provided training and professional development for teachers and administrators to implement HMH (digital learning) resources.

Was the consulting in both English and Spanish?

Yes, depending on the teachers' preferences. The Spanish materials weren't just translations. They had unique components. Some schools needed multiple sessions, others just one. I supported teachers and administrators in implementing HMH (digital) resources, providing training and professional development.

Was the consulting in both English and Spanish?

Yes, we delivered sessions in both languages, depending on the teachers' preferences. The materials in Spanish weren't just translations--they had their own components. Some schools needed multiple sessions, while others needed just one.

How did you get the materials? What was that process like?

When I was hired as an Ed Tech Consultant, we went through a four-week onboarding process to learn the company's workflows and curriculum. After that, I conducted both short workshops and longer coaching sessions, sometimes lasting several days, depending on the schools' needs. Some schools required multiple sessions, while others needed only one.

How many hours a day did that take?

It usually took longer than expected. We were paid for six to eight hours of learning, but it often took more time because there was so much to cover including the books, quizzes, and assessments. After training, we were then prepared to conduct professional developments at the schools.

Would you like to talk about why you decided to leave teaching?

Sure. There were several factors, and it wasn't an easy decision. One of the biggest reasons was work-life balance. I just felt like I wasn't making as much of an impact anymore, and that started to weigh on me over time. Teaching had become extremely stressful, and I started to feel anxious and even a little bit depressed. Managing students became more difficult, and principals were (very toxic and) micromanaging more than ever. I tried switching schools, thinking it might help, but the same issues kept coming up no matter where I went. Another major factor was the pay. I would see my friends with more energy, enjoying their weekends, while I felt completely exhausted. (I realized that it had changed me at my core and) It became clear that it was time for a change.

Do you miss having summer breaks? Have you been out of teaching long enough to experience that difference?

Not yet, but I know I will. It's a catch-22. You have those months of uninterrupted time off, but I envy people who can take vacations whenever they want. It'll be nice to take trips during quieter times of the year, not just in the summer or on school holidays when everything is more expensive. And with remote work, I can take my laptop and go anywhere.

Was the transition difficult?

Definitely. Learning new terms and putting in so many hours of research was hard, especially after burning out from teaching. I felt like I didn't really get a break before diving into something new. Also, connecting my teaching skills to corporate jobs was challenging. I knew I had the skills, but hiring managers wanted me to explain how they transferred, and I wasn't prepared for that at first.

I hear that all the time! Teachers just make things work without always explaining it.

Right. We analyze data as teachers, but in interviews, I had to dig deep to show how those skills applied to the job. Teaching interviews are different--you answer a few questions, and you pretty much know you're getting hired. Corporate interviews were a whole different world.

Yes, with those behavioral questions like "What would you do in this situation?" It's so different from what teachers are used to.

Exactly. It's a whole new set of questions to prepare for.

Anything else you want to share?

Just be kind to yourself. Transitioning to a new industry can feel overwhelming, but you've got this.

It really is a whole new world outside of teaching.

Yes, exactly. Education can keep you in a box, but once you're out, there's so much more freedom.

Senior Automation Engineer - Ryan

Taught for 4 years - Grades: 7 - 12 - Subject: Social Studies

What does it look like to be a Senior Automation Engineer?

I am part of the quality engineering department at a tech company. When we create technology, primarily web applications, we need to test them to ensure reliability. In the past, manual testers would click through and verify that everything worked as expected. We still have those, but I program computers to run those tests automatically. Instead of a person taking an hour to test something, automation allows me to run the same tests 100 times in ten minutes.

At what point in the development process do you get involved?

It's a constant iterative process, so I am involved throughout. I typically receive developed work toward the end of the cycle. The developers create something and hand it to me to verify that it works.

What languages do you have to know for your position?

My current work is in TypeScript, which is an offshoot of JavaScript. I have also done this work using Java, C Sharp, and JavaScript.

So, the language automates the testing process. Is that accurate?

Close enough. I use those languages to create scripts that automate tests.

I watched some videos on this profession, which is how I found you. I wanted to see if a former teacher had done this because it interested me. I am taking an SQL course right now to upskill and possibly explore database analysis. I was doing personal research and thought, let me find someone for my book.

Yeah, SQL is an important skill, especially for working with databases and automation testing. A lot of structured testing relies on clear logic, and SQL follows that same principle. In automation, we use structured testing methods like the triple-A pattern, Arrange, Act, Assert. Like a scientific experiment, we arrange the conditions, act by changing a variable, and assert that X should equal Y. If it does not, the test fails.

It seems like this is making sure it all works together and correctly.

Exactly. It is a common method, but there are variations. In automation testing, we often use a framework called Cucumber, which follows a different structure called Given-When-Then. Given a certain condition, when an action happens, then a specific result should follow. It provides clarity for both technical and non-technical people. Most of our scripts and tickets are written in that format.

Does Cucumber help structure the testing process?

Yes. The first thing I write is a feature file, which is written in Cucumber script. If we are working on something new, for instance, a banner component on our website, we need to ensure it works properly.

Is the feature file like a list of different situations to test?

Right. For example, one scenario might say, given a user has a banner with an image, when they click the image, then they should go to this link. Then they should see an expanded view of the image.

I think I follow. How do you take it from a written scenario to an actual test?

After writing the feature file, we define what each step means in code. That is done using a framework. There is Cypress and other major scripts. For example, I might write code that opens Chrome, accesses a URL, ensures a specific HTML element is present, and then works within the code at that level.

So the automation runs the test instead of a person having to do it manually each time?

Exactly. That is the core of the job. I hope that makes sense.

I think I got it. Where did you learn about the AAA pattern, Gerkin, and all these concepts?

I went to a 14-week coding boot camp called Tech Elevator.

It was a full-stack program, meaning we were trained to do everything related to development. Most of my graduating class got their first job at PNC.

I'm sorry, when you say full stack and everything, does that only have to do with web development?

That's a good question. Pretty much. I think it's most applicable to web development. The boundaries between web development and app development are becoming more blurred.

So with the same skill set, using about 75% of the same workflow and technologies, I could create something in a more old-school sense, like a computer program with its own desktop icon. That might be slightly different, but a lot of the skills would still apply. Generally, when people say full stack, 99% of the time, they are talking about web development.

Did the school cover both the front end and back end?

Yes. I received my training a while ago, but it prepared people in my graduating cohort for different roles. Some went on to work at small tech startups, some at robotics companies, and others became web developers.

From what I understand, very few people are hired as true full-stack developers outside of small startups. Who assigns the work? Who is giving you these tickets?

That is part of the agile scrum methodology. Software development needed a structured way to organize tasks. Before modern version control tools like Git, developers would pass code around physically, sometimes on floppy disks. Without coordination, changes could easily overwrite or break something. Until Git, version control was chaotic, requiring perfect organization to avoid conflicts. It was also difficult to ensure fair workload distribution. Not in a petty way, but in making sure tasks were divided properly. The old system used whiteboards full of post-it notes, called tickets, representing the smallest task units. There were three columns: To Do, Doing, and Done. Developers grabbed a ticket, put their name on it, and moved it through the workflow. Jira replicates that digitally, allowing more structured workflows. Instead of just To Do, Doing, and Done, teams can add stages like backlog, development, testing, and approval. Tickets can move between multiple people or be divided into subtasks, with testing as a subtask linked to the main ticket. Every company structures it differently, but the general system remains the same.

It sounds like once you've acquired the necessary skills, the work is fairly standardized. You went through a boot camp that walked you through the whole process. But if someone doesn't go through a boot camp, they're probably not going to see this workflow until they actually start working, right?

Yeah, they probably won't see it in action until they're on the job.

What about a portfolio? If a teacher decides to go this route and doesn't have a formal tech degree, would they need a portfolio?

If you don't have a degree in tech, then yeah, you need to have a portfolio. You need something to show. Even though we received a certification, it is not an industry certification, it just says we graduated. Every unit in the program had a capstone project, which we added to our portfolios, which was basically the same project. So we were very highly encouraged to take what little time we had to ourselves and make side projects to stand out, to do something slightly different from everyone else.

How long is a project in your current position? When you're given a task or assignment, when can you say "it's done"?

It's iterative, so it was constantly moving. I guess at the end of a project or the end of a sprint, a project is never really done anymore, in my experience. If it's a live service, it's not like LinkedIn is done. They're always going to add and tweak or address customer concerns when they come up. The lifecycle involves iterative improvement in a two-week cycle. At the start of the sprint, we get our work, and every day we have a stand-up process where we discuss what we did yesterday, what we are doing today, and what we need. At the end of the sprint, we look back on what went wrong, what went right, and what we can do better based on that. Sometimes we pass work to another team, and sometimes the process continues with refinement as another phase. That refinement phase connects the development team, the technical people, the business side, the people in suits--the fat cats on Wall Street or whatever. Based on customer feedback and company needs, they translate those needs into tasks, break them down into tickets, and decide what needs to be done. Every place handles this differently. In our case, we have a refinement meeting in the first week of the sprint, usually on Wednesday, where we take an hour to go through newly created tickets, ask questions, and clarify details. Tickets have points that represent estimated complexity and time. There is very little consistency, and estimating these can be frustrating because different development teams might use different metrics. One team might estimate a task as a three-point effort, while another team might rate the same task differently. We track velocity and points per sprint to manage workloads.

What is difficult about this?

I'll give you two answers, one generic and one personal. The generic answer is that some things are always outside your control. You can mitigate issues, but when our test environment goes down, it creates problems. I don't test on the real website; I use an internal version, sometimes with mirrored or simulated data. If real users number in the billions, our test site might have a large but scrambled dataset. Sometimes, we have to request data, which means waiting. Even when things are out of our hands, the expectation to deliver remains. Teachers can relate to high expectations and limited control. There's always pressure to get things done. On the technical side, UI testing has its own headaches, like page object locators. If I need to click a button, I have to tell the computer where it is, but website updates can change that. A lot of my job is updating those references rather than writing new code. My personal answer is that I was trained in a different field. What I learned years ago is outdated. This industry evolves fast. If I wanted to move beyond quality engineering, I'd have to push myself to relearn and adapt. I'm content, but I feel like I'm a little behind where I'd like to be.

Why did you leave education?

Teaching was never going to make me wealthy, and I accepted that, but my girlfriend, now wife, struggled with it. The first years were hard. It was one thing for me to go without, but watching her struggle was worse. Most successful teachers I knew had wealthier spouses. My wife went to art school, so we both had little income. The financial strain was heavy. I wanted my students to think critically. Anyone presenting political, historical, or social issues as simple was either lying or selling something. Hate requires understanding. You have to do the research and see people for who they are. That was my agenda. Social studies had been taught the same way for decades, and it was clear it wasn't working. If it were, we wouldn't be where we are. I felt increasingly useless. I made a difference to a few students, but it felt like polishing brass on the Titanic. Even the best teachers couldn't fix a system that wasn't producing engaged, informed citizens. I taught in an Orthodox Jewish school in Squirrel Hill, the Jewish neighborhood of Pittsburgh. I am Jewish but in a Larry David way... I took the job to connect with a heritage I barely knew, but I was a subversive element. I was married to a gentile, had a television, and had no fixed stance on Israel. The students were fascinated, but it was uncomfortable. Then the Tree of Life synagogue massacre happened, two blocks from my home. We heard sirens all day. The school's response broke me. That, along with the financial strain, made it impossible to continue. My fire burned out in an instant.

Do you miss teaching? And if so, what aspect of it do you miss the most?

I miss it every day. I dream about it a lot, just teaching a lesson or something. I miss the feeling that what I did mattered. The Trump administration kind of disillusioned me of that belief, but for a long time, I felt like my work had real purpose. The work I do now matters to me personally, and it affords me a really nice lifestyle. I can take care of my wife properly, we have a dog and a house, and it's great. Something that was completely unthinkable in my teacher lifestyle. But the actual work I do for this company, while good, doesn't feel like I'm saving the world. It doesn't feel like it serves any great purpose. I miss that feeling. I miss the connection with students. I was the teacher who made the weird kids feel seen because I was the weird kid. What really stuck with me was that some students, the ones who felt ignored, stuck in the corner, or who had no reason to go to school, saw my class as their reason to keep going. That mattered a lot.

Why did you become a teacher in the first place?

My grandfather was a teacher, and I spent a lot of time with him growing up. In many ways, I have inadvertently become a younger version of him, both for better and worse. Teaching always seemed obvious. My teachers knew I would become a teacher. My parents knew. It just felt self-evident. Beyond that, I believed I had a responsibility to give back. I was born into privilege and had the ability to make a difference. In a Spider-Man morality sense, with great power comes great responsibility. History, when studied authentically, fosters a deep understanding of people and the world. It builds empathy, something we desperately need.

Did you consider any other careers?

Yes, I looked into instructional design. I have always been fairly computer literate, and I worked summer jobs teaching kids coding. One day, while driving and listening to NPR, I heard a commercial for Tech Elevator. It sounded good, and with my background in coding camps, it aligned well.

Ok...last question...what advice would you give?

If you are burnt out, leaving is the compassionate thing to do. Think of it like a failing marriage. Divorce is often better for the kids than staying in a toxic home. I was a damn good teacher, but by the end, I wasn't. I knew that, and it was a disservice to the kids to keep going. Leaving does not mean you failed. The skills needed to thrive in a failing system are not the ones they teach you in education programs. Thriving in such an environment requires a skill set closer to what is needed in the medical field, particularly nursing. Nursing is another profession where people burn out quickly, but those who succeed have resilience and adaptability. Teachers have incredibly transferable skills--analyzing information, managing multiple tasks, and communicating effectively. Those abilities are especially valuable in the tech field, where many technically skilled people struggle with communication. If you can relate to people, be culturally aware, and convey information effectively, those strengths will carry you forward. If you are leaving because you were not a good teacher, that just means your gift lies elsewhere, and I am confident that it exists.

Senior Economic Research Analyst - Laurie
Taught for 19 years - Grades: MS/HS/CC - Subjects: Math, Economics, Statistics

Walk me through a project or just an assignment.

Projects vary depending on my involvement, which can range from six months to two or three years. Sometimes I get pulled into a project just for certain aspects, while other times I'm involved throughout. Most projects begin with proposal development, where I assist in writing proposals or grants. This is something I think people with teaching backgrounds would excel at because they can articulate the purpose of a study and why funding is needed. My focus, though, is on the technical aspects of research, such as what data to collect, who to collect it from, how to use it, and how to protect privacy. One current project started with proposal development and submission to the funding organization. Once the project was funded, project management began. This included staffing, planning tasks, and using project management software. Getting certified in project management software could be useful for joining a grant writing team. Another part of the process is forming an advisory board to guide the project. As labor economists, we handle the research and data, but the advisory board provides expertise on finding participants, forming relevant questions, and ensuring language fits the industry. For example, they help make sure the survey questions are well-formed and appropriate. For the current survey project, we used

Qualtrics to design and distribute the survey. This has been a multi-year process, and now we are in the final stages of data collection and beginning analysis. After that, we'll write reports and develop policy recommendations, which is the primary goal of the Health Policy Studies group I work with.

To go from teaching, to even go from being a stat teacher, economics teacher, or calc teacher, to writing a report—talk to me about that. How did you figure that out? Or where would someone who doesn't have that kind of background get that knowledge?

How was I able to just jump into this? Well, I didn't exactly jump into it—I had done it before I started teaching. I worked with the same group before, so I was able to pick up where I left off. I also used the skills I gained in the classroom, like communication, working with different groups of people, and organizational abilities. Those helped me come in at a higher level than where I left, even taking on leadership roles in projects. Not only did I have the analytical skills from my previous work, but because I had been contracting with them for a couple of years before returning full-time, I was able to stay sharp with the analytics.

Teaching also gave me leadership experience. Over time, you find yourself leading committees, facilitating workshops, mentoring, or becoming a department chair or site council member. All of that builds leadership, communication, and people skills, which are highly transferable. These soft skills are invaluable, and teachers should absolutely highlight them in interviews or on their resumes. I think many teachers don't realize how strong that skill set is and how relevant it can be outside the classroom. Even as a math teacher, I developed these skills, despite not teaching subjects like English or social studies that might seem more directly related to communication. Managing a math classroom involves significant organization and leadership too.

For me, having that contract work on the side really helped me re-enter this field at a higher level. For someone who doesn't have that background but wants to get into similar work, they could start by taking coding or data analysis classes during summers or breaks. A lot of people think data analysis might be a good path for them but don't know much about it. There are great free resources, like Codecademy, where they can get a feel for it. If they find it interesting, they might consider going back to school formally, if possible, to pick up new skills. I know that's harder for mid-career professionals with kids and other commitments, but it's not impossible. Many teachers have earned master's degrees while teaching full-time and raising families, so doing something similar in the summers or during breaks could work.

So if I'm thinking of my stat teachers, my economics teachers, my math teachers, where does the funnel begin for them? How should they start to upskill now to be prepare?

They would need to be proficient in a programming language and analytic tools like Stata, SAS, SQL, Python, or R.

Oh, okay, so do you use Python?

I don't use Python or R, but I use SQL, Stata, and SAS. SAS, in my opinion, is the Holy Grail of analytics software. I learned SAS first, then Stata, and now I'm learning SQL, which is completely new to me. I'm figuring it out on the job, and it's challenging. I'm working with big data, which surprises me, but my team believed I could handle it. I'm grateful to be learning something new, especially at this stage in my career. SAS and Stata are powerful tools, but they aren't free. On the other hand, R, Python, and SQL are free, and they teach the logic of data analysis. If you learn one, it's easier to pick up others because they use similar algorithmic thinking. When I started SQL, I thought it would be similar to what I already knew, but I quickly realized it was different. I grabbed some SQL books and started learning. The process has been rewarding. The work is challenging but fulfilling, and the team is supportive. It's a professional and respectful environment, and the shift has been a positive change for me.

What type of data are you analyzing, and can you provide an example of what you're working on?

Laurie:. Okay, let's discuss dentists, for instance. We know the medical field is losing a lot of people, right? Because of COVID. Sometimes it takes longer to see your doctor or dentist because people are leaving the field. But is that true for dentists? Are they leaving the field? I'm not sure, so I'd want to find out. To do that, I would start a study. First, I would need funding, maybe by writing a grant, because I cannot do this for free. To begin, I would do some preliminary work, like researching what others have written recently about the dental workforce, or more accurately, dental practitioners. I would look at official sources like JAMA, Health Affairs, or the American Dental Association's website to see what is happening. This step is essentially a literature review. Either I would do it myself or get a team to help, and we would read through the materials, keep track of them, and compile references, just like when you write a research paper in college or for a master's or doctoral thesis. The review would help us see what has been studied, what questions have been answered, and what gaps still exist. I would also look at the data sources others have used, how they collected their data, and what they did with it. Then I would gather publicly available data from places like the Bureau of Labor Statistics, which tracks professions, or the U.S. Census Bureau for population and geographic information. I might also check the CDC if there is a medical angle, like how many dentists use gas and in what quantities. Once I have that data, I would try to get a sample. For example, you can obtain lists of certified practitioners, like dentists or nurses, through Freedom of Information Act requests. I could create a sample from these lists, send out surveys, and match the responses with other data to analyze trends. I would start with descriptive analysis, which shows what the data says, and then move on to more complex methods, like regression analysis, to examine patterns. For instance, I would ask whether dentists are leaving Ohio for California, or vice versa, and if they are leaving the profession entirely or pursuing further education. I would also look at retirees to see how they factor into the trends. This response is actually based on a current study we are working on (not actually about dentists, though).

I'm trying to get a clearer picture...what exactly is the software doing with the data? I know SQL is used for data manipulation, but why do you need these other tools? What kind of data are you working with that requires this level of manipulation?

Excel can't handle the volume of data we work with. Excel can manage about a million records, but we typically deal with far more, along with numerous variables. Additionally, processing time is a factor. These languages are designed specifically for handling large datasets and performing a wide range of statistical analyses. For example, if we want to build multi-level models, we might analyze county-level data, looking at multiple professions, state policies, and time as a variable. We also incorporate demographics like race, age, education level, and political affiliations to understand their impact on our research questions. These tools provide capabilities far beyond what Excel can offer, especially for complex analyses involving diverse and large-scale data.

Is there anything else you want to convey, especially to math and stat teachers?

They should try to get a certification under their belt, like a coding or data analytics certification, and start connecting with people on LinkedIn. Following data analytics hashtags and engaging with the professional community on LinkedIn, or even Twitter, can make a big difference. Joining a professional group, attending conferences, and seeking out mentors are also great steps. For example, there's nothing wrong with reaching out to someone and saying, "Hey, I'm a transitioning teacher. I see that you've transitioned to or work in this field, and I'd love to ask you questions or get your advice." This can help them figure out their starting point. Teachers with degrees in economics or statistics, for instance, could directly apply for jobs in those fields. However, if they've been teaching for five to ten years, they might need a fresh certification. Short courses can make this transition easier. Ultimately, professional communities and networking will help them find valuable advice and responses.

Why did you leave teaching?

I left teaching for a lot of reasons, just as I joined for a lot of reasons. I stayed in it because I really enjoyed it, I loved the kids, and I felt like I was making a difference. All of that was still true when I left, but it was taking too much of a toll on my body and health. I was working so much, focused on the classroom and my workload, which always seemed overwhelming. What tipped the scales for me was teaching through COVID. First, during the shutdown, and then the year after. There was so much pressure to manage everything perfectly, even though we had never faced anything like it. Suddenly, we were addressing kids' emotional needs on a massive scale while dealing with everything happening nationally, including social movements and political tensions. It felt like there was a weight on all of us, teachers, students, and everyone in the United States. At the same time, I had to be there for kids dealing with enormous challenges. Living in a fairly wealthy area, I saw how some students fared well during the pandemic while others really struggled. The divide widened, and it was hard to witness. Some kids had such high academic, social, and emotional needs, and I often felt expected to do so much which required giving everything of myself. That constant stress affected my mental and physical health. At some point, you realize you have to move on. I had been thinking about leaving for a while, but those final straws, including COVID, the pressure, and the growing needs, pushed me to take that step. I think a lot of people are reaching those final moments now and realizing they need to step away, at least for a while, and try something else.

Do you think that you would have come to that conclusion had we not had COVID?

No, I left teaching for many reasons, just as I joined for many reasons. I stayed because I enjoyed it, I loved the kids, and I felt like I was making a difference. All of that was still true when I left, but the toll on my body and health became too much. I was working so much, focusing on the classroom and my workload, which always felt overwhelming. What finally tipped the scales was teaching during COVID, first during the shutdown and then the year after. There was intense pressure to manage everything perfectly, even though we had never faced anything like it. Suddenly, we were addressing kids' emotional needs on a massive scale while also dealing with everything happening nationally, like social movements and political tensions. It felt like a weight was on all of us. Teachers, students, and everyone in the United States. At the same time, I had to support kids facing enormous challenges. Living in a fairly wealthy area, I saw some students fare well during the pandemic while others really struggled. The divide widened, and it was hard to witness. Some kids had such high academic, social, and emotional needs, and I often felt expected to do so much while giving everything of myself. That constant stress affected my mental and physical health. Eventually, you realize you have to move on. I had been considering leaving for a while, but the final straws, including COVID, the pressure, and the growing needs, pushed me to take that step. I think many people are reaching those moments now and realizing they need to step away, at least for a while, to try something else.

Maybe. COVID did seem to tip the scales, and as soon as it started, I started consulting (very part-time) with my research group where I worked prior to teaching. I was lucky to have stayed in contact with my hiring manager. I had started my career in economic analysis, then went into teaching at a private school when my kids were little, then back to analytics. At some point around 2007 I decided to move into public school teaching and got my credential and MS in Education. Now, since COVID, I'm back to analytics. I realize that mine is an unusual career path, having one foot in each world for over 20 years, but it turned out to be a lucky one for me. My consulting practice grew as COVID progressed and after the 2022 school year, I reached a natural stepping-off point.

What was the breaking point that made you say, 'I'm done,' and how did you decide what to do next?

I think it depends a little on the field you are in. I know many teachers work too many hours and sacrifice their personal lives for their jobs. That was more the norm at the time. I can tell you about my last year. I taught in four different classrooms, and I had a physical problem with one of my feet. Last June was my last month teaching, and I left about a year ago. I had foot surgery because of the pain. I was in so much pain, moving from room to room. I had three different courses to teach in four different areas, and I was constantly lugging stuff around. At that point, I thought, this is too much. I will go work at the Container Store if I have to. I just needed to do something else. I ended up getting surgery on my foot after leaving, then was hired into a full-time research role six months later.

I was right there with you! There was an Aldi's down the street and I said I would go work there...work my way up to manager, then district manager...I had a whole plan. So let's get into your current role, what is that title?

I was able to craft my own title to some extent and landed on Senior Economic Research Analyst. Senior, because I have a good amount of experience. Economic research, because we do economic research. And then analyst, because somehow analyst needed to be part of the title. I could have been called senior economic researcher or economic analyst, but all of these words came into the title. I could have even been called senior statistician or something like that. I have a master's in economics, and that is what I really wanted to highlight. When I present myself professionally, I want people to think of me as an economist. Someone who can work with data, and that is how I see myself. I did not want just a title like statistician, which is easier for people to understand, but my dream is not in statistics. It is in economics. I like researcher because I also have a master's in education, and economic research reflects the need. There are other economists who work for banks and similar fields, but I am with the University of California, doing research on the healthcare labor market. This includes nurses, CNAs, and doctors, as well as looking at state policies and their ability to prescribe. For example, we look at differences between nurse practitioners and nurses, such as what nurse practitioners are allowed to do and how much practice they can do independently versus under a doctor's supervision. We explore all those aspects. I am with the School of Nursing, and we focus on nurses.

I always like to open the floor for any final word.

There are so many paths and variations in the experience of transitioning out of teaching. Everyone has a unique skill set, and they should pursue it. It's about putting one foot in front of the other until you get there. It's not always easy or fast, especially since you're not a new grad out of college, which is who many corporate employers are looking for. If you can accept that it might take some time and stay comfortable with that, it'll help. And honestly, don't hesitate to leave mid-year if that's what's best for you. Don't limit yourself to summer hiring. Many companies aren't hiring during the summer because people are on vacation.

Resources: Basic statistics courses and learning SAS, Stata, R or SQL, and Excel, Power BI or Tableau. (these are used for creating data visualizations). Alex the Analyst on YouTube - https://youtu.be/CUBfrdDwzn-Q?si=5oPqdW51_9aZGCJR

Senior Instructional Designer - Tandiwe
Taught for 15 years - Grades: K - 5

On LinkedIn and other job board, we have seen Instructional Designer and Learning Experience Designer as separate roles, but what are the differences?

So let me explain. My manager led a team discussion on differentiating the roles. Instructional Designers handle quick delivery, short-term projects, often receiving detailed direction on objectives and outlines. Learning Experience Designers partner strategically with program managers, SMEs, and stakeholders, advising on large-scale programs and user experience. Technically, I've always viewed the roles as the same because I'm always looking at the learner's mind and needs, ensuring content is learner-centered. On a team of eight, I was the only instructional designer before being promoted to Learning Experience Designer.

I have typically seen the development phase of ADDIE fall under roles titled eLearning Developer.

I've often seen the development phase of ADDIE assigned to roles titled 'eLearning Developer.' It's interesting how different companies define 'Instructional Designer'—some view it strictly as a storyboarder, while others expect involvement in everything from analysis to evaluation. This variation can be confusing for teachers transitioning into the field. When I do workshops, I guide them through the different types of instructional design roles roles so they can better understand job descriptions on LinkedIn and identify the positions that align with their skills and interests.

How did you gain the skills to become an instructional designer?

I started as a social services case manager and later became a field practice advisor, training new case managers and accompanying them on field visits. It became stressful, so I decided to return to teaching. I had previously taught pre-K at a nonprofit school, so I enrolled in Clayton County Public Schools' Alternative Teacher Preparation Program (TAPP). I took the GACE test, passed, and secured a teaching role, which was required for the program. At the same time, I started a graduate program in instructional design. We met monthly at Clayton County Middle School, and I applied everything I learned in my classroom.

Technology was limited then. We did not have Smartboards or laptops, but I advocated for technology integration, trained teachers, set up classroom equipment, and modeled best practices. In Clayton County, every new teacher had a teacher development specialist. Mine encouraged me to explore instructional design. I did not know the term at the time, but I knew I wanted to train adults.

I spent seven years in Clayton County facilitating professional development. When my husband received a job offer in Corpus Christi, Texas, we moved. I wanted a break from the classroom, so I worked at Theducation Service Center, Region 2 as a Corporate Consultant supporting K-12 schools, Head Start programs, and daycare centers. I modeled best practices, conducted observations, and trained principals on new initiatives, such as best practices for conducting classroom observations.. I also developed an assessment tool for classroom evaluations. My other role within the agency was a grant project director in which I partnered with the U.S. Department of Education to support three low-performing schools. I trained teachers and literacy specialists on running parent workshops and incorporating bilingual books. After a year, I returned to Atlanta to help raise my niece after my sister passed away.

Before moving back, I secured a job as an instructional technology specialist and instructional designer with DeKalb County Schools. I developed training for their new learning management system, created e-learning courses, and led instructor-led workshops. The work was intense but rewarding, though I disliked driving between schools. After a year, I returned to the classroom, teaching in Gwinnett County Public Schools. I taught fifth grade before transitioning into an Early Intervention Program role, working with students needing additional academic support. During that time, I completed my specialist degree in Instructional Design.

In 2019, we moved to Dallas for my husband's job. He suggested I might not need my Texas teaching certificate due to nearby corporate headquarters. He was right. I discovered instructional design through my specialist program and found IDOL Academy, bridging education and corporate terminology.

I joined IDOL Academy's first cohort, which was eye-opening. I had never heard of Storyline or Captivate, though I had used Camtasia and other tools. IDOL filled in the gaps. One year after joining IDOL Academy, I facilitated workshops and became a coach and mentor for the academy. That experience led me to establish my LLC. I was able to work with clients in various industries. . I sought coaching and mentorship to help me transition from previous roles since t my previous roles focused on training and team development. Even though I entered IDOL with experience, I learned from the students there and continue to learn every day.

I tell people I do not believe in the word expert. Once you consider yourself an expert, you stop learning. Every day, I hear something new on LinkedIn or from someone at IDOL Academy. The journey never stops.

Think about a project and walk me through it from top to bottom as if I know nothing, in your capacity, in your role.

At my company, when there is a request for a product or training, we start with a discovery workshop. It is set up in Miro, with presentations and embedded questions. I follow a similar process for my LLC using PowerPoint or Canva.

The discovery call helps us pinpoint needs and goals. We ask about the subject, intended audience, behaviors to change, business goals, expected outcomes, existing resources, past attempts, and supporting data. These overarching questions get stakeholders thinking. Workshops can last from a day to two weeks, and during this time, we work with subject matter experts who often realize gaps they had not considered. From these sessions, we develop learning objectives, which are essential for creating impactful learning experiences, whether e-learning or instructor-led.

Once we complete the discovery phase, we move into storyboarding, linking resources, and ensuring branding is consistent across products. Then, we develop the e-learning content. ADDIE incorporates agile elements, and the SAM model allows continuous updates. We use Review 360 for real-time feedback, which reduces the need for constant meetings. Previously, we had weekly or even daily meetings, but now feedback is immediate, streamlining the process. With Rise, we can create responsive e-learning courses efficiently, incorporating interactive elements while ensuring usability across devices.

Once approved, the course or script is sent to a voiceover vendor. I integrate the recordings, ensure proper timing, and send it back for SME review before final approval. I do not upload courses myself but send them to our learning management admin, who distributes them.

I also conduct training, and Miro and Monday.com are tools I rely on for identifying problems, managing projects, collaborating with colleagues, and structuring learning. It is highly effective, both in corporate settings and in my LLC. Learning should be application-based, beginning with problem identification, activating prior knowledge, and providing hands-on engagement. Every development decision needs to be intentional so that the learner experience can be meaningful and effective.

In terms of teachers transitioning, what would you tell them? What should they start or stop doing? Is there anything you have seen in the LinkedIn world or the teacher-transitioning space that you want to address?

Please stop debating about a job on LinkedIn. Not just being vague, but complaining. I have been there, and I get it. But I always tell people, find your community. A hiring manager may be watching. They may have pulled your resume, but if you are openly speaking negatively about an interview or financial struggles, that is not helping you. That is what your community is for. That is why you network. People use LinkedIn the wrong way. It is a networking tool, not a place to seek pity. I have never seen a manager hire someone because they feel bad for them. We have all struggled at some point. If your network is small, reach out privately, message a hiring manager, and put yourself out there. Complaining on LinkedIn does not make you look good.

Also, if you are working to transition out of the classroom, start creating opportunities within your local school or district by volunteering to develop and/or facilitate professional development workshops and curriculum. Those experiences can be documented on your resume. That is what I did to gather experience. Hand-on experience is very effective and can be a guide in helping to determine which area in Learning and Development is ideal for you.

Another mistake I see is people publicly posting their portfolio for feedback. Decision-makers can see that and may assume you lack experience. That is why I emphasize building a strong community. You would be surprised how many people will help you for free. I have been helped, and I have helped others. One thing you will never see me do on LinkedIn is complain. Nobody knew I was laid off last year. I cried real tears, but I kept it private. A week later, I found my current job. Not everything belongs on LinkedIn. If you are looking for a job, put your best foot forward, network, and use LinkedIn properly.

Why do you think so many teachers are leaving?

I had a good teaching experience overall, but there were years I needed more support. I had years in which my test scores were not great but I had to learn more strategies. Even at my 15th year of teaching, I was an effective, strong teacher but I was still willing to learn more to impact my students. The largest issue in education is leadership support. Principals are stressed, but they are not in classrooms enough to model their expectations. Students know when an observation is happening, and teachers often get vague feedback with little guidance.

Teachers are too nervous to challenge their evaluations. Principals outline expectations in meetings, but every teacher has unique needs. New teachers enter the field teaching the way they were taught or based on their training programs. Then they encounter a principal with their own teaching philosophy. Instead of vague directives, principals need to provide clear, structured support.

I will give you an example. In 2010, I was pregnant with my first child. I was 31 and had two students with severe behavioral challenges. I always had strong classroom management, but these students needed more support. I repeatedly asked for help, saying, "I need help. I am pregnant." Nothing changed. I was kicked in the leg, and the stress contributed to me going into labor early. I had my daughter at 34 weeks and six days. When I went on maternity leave, those two students were moved. I am writing a book about this experience actually.

It is not about education, but it is in the book. Those two students were moved to another classroom because the substitute teacher could not handle them. Some principals pick and choose who they want to help, and that was stressful for me. I have also had principals pull me aside and ask, "What do you think about the teacher next door? How is she teaching?" I told them, "I want to be your support, but I am not going to throw another teacher under the bus. My suggestion is to go in and model what you want to see.", Every school where taught had teachers who were burned out. They were stressed. I was one of them. Fortunately, I was able to create opportunities by offering training for the school because I knew it would lead to opportunities in another career outside the classroom.

Even with all of that, it was a great experience for me. Many teachers want to change mindsets and push their students to the highest level, but without support from administration, it is tough. We get it, some buildings only have one or two administrators, but if they took time to model what they expect, I believe more teachers would still be in the field.

SOC Analyst - Lance
Taught for 9 Years (Korea and US) - Elementary

Is this your first role after leaving the classroom?

Yes

What does a SOC Analyst do?

I work for what's known as a managed security service provider, which means that my company provides security services to other companies that don't want to outsource some of their security or all of their security. Specifically, I'm on level one, monitoring the network for events or alerts that come up on our system. When an incident occurs, I investigate by reviewing the alert and consulting various blogs and tools. I assess whether it's a critical threat, something that could be handled later, or merely a matter to inform my client about. I work for a dedicated team for a specific client, I notify their on-call contact whether the situation requires immediate action, can wait, or is insignificant—possibly a false positive. From there, I write up my notes and send it up. Another aspect is to protect the network and prevent server theft or unauthorized access. So, I'm all about protecting the network. A common task that you may be familiar with is that I deal with phishing emails that are reported by users.

How did you prepare for this position?

I'd never even thought about cybersecurity before my friend Sarah, in 2020, started studying for Security Plus, which is a big security certification. She was a teacher as well and she started talking to me about it. I started listening, and I was like, okay, I think I should do this too. She took the certificate test and a boot camp. A lot of people do a boot camp, but I am choosing to get a second bachelor's degree, through Western Governors University. Initially, I started with self-learning through Udemy, Coursera, online learning platforms that are self-paced. I then started mass applying to jobs. I submitted over 500 applications. I was desperate to get out of teaching. I loved working with kids, but the pay wasn't good, and I was tired of dealing with the politics.

Talk to me a little bit about that work-life balance.

I started taking courses towards my second bachelor's while I was still teaching, so it was a little tricky. It was also an emotionally exhausted time because we also had our son and I was studying. But I find that the work-life balance is a lot easier in the corporate world because I can do my work and then leave. I work remotely, so when my day ends, I close my computer and I'm done. When I was a teacher, even my last two years, when I made the decision to not bring work home (grading, planning, etc.), you still have all that in your head about what are you going to do tomorrow and everything. What about that kid that's living in the back of a pickup truck? I'm worried about little Johnny who doesn't come.

Why did you become a teacher?

So, I graduated college in 2012 in the middle of the recession...there were no jobs. I went to Korea (with my wife) to teach English. I never really thought about being a teacher because my degree is actually in Anthropology, but I got this opportunity to teach overseas.

Since you had the experience of teaching abroad, can you tell me a little bit about the differences?

In South Korea, many parents want their children to learn English and so they have after-school academies called hagwons. They're like private tutoring centers where kids go after their regular school day ends. Hagwons are a huge industry in South Korea - almost like a parallel school system. Parents sign their kids up to get extra instruction in subjects like English, math, science, and test prep for high school and college entrance exams.

So that is one difference...parents see hagwon as a way to boost their academics. But because it is a paid service, parents have certain expectations. We called it "edutainment", a combo of education and entertainment. You couldn't just educate them; you had to also make sure that they were having fun. Yes, we were educating them, but it really is a business model as well and there was lots of competition. Overall, the students were also, more or less, well behaved because they were trying their best to learn and understood the expectation.

Why did you leave education?

I love teaching, so I continued it. We returned to the states and I taught in Florida. The cost of living was lower and the pay was lower, but it was better than Korea. But I would say that one reason that I left is because education is under attack in Florida. My wife and I are very involved with our union and she actually works full time for our local teachers union and is no longer in the classroom. In my area they are union busting and passing laws on how to get rid of classroom libraries that aren't approved by the state. Implementing book bans and I have had parents accuse me of indoctrinating their kids. I was asked to sign a petition, saying that I wouldn't lie to my students about history. It caused an uproar and I even had to get my union rep to come in and represent me. I will say 95% of parents were fine. In fact, I am still in contact with a few and they ask how I'm doing now that I have left. But there was that small percentage that just made it really - UNFUN. In addition to that, the cost of living kept going up and the pay was not keeping pace. I was five years in and I was making the same as a starting teacher and also the same as a 13-year veteran. This was because the Florida legislature adopted a bell curve model and $47,500 was some magical number. Florida lawmaker hopes bill aiming to raise minimum salary for teachers gains momentum - Paola Tristan Arruda. What really drove the hammer home, like the final nail in the coffin, was, we had our son and thinking about them and the type of life that I wanted to provide for them...wanting to give them a better life...to be able to go on family vacations and I'd like to be able to afford to put him in sports and not have to worry about money. All of that caused me to leave. So, yeah, it was a big monetary thing for me on top of everything.

What advice do you want to give to teachers regarding making time for skills you need to transition?

Your teaching skills apply to so many different industries. I talk to teachers in various Facebook groups for transitioning teachers. There's so much that you do that can be leveraged towards other careers. For instance, if you want to be a data analyst, look at all the analysis that we do. If you have 40 students, the individual data for every single one of those kids...the curation of individual plans. Sure, you might have to learn some of the technical skills, but there's so much out there that you can do where you'll be more respected. Yes, it's worth the time and the effort to put in at night to get your life back.

I understand that teaching is a calling for a lot of people, but until it's treated better, I think until we leave en masse, they're just going to keep treating us poorly.

I would tell people to not get a teaching degree, but to get a degree in something else and minor in education if you're that interested in it. You can get a master's degree later if you find that you like it and you're willing to put up with all the b*&&$#!@!

Software Engineer - Ann
Taught for 10 years - Grades: 3 & 8 - Subjects: General and ELA

You mentioned your role is full stack. What exactly do you work on?

My position is full stack, which means I work on both the front end (user-facing) and back end (server-side) of our applications. But I'm often given front-end work because I'm passionate about accessibility. For example, I might be asked to adjust a web page's design so it's easier to navigate for users with disabilities, making sure the site can be used by people who rely on screen readers or keyboard navigation. I've attended a lot of accessibility conferences and follow experts in the field, so I'm always looking for ways to apply that knowledge. But I also work on the back end because I have a background in building complex spreadsheets from my teaching days. If you think of spreadsheets that can't communicate with each other, a database is essentially a tool that links all that information together. So, I often handle tasks like linking datasets, pulling information from multiple sources, and making sure everything is in sync.

Walk me through a typical project. What does the workflow look like?

I get work through two main sources. One is our ticketing system, where users submit requests for changes like deleting records, updating websites, or granting system access. If I know I can handle it, I grab the ticket and work on it. For example, if someone needs a specific access role for a new tool, I go into the system and assign those permissions. These tasks usually take an hour to half a day. But sometimes a ticket looks simple on the surface and ends up requiring coordination across multiple systems, turning into a full-day project. The other source is through larger projects run by our team leads. They break these into tasks and either assign them directly or ask me to collaborate with another programmer. I'm usually working on parts of projects that involve integrating front-end design elements with back-end data systems. For instance, if we're redesigning a form that users submit online, I might work on making sure that data goes directly into our database, updates correctly, and is displayed in a report for managers.

I see you know SQL. Do you also work with Power BI?

That's more on the data science and analytics side, which would have been a natural transition for me, given that so much of my work in teaching involved analyzing student data. But I realized I don't love maintaining those systems. I get a bigger kick out of building new tools, troubleshooting issues, and solving puzzles. With software engineering, that's the entire job. You get to constantly build and refine solutions.

You've learned several programming languages. How do they come together in your role?

Learning programming languages isn't like learning French or Russian. It's more like learning the rules of grammar and then applying them to different languages. Once you understand core concepts like variables, loops, and methods, you can pick up new languages more easily. I taught myself JavaScript and some Java in about a year and a half, so I know I can learn. The key is understanding how programming works fundamentally. For example, methods are actions that a program executes, while objects store data in a structured way to keep different parts of the program from interfering with each other. If someone wants to go this route, I'd say focus on building projects that put these concepts into practice. Then go back, refactor your work, and understand why your changes make a difference. One of the most common programming jokes is, "It doesn't work, and I have no idea why." Then, "It works, and I have no idea why." I don't want to be in that "I have no idea why" stage for long. I want to know what I did and how it made an impact.

If you work remotely, tell me what you like or dislike, and the advantages or disadvantages.

Working from home has been fantastic for me. I get more focus time than I ever did in an office. I don't have kids, my spouse is supportive, and I have a house with a dedicated office space, so I know my situation helps. I've gained back 60–75 minutes a day without a commute and love controlling my thermostat, lighting, and background music. I can set up my workspace however I like, fix ergonomic issues, choose my officemates, wear comfortable clothes, and enjoy coffee that's never burned. Plus, I get to work mask-free! There are downsides. Neighborhood noise can be distracting, and I'm responsible for my equipment and ensuring VPN access if the power or internet goes out. I often skip breaks because I don't want my Teams status to change unless I'm in a meeting or notify my supervisor. It's also harder to pick up on workplace norms since I can't observe colleagues, and ergonomic tweaks have added some expenses. Still, it's worth it to create a setup that supports my long-term health and career.

What skills or experiences from your teaching career have been helpful in your new role?

Knowing how to learn independently and break down large tasks into smaller steps translates well. My planning and pacing skills have been useful for running meetings, and while I haven't had to give presentations yet, my public speaking experience will be valuable as I move forward. There are also some unique skills from teaching that helped me: I was the webmaster at one of my schools, and I customized our district's Learning Management System, serving as informal tech support. Colleagues called me the "spreadsheet queen" because I designed master schedules and tracked student data.

As a teacher, the career path is pretty straightforward: teacher, lead teacher, assistant principal. Where do you see yourself going with this?

I started with a five or ten-year plan, but it's changing as I learn more and see new possibilities. I had no idea I'd enjoy C# so much, so I might shift again. The way C# works with .NET and Visual Studio is almost magical. You don't have to fight with it the way I did with JavaScript. I also stay open to new things. My dream job would be using AI and machine learning to build accessibility tools. Ideally, I'd create generative AI that adapts user interfaces based on how people interact with them.

So, you're diving into machine learning?

Right now, I'm focused on natural language processing because I want a solid foundation. I've got smaller projects, like building a poker trainer, but my main goal is a text-to-speech tool that reads contextually, more like an audiobook than the robotic voices we have now. Microsoft and Google are making great strides, so they may beat me to it, but I saw how much my students with dyslexia hated the browser's built-in tool. It's more than just sounding human. I would fluently read sentences naturally, not in chunks. I want to build something that captures that flow. But how do you do that ethically? How do you respect copyright? How do you make it work as one person? It's aspirational right now, but I want to use what I learn to create a system that predicts a user's next move. Some people find that creepy, but I grew up on Star Trek, so I picture technology responding to what you want, not just what you ask for. One joke in programming is that a computer will do exactly what you tell it. It doesn't matter what you meant; it does what you wrote. Why should a non-technical user need to understand that? I hope AI can make that smoother, especially for people with vision or dexterity issues.

Do you miss teaching, and if so, what aspects of it do you miss the most?

I feel like I should. It was my childhood dream and I spent the time, money and energy to earn a master's and substitute teach my way into my local district. (The teacher job

market here was fairly competitive back then). I don't miss it. If the job had stayed the way it was earlier in my career, I would probably still be teaching, but by the time I left, teaching felt a lot like the retail jobs I've held. I may feel differently as more time passes, but I've been away from the classroom for 18 months at this point and I've yet to wish to go back.

What did you do to prepare for your new career? Did you need additional training?

I took a free online course called #100devs, originally created to help 100 people get software jobs. While it gave me valuable web development skills and made me marketable, I realized I needed to upskill further to compete locally, so I took Python and Java classes through Sophia.org. #100devs was created by the founder of Resilient Coders, a program for marginalized people facing generational poverty. During the pandemic, he expanded it to help even more people. Although I've faced challenges like using food banks growing up, I've had access to education and stability, so I wasn't eligible for Resilient Coders. Still, I found it inspiring that he opened the program to a broader audience through YouTube under Learn with Leon and a community-focused Discord server. The program is unique. It's longer than traditional boot camps, self-paced, and requires self-motivation. Live classes on Twitch twice a week were optional, and no one checked attendance or assignments. You had to independently verify your work and ask the community for help when stuck, which encouraged collaboration and growth. As a graduate, I now contribute to the community by helping others with projects, interview prep, and troubleshooting. The alumni network and the support from previous cohorts and Resilient Coders participants have been invaluable. It's a pay-it-forward system that fosters a supportive learning environment.

Knowing what you know now, what would you have changed about your preparation, not necessarily the experiences that you have had?

I would have started sooner - I talked about learning to code for years before I actually I did it. I also should have made time to contribute to Open Source, because I would have learned more about how version control and collaboration work in larger codebases.

Before we talk about why you left, tell me why you became a teacher in the first place.

It was a combination of really loving the way my teachers made me feel important and wanting to help dyslexic students the way teachers helped dyslexic family members. And I was able to do that, for a little while - I was lucky enough to attend Orton-Gillingham training while I was completing my MAT & credential.

What made you decide to leave teaching?

It was a mix of the political climate and growing micromanagement in schools. I watched a community-focused district, known for its award-winning SEL program and valuing diverse learning, turn into a rigid, checklist-driven system of fear and compliance. Spot checks were done to ensure error-filled strategy posters were in specific places, and no unauthorized items were on walls. I was called into a disciplinary meeting with an assistant superintendent for turning a worksheet into a plot summary project and posting my students' work on a bulletin board. Then COVID hit. I listened to the school board argue over Zoom about whether ICU beds and teachers' lives mattered compared to the supposed harms of remote learning, while a board member who accused us of "not working" napped on camera. I was working double my contract hours. The breaking point came when we returned in person, and a student wrote stories about poisoning me. That's when I stopped thinking about leaving and began planning my exit. Ironically, those same board members later proposed closing multiple Title I schools to balance the budget.

The workload was crushing. Veteran teachers said I'd find my stride after a few years, but with curriculum changes, involuntary transfers, new principals, remote learning, and a switch from elementary to middle school, I never got my hours under control. My best year was 50 hours a week. By my last year, I worked 72 hours weekly, taking one Sunday a month off. I almost didn't leave. My dad had suggested IT, and in my pre-teaching jobs, I was the office IT guy at small engineering firms. People wondered why I didn't pursue tech, but back then, it felt impossible. In my city, in the 90s and early 2000s, you needed a CS degree and experience. I believed if you hadn't been programming since childhood, you didn't belong. It's still hard to break into tech if you expect a six-figure salary immediately or have strict criteria. But if you start entry-level, take a modest salary, and are willing to learn, there's room. It just took me time to realize that.

What advice would you give to someone considering leaving teaching for a new career?

Make sure it's really the job you're unhappy with. There's a big difference between getting out of a bad situation and expecting a career change to bring you happiness. If you're unsure, try volunteering or taking on side work over the summer. You'll gain experience and see if it's the right move. But if you know you're done, start making changes. Once you reach that point, staying won't make things better.

Resources: Project Odin, FreeCodeCamp, CodeWars engineers. https://leon-noel.com/100devs/

Software Engineer - Tyler
Taught for 12 years - Grades: Pre-K - 9 - Subject: Various

What tasks do you perform as a software engineer?

I've been a software engineer at for about two and three-quarters years. Someone took a chance on me. I started as an intern, but it felt more like an apprenticeship because I was 36 and started in February. I wasn't working alongside college kids in the summer. Initially, I was on what we called the Identity Team working on user profiles. When I started, I focused on what we call frontend work, which is writing the code your web browser executes to render things and fetch data. Backend engineers handle moving the data around and getting it ready to pass to the front end. Then there are iOS engineers for iPhone app development, Android engineers for Android app development, more data-focused roles, and infrastructure-focused roles. Most commonly, people work on Android, iOS, or back-end. Sometimes you will hear the term "full stack," which usually means doing both frontend and backend work. I started out mostly doing frontend work because it is the easiest to teach yourself and get into the industry. It is also where I thought I could become helpful to a company most quickly. I was on what we called a product team, working on projects that face users. Those projects are usually something like, "Hey, we want the profile to have this new module that lists local businesses you have favorited." The team would come together, a backend engineer, a frontend engineer, an iOS engineer, and an Android engineer, and we would scope or plan out the work as much as possible, then start tackling it. Every day, we would get together and say, "Hey, I got this done yesterday. Today, I am going to work on this. I am blocked by this, or I need help with that." That is the general workflow for a software engineer. That is mostly what life is like in this role.

I want to drill down into that a little more. What are you specifically given that allows you to say, "I'm goint to take that knowledge and do this?" What is that deliverable?

Usually the thing you're given is a design, basically a computer drawing, often created with a program called Figma. Figma is essentially a tool that produces something that looks like a screenshot of what the final product should look like. In an ideal scenario, the Figma design includes every possible flow.

For example, if a user clicks to favorite a business, the design shows the screen they should see before and after they favorite the business.. What is more common is that about seventy-five percent of the flows are mocked up. Then the engineers, because this is what we do all day, start identifying edge cases. For instance, we might ask, "What happens if the user is unverified and they click on a business that is not currently owned?" We call those edge cases. There is typically some back-and-forth with the designers about how to handle those edge cases. Once we agree on how to handle them, the deliverable is essentially making it happen. We write the code to implement the feature and ensure it looks and works the way the designers intended.

After you've done your dailies, do you do sprints?

My company is pretty flexible and lets each team develop a process that works for them, but we do something at least adjacent to sprints, generally. It's about iterating and breaking the work down into as small steps as possible. You make what's called a pull request, which is when you change some amount of code, ideally under 300 lines in one go.

Keeping it smaller makes it more manageable. A teammate reviews it, you make any changes based on their suggestions, and then you merge it into the main branch. Merging means the code is now part of the live code base that users encounter. You keep repeating this process until the feature is done. To handle partially completed features being merged into the main code, we use a feature flag system. This allows you to disable features based on users, locations, or other criteria. You can test the feature yourself while ensuring that users don't actually see it.

Do you want to tell me anything else about being a software engineer in the corporate world that you think teachers should know?

I would say the nature of the work can vary a lot. For example, I switched off my previous team, and now I am on our notification infrastructure team. The work I do now is much different. There are two main types of work I focus on most of the time now. One is project-based, similar to what I did on the profile team, but the projects are very independent. Instead of having multiple people working on different parts like someone on the backend and someone on the frontend I am usually handling one specific part of our infrastructure system. It usually doesn't make sense for multiple people to work on it, so it is a bit more isolated in that way. The second type of work I do involves digging into this big, complex system we have. For example, we send out billions of notifications a week. A lot of my time is spent analyzing data to understand when the system is not performing as expected or finding opportunities to improve the system, make it more efficient, or enhance its functionality.

It sounds like, from a layman's perspective, once the site and everything is built, you would mostly handle updates to correct errors.

Yeah, we call those bug fixes. There is kind of a never-ending stream of bugs to fix. These bugs can happen because you wrote bad code, or they might occur because something external changed. For example, the new Chrome browser might handle something slightly differently than you assumed it would. There are always lots of inputs that are changing.

Let's talk about how you learned to code. I guess the question I'm trying to get to is, once you learned the code, what was the gap between reading all the books, watching YouTube, doing the boot camp, and then sitting down in the actual position?

Before I decided to embark on this career transition, I already knew something about coding and computers. I was a big fan of Excel because I'm that kind of nerd. I could write complicated Excel formulas, which is really just programming in its own way. It's a little different from typical programming, but the logic is similar. After I got my master's in education and realized I didn't have anything I was officially learning at the time, I started exploring coding for fun. I did one of the open courseware courses, an introduction to programming. At that point, I knew the equivalent of what you might learn in the first two or maybe three weeks of a programming boot camp. That's where I started. The way I really learned to code was by building projects of increasing scope and complexity. I talked to a bunch of friends and second-hand connections to get suggestions and feedback about a roadmap to follow. Then I just started working through it. In the very beginning, I used platforms like Coursera to build a foundation of knowledge. Those were good for getting started. But pretty quickly, it became clear that I needed to start applying the knowledge to build things in order to really learn and grow.

What languages did you first begin to learn?

I started with JavaScript, which is the language that the browser runs. The idea was that I would be more useful and hireable by learning frontend development and web development. JavaScript is a great starting point because it is so widely used and practical.

Before I got hired, I also started working with a language called TypeScript. TypeScript builds on JavaScript and adds typing, which makes it easier to work with in some ways. It is essentially an enhanced version of JavaScript designed to make development more efficient and manageable.

Did you learn Python?

Python is one of the most popular programming languages. It is incredibly flexible and is commonly used for a lot of different things. That open courseware course I took a while ago was based in Python, but I didn't use it when I was studying because it's not often used for frontends. Most of the work I do now is in Python. We use it for a wide variety of things like processing new posts by users, creating notifications to send, and using machine learning models to personalize things for users.

Python is also one of the easiest languages to learn because it reads almost like English. It has tons of built-in features, so something that might take many lines of code in JavaScript can often be done in one line in Python. It is very popular for data science and machine learning too. It's everywhere and is a great first language to learn because of how accessible it is.

Did you go through a boot camp at all?

I didn't.

Since that was a couple of years ago, is there anything you've seen out there now whether it's a boot camp or something else that you would recommend if you were learning this on your own today?

That's a good question. I think it is a lot to break into the field now than when I did it. The economy has cooled off, and there have been a lot of tech layoffs. Many companies are only hiring experienced engineers now because there's a bigger pool of talent, and experienced engineers can be cheaper. There are also fewer companies investing in earlier-career engineers. We can talk more about this later, but the only time I regretted not going through a boot camp was when I was job hunting. My resume lost out to new grads with a computer science degree and to people who had completed boot camps. At least with boot camps, someone could vouch for the person by saying, "Hey, this individual finished the program and earned a certificate." However, once I got hired, I realized that doing it all myself had prepared me better than what I've heard about typical boot camp graduates.

What were the reasons you left education?

I've had this conversation a lot, and the metaphor I use is that there were things both pushing me out and pulling me toward something new. I was getting pushed out of education because I was starting to feel burned out. I worked in private schools because my undergraduate degree was in geosciences from a liberal arts college, and I didn't take education-specific classes. In 2008, during the financial crisis, the only job I could find was an internship at a private school, so I ended up staying in private schools. In private schools, there are even fewer career growth opportunities, and that was frustrating. On top of that, the job itself is incredibly hard. We were living near San Jose, which has an incredibly high cost of living, and I had just had my first child and then had my second. Finances were getting tighter, and all those things were pushing me away from education. At the same time, I had something else I was really interested in and enjoyed doing. I had taken a coding course for fun before I even considered transitioning careers because I was interested in computers and programming. It felt like there was an opportunity to do a job I enjoyed and be compensated much more generously.

With some research, I realized the transition was feasible. I didn't need to get another degree, and I figured I could make the switch without attending a boot camp. The only real risk was the job search period and managing without income for a while. Those factors combined led me to make the decision to switch careers.

If you work remotely, tell me about how you like or dislike it, and what the advantages or disadvantages are.

I love it! I absolutely love working remotely. Having young kids at home, except for my first grader, means I get moments with them during the day that I would miss otherwise. I also like having my office set up the way I want. Coding requires a lot of focus, and focusing in a traditional office would be tough for me. There are practical benefits too, like not needing to pack lunch and being able to take a midday run to unwind. I usually start work early, around seven, so I can focus in the morning and be available when the kids get home. The independence is great, but as an extrovert, I do miss interacting with people in person. It is a trade-off, but it works for me.

Do you have the opportunity to work in a hybrid setup, or not at all?

Not at all right now. I go into our headquarters in San Francisco about twice a year for a week. We used to have an office near where I live, outside Boulder, Colorado, but there are only six or seven of us in the area, and we are all spread out, so it doesn't really make sense to have an office anymore.

Have you faced any difficulties transitioning to your new career?

I felt some guilt leaving teaching because it gave me a sense of contributing to the greater good. Moving to a for-profit company was a big change, and my current role, sending notifications, does not feel as meaningful. I hope to find tech work that aligns more with my values, but at the time, I had to take what was available. Another adjustment was learning to schedule vacations. Since the age of five I have lived on a school calendar with breaks built in, so I initially went months without time off before realizing I had to plan it myself. While teaching relied on breaks to recharge, this job requires managing time differently. Although I miss the convenience of long breaks, tech offers generous vacation policies. You can take longer trips or even delay a job start date to create your own summer vacation. It is different, but it works.

Is there anything else you want to share? Whether it's advice, something about what you do, or anything I may have missed?

One thing I've done a lot recently is connecting with people who are trying to transition from teaching to software engineering. Earlier this year, I was also talking to a lot of undergrads from my college who were trying to get into the tech industry. Some of them were computer science majors planning to become software engineers, but others were coming from fields like anthropology or combining their major with computer science. I tried to help them think through their options.

If you could suggest one thing to improve education what would it be?

The obvious one is better compensation for teachers, but something more specific would be reducing the whiplash caused by constantly changing curricula and teaching approaches. I worked as a math specialist and coach, and the amount of stress caused by switching methods or materials without proper research is huge. In other countries, there are national curricula, so every school uses the same material every year. I'm not saying we need that exactly, but more consistency would be beneficial for everyone. For example, at my kids' school, the middle school recently switched from an investigative math curriculum to a very rote, drill-and-kill approach. I bet in five years, they'll switch back. That constant back-and-forth puts an unnecessary burden on teachers to smooth out the transitions.

Do you have any advice for teachers considering a career change?

It's okay to think about your own needs or your family's needs when deciding what to do next. You might feel some guilt about leaving education I definitely did but reframing it helped me. I realized that the sense of doing something good for the world, which we often substitute for adequate compensation, is still valid even if you decide to move on. The work you've done as a teacher is not any less valuable just because you choose to start working in another field. If the role you're in is not working for you, you don't have to plow through because you think you owe it to the kids. You also owe it to yourself to find something interesting and meaningful.

Wow, I love that. It's so true. Many teachers feel guilty and think they have to stay because of the kids and the nobility of teaching.

I've had managers and bosses use that argument, saying, "This is extra work for everyone, but we need to do it for the kids." That feeling is so ingrained in the role. Without it, fewer people would go into teaching. It's okay to feel conflicted, but making the best choice for yourself or your family doesn't make you a bad person. For example, recently when I had to get my dog's teeth cleaned, it led to additional costs for biopsies and other procedures. It was an unexpected expense, but I didn't have to panic about being able to afford it. That kind of stability allows you to take care of things in a way that feels reasonable. Making choices that improve your life doesn't mean you're selfish or bad.

Software Engineer Developer - Michael
Taught for 9 years - Grades: Pre-K, K & 2

Walk me through a project or about what you do as a developer.

Every morning, we start with a stand-up for our Software Engineering Department. The website I work on has various tabs, and our team is divided based on these tabs. Before my team stand-up, I review messages or emails. I attend my team stand-up and a tech stand-up, where we discuss what we did yesterday, what we'll work on today, and any blockers we might have so the team can offer support. Each day varies depending on meetings. We have specific and routine meetings, including refinements where we review and grade incoming stories (tasks for developers) based on difficulty and complexity. We also have a planning meeting for the upcoming two-week sprint. Developers start with their stories at the beginning of the sprint, aiming to finish them halfway through and then move them on to quality assurance. During this process, we support developers as needed. Our day involves coding, supporting developers, or addressing issues that come up.

Can you give me the definition of stories?

There are business requirements that need to be implemented on our site, such as new information or content added to a page for users, or more information about their specific claim. If a user clicks on their specific claim, that's what we work on. A new field might be added within a claim with new data. The story encapsulates the work that needs to be done for that specific business requirement. That can be broken down, usually into something that can be completed within a week.

How did you learn all of this? Not the software or the language, but everything else? The stand-ups, routines, sprints, and the overall workflow process.

I learned as I went. The acronyms and specific terminology varied from my school experience because different schools have different languages. I first had to learn what each term meant, often asking people about acronyms or specific words they used for so long they didn't realize I didn't understand. I usually do a bit of research on my own with a quick Google search. There's a lot of Googling to understand where they are. Even though the official methodology they follow is called Agile, they do it slightly differently at my company. I did my own research, was vulnerable, and made the team aware. I told them, "I don't understand this part. I'm still grasping this. Please help."

Give me an example of when you had to dig in and ask those types of questions.

A lot of it I try to do in person. My company is split up across five states. My specific team is in Chicago. I try to be vulnerable and ask questions in the office as much as possible. My team moves very quickly, but if something is happening, I'm always upfront and honest. For example, I'll say, "Hey, I'm still learning this. I'm not used to this methodology. I just want to understand this and that." If I don't understand or if I notice other teammates don't understand, as a former teacher, I set clear expectations for the whole team and document them. That way, we have somewhere to go and look at. It's not just evolving in our heads; we have a place to refer to.

Can you walk me through a project?

I would say when I first started, it was a very slow onboarding process.

After a while, contractors began working on front-end tasks. When their contract ended, I was utilized for my front-end skills because that was what I had been hired for. The team consisted primarily of back-end developers, so they gave this responsibility to me. I worked on it for a week, and every day, I was honest about where I was and what I was struggling with. By being upfront, I didn't run into any issues that completely stopped me. Over the course of about three weeks, I worked on the project, which eventually spilled over to the next sprint. When I encountered some challenges, I pulled in a teammate for support because I didn't understand certain aspects and needed their expertise. After resolving those issues, we submitted a pull request to a specific branch, which was then deployed to an acceptance environment accessible only to our team. I clarified what needed to be done, what required testing, and what had changed. Once that was complete, I requested deployment to the staging environment, which is the final step before production. After that, it was out of my hands, and I moved on to a new story.

Have you ever been in a situation where you had nothing to work with, or have you always been provided with something to start from?

I learned quickly from teaching not to reinvent the wheel and working at a bigger company provides the advantage of having access to other teams' code repositories. For example, the contractor we had was really skilled, and I learned a lot from reviewing his work. I Googled unfamiliar concepts in the code because it was more modern than what I was used to. I replicated his approach to maintain consistency within the code base. Additionally, I examined solutions other teams had implemented and adapted those where applicable. This approach saves time and ensures quality because the code has already passed at least one level of review before being shared with our team.

Can you walk me through something specific you worked on? Maybe testing new features or mentoring junior web developers. Also, can you explain what your transition into

this role looked like and give an example of what that process entailed?"

It's for a marketing agency. We worked for one specific client, based in Chicago, and I really enjoyed it. Marketing people are fun. My work was split evenly between email development and coding. For the email development, I used a website tool to build emails visually, like a click-and-drop interface. It was almost like working in a word processor but for emails. The other half of my work involved producing actual code. There was one senior developer who built the entire website, and the person in the junior position handled simpler tasks to support the website's ongoing updates. My role was to take on these tasks and help reduce costs for the client by not requiring a senior developer for everything. This role was designed to be short-term, usually one or two years, because there was no room for growth in a small company with long-standing senior developers. I stayed for a year, and while the role was limited in upward mobility, I genuinely enjoyed it and found it fun.

What did you do to prepare for this field? Have you had to go back to school or receive any additional training for your new career? How did you learn software and languages?

My friend gave me the idea of being a software engineer. He worked at big companies. I thought there was no way, but the more I researched it, I knew I wanted to look for something that was really interesting because I didn't want to just get out of teaching. I wanted to make it a career that I wanted to do. I watched documentaries about coding and the field, watched YouTube videos, read some articles, but I never actually did coding.

The pandemic hit, the world shut down. I was working from home. I was a really well-oiled machine. Once after a few weeks with my classroom, I realized the world was changing. I started looking for a coding boot camp that fit between the end of the school year and the beginning of the next school year for summer. Everything was shut down so I wouldn't have FOMO. I looked at boot camps and found one that was good quality.

Once I narrowed it down, I chose General Assembly. They have really good data and supportive career coaches that honestly help you get into the field. I did twelve weeks, spending my nights coding, trying to network as much as possible. It took me an entire year of networking and trying to find interviews. I continued learning because I had to continue pushing myself to get that job. It was full stack, so it was front and back end, but I really like the front end. It made more sense to me. I got a lot of feedback from people I networked with who said to focus on one or the other because they knew I wouldn't be an expert in both. I chose front end. That's how I got my job.

Would you say you have a talent for graphic art or design? Are you visually astute?

Yes. I was teaching. Through teaching, I learned I am a visual learner. I like to be creative as well. This is perfect. When we were taught the Framework React by Facebook, I really liked it. I love the story. I loved how it was used. These things were happening on a website that I didn't even realize how significant they were. I just honed in on that because it was fun.

Knowing what you know now, would you have changed anything about your preparation? Not necessarily your experiences, but anything else?

The only thing I would change is I wish I would have just started coding to see if it was fun. I felt overwhelmed with teaching and didn't want to feel like I was failing or just overwhelmed. At the end of a teaching day, when you get off, you just want to go home. Transitioning and working full-time while trying to do a coding boot camp was challenging, but I am happy with how it worked out. Unfortunately, the pandemic was a pandemic, but it gave me the opportunity for the world to stop, allowing me to focus 100% on myself for the first time and make the transition I wanted to make.

Do you think you would have made the transition if we had not had the pandemic? When did you make the decision to leave teaching?

I made that decision in 2018. I was at a charter school in Chicago and had tough classrooms every year. Everyone at the school would say, "Wow, that's a really tough classroom." One year, after a half day of kindergarten, staff came in, and my coaches and I had to choose a child to move to another classroom so I could manage.

It was my third year at the school. I had taught kindergarten for two years and wanted to move up to second grade. Many challenging students had moved away, so I thought it would be easier. But right before the school year started, those children moved back to the neighborhood. As the year went on, the students faced more challenges, and I was really struggling and not mentally well. Then, on a late Friday at dismissal, the administration pulled me in.

Previously, the administration had been supportive, especially during my tough kindergarten class the year before. Nobody knew how to handle my classroom, and none of the special teachers wanted to take my students. Some even threatened to quit if assigned to my class. Despite this history, the administration suddenly blamed me, saying it was my fault for not connecting enough with a particular student.

I had a strong relationship with his mom and was in regular contact with her. The student, however, was often angry for no clear reason, even though he came from a supportive family. They told me it was still my fault for not connecting with him enough. At the time, we only had 20 minutes for lunch, which included dropping off the kids, going to the second floor, microwaving my lunch, using the restroom, and coming back down. I had wanted to use my lunch break to sit with him and build a relationship, but the time constraints made that unrealistic.

Over 70 percent of my students were dealing with untreated trauma, and the entire class was struggling. That weekend, a friend suggested I look into a coding boot camp. I was also considering a master's program in school leadership and debating whether to discuss it with my principal and vice principal. Ultimately, that conversation led me to consider a new direction for my career.

I'm so glad that happened, and I was able to get out because I really needed to do it for my health. My family was concerned about my health. My friends were tired of hearing my stories. That's how I got out.

I get all of that! That mental trauma when you're dealing with students is real.

I was talking with some friends who are still in education about how I'm working on lowering my work anxiety. I feel like I have to do everything immediately because of my teaching background. He said many of his teacher friends have the same issue. This is a real problem.

It's because of that urgency. I don't know where it comes from, but there's always this sense of urgency, even with lesson plans. We do all that work, but the urgency is still there. How have the skills and experiences from your teaching career helped you succeed in your new role?

First and foremost, soft skills. I actually got my job because I'm a teacher. A recruiter reached out after I turned on the "open to work" sign. Within a week, she messaged me. During the interview, I focused on my soft skills because I knew they were a strong point. After the interview, she said she reached out because she searches for teachers turned software engineers. She mentioned that there's something about teachers turned software engineers that works really well at their company. Honestly, it's our soft skills; we aren't afraid to have conversations and we get to the point directly. I'm humble and always asking questions. I have very serious team members who, if anyone makes a mistake, don't address it directly. Instead, they say, "Hey team, reminder of blah, blah, blah," which is so passive-aggressive. I'm the opposite. I say, "Oops, you made a mistake. Oh man, I would have made it too." I open up to be vulnerable, and that's often missing. I'm leading a large effort as a front-end developer, but my team has been leaning on me. I'm just doing my job, and many people have said, "You're doing a great job." I'm not coding something and solving a world issue, but I think those soft skills aren't really highlighted in teaching. It's hard for me to see myself from the outside, but I know I try to have my stuff together. I'm honest about what I'm not doing well. I've told the team, "Hey, this is something I don't understand at all. Does anybody want to do this?" My team has really appreciated that. We talk about work a lot, but we have yet to talk about anything else. I've been there six months, and I barely know anything about my team. As a teacher, I know how to solve issues. I know how to Google things and solve problems. I know when I need to stop and ask for help.

Do you miss not having a summer break? Explain why or why not.

No, I didn't really have summer breaks. One summer, I studied for the GRE. Before that, the LSAT. I spent one summer in New York between school years, mostly in bed. I didn't realize I was depressed until I left New York and processed my emotions. The school year ended, and I went from 200% to nothing. I avoided people and went to a few museums, but those were just distractions. Even spring breaks were just about surviving. I like my routine now. I manage my time at work. My hours are mine, and I do not respond outside of them. When teammates message me at 6:00 a.m., I wait. I enjoy life outside of work. I probably need a vacation soon, but a short one will do.

That's what I'm finding. A lot of people don't miss those breaks because they were always recouping. Always recovering, trying to get ready to go back. What advice would you give teachers regarding the transition?

Do what truly makes you happy and what you enjoy because you deserve it after everything you've done. My therapist helped me realize that leaving the classroom is hard. No matter when you leave, it's the right time for you. You've done so much in this field, and you don't need to make up for the challenges of our educational system. It's not something you can solve right now. If you're at your endpoint, you need to focus on yourself and give yourself the energy you deserve. I also worked with my parents through this process because I could have left during the school year. I received a job offer and wasn't initially thinking about taking it. Luckily, it came two weeks before the school year started. I already had all my stuff home, and I emailed my resignation letter to leadership, thanking them for the time. I was there for two years. I told them my classroom items were available for any teachers. I was done, washed my hands clean, and it felt great.

Solutions Consultant - Jenni
Taught for 17 years - Grades: 1 & 3

Tell me about your career in education.

I'm a former teacher and what I can most easily describe as a building teacher leader which is kind of like being the principal's right-hand person. I supported the development of school policies and procedures, was the chair of the safety committee, and a member of both the building response team and the response to intervention team. I was really hands-on and deeply involved in a lot of the structures we put in place, which was great.

What have you been doing since leaving education, and what is your current role?

After leaving education, I became a quality assurance analyst at Paper Education. I reviewed chat sessions and transcripts from tutoring sessions, providing coaching and feedback to improve tutors' interactions with students across all grade levels. I also trained new team members, including tutor managers and advanced-level tutors, on conducting peer quality assurance. Training new quality analysts on our marquee platform was another exciting part of my role. Now, I am a solutions consultant at Navigate360, specializing in three products: our behavioral threat assessment case manager, detect scanning service, and P3 anonymous tip reporting system. I work closely with the sales team and meet with prospective clients to present these tools and answer questions about how they can support schools and other organizations. In my first two months, I have immersed myself in understanding our products and how they solve challenges for clients. This role has been a learning experience, but I am energized by the opportunity to apply my teaching skills in a completely new field. Leaving education was not an easy decision, but it is rewarding to see how my background as an educator translates to this work. I feel like I am still making a difference, just in a different way.

What did you do to prepare for this field or career?

All of the skills I have used in both my role as a quality assurance analyst and now as a solutions consultant are those I developed and strengthened throughout my 15 years as a teacher and building teacher leader. I did not need to acquire a new degree, go back to school, or take additional training beyond job onboarding. However, I have chosen to take courses to enhance my practice. For example, I completed Google's project management course on Coursera, which introduced me to methodologies like Agile and their application in corporate settings. On Udemy, I have taken courses on project management to refine how I balance, organize, and prioritize tasks. Currently, I am taking a course on mastering sales skills. This is not required for my role, but it helps me understand my team's work and equips me to do my best when sharing information. Understanding the sales cycle and the client's stage in their journey helps me tailor demos effectively. For example, with an IT director, I focus on technical aspects, while a district administrator's conversation centers on administrative needs. I pursue these courses because I want to grow. Even after training hundreds of teachers and delivering countless presentations, I know I can always improve. I actively seek opportunities to learn by asking my manager and colleagues questions. While I did not need to take additional courses or return to school, the extra learning I have pursued has been my choice, driven by a desire to grow and continually improve.

If you work remotely, tell me what you like or dislike, disadvantages, and advances.

Remote work has its pros and cons. One of the biggest pros is being there for my two children, my seven-and-a-half-year-old daughter and four-year-old son. Being remote means I can be home when they are sick or if there is a half day at school. More importantly, I can give them a full and peaceful morning. When I was teaching, my husband and I worked an hour away and had to drop off the kids at 6:30 a.m., even though my daughter's school did not start until 9:00 a.m. She stayed in early care until her bus arrived. Rushing them out the door to beat traffic toward New York City was frustrating.

Now, we have home-cooked breakfasts and take our time. My daughter practices reading and math, my son traces to prepare for pre-K, and we all sing along to music in the car. Starting the day calm and happy makes a huge difference. Remote work also lets me handle small household tasks, keeping weekends free for family time. When we were commuting, coming home at 4:30 to cook, help with homework, and manage bedtime routines was exhausting. Now, I can cook dinner or do laundry during the day, so weekends feel like a break. Flexibility is another pro. Both Paper Education and Navigate360 allow schedule adjustments for unexpected events. After a rough night with a sick child, I can start later and make up the time. This was impossible in teaching, where you have to be "on" in front of the class. Remote work does have its cons. It can feel lonely, and the line between work and home often blurs. At Paper, I worked late into the night, often returning to work at 9:00 p.m. My team encouraged me to set boundaries, which I am now better at following in my current role. Another downside is how sedentary it can be. In school, I was constantly moving, attending meetings, and walking between wings. Now, even with breaks to do laundry, it is not the same level of activity. I have learned the importance of setting boundaries and prioritizing balance for both physical and mental health. Without it, things can spiral out of control.

As a teacher, sometimes we didn't have much autonomy and tell me how that's changed.

My manager in both roles, my former manager and my current manager, are not micromanagers, which is great. They would give me a task, and I would ask questions to make sure I understood the purpose, the goal, the deadline, and their vision. Then I went to work, and they trusted me to get the job done. That autonomy allowed me to produce great work with minimal stress. I didn't have to worry about small details or preferences from my manager because they trusted my ability and skill. Every time, they were pleased with the results. It was nice to be appreciated and have control over how I approached the project.

What skills or experiences from your teaching career have been helpful in your new role?

Some of the skills that have been helpful include my ability to multitask. In the classroom, you manage students working independently, a small group lesson, and an assembly starting in ten minutes. You have to wrap up your group while ensuring the whole class gathers and puts away their materials. That ability to juggle multiple tasks has been very useful. Another helpful skill is planning projects thoroughly. In teaching, unit planning involves considering the end goal and working backward. You think about all the pieces, like the questions to ask, materials to use, and homework to assign while integrating other disciplines. This same approach applies to my current role, where I plan training or create demos. For example, when I trained an onboarding specialist on the QA team, I developed supplemental resources to support the trainees. This thorough planning skill, developed in teaching, continues to serve me well. Communicating with different stakeholders has also been essential. As a teacher, I adapted my style for parents, colleagues, and building leaders. Later, as a building teacher leader, I gained experience speaking with district leaders, superintendents, and politicians. For example, as a test coordinator, I worked with our middle school to administer their honors test. These experiences taught me to tailor my communication based on the audience, a skill I now use regularly in my role. Conversations with the CEO or director of corporate recruitment range from formal project updates to casual coffee chats. Learning to communicate effectively has been invaluable. Problem-solving under pressure is another skill I have carried over from teaching. Remote work often brings asynchronous communication and unexpected technical issues, but staying calm and finding solutions quickly feels natural. In the classroom, you are constantly managing surprises like a class trip, a spilled bottle of water, or a sick student. These experiences prepared me to handle challenges efficiently. Another skill I brought from teaching is creating engaging and purposeful training. Over time, I became intentional about simplifying complex information and tailoring it to my audience. Whether designing a unit plan or creating a training presentation, I focus on helping people grasp background knowledge and actionable steps. This skill has been critical in my current work.

Knowing what you know now, what would I have changed about my preparation?

Even with everything I know now, I would not change my preparation. I loved teaching and education, and I still do. I miss the people, the families, and my colleagues. Teaching gave me skills and experiences I might not have gained in corporate. I no longer manage 32 emotionally dysregulated students or clients with five-minute attention spans, but those experiences shaped me. I understand child development well, which helps me as a mother and in connecting with other moms and their children. I do wish the corporate world better understood how prepared teachers are and how transferable our skills can be. Teachers present daily, keeping students engaged and conveying information in ways they can understand, whether in first grade or high school. Teachers accomplish so much in a day, a week, a month, and a year. We are hardworking, self-motivated, and flexible. I want the corporate world to appreciate that more

Have you faced any difficulties transitioning to your new career? And if so, describe them.

Imposter syndrome is definitely a challenge. You go on LinkedIn, and there are 2,000 applicants. It makes you think, "Forget this. I'm never going to make it." There are also many auto-generated rejection letters, and those are really deflating. Networking is very different from the education space. I never had to network with a principal before applying for a teaching job or with other teachers at a school. This is completely new for me in this industry, and it can be intimidating. What do you say? How do you sound genuine about wanting to get to know someone while also wanting the job? It can feel impossible to get it right. What I have found is to just be myself. I apply only for roles that genuinely interest me, with companies I care about—companies I have worked with as an educator or as a mother. This helps because I can speak honestly about how much I love the product, the people, or the service. From there, I focus on building a connection and working my way forward.

How has your new career impacted your work-life balance compared to teaching?

My first role at Paper as a QC Analyst was a challenge. I was really eager to prove myself. They were a startup company, and I had heard from so many people I networked with that you could grow quickly. I wanted to prove myself and grow because I love being challenged, and I knew the role I was coming into was very entry-level. But as a result, I failed miserably at setting boundaries and burned myself out. I said yes to everything. In my new role at Navigate360, my work-life balance has been a really positive change. It is very important to my team, and we are all adamant about holding boundaries. This has been a great thing for me and my family. In teaching, I was lesson planning on weekends and answering emails and calls before and after school. So in that respect, it's been a positive change.

How has your teaching background helped or hindered me in my new career?

My teaching background has helped my new career in many ways. I have become a go-to for training because I can break down complex information. Sometimes, I thrived on the positive energy of being "on" with my first graders, students, friends, and colleagues – it's only natural that I miss that environment. My project management skills and go-getter attitude have also been invaluable. I often manage multiple projects at once, creating timelines, prioritizing tasks, and meeting deadlines. These skills have been crucial in my career growth.

Do you miss teaching? And if so, what aspects do you miss the most?

I really miss the daily interaction with fellow educators who often stopped by my office. I do not miss feeling undervalued, disrespected, overworked, or micromanaged by the system. Sometimes, when volunteering at my daughter's school, I realize I miss teaching more than I thought. Teaching gave me so much, but it also showed how much support new teachers need. That understanding led me to start Pencils & Planners. Teachers spend so much time with our children but are rarely taught how to balance or prioritize their work. Many feel pressured to create Pinterest-worthy classrooms, which is not real teaching. It takes about three years to feel confident. Without support, the job feels overwhelming, driving many teachers to leave within one or two years. As a mentor teacher, I co-taught, demonstrated strategies, provided behavior management support, and helped teachers adjust approaches. Hands-on mentoring made the job feel possible and retained teachers. During the pandemic, I started Pencils & Planners to support new teachers. I fell in love with this work, though balancing it with a new job has been challenging. There is a growing community of teachers with side hustles that become businesses. I found a business coach, Kayse Morris, who taught me to grow passive income while doing something fulfilling. That became Pencils & Planners.

Why did you decide to leave education, and was there a specific event or situation that inspired you to pursue a new career?

A year and a month ago, I decided to leave education. I had come to a point in my career where I hit a crossroad. It was either officially becoming a principal or moving toward becoming a superintendent, but those weren't pathways I was interested in. I still wanted to have an impact in education. I wanted to support teachers, students, and families in some way, so I decided to explore opportunities in the corporate world that would allow me to stay connected to education but in a different capacity.

My reasoning was twofold. First, I live for my children. I was dropping my daughter off two hours before her school day started. She was losing two hours of sleep and missing a homemade breakfast. She was losing the calm and peace of good starts to the day. Instead, she was spending those two hours in early care with other kids in an unstructured setting. At some point, when you give kids two hours of unstructured time, problems happen. She was getting in trouble leading to my husband and I punishing her, but I felt like it was my fault. She was there for two hours before she really needed to be anywhere, in a space that didn't have staff to entertain them or lead activities. The kids were just left in a room with supervision but no structure. We sent her to practice work and activities, but it felt like punishment. I hated that for her. Second, my job has become second nature. I could do it in my sleep. I could do it during a pandemic. I could do it from afar. I could do it in person. But I crave new learning and challenges. Mommy guilt, combined with my desire for a new challenge, made me decide it was time to make a change.

What advice would you give to someone considering leaving for a new career?

My advice has a couple of key points. First, don't be afraid to go, because nothing is ever set in stone. You can leave and go back to teaching, or you can find another job in the industry. My sister-in-law, who has been in corporate her whole life, taught me that there's nothing to feel bad about. Teachers are used to staying in the same school for decades, but in corporate, it's normal to change jobs every few years. Don't be afraid to leave if you're unhappy, and don't be afraid to come back if you miss teaching. Sometimes you just need a break or a sabbatical. Would I go back to my job if it were offered? I don't know. Sometimes I say yes, sometimes no.

My other advice is to look at job descriptions for roles you're unsure about. In education, a teacher is a teacher, and a principal is a principal. In corporate, roles like solutions consultant or solutions engineer might mean the same thing. Don't hesitate to take a chance on a job you think you can do, even if you're missing one or two requirements. You can learn new skills. What you can't learn is drive, dedication, motivation, and initiative, and teachers already have those. Teachers are asked to pivot and learn new things all the time. Every year, we have to adapt to a new curriculum. Be able to explain what you already know in the job description and how you can fill in the gaps. Don't be afraid to say, "Here's where I'm not experienced, but here's how I plan to get better." Share your excitement and be yourself. You want to work for a place that values you. I'm a quirky, goofy kind of person, and that's how I am in my interviews. I take them seriously, but I stay true to myself. That's what you'll get if you hire me.

Update:

Jenni left her corporate position and returned to a school setting, working closer to home and is available in the mornings for her kids. She is now a Literacy Coach and AIS Reading teacher and is now happier than she's been in a long while.

Resources:

www.KayseMorris.com

https://pencilsandplanners.com/

Solutions Consultant - Haley
Taught for 5 years - Grades: 6 - 8 - Subject: ELA

Talk to me a little bit about that first leap.

Basically what you had shared. I knew I was ready to leave. I had taught all through Covid virtually. I was relocating from Wisconsin to South Carolina, and I pretty much knew I wasn't going to teach down here. I was in a position where I would do literally whatever, even if I had to jump in at an entry-level sales role. Educational sales consultant was a fancy name for entry-level sales which involved a lot of cold calling.

Did you decide that you wanted to go into sales?

Sales definitely wasn't on my mind. I felt this need to get into a tech company because I had no sense of my skills being transferable in the tech world. I thought maybe educational technology companies would look at me and see that I understand education.

Talk to me about your role as the educational sales consultant?

The ramp-up process was three months, and then I got a bunch of accounts assigned to me. My role was to call out, check-in, email, and leave voicemails. It was based on hitting a quota, so if they were getting low on hours, I would call to see how tutoring was going. If they were having issues with their tutor, I would get a new tutor assigned. If they had a new subject that they needed a tutor for, I would get that taken care of. It was a lot about hosting a discovery conversation, figuring out what they needed, and then being able to provide recommendations.

You said there was a three-month ramp-up process. What were you learning in those three months?

It was a lot of cold-calling people who were not interested. My heart is on my sleeve at all times, no matter how much I've tried to hold that back. I was in tears many days because people would just hang up on me. They would ask me why I was calling. It was really defeating. That period taught me how that side of sales can be. It did teach me to pivot conversations really well. If something isn't going great, let's try to use a different value proposition or dig into another avenue that we can support. Engagement and re-engagement strategies were things that I learned.

How did you then go into customer success management?

My sales experience really served as a springboard for me. I had heard that Varsity Tutors was launching a separate department called Varsity Tutors for Schools. I just lit up because I thought, schools—that's for me. In this role instead of finding tutors for just one family, we were finding tutors for hundreds of kids in small groups. It resonated with me as something I wanted to do—getting back closer to working with teachers and principals. I started out doing more of an implementation specialist role. I had a hand in the entire team's new programs and the implementation or onboarding process. It's interesting as I look at my career trajectory now, how involved in the onboarding phase I've been for the last almost two years.

Where in the process did your roles start?

Everything customer success-related is typically post-sale. Our sales folks would be calling, doing the discovery, trying to get a program proposed, and getting a contract signed. Once that contract was signed, they would bring in an implementation specialist and the customer success manager to have that first kickoff call and determine the direction of the program.

In terms of onboarding versus customer success, customer success is a newer function to companies. They're realizing the importance of long-term proactive customer retention strategy. Now that it's showing its worth, companies recognize that CSMs spend so much time in the onboarding phase. Companies have established success teams and are starting dedicated onboarding teams. When I switched to Intuit Mailchimp, I was excited to have that dedicated onboarding focus. We have customers for the first 30 days or so, and our metrics

are based on 90-day retention.

Talk to me about the kickoff meetings and what that kickoff meeting looks like.

A kickoff call—I usually run them. I have a slide deck with an agenda. I do the welcome and introduction first. I try to get as personal as possible. I share stuff about myself outside of work so they can know my background and who I am. I invite them to do the same because the most important thing is to get that connection and relationship going. That's what solidifies the customer's trust in the long run—at least that's my opinion. Once that's out of the way, I ask a lot of questions to get to know their goals, their most immediate priorities. In my current role, I start making recommendations about what tools will be most beneficial to them.

Are you at liberty to say why you left Varsity Tutors for Mailchimp?

Basically, I was seeking growth. I wanted to branch out of EdTech. I had already left the classroom, but I was still in EdTech. I wanted to see what other opportunities my career could take me to.

How many years did you teach, and did you switch schools?

I taught for six years, and yes, I switched schools.

It seems there's a lot of movement in the corporate world, and it's a non-issue. But in the education world, it's almost taboo.

I'm trying to pinpoint where the taboo is. Is it just leaving education in general?

Yeah, I think it's hard. It's the yearly contract, the cycle of summers off, holidays, and Christmas break. I have an eight-year-old, and part of me was like, I can never leave teaching because what would I do over summer break? There's so much. And also, the pressure of not renewing your contract in February or March and then knowing you have to find something by June. I have so many friends who still teach, and that time frame always gets to people. I was part of one school in particular where you had to pay a couple thousand dollars if you broke your contract. But you mentioned we never leave because of the kids, but we always stay because of them. That's the biggest thing that keeps people in it. I struggled with it for a good year and a half when people would ask, "Are you still teaching?" and I'd say no, then follow up with a justification for why I wasn't teaching. Deep down, I did feel bad or guilty for leaving. But once you get out, you realize how much money you can make, the experience you can get, the leadership opportunities. This was never in my realm of possibility before—almost double what I was making in my first year of teaching. It's a no-brainer.

Everybody makes such a big deal about Salesforce. Talk to me about the onboarding for yourself, the learning process, how you learned to use it. Walk me through anything about your current position so someone who doesn't know anything can understand.

Salesforce—we're moving towards using it all the time. Right now, it's more on the sales side, and I have to access that system. I use TurnZero as a CRM to manage my book of business. As a former teacher, I had technology after technology thrown at me, and I just spent enough time figuring out how it works, watching YouTube, asking experts. It comes pretty naturally, so I'm thankful I was exposed to that in the teaching world. None of it is too hard to figure out.

Talk to me a little more about when a new client comes on. Walk me through that process until you drop off.

We get assigned a new client and then send out an initial welcome email if they haven't already booked a kickoff call with us. There are two different types of customers: some that come through sales and are already engaged, and others that are web sign-ups where I have to try to get them to meet with me. It's a mixed bag of unengaged and engaged clients. For the engaged, we meet for our kickoff, I develop a customized action plan for them, send it to them, and check in based on the cadence they set—could be bi-weekly. I get to use a lot of my personal judgment calls, which is nice. For the unengaged, it's weekly outreach, giving them educational resources, trying to get them to book a call with me. Depending on their requirements, they could be transitioned to a Customer Success Manager. In that case, I host a transition call where I, the customer, and the CSM join to talk about their progress and give them ideas on where they're headed.

Did someone give you a document that said, this is what you need to do with a new client?

For each customer, it's different.

How do you dig into that to cater to what they need and understand their needs?

I work with small and mid-sized businesses. Sometimes I'm dealing with the owner, other times it's a full-blown marketing team or an IT person, so it varies. Both teams I've been a part of in customer success didn't have much for us. I use my skills from creating curriculum for that purpose. I'm a big proponent of, if it's not there, I'll make it and share it with the team. I created documents on how to prepare for a kickoff call, what questions to ask, what to do for follow-up. I've created several docs outlining situations that might happen, and I go to leadership to get them approved, just so we have everything visible. In startup teams, when it's all in people's heads, it doesn't benefit anyone. So I'm all about documenting procedures. I like to use templates for everything because it allows you to customize for the customer and avoid recreating every communication from scratch. Big fan of email templates with customizable parts to keep it relevant.

Why did you become a teacher in the first place?

I originally wanted to be a guidance counselor, and teaching was my path to that. It's kind of funny this is where I ended up.

Do you miss summer breaks?

I miss it less than I thought I would because I have PTO and can take a week off. I work remotely and have flexibility, so I don't feel that intense need to recharge for eight weeks since my cup is pretty full most of the time.

Knowing what you know now, what would you have changed about your preparation? Not necessarily the experiences you've had.

Honestly, the only thing I wish I had done differently was believe I could make the transition sooner and gotten out sooner.

You just touched on something—you said you would have gotten out sooner. Talk to me about what that means to you.

I didn't teach very long, but where I was, I felt burnt out. After one year at a particular school, I was coming home with nothing left, so depleted mentally and physically, often in tears. I knew it wouldn't get better the next year, but the obligation kept me. I wish I had seen sooner how unsustainable it was because I really put myself in a tough spot with my mental health. It took a long time and a lot of work to retrain my mind to put myself first after years of neglecting that. It's hard to come back from, and I wish I had recognized the impact sooner and left earlier.

Any advise?

I just wish people would realize how capable teachers are of working in tech and things like that. I get a lot of teachers reaching out to me on LinkedIn—how did you end up where you're at? What do I do? And even friends. The one thing that I would say is, don't limit yourself to customer success and don't limit yourself to edtech, because those two are like the comfort zones for former teachers. And, gosh, the skills are so usable in so many other fields.

Sr. Client Support Specialist - Neta
Taught for 13 years - Grades: PK, K, 5, Adult Education & ESOL

I really want to stress to teachers to look at all the tools in their toolbox. The years of experience in and out of the classroom. Many have had other careers and interests prior to teaching...

Collecting skills for the toolbox. This is always what I come back to when working with people transitioning into new careers. The first step is always focus, right? How many opportunities are out there? The first thing to consider in a transition is not even the process itself. It is figuring out your focus. The focus begins as a wide umbrella. What industry do you want to be in? Forget about roles for now. Do you want to be in EdTech? In tech at all? In retail? Restaurants? Health? What interests you? Once you have identified the industry, you look at the fields within it. The fields are similar across industries, but they take different shapes. Project management in healthcare is not the same as project management in construction. The titles are the same, but the roles are not. Once you have narrowed the industry, focus on the field of work, not specific roles. What do you want to do? Sales? Client experience? Data analysis? Coding and development? What about that field excites you?

From there, you start looking at the roles. Within a client experience field, for example, you could be a success manager, support specialist, implementation manager, or do coaching, depending on the company and product. These are the roles within this field, within this industry. It is the hardest part of the transition when you are stepping into unfamiliar territory. We do not always know where we are heading, but research is key. Research, research, and narrow it down.

Where do you want to begin?

When people ask what I do, I say I'm a Jill of all trades--whatever you want to call it. My journey has been long. I started working at 14, coming from a humble background. My family didn't have much, but I attended a private high school on a scholarship. That gave me a strong foundation. At 20, I began studying psychology and communication in college but quit after a semester. I didn't know what I wanted, and my learning disabilities made school challenging. I spent eight years working retail during the day and bartending at night, doing what I could to get by. At 28, I realized I needed a change. I found a teaching credential program combined with a bachelor's degree, designed for working people. It allowed me to study three days a week while working the rest. I chose early childhood education because I loved working with kids, though I doubted my ability to master a single subject like math or history. I earned my degree and started teaching. I loved the kids and was good at it, but the work didn't excite or challenge me. While in school, I received a scholarship that required me to mentor high school and college prep students. That experience introduced me to the nonprofit world. My first career change was becoming a project manager in the nonprofit sector. My background in education helped me understand the system and work with teachers. I excelled at taking programs from ideas to reality and loved seeing the impact on people's lives.

Much of what we do as teachers aligns with the work nonprofits are doing.

Exactly. Looking into the nonprofit world is definitely something I recommend a lot of teachers to consider. If you want to become a project manager but can't get your foot through the door, go to your local nonprofit and say, "Hey, I want to volunteer my time. Here's what I'm good at. Give me something to do." That experience opens doors and introduces you to people. Nonprofits match well with the characteristics of a teacher. We want to heal the world, do good by everyone, and feel the meaning and the impact. Speaking on behalf of most teachers, I think there's that element of wanting to contribute. That's why I transitioned into nonprofit work and stayed there for about six years. During that time, I got married and had a child in Israel. Then we moved to the US when we got our green card. When we got here, I had nothing lined up. But I knew the easiest job for me to find would be teaching because a teacher is a teacher no matter where you go. An early childhood education teacher, even more so. I knew it was going to be back to the classroom. Within a month, I was teaching again. Going back to the classroom in a new country, teaching in English, which isn't my native tongue, and adjusting to a new culture was like learning to teach all over again. The first year was about getting my bearings and figuring out how things worked here. But as I've said before, I love teaching, and I was good at it. I started talking to my directors and people in administration about what else I could do within the system to develop myself professionally. They had a lot of suggestions. I already had a bachelor's degree. So I didn't need to go back to school. Instead, I focused on becoming a mentor, sharpening my skills as a people manager and supervisor, and becoming certified as a mentor teacher. That changed my experience in the classroom completely. I was working at a private Jewish preschool with three other teachers, four of us for a classroom of 22 kids. I was also mentoring between four to six students every week. These were additional adult helping hands coming into the classroom two or three times a week. I was helping them with their fieldwork, and that was, I think, the happiest time I had in the classroom. Then I got pregnant again. When I went on maternity leave, I left the classroom in capable hands. When I returned, my director said, "Those three teachers you've been grooming all these years are leading the class now. They're doing great work. I want you back, but on paper, as the lead teacher. I want you to continue teaching the adults, not the kids." I said, "No problem. That sounds good." While I was working there, I started exploring other opportunities. I started looking into academy positions and private sector opportunities where I could offer my expertise to other teachers. Then I saw a job listing for an ed-tech company. I was interested, but I was nervous about leaving mid-school year. When I went to tell my director, I was shaking. My hands were shaking as I prepared to meet with her. She is a formidable personality, well known in Los Angeles, and a professor who lectures all over the world. I expected a scolding, but instead, I got a hug, a kiss, and a "Good luck. Stay in touch. The door is always open." I was relieved. This was a positive experience for me. I wasn't used to that. Instead, she said, "You did a good job preparing those teachers. They're leading the class already." I was happy and grateful for her support.

I just read about a teacher who posted on Facebook, thinking it was private, that she might be job hunting. Her principal found out, and now she has to meet with the principal and her union rep. She's terrified, but I told her she owes no explanation unless her contract says otherwise. She should stay quiet. That fear is exactly what you said you felt too.

"Yes, they say, 'I don't want people to dislike me.' I have heard things like, 'You are a traitor, betraying your families and students just to advance yourself.' The reason does not matter, right? We are trying to better our lives. People react like, 'How could you? Did you not have a calling? Now you are leaving it behind?' Thankfully, my director was very supportive. We are still in touch, and we are good friends.

At WonderSchool, I was hired as their first mentor. My job was to help directors with childhood education by raising quality, designing better environments, and discussing best practices. I also worked with them to increase enrollment while improving education. Startups are always changing. About two weeks in, I was working with two salespeople and a customer success person. Suddenly, both salespeople were gone. One was planned, but the other caught everyone by surprise. He went with the rest of the revenue team to a summit, I tried reaching him, but I could not. Then I called Annie, our operations director, and she told me he had been fired. She asked me if I could take over some of his sales meetings. I said yes and ended up doing sales until new people were hired along with my own job responsibilities.

The job kept changing. It started with mentoring in early childhood education but grew into business strategy and customer success. It was not just about education quality anymore. I was managing relationships and growing the business. When I started, I worked with 30 small businesses, and in a few months, that number grew to 300 across Southern California. We knew one mentor was not enough, so the company hired more. Even then, I still had the largest portfolio. Eventually, I asked for another mentor in my region, and we expanded the team to include a Spanish speaker.

The roles kept growing. We took on planning, leadership, and quality standards. At one point, we were even designing websites. No one had a clear job description, but we all did whatever needed to get done. That is what I love about startups. If there is something that needs doing, you can step up and do it. That is how I built my skills.

We were doing so well. Then Covid hit. Everything changed. Parents started pulling kids out of programs. Teachers and directors were closing their doors because they were afraid. The industry took years to recover. Seventy-five percent of us were laid off, though they gave us three weeks' notice and made sure our benefits carried through the month. It was still hard. Everyone warned me about startups, saying they could fail overnight. I thought, 'I am a teacher. I can always go back.' But during Covid, there were no teaching jobs. I felt stuck. The jobs I found paid so little that unemployment was more. I had a family to support.

So I started applying. 2020 was a hard year. I also knew people in different industries, which helped. Some friends who ran a co-working space with childcare had to close their doors to . Together, we started brainstorming. Parents still wanted education for their kids but did not feel safe sending them to school. That is how we came up with PodSkool.

PodSkool was about helping families organize small groups of children.

We provided the teacher, curriculum, materials, and scheduling. We sent a teacher to them. It was different from other pod setups because we focused on early childhood education, not school-age kids. We did not just stick kids in front of a Zoom screen all day. It worked really well. We ran it for over a year, but once schools reopened, it became unnecessary, so we closed it. During that time, I was the director of education. I created the curriculum, trained the teachers, and supervised the programs. I was not a classroom teacher anymore. I was designing programs and running a business. It was really cool.

In the meantime, I did odd jobs because I knew people. Someone at an ed-tech company needed help placing teachers part-time, so I took that. I also interviewed for the company I work at now. I knew PodSkool would not last forever, so I kept looking for full-time work. Part-time jobs were okay while PodSkool was my main work, but they were not enough to provide for my family.

That is something I think teachers transitioning out need to understand. Some influencers say, 'Just quit and go for it.' But if you have rent, a mortgage, or kids to feed, you cannot just quit and wait for months to find a job. That is not realistic.

Right. I see that happening all the time in the online communities that I'm in. They're like, "I quit! I'm so happy!" and I'm thinking to myself, if you have responsibilities...

Some people can afford to do that. If you can, by all means, go for it. If you are unhappy in teaching, suffering every day, and have a spouse providing for you or savings to carry you through a year, then do it. Most people are not in that position. You are not making that kind of money unless you are on the coast. Even there, I have friends teaching high school math in LA making six figures, but they are paying a million dollars for a house. You live on the coast, you make more, but you spend so much more. It is wild when you think about the percentage difference.

I ran into Formative when they were still very small, maybe ten employees. They started in 2013, hit the market in 2016, and blew up in 2020. During Covid, they did something brilliant. They gave their product free to any district that asked for it. It was a formative assessment platform designed to provide real-time data from students and close the feedback loop real time. It was exactly what schools needed for remote learning and worked beautifully in classrooms too.

When I first tried Formative, it looked nothing like it does today. We have come a long way. But even then, I kid you not, it took me 90 seconds to slap my forehead and ask myself, "Oh my God, why didn't I think of this?" I immediately fell in love with the product. It was brilliant. A formative assessment platform that was not just about assessments. It was a holistic pedagogical system. It gave real-time data from students, let teachers see their work live, and closed the feedback loop instantly. I thought, "This is exactly what teachers need."

They posted a job for a customer success manager. I applied, even though I had never seen the product before. I loved the people I interviewed with. The VP of sales and I hit it off in what was supposed to be a 30-minute interview that lasted two hours. The co-founders were amazing too. It didn't feel like an interview. It felt like we were just talking and getting to know each other.

For the final round, I had to do a presentation, but at the same time, PodSkool was really gaining momentum. Over the weekend before the final interview, we started getting a lot of interest from clients. It became obvious I would not have the time for a full-time job if PodSkool was going to work. I talked to my co-founders and told them, "I know I am going to get an offer from Formative, but I need to know if we are going all in on this." They confirmed we were, so I let Formative know I had to step back. It was a hard decision because I loved them, but I felt confident it was the right call for that moment. They were so understanding.

A year later, I posted on LinkedIn about how great Formative was and how much I loved their team. The very next day, one of the co-founders reached out and asked if I could help with recruiting. They were growing fast and needed someone with connections. I started with ten hours a week, but within two weeks, it turned into full-time contract work. The startup was scrappy. I focused on hiring leadership roles like VP of marketing and HR. By then, PodSkool was winding down, so the timing was perfect.

After about seven months, they asked if I wanted to stay on full-time. I had a meeting with their VP of Revenue, and she asked me what I was good at. I told her, "I am good at getting things done." That was my strength, and it stood out. They offered me a senior role in support where I could build processes. My job became defining responsibilities, creating escalation procedures, and setting up systems.

That is how I got here. The role has grown with the company. I still do what I was hired to do, but I am always finding ways to help. That is the beauty of startups. When you see a gap, you can step in and make things happen.

Training Coordinator, Senior- Rozina
Taught for 4 years - Grades: 6 -11 - Subject: Math

How long have you been in this position?

It's going to be a year.

Tell me what you do. You can walk me through a project, or provide details about your position.

I have a team of five people. If you look at the ADDIE model, I handle the first A, the analysis part. My team relies on me to bring in training projects. I serve in an IT training environment, where we train on applications. The work for a waste management company based across North America. Sometimes the systems and applications can be numerous. We conduct many mergers and acquisitions, so my team is responsible for onboarding new people onto our organizational applications. Whenever we onboard new people or launch new applications, I'm the frontline person who analyzes the project. I assess the requirements, identify the users and their locations, determine gaps, and define training needs, such as content creation or training delivery.

When you talk about gaps, how do you determine them? Without having specific experience in the domain you're training for, how do you identify these gaps?

For instance, I rely heavily on stakeholders. We always have existing systems; there's never a complete void. There's a current state and always a future state. That's how we identify the gap or delta--what additional tasks are needed. My team evaluates our current state, what's existing and working, and what changes are incoming. That's how we reevaluate our training materials or training deliveries, adjusting our content. That's gap analysis. Again, I rely on my SMEs. For example, we recently implemented multi-factor authentication to provide companies with an extra security layer for their devices. After creating training materials in January, they became obsolete within months when an additional authentication step was added, requiring users to enter a location-specific number. This situation required us to identify the delta--the change--and collaborate with SMEs to update our documentation by removing outdated information and introducing the new processes.

As you're speaking, I'm hearing a lot of jargon: delta, future state, current state. Good jargon--I knew delta because I taught math--but how did you learn all this jargon? Coming from teaching, I can't recall if you were previously in the workforce outside teaching.

I have an engineering degree and worked in the corporate sector, though not in North America. I worked as an engineer in Dubai. Then, I pursued my master's in education. I didn't necessarily plan to enter classroom teaching, but around that time, I moved to Canada. Teaching was an easy and natural fit for me. I genuinely loved teaching and stayed with it for four years. The IT side of things came organically. Although I don't hold a formal IT degree, I became an LMS administrator at my school because of my IT skills. Teaching combined with my affinity for technology helped me develop relevant skills. Those became my transferable skills for getting into a training role. Obviously, your help and the support of so many people in my network guided me toward specific academy-based courses about adult education, which specifically paved my way to this role. So, yes, I had somewhat of a background in what I currently do.

What else do you want the audience to know about your current role? If someone is interested, what should they know

to prepare? What details about your position should they understand?

There is a strong connection between being a teacher and a leading a corporate training team. In former you teach young kids and in latter you teach adults, and they listen :) To anyone interested in stepping outside of the classroom thinking what else they got, I would say mapping their current skill set to what they wish to become. As a teacher we hold several transferable skills to Instructional Design, Learning & Development and Training, the core is to identify what one wish to become if not a teacher and what bridging program/ courses they must participate in to enter the new paradigm of their careers.

Sometimes I speak with people, and I've experienced this myself, who have a position but no existing materials. I had to create my own documentation and procedures. I'm sure you company provides what you need, but could you talk about your experience with this? For instance, I often see questions online asking about how to conduct a needs analysis or what types of questions should be asked. In your process, did you come into the role with documentation, or did you have to create it yourself?

You're correct in asking this question. Standardized templates for conducting various training steps are scarce, or rather, one size doesn't fit every organization. Every template requires some customization. Thanks to my LinkedIn community, I encountered many useful resources during my transition out of the classroom that I now utilize in my current role. The needs analysis template I use guides my conversations with stakeholders or SMEs through targeted questions. My focus is on analyzing the business need, understanding why it exists, and determining what we must do to address it, including identifying potential training solutions. If training is the solution, I further explore design needs and training modalities. Since our company operates across multiple time zones and regions, I need to understand the locations of our participants.

For example, if conducting a live webinar, I must consider participants on the Pacific side to ensure timing is reasonable for those on Eastern Standard Time. Small nuances like this must be addressed. French compliance is crucial for us because we are in Canada, so we anticipate French translations ahead of time. Spanish translations may also be necessary in certain U.S. regions with predominantly Spanish-speaking populations. All of these details are captured through my template, and I ask specific questions to obtain more information on each aspect.

As you're speaking, I'm thinking about content creation. I want to distinguish between creating content for students who have limited prior knowledge and need instruction on entirely new content, versus your role as a trainer and content developer. Can you distinguish these two experiences?

This is definitely different experiences, though the strategies of creating a curriculum and lesson plans may stay similar, however in the corporate world holding adult learning principles in the back of your mind are crucial. As a former teacher I stayed firm on the pedagogical concepts, on student's motivation and prior knowledge, now I value and recognize adults requiring concise relevant information pertinent to their work without unnecessary content. These adult learning principals allows to stay consistent with the quality of the product my team creates for the larger audience we serve.

You mentioned you're primarily on the analysis side of the ADDIE model, and I feel the analysis and evaluation components often overlap. Do you consider evaluation during your analysis?

I'll address the behavior and performance aspect first. That actually intersects more with HR. I occasionally facilitate HR initiatives because our team has the capability, but behavior and performance aren't strictly part of our IT training focus. We're primarily centered on knowledge.

Regarding your observation about evaluation, your point is well taken.

Currently, our evaluation processes mostly involve pre and post-surveys, quizzes, and polls to measure impact. Although we don't yet have a dedicated Learning Management System and instead rely on SharePoint, we do our best to track and analyze data manually using Excel whenever possible. Evaluation is definitely important to us, and while we have room to grow in this area, our team continues to find creative ways to work effectively with the resources available.

Many professionals I've spoken with conduct Kirkpatrick level one or level two evaluations but rarely reach level three or level four, which measure actual behavior change and organizational impact. Honestly, that's because we're usually busy keeping up with daily business demands. Is there anything else you'd like teachers to know?

Readers should understand there's significant growth potential in this role. However, if someone particularly enjoys teaching perks such as summer breaks, March breaks, decorating classrooms, and reflective time, they might miss those elements in a corporate environment. Nevertheless, corporate roles offer many advantages like flexibility, creativity, and the chance to influence larger-scale changes. Although corporate positions can occasionally be stressful, workload stress exists in all professions, including teaching. The primary advantage here is flexibility. Working hours are not fixed, unlike teaching, where punctual daily attendance is mandatory. Corporate roles allow work-from-home opportunities, flexible schedules, and virtual meetings, even when you're not feeling your best. These are some important benefits I'd like readers to consider.

Wonderful. Now, shifting gears slightly, if you're comfortable, I'd like to discuss your teaching experience. You've already shared why you entered teaching, but could you elaborate on your reasons for leaving education?

I entered teaching naturally, having a master's degree in education and easily obtaining my Ontario teaching license since math teachers are always in demand. Finding initial teaching roles was straightforward, making teaching a practical starting point in a new country. Ultimately, I left teaching because I reached a saturation point regarding financial growth and opportunities for creativity. After four years, I felt stuck in repetitive routines. Teaching middle and high school during and after the pandemic revealed significant shifts in education. Students frequently misused digital tools like PhotoMath, which undermined genuine learning. The lack of consistency, accountability, and declining classroom culture became increasingly frustrating. Teaching became more administrative, with much of my time spent chasing assignments and evaluations rather than truly instructing. Only 20 to 30 percent of my day involved actual teaching, while 70 percent involved managing student behavior, engagement, and integrity issues. I realized I wasn't enjoying my work anymore and knew it was time to move on.

Thanks for sharing that. How long did it take you to secure this role...from when you decided to leave teaching until you got the position?

Honestly, I was fortunate. It didn't take me long because I had a strong resume highlighting my training skills, attracting numerous recruiters. After modifying my resume and LinkedIn profile, the results came quickly. Within six to eight weeks, I had multiple offers. I remember reaching out to you and Alex for advice on choosing between instructional design and training coordinator roles. Your guidance helped me make a decision I'm happy with. By August, I had already secured my position and ironically, yesterday marked my first anniversary there.

That's great. It goes by quickly. I'll reach my one-year mark this October too. Lastly, any additional advice or insights?

My advice to teachers is never underestimate your skills and experience. Even if it feels like your teaching experience limits you, the skills gained in the classroom are extraordinary. Transitioning to training or project management roles is achievable without expensive courses. Leverage resources like LinkedIn, YouTube, and community workshops to enhance your credentials. Imposter syndrome is common, and I've felt it too, but it fades with experience. You'll discover you can manage your new responsibilities as effectively as you did in teaching. Transitioning from classroom teaching to virtual or corporate roles is possible, affordable, and beneficial for your personal growth. If you feel inclined to make that move, go for it.

Update:

When we first spoke, I was part of the Technical Team at GFL; now I'm leading a team of six training specialists as the Enterprise Training Manager. Initially, I was following a strategy, and now I'm driving one. These are interesting times. I sit at the forefront of technical and people training needs across our 10,000-employee organization, implementing an enterprise-wide LMS strategy to accommodate varied training requirements, completion records, and reporting. I manage a team of bilingual Instructional Designers (English and French) and lead the LMS Implementation Team, which serves as internal consultants for different departments. Thorough needs analysis and project management are at the core of successful training delivery in my world. I get excited to introduce myself as a former teacher now facilitating training in corporate settings.

Virtual Assistant - Nicole K.
Taught for 12 years - Grade: Preschool

Why did you get into education?

Ever since I was a young child, I wanted to be a teacher. My fourth-grade teacher was amazing. I still remember everything about her and how great she was. I think she really instilled in me the idea of wanting to be like her. What I wanted to teach changed over the years, but the desire to be a teacher never did.

What is one aspect of why you left education?

I want to say resources, but I am not sure that is entirely true. Thinking back to elementary school, it was fun. I do not recall much talk about budgets or being told, "No, we cannot have or do things." I remember being in fourth grade and thinking about how inspiring one teacher could be.

You're right! I remember how we used to go to skating parties and take a lot of field trips. We went to the theater and did so many activities. But when I compare that to my own children's experiences, they had fewer opportunities like that. They did attend some events, but they were in a more affluent school district. I also taught in a similar district, so I can see how resources might play a role. All right, let's talk about why you left education. What part of your story do you want to share?

How much time do we have? Essentially, it comes down to boundaries. I poured so much of myself into teaching and into my classroom that by the time I left, there was nothing left to give. I have a five-year-old, and raising him during COVID was challenging. COVID itself was a huge factor. I reached a point where I was so sick of fighting the red tape of the system. I was a special education teacher, and it felt like I was constantly fighting to get kids the services they needed. It was exhausting.

Did you have these thoughts before COVID?

I would say I had some general thoughts about it before COVID. I remember thinking there is no way I am going to do this until I am 65. It just felt impossible. I think there was another major shift when my youngest was born. He just turned five, and I realized I was working so much that I was missing out on moments with him. Then COVID happened. Teaching preschool special education online was incredibly hard, almost impossible. With parent support, we managed, but it made me realize something. We do not have to push ourselves to the limit. We can slow down. It does not have to be a constant rush. The final shift came with poor decisions from administration during and after COVID. These decisions were made by people who were not in the classroom and did not provide the support or resources they promised. That was the breaking point for me.

I hear that a lot. There is just no give. Can you provide one specific example that would help someone outside of education understand?

It is like going to the doctor with a sinus infection. The doctor diagnoses you and says, "You have a sinus infection," and then just tells you to take care without giving you any medication. You are left asking where the treatment is. That is how it felt. We identified the problems, but there was no real solution or follow-through. It was like saying, "Good luck, you are on your own."

Did you explore other careers when you decided to leave? What were some of the things you considered, or how did you approach it?

Honestly, I did not know what I was going to do at first. The initial part of leaving was about healing. I felt so broken. I joined Facebook groups and got on LinkedIn to see what other transitioning teachers were doing. I explored a few options, like project management. As a special education teacher, I felt like I was managing projects every day. I looked into it and a few other things, but nothing felt right. Part of me was just done with systems altogether. I wanted autonomy and flexibility. I needed time to be myself, a wife, a mom, a friend. The roles I explored, like typical eight-to-five jobs, felt like they would take me further away from my kids. It was not that I was unwilling to learn something new, I absolutely could have, but I needed flexibility, and I could not find that in the options I considered.

What are you doing now? Are you currently doing it, aspiring to do it, or where are you in the process?

I'm doing it now. What really helped was being in so many Facebook groups and hearing guest speakers. People were really focused on helping teachers transition into other careers. One speaker, Julie Taylor with the Geek Pack, led a session where she showed some brief coding basics. My husband is a programmer, so I've seen the deep back-end work he does to make things function. I'd always thought coding seemed overwhelming, but seeing the small changes I could make on the front end, like on websites, made me think, "I could do that."

I joined her five-day challenge and thought, "Wow, look at that." That led to me purchasing her program. It's been challenging to learn something so completely different since child development is second nature to me. However, it's been nice to engage my creative side.

Another group introduced virtual assistant work, and I bought that course too. I thought these were two good options. When one wasn't going well, I could rely on the other. That's how I built my LLC, which is based on both services. Now I work as a virtual assistant and create websites. It's so different from what I was doing before, but I needed that. It also allows me to volunteer at my kids' school. I now do part-time work for them, which includes some of the same tasks I do as a virtual assistant.

How long did it take you to go from leaving the classroom to establishing your own company/services?

It's hard to give an exact timeline. It wasn't like it took me three months or something definitive. It was a much larger, deeper process. A lot of it was about healing. Mentally and emotionally, I felt broken. That's the best way to describe it. Leaving teaching left me feeling defeated. I spent a lot of time working through that before I even began focusing on the courses. I started picking at them little by little. By December or January, I finally felt like I had the energy and mental clarity to dive in fully. I launched my business in March.

You mentioned feeling broken a couple of times. Why did you feel that way? Can you explain it to someone who's not a teacher? I hear it a lot, and I understand it, but what does it mean to you?

It's hard to describe to someone who hasn't been a teacher. People who don't prioritize self-care might not understand it, no matter their profession, unless it's something demanding like being a doctor. They might say, "Oh, you're performing surgeries or on your feet all day," but they don't always extend that understanding to teaching.

Many people I've spoken to view teaching as "just a job," like any other. Teachers don't go into it just for the paycheck. There's a deeper attachment, a passion. For many, it's a calling.

That's an important distinction. Passion versus just a job. Many of us stay in teaching despite the poor pay and challenging conditions. While there are some teachers who

treat it like any other job, most are there because they truly believe in it, even if they don't always consciously acknowledge it.

That's exactly it. Imagine a well that you keep drawing water from, but eventually, it dries up. Every day, there's no water left. That's how I felt in my last few months of teaching. I lost the joy in it. That was my sign that something was wrong. I still loved the kids and enjoyed spending time with them, but everything else...the IEP paperwork...just made me wonder, "Why am I doing this?" My well was bone dry.

Talk to me about some of your latest projects. What kind of work are you doing, especially in the virtual assistant space?

I think being a special education teacher really ingrained in me the importance of organization and time management. Those strengths have carried over into what I do now. I'm currently working for a client, helping her set up systems. I'm streamlining her processes and consolidating everything into one place instead of using multiple apps and tools. It's been great to apply those skills in a new way.

If someone wanted to become a virtual assistant, what advice would you give them?

Julia Taylor's Geek Pack was one of them, and I'm still a member. I think I'll probably stay a member for life. The other one was Michaela Quinn's Live Free Academy for virtual assistant work.

If someone said they wanted to pursue this path, what advice would you give them about getting started? What would you tell them to focus on?

I'd start by asking them what they enjoy doing. You don't want to end up doing something you don't like. For example, a lot of virtual assistants offer social media management, but I don't enjoy that. It's important to find something that fulfills you. For me, I'm a helper, so it was important to find roles where I could continue helping people while also maintaining the boundaries I've worked so hard to establish. Forming my own LLC has made that possible. I can help others, do meaningful work, and still prioritize my own self-care. I had a call today with someone who wants to focus on social media management. I couldn't help with that directly, but I could guide her in thinking about the kinds of services she wants to offer and how to value her time. Knowing what you enjoy makes it easier to price your services and manage your workload effectively.

You've learned a lot from the virtual assistant programs. What's something you learned from them that you didn't already know? What did they provide that helped you build your business? Why couldn't you have done it without them?

I think the community aspect was a big part of it. Both programs include a lot of former or transitioning teachers, so the people in these groups understand what it's like to redevelop yourself. That shared experience made a difference for me. Julia Taylor, in particular, felt like a personal cheerleader. Even though there are tons of people in the group, she made it feel like she was speaking directly to you, encouraging you by showing how doable this all is. Both programs also offer coaching from experts in various areas, which was incredibly helpful. The Facebook groups are another great resource. You can post a question, and someone will always answer, no matter how simple or complex it might seem. Both programs also tackle imposter syndrome, which is huge for people coming from teaching or other fields. So many of us think, "I'm just a teacher, I can't do this," but they remind you that your skills are transferable to so many things. That mindset shift is invaluable.

You mentioned your LLC, and I imagine other teachers might want to start their own. Can you walk me through the process? Talk about timing, costs, or any tips. Things like "make sure you do this" or anything along those lines.

Sure. I actually have a business coach because I had never run a business before. There was so much I didn't know. Initially, I met with her as a career coach, but when I realized I didn't want an established corporate career and wanted to reinvent myself, she helped guide me through that process. I really wanted my LLC in place when I launched because I felt it was important to protect myself and my business. For me, the process was easy. In California, at the time, they were waiving the fee for creating an LLC, which helped. I applied for my EIN first, then used that to apply for the LLC. It took about a week, and I was up and running. I'm not sure if it's always that fast, but it was surprisingly simple.

That's great to know. I feel like other teachers might find that encouraging. You mentioned earlier you had a career coach. What were the advantages of having one?

I found my coach, Mollie Lo, on LinkedIn. At the time, I was floundering, trying to figure out what I was going to do next. I attended a few of her webinars, one of which focused on confidence, and I realized I needed her guidance. Initially, I thought I needed help transitioning into the corporate world, but when I decided to start my own business, I asked if she would coach me on that instead. She agreed, and now we have an ongoing agreement.

You do have to be willing to invest in services like this, but I needed her expertise. She helped with the business side of things, like social media, marketing, and creating a sales pitch, areas where I had no experience. She has been incredibly helpful, walking alongside me through the process. She's also very extroverted, which complements my introverted nature. She knows when I'm overthinking and will call me out on it. Mollie is with LoTus Mentoring, and she has been amazing.

My last question is always this: what advice would you give to other teachers about their journey?

I think the biggest advice I can give is to stay true to yourself. So many teachers fall into this mindset of, "I have to do this for the kids, I have to stay because they need me." While that's noble, I'd urge them to remember that they need themselves first. Your family needs you first, and it's okay to make changes.

One of my favorite movies is A Knight's Tale with Heath Ledger. There's a line where the main character asks, "Can it be done, Father? Can a man change his stars?" He's from a poor part of London where becoming a knight seems impossible, but by the end of the movie, he becomes one. That idea has stuck with me. I wanted to be a teacher since I was young, and I pursued that dream. I got my master's degree and built my career, but I've realized it's okay to change paths. Changing your stars doesn't mean the work you did before was wasted.

That's also where the name Purple Lotus for my business came from. Purple is my favorite color, and a lotus grows in mud, thriving in harsh conditions. That's what I went through. I broke after pouring my entire adult life into teaching. When I left, I had to regrow, which was painful at times, but I did it. On my website, I call myself a purple lotus because I've grown through the mud and recreated myself.

Resource:

https://geekpack.com/

https://purplelotussolutions.com/

https://www.lotusmentoring.net/

AFTERWORD

I prayed and asked God to give me an idea. One day, the idea came to me to write this book!

In March 2023 I began reaching out to former teachers...I didn't think it would take me this long (two years). I originally talked to over 100 teachers, but as I began to edit the raw transcripts, two things became clear: It would be way too long and as they began to tell their stories, a common theme emerged and that was mental anguish. The lack of support came up in so many ways, the stress and frustration. That's when I realized that "Why did you leave teaching?" was just as important a question as "What are you doing now?"

The interviews were an experience in themselves. Some of them absolutely surprised me...our banter and the way we hit it off immediately...like old friends with a shared struggle. However, there were some that were raw and the hurt and guilt was palatable. Each former teacher's story was unique, yet there were obvious threads running through them all. This has to mean something. This many people, from different backgrounds, different schools, different districts, all saying the same things in their own ways and it must say something about the state of teaching/education in 2025. Why did we all leave for so many different reasons, yet the same reason? With so many leaving, it is not just an individuals issue, but a systemic failure.

If I had my way, no one would become a teacher in the education system as it stands now. If teaching is to continue, it should be through micro schools with programs such as Amar Kumar's KaiPods or Jessica Shelley a former teacher, founder and CEO of Dailies

I beg you, I implore you that if you are thinking about leaving, take the time to find something new. Yes, it may take time. It may take sacrifice. Actually, it will take time and sacrifice, but where is your time going now...what are you sacrificing now?

1. _____

2. _____

3. _____

You may have to learn something completely different.

But it is worth it.

You are not stuck.

Even if it takes two to five years to make the transition, it is still worth it.

True freedom, as I have heard from so many, is being treated like the professional you are. It's being able to do your job without the constant overreach, the lack of trust, and the never-ending demands that follow you home. It's knowing that while every job has challenges, few of them compare to what we endured and you are enduring as a teacher.

I want to express my deep gratitude to the teachers who shared their stories with me. Their honesty and vulnerability.

If I found 100 teachers who left, then there are probably 1,000 more. And if there are 1,000, then YOU can be the next one.

ACKNOWLEDGEMENTS

To my Lord and Savior Jesus Christ. This book was a gift from God. He orchestrated and granted me favor with many of the people I interviewed.

To my husband, Louis, who didn't know he was marrying a "project-nerd", someone who is always working on "some project". Thank you for your patience as I "holed" myself up in my office night after night. I ♥ U, boy.

To my sons, Chadwick and Donovan: If I can do this, you can do ANYTHING! Mommy loves you so much...and stop biting me!

To my parents William Jr. and Patricia Seymour. I am blessed beyond measure to have you as my parents. You gave me a wonderful life and I love you both so very much.

Teachers run in my family, and I want to acknowledge them for obtaining the education needed to change the trajectory of our lives, especially considering the period during which they lived: Father's side: William Seymour, Jr. – father, Virginia Dodd – grandmother, Marilyn Hatch – aunt, Alisha Seymour – cousin Mother's side: Nellie Lane – great aunt, Francine Wiley – aunt

Bishop Truman & Dr. Beverly Martin, Founding Pastor & Co-Pastor of Maranatha Worship Centre - Dayton, OH, where I learned about loving God and discovering His promises in His Word and where you modeled for me how to BE a Believer. Thank you. I love and miss you.

Pastor Scott & Co-Pastor Cynthia Sanders, Founding Pastor & Co-Pastor of Rhema International Ministries - Albany, GA, where I am learning more about His promises and allowing the Holy Spirit to have His way. I love and thank you.

Dr. Robin Sargent, founder of IDOL Courses Academy. This is where my transition to a new career began. I would not have been able to gain the skills needed to become an Instructional Designer had you not pursued your dream. Thank you.

Lyn C., my mentor from ATL-ATD; it was not by chance that we were partnered together. Your words of encouragement and sharing your expertise and experiences laid the groundwork for me to mentor others Thank you..

Lisa K.R., my first supervisor out of the classroom, who gave it to me straight but provided me the opportunity. Thank you.

Kizzie and Dr. Robin R. – Our Saturday accountability sessions during IDOL, tweaking our resumes and portfolios, eventually led to all three of us leaving teaching. Your support, countless voice messages on Facebook Messenger, and so much more made it happen.

Shanique and Dr. Robin R. – Thanks for listening to me talk only about "this one thing, because that is all that there is." :)

Kight and Zach – Thank you for stepping up and spreading the word to other former teachers featured in this book, letting them know I was working on it and looking for more people to interview.

Tiffany Aliche, "The Budgetnista" – Thank you for holding your mentoring sessions and sharing the steps you took to launch your book.

Terri Savelle Foye – Your message on YouTube entitled, "Ask Big" was life-changing!

Dr. Briana Whiteside – It was during your "Let There Be" challenge in November 2022 that I asked God to remove all hindrances to witty ideas, and in March 2023, I began this book.

Canvas and Pixels YouTube Channel – Thank you for the video that showed me how to use Adobe InDesign.

Kathy and Ja'Mya, "my cheerleaders" at the Lee County GA, Walnut St. Branch Public Library.

Ya'Shu'a at Panera Bread-Albany, GA, Morning Cafe and Temp Cafe – Leesburg, GA where I spent many-an-hour on this book.

I would like to express my gratitude to the following individuals who generously participated in interviews for this book, although I was unfortunately unable to include their contributions in the final publication:

Account Director - Karin
Account Executive – Shanna
AI Technical Product Manager – Peyton
Comedian and Podcaster – Chris
Corporate Training Coordinator - Jonathan
Curriculum and Instructional Design Specialist – Ronald
Curriculum Developer - Jennifer
Curriculum Specialist – Chris
Customer Success Manager – Danielle
Director of Learning and Development – Brandon
Early Childhood Specialist and National Trainer – Dr. Nefertiti
Executive Vice President of Global Learning and Dev. – Doug
Founder and CEO of Dailies – Jessica
Hypnotherapist (UK) – Helen
Instructional Coach - Jacob
Instructional Designer – Heidi
Instructional Designer – Ryan
Personal Trainer – Elaine
Product Management - Gary
Professor – Ja'lia
Program Specialist and Consultant for Prof. Dev. – Stacey
Recruiter – Aurora
Sales Development Representative – Joshua
Senior User Experience Researcher – Jon
Software Engineer – Katie
Social Worker–Case Manager – Rebecca
Senior Learning and Development Consultant – Kristyn
Senior Project Manager - Joel
Talent Development–Mgr. Development Director – Stephania
Transitioning Teacher - Fiona (UK)
Transitioning Teacher - Kelsey
Transitioning Teacher - Margie

Still stuck on where to begin?

"Transferable skills on your resume"

"Non-teaching interviews are different"

"Optimize your LinkedIn page"

As a former teacher, I remember what felt confusing, overwhelming and unclear when I <u>had</u> to choose a new career.

You don't know what you don't know... but I *do* and it's in my AFFORDABLE course.

Join the waitlist now, for the Future Former Teachers Course.
email "Switch Soon" to:
Futureformerteachers@gmail.com

don't forget to add the "s"

www.ingramcontent.com/pod-product-compliance
Lightning Source LLC
Chambersburg PA
CBHW070605030426
42337CB00020B/3695